Maya Mandery

# Party Autonomy in Contractual and Non-Contractual Obligations

A European and Anglo-Common Law perspective
on the freedom of choice of law in the Rome I Regulation
on the law applicable to contractual obligations
and the Rome II Regulation on the law applicable
to non-contractual obligations

PL ACADEMIC RESEARCH

**Bibliographic Information published by the Deutsche Nationalbibliothek**
The Deutsche Nationalbibliothek lists this publication in the Deutsche
Nationalbibliografie; detailed bibliographic data is available in the internet at
http://dnb.d-nb.de.

Zugl.: Köln, Univ., Diss., 2014

**Library of Congress Cataloging-in-Publication Data**
Mandery, Maya.
  Party autonomy in contractual and non-contractual obligations a European and
Anglo-Common Law perspective on the freedom of choice of law in the Rome I
regulation on the law applicable to contractual obligations and the Rome II regulation
on the law applicable to non-contractual obligations / Mandery, Maya.
    pages ; cm
  Includes bibliographical references.
  ISBN 978-3-631-65321-0
  1. Conflict of laws--Contracts--European Union countries. 2. Conflict of laws--
Obligations--European Union countries. 3. Contracts--European Union countries. 4.
Obligations (Law)--European Union countries 5. Conflict of laws--European Union
countries. I. Title.
  KJE983.C66M36 2014
  346.2402'2--dc23
                                    2014013247


                                        D 38
                                 ISSN 0930-4746
                            ISBN 978-3-631-65321-0 (Print)
                            E-ISBN 978-3-653-04496-6 (E-Book)
                             DOI 10.3726/ 978-3-653-04496-6

                                 © Peter Lang GmbH
                         Internationaler Verlag der Wissenschaften
                                 Frankfurt am Main 2014
                                   All rights reserved.
                    PL Academic Research is an Imprint of Peter Lang GmbH.

                  Peter Lang – Frankfurt am Main · Bern · Bruxelles · New York ·
                                Oxford · Warszawa · Wien

              This book is part of an editor's series of PL Academic Research
                      and was peer reviewed prior to publication.

                                 www.peterlang.com

# Acknowledgements

This thesis is the product of a series of serendipitous encounters with people who have changed the course of my academic career and it is a pleasure to thank them. First and foremost, my utmost gratitude to my supervisor Prof. Dr. Heinz-Peter Mansel, Director of the Institute of Foreign Private and Private International Law at the University of Cologne. I am indebted to him for his continual guidance, expertise and invaluable advice and it was an honour to complete my research under his supervision. I am most grateful for the financial assistance received from the Dr. Carl-Arthur Pastor-Stiftung, which enabled me to pursue this research. I also owe my deepest gratitude to Associate Professor Dr. Elsabe Schoeman from the University of Auckland who has been and continues to be my inspiration. Without her consistent support, both academic and personal, I would not have had the opportunity to undertake and successfully complete this study. I also gratefully acknowledge the generous funding received from the Faculty of Law, University of Auckland towards the publication of this book. Finally, I thank my family, friends and especially Thorsten, for the unfailing support they have provided me throughout the various stages of my research. I dedicate this with love to the most important people in my life – Timothy, my daughter Jada and my wonderful mother Christa.

# Table of Contents

# Abbreviations

| | |
|---|---|
| ALRC Report | Australian Law Reform Commission (*ALRC*) Report No. 58, 1992, Choice of Law |
| BGB | *Bürgerliches Gesetzbuch* (German Civil Code) |
| BGH | *Bundesgerichtshof* (German Federal Supreme Court) |
| Brussels Convention | Convention of 27 September 1968 on jurisdiction and the enforcement of judgments in civil and commercial matters |
| Brussels I Regulation | Council Regulation (EC) No 44/2001 of December 2000 on jurisdiction and the recognition and enforcement of judgments in civil and commercial matters (OJ L 12, 1 [16.1.2001]) |
| CA | Court of Appeal |
| CISG | United Nations Convention on Contracts for the International Sale of Goods, Vienna, 11 April 1980, S.Treaty Document Number 98–9 (1984), UN Document Number A/CONF 97/19, 1489 UNTS 3 |
| Commission Amended posal | European Commission, Amended Proposal for a Regulation on the law applicable to non-contractual obligations (Rome II) (COM (2006) 83 final) [21.2.2006]) |
| Commission Proposal | European Commission, Proposal for a Regulation on the law applicable to non contractual obligations (Rome II) (COM (2003) 427 final of 22 July 2003 [22.7.2003]) |

| | |
|---|---|
| DCFR | Draft Common Frame of Reference Study Group on a European Civil Code/ Research Group on EC Private Law (Acquis Group) (eds.), Principles, Definitions and Model Rules of European Private Law. Draft Common Frame of Reference (DCFR), Interim Outline Edition, 2008 |
| EC | European Community (1993-) |
| EC Treaty | Treaty on European Union (consolidated version) (OJ C 321E [29.12.2006] p. 203–224) |
| ECJ | European Court of Justice |
| EEC | European Economic Community (1958–1993) |
| EGBGB | *Einführungsgesetz zum Bürgerlichen Gesetzbuch* (Introductory Act to the German Civil Code) |
| EP | European Parliament |
| EP 1st Reading Report | 1st Reading Report of the EP JURI Committee on the proposal for a Regulation on the law applicable to non-contractual obligations (Rapporteur: Diana Wallis) (EP document A6-0211/2005 FINAL [27.6.2005]) |
| EU | European Union |
| European Parliament's sition 2005 | Position of the European Parliament Po-adopted at 1st reading on 6 July 2005 with a view to the adoption of a Regulation on the law applicable to non-contractual obligations (OJ C 157E, 371 [6.7.2006]) |
| Explanatory randum | Explanatory Memorandum of the Memo-Commission of the European Communities accompanying the Proposal for a Rome II Regulation (see Commission Proposal above) |
| GEDIP | *Groupe européen de droit international privé* (European Group for Private International Law) |

| | |
|---|---|
| GG | *Grundgesetz* (German Basic Law) |
| Giuliano & Lagarde | M. Giuliano & P. Lagarde, Report Report on the Convention on the Law Applicable to Contractual Obligations, Official Journal of the European Union (OJ C 282 [1.10.1980], 0001–0050) |
| HC | High Court |
| HCJ | High Court of Justice |
| HGB | *Handelsgesetzbuch* (German Commercial Code) |
| HL | House of Lords |
| ICC | International Chamber of Commerc |
| JURI | European Parliament Committee on Legal Affairs and the Internal Market |
| Lando-Commission | Commission on European Contract law (1980) |
| OJ | Official Journal of the European Union |
| OLG | Oberlandesgericht (German Higher Regional Court) |
| PC | Privy Council |
| PECL | Principles of European Contract Law, prepared by the European Commission on Contract Law (Lando-Commission), 1999 |
| PICC | UNIDROIT Principles of International Commercial Contracts 2010 |
| PIL | Private International Law |
| Restatement of the Law | US Restatement of the Law, Con flict of Laws (1933) as adopted and promulgated by the American Law Institute at Washington, D.C., May 1934 |
| Restatement Law (Second) | US Restatement of the Law (Sec of the ond): Conflict of Laws (1971) as adopted and promulgated by the American Law Institute at Washington, D.C., May 1969 |
| Rome Convention | Convention on the law applicable to contractual obligations (OJ L 266, 1 [9.10.1980]) |

| | |
|---|---|
| Rome I | Regulation (EC) No 593/2008 on the law applicable to contractual obligations (Rome I) (OJ L 177, 6 [4.7.2008]) |
| Rome I Regulation | See Rome I (above) |
| Rome II | Regulation (EC) No 864/2007 on the law applicable to non-contractual obligations (Rome II) (OJ L 199, 40 [31.7.2007]) |
| Rome II Proposal | Commission Proposal (see above) |
| Rome II Regulation | See Rome II (see above) |
| SC | Supreme Court |
| TFEU | Treaty on the Functioning of the European Union (OJ C 115/47, [9.5.2008]) |
| The Green Paper | Green Paper on the conversion of the Rome Convention of 1980 on the law applicable to contractual obligations into a Community instrument and its modernisation COM (2002) 654 [14.1.2003] |
| The Proposal | Proposal for a Regulation of the European Parliament and the Council on the law applicable to contractual obligations (Rome I) COM (2005) 650 final [15.12.2005] |
| Treaty of Amsterdam | Treaty of Amsterdam Amending the Treaty on European Union, the Treaties Establishing the European Communities and Certain Related Acts of 10 November 1997, OJ C 340/01 |
| UK | United Kingdom |
| UK PIL Act 1995 | Private International Law (Miscellaneous Provisions) Act 1995 (1995 c 42) (UK) |
| UNIDROIT | The International Institute for the Unification of Private Law |
| US | United States of America |
| ZPO | *Zivilprozessordnung* (German Civil Procedure Code) |

16

# Introduction

The principle of *party autonomy*, in the sense of freedom of choice, or the self-arrangement of legal relations by individuals according to their respective will, broadly encompasses the idea that parties should be free to choose the law to govern their relations and the forum to adjudicate any disputes that might arise between them. It is one of the leading principles of contemporary conflicts theory and forms the cornerstone of the intersection between international commerce and private international law. In cross-border litigation, one of the key questions a court will be required to solve is how to determine the applicable law. This study focuses on the extent and scope of the parties' freedom to choose the substantive law to govern their cross-border contractual dispute and in particular, the significant developments extending this right into the area of non-contractual disputes, an area previously thought to be unable to provide for party autonomy.

In contrast to rules, which generally seek to connect the contract or tort to the law having a connection or most substantial relationship, the principle of party autonomy puts the will of the parties at the centre of the search for the applicable law. It is not longer the belief that a territorial connection should be the determining factor or that the objectively ascertained choice of law identified through objective connecting factors should be at the forefront, but rather that the will of those involved should be determinative of the applicable law. Parties are given the freedom to displace and by agreement rise above the otherwise applicable law. This freedom of choice is generally regarded to be the conflict of laws aspect of freedom of contract or market autonomy. It is common in international litigation and commercial arbitration and recent significant developments at a European level strongly underscore the trend in favour of party autonomy. Both the Rome I Regulation on the law applicable to contractual obligations[1] and the Rome II Regulation on the law applicable to non-contractual obligations[2] have elevated party autonomy to be the central choice of law rule within European private international law. Indeed,

---

1    Regulation (EC) No 593/2008 on the law applicable to contractual obligations (OJ L 177, 6 [4.7.2008]) (reproduced in Appendix 1).

2    Regulation (EC) No 864/2007 on the law applicable to non-contractual obligations (Rome II) (OJ L 199, 40 [31.7.2007]) (Reproduced in Appendix 2).

the parties' right to choose the applicable law not only forms an integral part of European choice of law rules but also in many other common law countries including the USA, Canada, Australia, New Zealand and Singapore. Has party autonomy become the most important universal principle in the conflict of laws?

# i. Research aims and methodology

Party autonomy encompasses the parties' right to choose the *forum* to adjudicate any disputes that arise between them and the *law* to govern their relations. However, only the power of parties to determine the substantive law by which they will be bound is the subject of this study. The aim is to examine the freedom of choice of law provided for in both the Rome I Regulation on the law applicable to contractual obligations and the Rome II Regulation on the law applicable to non-contractual obligations. The examination follows an integrated comparative method, whereby the principle of party autonomy as provided for in the Regulations is compared with the pre-regulation position in Germany and England. In particular, the innovative inclusion of party autonomy in the Rome II Regulation and the rationales underpinning the principle within non-contractual obligations is explored. The examination of European developments provides the basis for the subsequent critical reflection on the position of party autonomy in contract and tort in the Anglo-common law jurisdictions of Australia, New Zealand, Canada and Singapore. An assessment of the scope for party autonomy within the tort and contract choice of law rules of these common law systems will be made. Since all of these common law jurisdictions are based on English law, it is particularly pertinent to analyse and compare the European developments to those systems still clinging to the pre-legislative and pre-regulation reform position in England. Moreover, can these European developments make a contribution to the call for reform of the common law position concerning party autonomy in contractual, and perhaps more radically in non-contractual obligations?

This study is set out into the following five parts: *Part I* considers the place of party autonomy within the Rome I Regulation on the law applicable to contractual obligations. It provides a brief summary of the history of the Convention on the law applicable to contractual obligations and an outline of the background developments leading to the enactment of the subsequent Rome I Regulation. It focuses on the central position given to party autonomy in Article 3 of the Regulation. In addition, the inclusion of limitations on the parties' freedom to choose the governing law is also examined.

*Part II* similarly presents an exposition of party autonomy within the Rome II Regulation on the law applicable to non-contractual obligations. A brief summary of the history of the Rome II Regulation and an outline of the background developments leading to its enactment are presented. But given that choice of law in non-contractual obligations has largely been considered unworkable, it is thought important to consider the possible justifications for granting a freedom of choice in this area of law. Accordingly, the rationales that underpin the general rise in the status of party autonomy, and more specifically, the acceptance of the principle within the field of non-contractual obligations are set out. Following this, the primary choice of law rule established in Article 14 of the Rome II Regulation dealing with the principle of freedom of choice of law is examined. The requirements for a valid choice of law as well as the inclusion of limitations on the parties' freedom to choose the governing law are presented and dealt with separately.

*Part III* considers the procedural treatment and application of the parties' chosen foreign law according to Rome I and Rome II. Section A examines the introduction of the chosen law in national courts and the relationship between the law of the forum and the chosen foreign law. Section B focuses more specifically on the national procedural approaches taken to the introduction and ascertainment of foreign law in both German and English courts.

*Part IV* provides a critical reflection on the English common law origins and development of the principle of party autonomy in light of European developments. More specifically, a cross-national examination of party autonomy in the common law jurisdictions of Australia, New Zealand, Canada and Singapore is given. The conflict choice of law rules for contractual and non-contractual obligations in each legal system are dealt with in turn. For contract, the reception and application of the English doctrine of the proper law in each common law jurisdiction is set out. For non-contractual obligations the general English rule of double-actionability and its exception, followed by its reception and application in each common law jurisdiction is presented. Subsequently, the narrow scope for party autonomy within the common law approaches is summarised, followed by the suggestion of four general approaches that may accommodate party autonomy.

*Part V* summarises the conclusions drawn in the foregoing analyses and reflects upon these. From this three main themes emerge. The first is that both the Rome I and Rome II Regulations have clearly elevated the principle of party autonomy to the central choice of law rule within European private international law. More specifically, the Rome II Regulation has clearly confirmed the applicability of the principle in non-contractual obligations, including *ex ante* agreements. The second is, after an analysis of the procedural treatment and application of a choice of foreign law it is evident that there remains room for divergent approaches taken by national courts to this issue. It follows that there is a need for uniform procedural rules to supplement the uniform choice of law rules contained in the Rome I and

Rome II Regulations. Thirdly, both Regulations provide a great platform upon which to reconsider the common law approach to party autonomy within contract and non-contractual obligations. In particular in the area of non-contractual obligations it is suggested that the approach taken in the Rome II Regulation, permitting the freedom of choice and the benefits that derive from recognition of party autonomy within a structured choice of law regime, offers a great opportunity to rethink the traditional common law tort choice of law approaches.

By way of preceding information it is believed that the importance of the Rome I and Rome II Regulations should be understood within the context of the communitarisation or unification of private international law. The following point briefly sets out the impetus behind the unification of private international law, precipitating the significant rise in the status of party autonomy within European choice of law rules.

## ii. The unification of private international law within Europe

The international harmonisation and unification of commercial law is a well-known phenomenon, facilitated by various methods such as through the adoption of Conventions,[3] Regulations,[4] Principles,[5] general rules in the form of European Directives,[6] or model contracts[7]. The impetus behind these developments stems from the difficulties encountered in international commercial transactions. A single transaction may involve multiple legal relationships, which may be subject to several different laws. Those who engage in cross-border transactions

---

3    E.g. CISG – United Nations Convention on Contracts for the International Sale of Goods, Vienna, 11 April 1980, S.Treaty Document Number 98–9 (1984), UN Document Number A/CONF 97/19, 1489 UNTS 3· See further, *Matthias Lehmann*, The State of Development of Uniform Law in the Fields of European and International Civil and Commercial Law (7/2008 EuL Forum) 266–270.

4    E.g. Regulation (EC) No 593/2008 on the law applicable to contractual obligations (Rome I) (OJ L 177, 6 [4.7.2008]); Regulation (EC) No 864/2007 on the law applicable to non-contractual obligations (Rome II) (OJ L 199, 40 [31.7.2007]).

5    E.g. UPICC – UNIDROIT Principles of International Commercial Contracts 2010; PECL – Principles of European Contract Law, prepared by the European Commission on Contract Law (Lando-Commission) 1999.

6    See e.g. directives at http://ec.europa.eu/legislation/index_en.htm.

7    See e.g. ICC (International Chamber of Commerce) model contracts listed at http://www.iccwbo.org/policy/law/id272/index.html.

will be required to have adequate knowledge of the legal conditions governing the interpretation and performance of the general obligations. In the case of litigation, courts or arbitral tribunals will be required to determine the law applicable to the contract and possibly to the different aspects of the transaction. For both the parties involved and the courts, ascertaining the applicable law will clearly prove more difficult where the transaction is subject to divergent national laws. It may be a relatively uncomplicated task where the parties have clearly specified the law applicable to the parts of the transaction. However, where the parties have not included a choice of law clause or have failed to clearly express the law intended to govern the transaction, the various rules of private international law of the forum will govern. The uncertainty surrounding the ascertainment of the governing legal system may prove costly and time consuming and the application of different national laws may result in divergent solutions to the same problem. It is thought that the harmonisation or unification of private international law rules will promote legal certainty, economic efficiency and prevent divergent results.

Although the concepts of unification and harmonisation are often referred to as analogous activities, they are distinct in their objectives and results.[8] Harmonisation refers to the approximation of the laws of different jurisdictions. It does not lead to a uniform set of agreed rules, but rather it directs a change of rules, standards or processes in order to bring about equivalence.[9] Unification means the adoption of agreed set of rules, standards or guidelines for application to cross-border transactions without any room for different implementation.[10] Within the European context, this is predominantly achieved through Conventions or Regulations. The unification of choice of law rules for contract was initially achieved by the Rome Convention of 1980.[11] Although it unified the law applicable to contractual obligations, the creation of real

---

8    *Katharina Boele-Woelki*, Unifying and Harmonizing Substantive Law and the Role of Conflict of Laws, Collected Courses of the Hague Academy of International Law 340 (2010) 299. On terminology see also *Luke Nottage*, Convergence, divergence and the middle way in unifying or harmonizing private law (2004) 1 Annual German and European Law 166–245; *Christian Twigg-Flessner*, The Europeanisation of Contract Law (2008) 9–19.

9    Note however, that the term harmonisation is commonly used to denote all efforts to achieve an approximation of the laws of states.

10   See further, *Camilla Baasch-Andersen*, Defining uniformity in Law (2007) 12 Uniform Law Review, 5–56.

11   The Convention on the Law Applicable to Contractual Obligations, 1980 (OJ L 266, 1 [9.10.1980]). The consolidated text of the Convention is published in OJ C 27, [26.01.1998] 0034 – 0046 (English text).

unified or uniform law still required the ratification of the Convention by the individual states. It was not until the Treaty of Amsterdam[12] expressly granted the European Community the competence to deal with matters of private international law that it was possible to codify choice of law rules for both contractual and non-contractual obligations in the form of Regulations. This means that in accordance with the Treaty on the Functioning of the European Union (TFEU)[13], a Regulation shall be binding in its entirety and directly applicable in all Member States[14] on the date of its entry into force[15] and no measures to incorporate it into national law are required.

For the purposes of this study, the unification of private international law is relevant. Compared with the unification of substantive law, the unification of the rules of private international law is more practicable, since the rules apply solely to legal relations involving an international element.[16] In Europe, the unification of choice of law rules, also referred to as the europeanisation of the rules of private international law, was achieved by the Rome Convention of 1980 and more recently by the Rome I Regulation for contractual obligations and the Rome II Regulation for non-contractual obligations.[17] According to Article 81 TFEU,[18] measures in the field of judicial cooperation having cross-border implications, and insofar as necessary for the proper functioning of the internal market, include among others those aimed at ensuring the compatibility of the conflict-of-law rules.[19] Accordingly, Recitals of both the Rome I and Rome II Regulations affirm that the proper functioning of the internal market creates a need to establish uniform conflict-of-law rules irrespective of the nature of the court or tribunal seized.[20] The justification for the unification of the choice of law rules is based on the argument that the differences between the legal systems

12   Treaty of Amsterdam Amending the Treaty on European Union, the Treaties Establishing the European Communities and Certain Related Acts of 10 November 1997, OJ C 340/01.
13   Treaty on the Functioning of the European Union (TFEU), consolidated text of the Treaty is published in OJ C 115/47, [9.5.2008].
14   See Art. 288 TFEU.
15   I.e. 20 days after their publication in the Official Journal.
16   *Mario Giuliano & Paul Lagarde*, Report on the Convention on the Law Applicable to Contractual Obligations, OJ C 282 [1.10.1980] (hereafter: *Giuliano & Lagarde* Report) 1.
17   For a useful overview of the methodological background in Europe, and, in particular on the objectives of the Rome II Regulation see, *Th. de Boer*, The purpose of uniform choice of law rules: The Rome II Regulation (2009) NILR 295–332.
18   Formerly Article 65 Treaty on European Union (consolidated version) OJ C 321E [29.12.2006], 203–224 (EC Treaty).
19   Article 81(c) TFEU (*ex* Article 65(b) EC Treaty).
20   See Recitals (6) Rome I; Recital (6), (8) Rome II.

hinder commercial cross-border transactions, bring about unequal conditions of competition, and that the uncertainty surrounding the ascertainment of the governing legal system may prove costly and time consuming.[21] The advantage of a unified European system of conflict-of-law rules is that it will increase the level of legal certainty, promote confidence in the stability of legal relationships, and augment the protection of rights over the entire field of private law.[22] The consolidation or strengthening of legal certainty implies substantial predictability of "the outcome of litigation",[23] and as a result will promote settlements. It also implies decisional certainty whereby different courts in different countries will decide disputes according to the same law and consequently recourse to 'forum shopping' is prevented.

Nevertheless, a unification of choice of law rules will not guarantee absolute decisional harmony. Inherent in the creation of a unified system of conflict-of-law rules is the persistent struggle to find a balance between certainty and predictability on the one hand and flexibility on the other. Inevitably, such a system will need to include specific rules coupled with rules of displacement and rules that provide for recognition of national interests and policies. Choice of law criteria must be based on the premise that forum law and foreign law are equally suited for application and that any choice between them should be made on a neutral basis.[24] Thus, because the European choice of law rules contained in the Rome Regulations must be autonomously applied and interpreted, there should be no room for any divergent

---

21    *Helmut Koziol*, Comparative Law – A Must in the European Union: Demonstrated by Tort Law as an Example (2007) Journal of Tort Law Vol. 1 Issue 3 Article 5 1–18, 2. Further on the importance of harmonisation and unification in Europe see, *Stefan Leible*, Wege zu einem Europäischen Privatrecht – Anwendungsprobleme und Entwicklungsperspektiven des Gemeinschaftsprivatrecht (2005); *Thomas Kadner Graziano*, Die Zukunft der Zivilrechtskodifikation in Europa – Harmonisierung der alten Gesetzbücher oder Schaffung eines neuen? 2005 Zeitschrift für Europäisches Privatrecht 523; *Elsabe Schoeman*, Third (Anglo-Common Law) Countries and Rome II: Dilemma or Deliverance? 2011 Journal PIL Vol. 7 No. 2 361–392. See also the *Giuliano & Lagarde* Report at 2: "The number of cases in which the question of applicable law must be resolved increases with the growth of private law relationships across frontiers."

22    See also *Erik Jayme/Christian Kohler*, Europäisches Kollisionsrecht 2007: Windstille im Erntefeld der Integration (2007) IPRax 493–499, 495 with further references.

23    Recital (6) Rome I and Recital (6) Rome II.

24    See *Th. de Boer*, The purpose of uniform choice of law rules: The Rome II Regulation (2009) NILR 295, 297; *idem*, Forum Preferences in Contemporary European Conflicts Law: The Myth of a Neutral Choice, FS Jayme Vol. I (2004) 39–55 who posits that the possibility for forum bias remains.

application of the *lex causae*. However, both Rome Regulations include mandatory rules designed to protect the weaker party[25] and special rules as a means to further commonly accepted social policies.[26] The inclusion of these rules recognises that substantive values, interests and policies of the forum should be permitted to influence the outcome of the choice of law process, but at the same time may cause a degree of legal uncertainty. In this respect, the role of the European Court of Justice (ECJ), as having substantive control over the choice of law rules contained in the Regulations, provides the potential to remove discrepancy in the application of the choice of law rules by national courts and further the absolute unification of European private international law.[27] Moreover, both Rome Regulations expressly exclude issues of procedure. This means that the general principles of procedural conflict-of-law rules may be applied in different ways by national courts, leaving open the further potential for discrepancies amongst fora and possibly the ability to 'forum-shop' for procedural advantages. Leaving this issue unresolved on the European level will continue to represent an obstacle to the underlying aims of both Rome Regulations, namely to achieve uniformity, certainty and predictability of results within European private international law. It is suggested in Part 3 below that in order to reach these objectives, the Rome Regulations need to be supplemented by uniform procedural rules governing the introduction and ascertainment of foreign law in court.[28]

---

25 See for example Arts 6(1) and 8(2) Rome I Regulation.

26 *Th. de Boer*, The purpose of uniform choice of law rules: The Rome II Regulation (2009) NILR, 297–298; on this also *Felix Maultzsch*, Rechtswahl und ius cogens im Internationalen Schuldvertragsrecht, RabelsZ Vol. 75 (2011) 60–101.

27 National court decisions are subject to review by the ECJ. In particular, the ECJ has full jurisdiction to control the application of the notion of public policy in any particular case where it was invoked: Case C-7/98 *Krombach v Bamberski* [2001] QB 709 at [22] (recourse to the public policy exception could be envisaged only if recognition or enforcement constitutes a manifest breach of a rule of law regarded as essential or as a fundamental right in the legal forum; Case C-38/98 *Régie Nationale des Usines Renault SA v Maxicar SpA* [2000] ECR I-2973 at [27] (equality of national and Community law).

28 Note Article 30(1)(i) Rome II: "Not later than 20 August 2011, the Commission shall submit to the European Parliament, the Council and the European Economic and Social Committee a report on the application of this Regulation. If necessary, the report shall be accompanied by proposals to adapt this Regulation. The report shall include: (i) a study on the effects of the way in which foreign law is treated in the different jurisdictions and on the extent to which courts in the Member States apply foreign law in practice pursuant to this Regulation." On this see project JLS/CJ/2007-I/03,

24

# Part 1: Freedom of choice of law under the Rome I Regulation on the Law Applicable to contractual obligations

Freedom of choice or party autonomy is an internationally accepted principle in the area of contract choice of law.[29] The justifications normally given for party autonomy are: freedom of contract, certainty and economic efficiency.[30] Where parties are given the freedom to enter into any contract they wish and to choose and design the legal aspects of their relationship, it necessarily follows that the parties should have the liberty to choose the law by reference to which their contract will be construed. Hence, when the choice of the parties is respected, the legitimate expectations or interests of the parties will be protected.[31] In addition, all contracts whether international or domestic require certainty and economic efficiency,[32] both achieved by enabling the parties to know their rights and liabilities under the contract in advance.[33] In most contractual cross-border disputes, no difficulty will arise as a court will simply be required to give effect to the parties' expressed choice of law. However, problems arise

---

Principles for a Future EU Regulation on the Application of Foreign Law (Madrid Principles), discussed further below at Part 3/B *Introduction and ascertainment of foreign law in national courts.*

29　For commentary on the principle of party autonomy in the law of contracts see generally e.g. *Peter Nygh*, Autonomy in International Contracts (1999); *Stefan Leible*, Parteiautonomie im IPR – Allgemeines Anknüpfungsprinzip oder Verlegenheitslösung? FS Jayme (2004) 485 *et seq.*; *Gisela Rühl*, Party Autonomy in the Private International Law of Contracts: Transatlantic Convergence and Economic Efficiency, CLPE Research Paper 4/2007 Vol. 03 No. 01 (2007) available at: http://ssrn.com/abstract=921842.

30　*Peter Nygh*, Autonomy in International Contracts (1999) 2. See also *Jan Kropholler*, Internationales Privatrecht (2006) 295 *et seq.*

31　See generally *Axel Flessner*, Interessenjurisprudenz im IPR (1990).

32　Professor *C.G.J. Morse*, The EEC Convention on the Law Applicable to Contractual Obligations (1982) 2 YB Eur.L., 107 at 116 maintains that the justification for the principle is found in international commercial convenience. See also *Peter Nygh*, Autonomy in International Contracts (1999) 2–3; *Stefan Leible*, Außenhandel und Rechtssicherheit, ZVglRWiss 97 (1998) 286, 288.

33　These issues are further dealt with below, see Part 2/A.III *Justifying party autonomy in the conflict of laws.*

when the existence of a valid choice of law to govern the contract is denied or when the contended choice of law is unclear. In such a situation, a court will be required to determine the parties' choice of law in contract, analysing consent and agreement and possibly draw on divergent national practices in doing so. The European unification of choice of law in contracts provides courts with a systematic and congruent conflicts system in order to resolve such issues. The 2008 European Regulation on the Law Applicable to Contractual Obligations makes the doctrine of party autonomy the general choice of law rule for contractual obligations. The approach of the Regulation reaffirms the approach embodied in the private international law of all of the Member States of the Community, and indeed most other countries.[34] In England, the leading authority *Vita Food Products Inc v Unus Shipping Company Ltd*,[35] firmly established that the law chosen by the parties will govern the contract, provided that the choice is *bona fide*, legal and not against public policy.[36] In Germany, *Freiheit der Rechtswahl* or *Parteiautonomie*, conferring the power of parties to specify the law applicable to their contract is also recognised and founded on case law.[37] The following exposition will examine the unified approach to be taken within Europe to the Rome I Regulation and will integrate a comparison of the pre-regulation civil law position in Germany and the common law position in England.

---

34   See *Giuliano & Lagarde* Report at 14–16.

35   [1939] AC 277 at 289–290 (PC).

36   See also *R v International Trustee for the Protection of Bondholders Aktiengesellschaft* [1937] AC 500, 530. Note, however that the position taken in the *Unus Shipping* case has been subject to vigorous criticism, see e.g. Denning LJ in *Boissevain v Weil* [1968] 1 KB 482 at 491; Upjohn J in *Re Helbert Wagg and Co* [1956] 1 All ER 129 at 136. For academic criticism, see e.g. *J.H.C. Morris/G.G. Cheshire*, The Proper Law of a Contract in the Conflict of Laws (1940) 56 LQR 320. Nevertheless, the proposition in the *Unus Shipping* case on the effect of a choice of law by the parties was reaffirmed in *The Komninos S* [1991] 1 Lloyds Rep 370 (CA) at 373. See further discussion of the English position below under Part 4/A.I. *The English doctrine of the proper law*.

37   *Christoph Reithmann/Dieter Martiny* (eds.), Internationales Vertragsrecht (2010) marginal no. 87 with further references; *Dieter Martiny* in: Münchener Kommentar zum Bürgerlichen Gesetzbuche (2010) (hereafter: *Martiny* in: MünchKomm (5th ed.) Art. 3 Rom I-VO, 461; *Volker Triebel*, The Choice of Law in Commercial Relations: A German Perspective (1988) 37 ICLQ 935, 937.

# A. The Rome Convention and the Rome I Regulation

The harmonisation of jurisdiction and enforcement in international civil or commercial disputes achieved by the Brussels Convention[38] (now Brussels I Regulation[39]), did not provide for the unification of European choice of law for contracts. A sufficient amount of uniformity in the commercial sphere was unattainable if there continued to exist diversity of choice of law rules at the substantive level. A first move towards a unification of substantive law was made in 1972, when the original six Member States of the European Community presented a first preliminary E.E.C. Draft Convention on Contractual and Non-Contractual Obligations.[40] However, in 1978 the decision was made to abandon the non-contractual provisions of the draft convention and to rather focus attention only on contractual obligations. In 1980, negotiations led to the adoption of the Convention on the Law Applicable to Contractual Obligations, commonly called "Rome Convention", which came into force on 1 April 1991.[41] The Convention was regarded a natural follow-up to the Brussels Convention, facilitating unification within the field of private international law. It established uniform rules of choice of law in contract in order to advance the unification of and eliminate the inconveniencies arising from the diversity of the rules of conflict within the European Community.[42] By the end of 2005, the European Commission tabled a proposal for a Regulation on the Law Applicable to Contractual Obligations (hereafter 'The Proposal'[43]), following

---

38    OJ L 299/32 (1972).

39    In 2001 the European Union converted the Brussels Convention into a Regulation: Council Regulation (EC) No 44/2001 of 22 December 2000 on jurisdiction and the recognition and enforcement of judgments in civil and commercial matters, OJ L 12/1 (2001).

40    For comments on the draft see amongst others *Ole Lando*, The EC-Draft Convention on the Law Applicable to Contractual and Non-Contractual Obligations, (1974) RabelsZ 6–55.

41    Hereafter referred to as the "Rome Convention". The consolidated text of the Convention is published in OJ C 27, [26.01.1998] 0034 – 0046 (English text). See also Rome I Regulation (EC) No 593/2008 on the law applicable to contractual obligations (Rome I) OJ L 177, 6 [4.7.2008], which replaces the Rome Convention. For text of Rome Convention in various languages, see http://eurlex.europa.eu/LexUriServ/LexUriServ.do?uri=CELEX:41998A0126(02):EN:NOT.

42    See Giuliano & Lagarde Report.

43    Proposal for a Regulation of the European Parliament and the Council on the law applicable to contractual obligations (Rome I) COM (2005) 650 final 15.12.2005. For further commentary on this text see e.g. *Franco Ferrari/Stefan Leible* (eds.),

the Green Paper[44] and public consultations[45], which proposed to introduce a large number of changes to the Convention.[46] The Proposal adopted by the legislature integrated some of the proposed changes, rejected others and introduced further changes not previously proposed.[47] The final text was adopted on 17 June 2008 and superseded the Rome Convention on 17 December 2009 as the Rome I Regulation (hereafter abbreviated as Rome I or the Rome I Regulation).[48] In accordance with Article 288 TFEU, the Rome I Regulation will be directly applicable in all

---

Ein neues Internationales Vertragsrecht für Europa – Der Vorschlag für eine Rom I-Verordnung (2007); *Peter Mankowski*, Der Vorschlag für die Rom I-Verordnung (2006) IPRax 101.

44 Green Paper on the conversion of the Rome Convention of 1980 on the law applicable to contractual obligations into a Community instrument and its modernisation COM (2002) 654 14.1.2003COM (2002) 654 14.1.2003. For comments on this text see, *Andrea Bonomi*, Conversion of the Rome Convention into an EX Instrument: Some Remarks on the Green Paper of the EC Commission, Yearbook PIL (2003) 53–98; *Stefan Leible* (ed.), *Das Grünbuch zum internationalen Vertragsrecht* (2004).

45 More than eighty replies were received from academics, institutions and other organisations. These are available at: http://ec.europa.eu/justice_home/news/consulting_public/rome_i/news_summary_rome1_en.htm. Detailed commentary was provided by *Jürgen Basedow* (et al.), The Max Institute for Comparative and International Private Law, Comments on the European Commission's Green Paper on the Conversion of the Rome Convention of 1980 on the Law Applicable to Contractual Obligations into a Community Instrument and its Modernization, 68 RabelsZ (2004) 1–118. See also *Ulrich Magnus/Peter Mankowski*, The Green Paper on a Future Rome I Regulation – on the Road to a Renewed European Private International Law of Contracts, (2004) 103 ZvglRWiss, 131; *Jürgen Basedow* (et al.), Max Planck Institute for Comparative and International Private Law, Comments on the European Commission's Proposal for a Regulation of the European Parliament and the Council on the Law Applicable to Contractual Obligations (Rome I), 71 RabelsZ (2007) 225–344.

46 See for example Article 7 and 16 of *The Proposal*. *The Proposal* also suggested radical reform of Articles 3, 4 and 5 of the Rome Convention.

47 Changes made, include *inter alia*, to Articles 3 (party autonomy), 4 (applicable law in the absence of choice), 5 (contracts of carriage), Article 6 (consumer contracts), 7 (insurance contracts) and Article 9 (overriding mandatory provisions). This essay will only focus on Article 4 and the freedom of parties to choose the applicable law and the effect of Article 9 on party autonomy.

48 Article 28, Rome I. The Rome Convention will continue to determine the choice of law governing contractual obligations for contracts concluded prior to 17 December 2009. See also Article 24(1) that states that Rome I will replace the Rome Convention.

Member States, except Denmark[49], without the need for ratification by the States.[50] The Member States will be required to apply Rome I even where the law specified by it is not the law of a Member State.[51] According to Article 29, the Regulation entered into force 20 days following its publication in the Official Journal of the European Union (i.e. 24th July 2008).[52]

The Rome I Regulation presents a revised version or modernisation of the Rome Convention of 1980.[53] It applies in situations involving a conflict of laws and designates the applicable law for contractual obligations in civil and commercial matters.[54] Due to the recent adoption of the Regulation and therefore the lack of case law on it,[55] it will be necessary to deal with cases, texts and commentary on both the Rome Convention and the Rome I Regulation. The Rome Convention

---

49  See Recital (46) of the Rome I Regulation. Denmark will continue to apply the Rome Convention.

50  Compare the incorporation of the Rome Convention: In England the Convention was enacted by virtue of the Contracts (Applicable Law) Act 1990, for Germany see *EGBGB* Arts 27–42.

51  Article 2, Rome I. This approach is also taken in the Rome Convention (Article 2) and the Rome II Regulation (Article 3).

52  The Rome I Regulation makes a distinction between the date of entry into force and the date of application (Article 29). However, it is unclear why the Regulation insists on making such a distinction as the Regulation is not *in force*, i.e. its rules cannot be applied, until the date of its application. Arguably therefore the distinction appears unimportant – the date of application being in effect the date of *entry* into force. Compare for example the Brussels I Regulation which only uses entry into force. On this see *Michael Wilderspin*, The Rome I Regulation: Communitarisation and modernisation of the Rome Convention, ERA Forum (2008) 259, 260 n 2.

53  All private international law instruments have been adopted in the form of regulations. The Commission in its Green Paper stated that: "rules on jurisdiction and choice of law applying to contractual and non-contractual obligations of a civil or commercial nature form an entity, the fact that the Rome Convention takes a different form from the other Community instruments of private international law does not improve the consistency of this entity", Green Paper at 2.2. See also Recital (7) of the Regulation. See generally *Ole Lando/Peter Nielsen*, The Rome I Regulation, (2008) 45 CML Rev 1687–1725; *Ulrich Magnus*, Die Rom I-Verordnung (2010) IPRax 27–44.

54  Article 1(1) and Recital (7), Rome I. Rome I will not apply to revenue, customs or administrative matters (Article 1(1)) and several further exclusions listed under Article 1(2) Rome I. These will not be dealt with in this essay.

55  The Regulation applies to contracts concluded after December 17, 2009. Decisions made on the Convention will continue to remain authoritative as to those provisions not amended in the Regulation.

is accompanied by the Giuliano and Lagarde Report (hereafter referred to as the *Giuliano & Lagarde* Report),[56] a commentary by members of the Working Group responsible for drafting the Convention. The Report has been published in the Official Journal of the European Union enabling it to be considered in interpreting the Convention. Much of the wording of the Convention has been simply adopted in Rome I with only minor modifications.[57] In particular, Article 3 and the freedom of choice of the applicable law by the parties, is reaffirmed in Rome I with only minor amendments.[58]

## B. The Applicable Law and Freedom of Choice under the Rome I Regulation

Chapter I of the Rome I Regulation contains two Articles (Articles 1 and 2) dealing with the material scope and universal application of the Regulation. The general conflict-of-law rules are set out in Chapter II (Articles 3–18), entitled "Uniform Rules". Chapter II contains further Articles dealing with specific types of contracts and placing limitations on the effect of party autonomy in terms of mandatory rules[59] and in relation to consumer[60] and employment[61] contracts. Chapter III (Articles 19–28), entitled "Other Provisions" deals, *inter alia*, with description of habitual residence, public policy and the Regulation's relationship with existing legal provisions. Finally, Chapter IV (Article 29) includes only one Article governing the entry into force and application of the Regulation.

---

56 Giuliano & Lagarde Report.
57 In part, the changes made were necessary in order to make the language of the Rome I Regulation consistent with both Rome II and the Brussels I Regulation. See Recitals (7), (15), (17) and (24), of Rome I.
58 The amendments made in the Regulation will be pointed out under the relevant points below.
59 Mandatory laws of the country with which all the elements relevant to the situation at the time of choice were connected: Article 3; mandatory rules of the country in which the consumer has his habitual residence that protect him: Article 6; mandatory rules of the country of the country whose law would have applied to the employment contract, in the absence of choice that would have protected him: Article 8; mandatory rules of the *lex fori*: Article 9, Rome I.
60 Article 6, Rome I.
61 Article 8, Rome I.

The central provisions of the Rome I Regulation are Articles 3 and 4 in Chapter II of the Regulation. Article 3 embodies the principle of party autonomy and governs cases in which parties have made a choice of law, whereas Article 4 provides a set of rules for the determination of the applicable law where parties have not made a choice. In cases where a choice is made pursuant to Article 3 of the Regulation, the parties' intention, either express or inferred, will be relevant.[62] Where the parties make no choice, reference to objective connections will be required under Article 4.[63] These two central provisions are intended to provide legal certainty through clearly set out rules in order to determine the law that should be applied to contractual obligations, while at the same time providing courts with enough flexibility and discretion to determine the law that is most closely connected to the situation.[64] The applicable law, whether chosen or not, refers only to the domestic law of the country, the operation of *renvoi* is excluded.[65]

# I. Principle of Party Autonomy under Article 3 Rome I Regulation

The fundamental principle generally underpinning choice of law in the Rome I Regulation is that parties have substantial autonomy: parties may make a choice as to the applicable law and when a choice is made by the parties this should be decisive and only in situations where no choice is made, should courts resort to determining objective connections. This principle of party autonomy is embodied

---

62    Article 3, Rome I.
63    Article 4, Rome I, provides specific rules for determining the applicable law in the absence of choice. This Article will not be considered further here.
64    This being the general objective of the Rome I Regulation according to Recital (16).
65    Article 20 of the Rome I Regulation (Article 15 Rome Convention) states that the choice of law of a country means: "the application of the rules of law in force in that country other than its rules of private international law." See also *James Fawcett/Janeen Carruthers* (eds.), *Cheshire, North & Fawcett Private International Law* (2008) (hereafter: *Cheshire & North* (14th ed.)) 689; *Richard Plender/Michael Wilderspin*, The European Contracts Convention, (2001) 57; *Giuliano & Lagarde* Report 43. See reasons for exclusion of *renvoi* in the event of an express choice of law given by Lord Diplock in *Amin Rasheed Shipping Corp v Kuwait Insurance Co* [1984] 1 AC 50. Compare also Article 24 Rome II Regulation which also explicitly excludes the application of *renvoi*.

in Article 3 of the Regulation and entitled "Freedom of choice".[66] Article 3 paragraph (1) states:

> A contract shall be governed by the law chosen by the parties. The choice shall be made expressly or clearly demonstrated by the terms of the contract or the circumstances of the case. By their choice the parties can select the law applicable to the whole or to part only of the contract.

The rule enunciated in paragraph (1) clearly establishes the supremacy of party autonomy. It is considered to be the most central and dominant rule in the Regulation, authorising the broad recognition of the principle of party autonomy.[67] Not only does it permit the parties to a contract to choose whichever law they wish, whether or not it has a connection to the contract, but also allows the parties to choose different laws for different parts of the contract, to exercise their choice at any time, and to change their choice. The supremacy of party autonomy flows from the recognition of the principle of freedom of contract. Parties are free to enter into any contract; so, providing parties with the liberty to choose the law by reference to which their contract will be construed will in practice facilitate international trade and commerce.[68] Recital (11) to the Regulation affirms that: "The parties' freedom to choose the applicable law should be one of the cornerstones of the system of conflict-of-law rules in matters of contractual obligations".[69] The parties' choice therefore is to be decisive – a choice that can only be restricted or displaced in clearly specified situations.[70]

Inherent in the first two sentences of Article 3 paragraph (1) are two requirements:

(1)   that a choice was made by the parties; and,
(2)   that the choice must be express or clearly demonstrated by the terms of the contract or the circumstances of the case.[71]

These two requirements and related issues will be now dealt with in turn.

---

66   In the German text *"Freie Rechtswahl"*, in French text *"Liberté de choix"*. Compare Article 3 Rome Convention; Article 27 German *EGBGB* and further discussion in *Ulrich Magnus*, Die Rom I-Verordnung (2010) IPRax 27–44, 31 *et seq.*
67   *Dieter Martiny* in: Münchener Kommentar zum Bürgerlichen Gesetzbuche (Vol. 10 2010) (hereafter: *Martiny* in: MünchKomm (5th ed.) Art. 3 Rom I-VO marginal no. 8; *Peter Nygh*, Autonomy in International Contracts (1999) 87.
68   *Martiny* in: MünchKomm (5th ed.) Art. 3 Rom I-VO marginal no. 8.
69   Recital (11) of Rome I.
70   These are briefly discussed below, see Part 1/B.II. *Restrictions on Party Autonomy.*
71   *Adrian Briggs*, The Conflict of Laws (2002) 159.

## 1. The choice made by the parties

As indicated above, Article 3(1) of the Rome I Regulation clearly establishes that parties can exercise a choice of law. Consequently, the ensuing issues concern 'consent and validity' of the choice exercised.[72] This involves consideration of issues such as: whether the choice has been lawfully and effectively made and whether there was agreement between the parties as to the choice of law made. But in order to do so, the difficult question of which law will govern these issues will first be discussed. In addition, the problem of agreement between the parties as to the choice of law and the effect of silence on consent will also be considered below.

*a. Has the choice been lawfully and effectively made?*

The Rome I Regulation takes a very liberal approach to issues of formal validity of the contract. Article 11 of the Regulation (Article 9 of the Rome Convention) contains the rules concerning formal validity. Article 11 does not define the expression *formal validity*. According to the *Giuliano & Lagarde* Report, formal validity encompasses "every external manifestation required on the part of a person expressing the will to be legally bound and in the absence of which such expression of will, would not be regarded as fully effective".[73] The rules contained in Article 11 – although somewhat confusingly set out – provide a list of applicable laws, which when complied with, will establish formal validity. As regards the choice of law made by the parties, Article 11(1) of the Regulation refers the formal validity including the formal validity of a choice of law clause[74] either to (a) the law of the country or countries where both the parties are at the time of conclusion of the contract[75] or (b) the law which governs the contract in substance, i.e. the law chosen by the parties pursuant to Article 3 (or Article 4) of the Regulation. Accordingly, the formal requirements as stipulated under the law identified by Article 11(1) must be fulfilled.

A further issue that is raised is whether Article 3 of Rome I permits the scrutiny of a pre-formulated choice of law clause contained in a standard form contract (*Inhaltskontrolle von AGB-Rechtswahlklauseln*). In other words, whether the Regulation requires scrutiny of such a clause according to the *lex causae*,

---

72 *Peter Nygh*, Autonomy in International Contracts (1999) Chapter 4.
73 Giuliano & Lagarde Report 29.
74 See *Giuliano & Lagarde* Report 30–31.
75 Or, if they are not, the law of either country in which they are present at the time.

over and above the control mechanisms governing formal validity provided for within the Regulation. Article 11 of Rome I does not make any mention of specific control of choice of law clauses contained within standard form contracts. The prevailing academic opinion appears to be that although a choice of law clause is to be examined as to whether it has been lawfully and effectively made, an additional specific control of a choice of law clause contained in a standard form contract is inadmissible.[76] As a result, a choice of law clause will be valid if expressed either in an individually negotiated contract or in a standard form contract.[77]

*b. Was there an agreement on choice of law?*

Party autonomy is centred on the intention of the parties in freely negotiated contracts[78] substantiated by the existence of *consensus ad idem* or agreement as to the choice of law.[79] Courts will readily give effect to the parties' intention if there was manifest agreement and will understandably be less willing to do so in cases where the existence of agreement is denied. Under English law, it appears to have been accepted that where there is a choice of foreign law or jurisdiction that this choice may still be ineffective if by English law there had been no *consensus ad idem*.[80] Accordingly, there will be no consensus where there is a clear rejection of a proffered choice of law clause, such as where a choice of law clause in the agreement is crossed out by one party.[81] Similarly, the use of inconsistent terms in a contract will also indicate a lack of consensus.[82] But under

---

76    *Rolf Wagner*, Der Grundsatz der Rechtswahl und des mangels Rechtswahl anwendbarer Recht (Rom I-Verordnung) – Ein Bericht über die Entstehungsgeschichte und den Inhalt der Artikel 3 und 4 Rom I-Verordnung (2008) IPRax 14; *Erik Jayme*, Inhaltskontrolle von Rechtswahlklauseln in Allgemeinen Geschäftsbedingungen, in: *Bernhard Pfister/Michael Will* (et al. eds.), FS Werner Lorenz (1991) 435.

77    *Martiny* in: MünchKomm (5th ed.) marginal no. 42 and 109.

78    *Ole Lando*, Contracts in: *Kurt Lipstein* (ed.) International Encyclopedia of Comparative Law 3, Private International Law 3 (1976).

79    *Adrian Briggs* (ed.), Agreements on Jurisdiction and Choice of Law (2008) 37; *Dicey & Morris* (14th ed.) Vol. II 1577–1578.

80    *Dicey & Morris* (14th ed.) Vol. II 1577 citing e.g. *Mackender v Feldia AG* [1967] 2 QB 590 (CA).

81    As in Land Rover Exports Ltd v Samcrete Egypt Engineers and Contractors SAE [2001] EWCA Civ 2019, [2002] CLC 533.

82    See e.g. Iran Continental Shelf Oil Co v IRI International Corp [2002] CLC 372.

application of the Regulation, which law is to govern the issue of agreement in regard to choice of law?

aa) The general rule under the Regulation

Article 3(5) of the Rome I Regulation expressly refers the question of validity of *consent* of the parties as to the contract in general (*Hauptvertrag*), including the choice of the applicable law (*Verweisungsvertrag*), i.e. whether the choice has been lawfully and effectively made, to be determined in accordance with Articles 10, 11 (Formal validity) and 13 (Incapacity) of the Regulation. Article 10 of the Regulation (Article 8 of the Rome Convention)[83] is headed "consent and material validity" and comprises two paragraphs: the first contains the general rule; the second contains the exception. Paragraph (1) provides that "the existence and validity of a contract, or of any term of a contract, shall be determined by the law which would govern it under this Regulation if the contract or term were valid". This suggests that where there is a disputed agreement on choice of law, courts will be required to assume that the choice of law is valid and that this 'chosen' law is to be applied for the determination of whether the choice was lawfully and effectively made.[84] The mere 'appearance' of a choice of law is for the purposes of validity treated as a manifest declaration of the will of the parties. The law chosen is to therefore initially govern the validity of the actual choice and subsequently the validity of the contract as a whole.[85]

This approach has been criticised as being logically unclear. Questions of formation cannot be governed by the applicable law, for until such questions are resolved it has not been established that there is a contract.[86] However, the Regulation ignores this problem of logic and in the terminology of the common law provides for the application of the 'putative proper law', i.e. the law that the parties purported to choose or the law that would govern the choice of law clause if the clause were

---

83 The wording of the Article is virtually identical to the former Article 8 Rome Convention.

84 This is the approach taken by the common law: Compania Naviera Micro SA v Shipley International Inc 'The Parouth' [1982] 2 Lloyds Rep 351; Union Transport plc v Continental Lines SA [1992] 1 WLR 15, 23 (HL); Seapremium Shipping Ltd v Seaconsortium Ltd ('The Gilian') [2001] EWHC (Admlty) (Steel J).

85 *Jan Kropholler*, Internationales Privatrecht (2006) §40 III, 1 and §52 II, 2; *Christoph Reithmann/Dieter Martiny* (eds.), Internationales Vertragsrecht (2010) marginal no. 89.

86 *Christopher Clarkson/Jonathan Hill*, The Conflict of Laws (2011) 246.

valid.[87] The English High Court in *Egon Oldendorff v Libera Corporation*,[88] in considering the question whether an arbitration clause had been validly incorporated, held that the putative proper law applied. Similarly, the German *Bundesgerichtshof* in 1986 also applied the putative proper law analysis holding that the validity of a choice of law clause contained in a bill of lading was to be determined in accordance with the law which would be applicable if the clause were valid.[89]

Other solutions have been suggested, such as the application of the *lex fori* or the law which would be the proper law in the absence of an express choice[90]. But as the authors of the *Giuliano & Lagarde* Report make clear, the approach taken under the Regulation is necessary in order to "avoid the circular argument that where there is a choice of the applicable law no law can be said to be applicable until the contract is found to be valid".[91] Although this presents a pragmatic solution to the question, it has been pointed out that the application of the putative proper law in order to determine the existence of a choice may be unfair and arbitrary and that the law of the forum, through the application of its rules of private international law, should determine whether a particular choice of law is legally effective.[92] However, by opting for the application of the putative law, there will at least need to be an apparent acceptance by each of the parties of the relevant choice of law.[93] Further, the application of a law based on the apparent acceptance

---

87   This is the approach also taken in the Hague Convention on the Law Applicable to International Sale of Goods, 1955, Art. 2(3) and the Hague Convention on the Law Applicable to Contracts for the International Sale of Goods (1986), Art. 10. See *Dicey & Morris* (15th ed.) Vol. II 1814; *F.A. Mann*, The Proper Law of Contract – An Obituary, (1991) 107 LQR 353; *Peter Nygh*, Autonomy in International Contracts (1999) Chapter 4; *Jonathan Harris*, Does Choice of Law Make Any Sense?, (2004) Vol. 4 57 Current Legal Problems 305–353, 316 *et seq.*

88   *(No 1)* [1995] 2 Lloyd's Rep 64 (per Mance J). See also *Mackender v Feldia AG* [1967] 2 QB 590 (CA) at 602 (per Diplock LJ); *Compania Naviera Micro SA v Shipley International Inc The 'Parouth'* [1982] 2 Lloyds Rep 351.

89   *Bundesgerichtshof* judgment of 15.12.1986 *The Lankya Abbaya* (1988) IPRax 26.

90   See *Peter Nygh*, Autonomy in International Contracts (1999) 92–96; *Dicey & Morris* (15th ed.) Vol. II 1814–1815.

91   Giuliano & Lagarde Report 30.

92   *Peter Nygh*, Autonomy in International Contracts (1999) 95; but c.f. critically *Adrian Briggs* (ed.), Agreements on Jurisdiction and Choice of Law (2008) 426 *et seq.*; *Martiny* in: MünchKomm (5th ed.) 497.

93   In German "Rechtsschein einer vertraglichen Vereinbarung", see e.g. *Christoph Reithmann/Dieter Martiny* (eds.), Internationales Vertragsrecht (2010) marginal no. 89 with further references.

of the parties is far less arbitrary and uncertain than the application of the *lex fori* to determine the existence of a choice made by the parties, and is in keeping with the spirit of the Regulation.[94] In this way the application of the *lex causae* clearly promotes a uniform determination of agreement in regard to choice of law.

bb) The exception

Article 10(2) of the Regulation adds, by way of corrective that:

> [...] a party, in order to establish that he did not consent, may rely upon the law of the country in which he has his habitual residence if it appears from the circumstances that it would not be reasonable to determine the effect of his conduct in accordance with the law specified in paragraph 1.

This suggests that even though the validity of a choice of law, in cases where it is denied that there was agreement on the clause, may be assumed under paragraph (1), a party may nevertheless invoke the law of his place of habitual residence to establish that he is not bound by the clause.[95] In other words, where the validity of a choice of law clause is contested, its validity will be assumed for the purpose of deciding if the parties are bound (under Article 10(1)), but a party may still contest this by appeal to his own law. In this way, Article 10(2) provides an exception to the application of the putative proper law if it appears from the circumstances that it would be unreasonable to do so. Although courts have reacted cautiously when evaluating this defence,[96] it does provide a balance between the conflicting positions of the parties on the issue of the existence of consent. Where there is consent it clearly provides for the application of the putative law and in cases where consent is contested avoids the taking of sides by allowing a party to rely on his own law to show that there was no consent. Thus, while logical objections can in general be

---

94    *Peter Nygh*, Autonomy in International Contracts (1999) 95; *Dicey & Morris* (15th ed.) Vol. II 1815.

95    See critically *Adrian Briggs* (ed.), Agreements on Jurisdiction and Choice of Law (2008) 398–399.

96    See e.g. *Egon Oldendorff v Libera Corporation (No 1)* [1995] 2 Lloyd's Rep 64, one of the first English cases reported that considers Article 3 of the Rome Convention. Mance J in rejecting the defendant's arguments explained that the court should adopt a dispassionate, internationally minded approach and that the onus is on the party invoking the provision. See also *Welex AG v Rosa Maritime Ltd* [2002] 2 Lloyd's Rep 701, Steel J holding that nothing in the circumstances rendered it unreasonable to determine the effect of Welex's conduct by reference to the putative proper law (English law); upheld in [2003] 2 Lloyd's Rep 509 (CA); *Morin v Bonhams & Brooks* [2003] 2 All ER (Comm) 36.

made to this approach, the solution taken by Article 10(1), together with the protection afforded by Article 10(2) to a party who denies having agreed to the choice of law asserted by the other party, appears sufficiently rational.

A further problem arises in cases involving a so-called 'battle of the forms'. This is a situation involving the exchange of conflicting contractual standard forms, where one contains a choice of law and the other does not, or where each contains a different choice of law clause. For example, A makes an offer to B on A's standard form including standard terms and conditions. B accepts, but does so on his standard form including standard terms and conditions. At this stage the acceptance by B would, under English law, not be regarded as an acceptance of A's offer but rather as a counter offer. However, an enforceable contract may still exist if A performs his side of the agreement. This would be regarded as an acceptance to B's counter offer.[97] The question thus arises as to which terms and conditions will be applicable under the Rome I Regulation, when each of the parties argues for the application of its choice of law.

Article 11 of the Rome I Regulation (Article 8 of the Rome Convention) deals with the existence and validity of a contract but does not expressly provide an answer to the question of which law should apply in situations involving a battle of the forms. Courts have tended to apply the *lex fori* to determine what the terms of the contract are. As mentioned above, under English law the last counter offer made before performance will render all preceeding offers void.[98] Other solutions that have been suggested include applying the law which would govern the contract in the absence of an express choice of law, i.e. the objective proper law,[99] or that the later-formed contract supersedes the earlier to the extent of the

---

97 See e.g. *Butler Machine Tool Co Ltd v Ex-Cell-O Corporation (England) Ltd* [1979] 1 All ER 965.

98 This is referred to as the so-called "last shot" doctrine. See e.g. *Hugh Beale* (ed.), Chitty on Contracts (2012) Vol. 1, at para. 2–037. The doctrine is also referred to in Germany as the *Theorie des letzten Wortes*. Article 19 CISG (United Nations Convention on Contracts for the International Sale of Goods) may also be applicable in the cases concerning the international sale of goods (note: the UK has not ratified this Convention). However, the application of CISG appears to be disputed, compare e.g. *Volker Triebel*, The Choice of Law in Commercial Relations: A German Perspective, (1988) 37 ICLQ 935, 939 who states that under German law those standard terms that are identical will be incorporated into the contract and those terms that are contradictory rejected; the remaining terms and conditions will be filled by the law governing the contract.

99 *Lawrence Collins et al.* (eds.), Dicey and Morris on the Conflict of Laws (1993) (hereafter: *Dicey & Morris*, 12th ed.) Vol. II 1251; also *Lawrence Collins et al.* (eds.), Dicey and Morris on the Conflict of Laws (2012) (hereafter: *Dicey & Morris*,

inconsistency[100]. This issue was considered by the English Court of Appeal in the case of *Tekdata Interconnections Ltd v Amphenol Ltd.*[101] The judge at first instance had held that Tekdata's terms applied despite the fact that Amphenol's acknowledgment was the last act made before performance. The judge held that this was what the parties had intended, taking into account the trading history between the parties. The Court of Appeal reinstated the traditional English approach taken to contract formation, stating that the judge had concentrated more on what would have happened rather than what had happened. Thus, it appears that English courts will not easily displace the traditional approach whereby the last contractual document sent before performance will prevail, unless there is sufficiently strong evidence to suggest that the parties intended otherwise.[102] However, it is noted that resort to the *lex fori* in such cases must be avoided and that instead the *lex causae* be applied. This is deal with further in detail below.[103]

### c. The problem of silent consent

An additional issue concerning agreement of the choice of law made by the parties is whether mere silence by one of the parties in certain circumstances can indicate consent. This issue should not be confused with general silence by both parties as to the choice of law made by the parties (dealt with under Article 3(1) second sentence, inferred choice of law).[104] Instead, this issue is referred to as the problem of silent consent.[105] Different national approaches have been taken to this problem. Under English law, it is generally regarded as settled law that silence may not amount to consent.[106] Unless heard to the contrary or previously agreed

---

15th ed.) Vol. II at 1816. The authors note that this solution was more in keeping with the spirit of the Convention and thus preferable to the *lex fori* solution.

100   *Peter Stone*, EU Private International Law: Harmonization of Laws (2006) 296.
101   *Tekdata Interconnections Ltd v Amphenol Ltd* [2009] EWCA Civ 1209. But compare *Evialis SA v SIAT* [2003] EWHC 863 (Comm) at [38] where the High Court, citing *Lawrence Collins et al.* (eds.), Dicey and Morris on the Conflict of Laws (2000) (hereafter: *Dicey & Morris*, 13th ed.) applied the law which would govern the contract in the absence of an express choice.
102   *Tekdata Interconnections Ltd v Amphenol Ltd* [2009] EWCA Civ 1209, at [21].
103   See Part 3/A.II.2. Issues of interpretation.
104   General silence by the parties indicating an inferred choice of law. See Article 3(1) second sentence a "clearly demonstrated" choice of law. Dealt with further below, see Part 1/B.I. 2.b. *Inferred Choice of Law.*
105   *Peter Nygh*, Autonomy in International Contracts (1999) 96–97.
106   See leading case of *Felthouse v Bindley* [1862] EWHC CP J 35.

by the parties that an acceptance may be presumed, English law would not allow the *offeror* to bind the *offeree* in this way. An acceptance may however, be inferred from conduct of which silence may form part.[107] This is also the approach taken in French law, where the established rule is that silence cannot imply acceptance unless so established by statute, usage, or prior relations as between the parties.[108] Under German law silence may in some circumstances amount to an acceptance, depending on the individual circumstances of the case. This will be particularly in cases where the offer has been made in the context of existing commercial relations between the parties.[109] German courts have taken this approach to commercial letters of confirmation (*kaufmännisches Bestätigungsschreiben*).[110] If for example, a letter of confirmation is sent containing the same terms agreed to in prior oral negotiations, the letter is treated as evidence of the negotiations. However, if a letter of confirmation contains different terms to those agreed to orally, but is subsequently accepted without comment, the agreement will be treated as having been modified by the written terms contained in the letter.[111] Under English law, such correspondence would be regarded as being either a request for information (not affecting the original offer) or a counteroffer (requiring acceptance).

German legal practice has often placed a low threshold on silent consent to a choice of law.[112] Thus, it has been considered sufficient if both parties relied on German law during legal proceedings (or where reliance on German law was unchallenged by one party), to infer a silent consent of German law by the parties as the applicable law to their contract.[113] Similarly, German courts have deduced the

---

107  E.g. *Rust v Abbey Life Insurance Co* [1979] 2 Lloyd's Rep 355; *Wettern Electric Ltd v Welsh Development Agency* [1983] QB 796; *Hugh Beale* (ed.), Chitty on Contracts (2012) Vol. 1 at 2–076. Also *Giuliano & Lagarde* Report 28.
108  See *Parviz Owsia*, Silence: Efficacy in Contract Formation. A Comparative View of French and English Law, (1991) ICLQ 784–806.
109  *Christoph Reithmann/Dieter Martiny* (eds.), Internationales Vertragsrecht (2010) marginal no. 129.
110  Paragraph 346 *HBG*; Article 31 II *EGBGB*.
111  *Bundesgerichtshof* judgment of 9.7.1970 – VII ZR 70/68, BGHZ 54, 236, NJW 1970, 2021.
112  See *Christoph Reithmann/Dieter Martiny* (eds.), Internationales Vertragsrecht (2010) 111–128.
113  Compare cases where the German *Bundesgerichtshof* has held that a silent acceptance by the parties of German law as applied in legal proceedings indicated a choice of law, see e.g.: *Bundesgerichtshof* judgments from 28.11.1963, BGHZ 40, 320, 323; 27.3.1968, BGHZ 50, 32, 33; 23.10.1970, NJW 1971, 30.9.1987, NJW-RR 1988, 159, 160; 323, 324; 12.12.1990, NJW 1991, 1292, 1293; 28.1.1992, NJW 1992, 1380;

applicable law from the parties' conduct or attitude during legal proceedings.[114] As a result, the applicable law has been inferred through the silent consent to a choice of law where the parties relied on particular legal provisions of a specific legal system during proceedings.[115] However, such an inference has not been extended to situations where a silent acceptance and therefore choice of English law was argued on the grounds that the contract had been concluded in the English language.[116] Nevertheless, the assumption of silent consent based on the use and apparent acceptance by the parties of a law during legal proceedings is problematic.[117] In cases where the law relied on is the *lex fori*, this obviously allows for the convenient application of familiar national law. But often parties will, during proceedings, be under the mistaken belief that because the proceedings are brought in a particular forum that the law of the forum is also applicable, when in fact a different law is applicable.[118] Hence, they will not even be aware of having made the assumed choice of law. Application of that law would then be no less than an involuntary and ignorant choice of law. Furthermore, a hasty acceptance of the *lex fori* will almost always place one of the parties at an unjustified disadvantage. Accordingly, national courts should cautiously approach situations in which an application of the *lex fori* is argued for on the basis of silent consent during proceedings, especially where the application of such is contested.

---

21.10.1992, NJW, 1993, 385, 386; 12.5.1993, NJW 1993, 2753; 20.9.1995, BGHZ 130, 371. Also judgments from the German *Oberlandesgericht* Hamm from 9.6.1995, NJW-RR 1996, 179; Düsseldorf 19.12.1997, NJW-RR 1998, 1716.

114 *Heinz-Peter Mansel*, Kollisions- und zuständigkeitsrechtlicher Gleichlauf der vertraglichen und deliktischen Haftung, ZvglRW 86 (1987) 1; *Edgar Steinle*, Konkludente Rechtswahl und objektive Anknüpfung nach altem und neuem deutschen internationalen Vertragsrecht, ZvglRWiss 1994 303; *Haimo Schack*, Keine stillschweigende Rechtswahl im Prozeß! (1986) IPRax 272–274.

115 See e.g. *Bundesgerichtshof* judgment of 19.1.2000 – VIII ZR 275/98, NJW-RR 2000, 1002, 1004.

116 See e.g. *Bundesgerichtshof* judgment of 22.11.1955 – I ZR 218/53, BGHZ 19, 110, 112; *Bundesgerichtshof* judgment of 26.10.1989 – VII ZR 153/88, NJW-RR 1990, 183, 184; also *Edgar Steinle*, Konkludente Rechtswahl und objektive Anknüpfung nach altem und neuem deutschen internationalen Vertragsrecht, ZvglRWiss 1994, 300, 313.

117 *Heinz-Peter Mansel*, Kollisions- und zuständigkeitsrechtlicher Gleichlauf der vertraglichen und deliktischen Haftung, ZvglRW 86 (1987) 1.

118 *Jan Kropholler*, Internationales Privatrecht (2006) §40 IV, 4 and §52 II 1; *Axel Steiner*, Die stillschweigende Rechtswahl im Prozeß im System der subjektiven Anknüpfungen im deutschen IPR (1998); *Martiny*, in: MünchKomm (5th ed.) marginal no. 55 with further references.

Under the Rome I Regulation, matters of formation including the effect of silence are regulated in Article 10.[119] As seen above, Article 10(1) provides for the application of the putative proper law to issues of material validity and Article 10(2) allows for displacement of this law if it appears from the circumstances that it would be unreasonable to apply the putative proper law. The inclusion of this exception was specifically devised with the issue of silence constituting acceptance of an offer in mind.[120] But again, surely the allegedly agreed to choice of law should not itself govern the issue of silent consent. The following example helps to demonstrate the issues stemming from the problem of silent consent:[121]

Party A makes an offer to Party B and inserts a choice of law clause in the contract stating that the law of 'X' will govern all disputes between the parties. B remains silent, neither expressly accepting nor rejecting the offer. Under the law of X silence can constitute an acceptance. According to Article 10(1) of the Regulation the law of X, as the putative proper law of the contract would be applicable and an enforceable contract between A and B would exist. However, B contests this and wishes to rely on Article 10(2) and the application of the law of his habitual residence 'Y', under which silence does not constitute an acceptance. In order to apply this exception, a court would have to find that it would not be reasonable to determine the effect of B's conduct under the law of X.[122]

On the above facts, it is generally accepted that it would be manifestly unfair for B to be contractually bound.[123] Consent to choice of law should involve a voluntary and conscious choice of law. Circumstances that a court would take into account when assessing the 'unreasonableness' of applying Article 10(1), include the practice followed by the parties *inter se* as well as their previous business relationships.[124] The overall effect of Article 10 Rome I is that an alleged choice of law may be invalidated either by reference to the putative applicable law under paragraph (1), or by reference to the law of the habitual residence of the party denying consent under paragraph (2). However, although a party may be released from being bound under a contract under paragraph (2), it may not be used to produce the opposite effect,

---

119  *Dicey & Morris* (15th ed.) Vol. II 1842; *Cheshire & North* (14th ed.) 746.
120  Giuliano & Lagarde Report 31; Cheshire & North (14th ed.) 746.
121  This example is based on the example offered in *Cheshire & North* (14th ed.) 745.
122  In *Egon Oldendorff v Libera Corp (No 1)* [1995] 2 Lloyds Rep 64 at 70, the court notes that a "dispassionate, internationally minded approach" should be taken to this issue.
123  *Cheshire & North* (14th ed.) 745.
124  Giuliano & Lagarde Report 31.

i.e. that a contract exists which is non-existent under the putative applicable law.[125] Or, in other words a party may not claim that a contract exists on the grounds that under the law of *his* habitual residence silence constitutes an effective consent. In sum, when a court is faced with the argument that law 'X' is the applicable law (based on the silent acceptance of the law during negotiations), the correct approach under the Regulation would be to first apply Article 10(1), i.e. the putative proper law as established in accordance with Article 3(1) Rome I. Then, in cases where one party denies consent to the putative proper law, the party may be able to rely on the law of his habitual residence according to Article 10(2) if and only if it would not be reasonable to apply the alleged chosen law. Further, in situations where there is not even an alleged choice of law between the parties (albeit the argument that reliance on a legal system during proceedings constitutes a choice of law), Article 4 of the Rome I Regulation should be applicable. Accordingly, the approach previously taken by the German *Bundesgerichtshof* is not maintainable under the Regulation.

## 2. The way in which the choice may be made

The second requirement under Article 3(1) of the Rome I Regulation is that the choice must be "expressly or clearly demonstrated by the terms of the contract or the circumstances of the case". According to Article 3 Rome I, the choice of law by the parties is to be decisive. A choice by the parties will be effective if the parties' intent to choose a particular law is determinable. In other words, in order to establish that the parties have made a choice of law, a manifest intention must be established. As demonstrated above, the parties must voluntarily and consciously choose a law. Yet, although Article 3 Rome I states that the law shall be chosen by the parties, this does not necessarily require that the choice be made by the parties themselves.[126] It could be agreed that the choice be reached by one party only, a third party, or even chosen by lot.[127] Further, parties may also choose to restrict the application of one or more specific legal systems to their contract. Such a 'negative choice of law' is permissible under the Regulation.[128] In such a situation the law would be determined on the basis of Article 4 Rome I subject to the exclusion of the nominated legal systems.[129]

---

125  *Giuliano & Lagarde* Report 31. Article 10(2) uses the wording "in order to establish that he did *not* consent" [emphasis added].
126  *Martiny*, in: MünchKomm (5th ed.) Art. 3 Rom I-VO marginal no. 17.
127  ibid.
128  *Martiny*, in: MünchKomm (5th ed.) Art. 3 Rom I-VO marginal no. 19.
129  ibid.

Article 3 paragraph (1) of Rome I provides two alternatives from which an intentional choice may be drawn. Such an intention may either be evident either in the form of an express choice of law clause in the contract, or in the form of a tacit choice, i.e. inferred from the circumstances of the case. The determination of the parties' choice of law whether express or inferred, is a matter of interpretation and therefore should be governed by the applicable law or putative proper law, rather than the *lex fori*.[130] The *Giuliano & Lagarde* Report does not offer any guidance on this point. However, Article 3(5) refers the question of the existence of a choice of law to be governed by Article 10(1); i.e. the law, which would govern it under the Regulation if it existed. Moreover, even if such an issue is preferably dealt with as a matter of interpretation, the Regulation provides in Article 12(1)(a) that interpretation is also governed by the law applicable under it. Thus, whether a choice of law clause stipulating German law as applicable amounted to an express choice of law, is to be determined according to German law; an English choice according to English law, and so on. The approach is to assume what is set out to be proven. A court will be required to assume that a contract and its terms are valid and to ascertain the putative applicable law from those terms in order to determine whether the contract is valid.[131] This approach is also referred to as the "bootstraps" approach. Effectively parties are able to pull themselves up by their own bootstraps. In other words parties may use choice of law clauses to ensure the determination of all issues according to their choice and avoid application of the objective governing law (under Article 4).[132] Although such an approach may lead to unfairness to one of the parties, the effect is resolved to some extent by the safeguard provided for in Article 10(2) in relation to consent to the contract.[133]

---

130 Further discussed under Part 3/A.II.2. *Issues of interpretation.* See also *Richard Plender/Michael Wilderspin*, The European Contracts Convention, (2001) 80 and 99. But see *Dicey & Morris* (14th ed.) Vol. II at 1802, the authors state (somewhat vaguely) that such an issue is one of interpretation and should be looked at from a "broad Regulation-based approach, not constrained by national rules of construction". Statement approved in *Egon Oldendorff v Libera Corporation (No 2)* [1996] 1 Lloyds Rep 380, 387. Cf. the earlier English approach in *Compagnie d'Armement Maritime v Compagnie Tunisienne de Navigation, SA* [1970] 3 ALL ER 71.

131 *Jonathan Harris*, Does Choice of Law Make Any Sense?, (2004) Vol. 4 57 Current Legal Problems 305–353, 316–317.

132 *Cheshire & North* (14th ed.) 745.

133 See *Cheshire & North* (14th ed.) 745; *Peter Nygh*, Autonomy in International Contracts (1999) 75, 84; *Jonathan Harris*, Does Choice of Law Make Any Sense?, (2004) Vol. 4 57 Current Legal Problems 318–319 who suggest that a choice of law clause clearly agreed upon by the parties is independent of the contract and can therefore

*a. Express choice of law*

The first alternative under Article 3(1) Rome I is that a choice may be made expressly. Accordingly, the simplest way to ensure that the law intended by the parties is applied is to include an express choice of law clause in the contract. This alternative may be satisfied when for example a choice of law clause is formulated as: 'this contract shall be governed by the law of Germany', 'any dispute arising out of this contract shall be decided according to German law', or 'this contract is to be construed in accordance with German law'.[134] A clause containing a qualifying sentence specifying particular laws, will not affect the validity of the express choice of law made. Thus, the formulation 'this contract shall be governed by the law of Germany, particularly with regard to the regulations contained in paragraphs 123 *et seq.* of the German Civil Code', will be regarded an express choice of German law governing the contract.[135] In most cases, the determination of a choice of law clause as being an express choice agreed to by the parties will be straightforward and the parties will get what they expected.[136]

However, an express choice of law should not be confused with incorporation.[137] Incorporation is the inclusion of some provisions of a foreign law as a term or terms of the contract. The incorporated provisions of foreign law are interpreted in the same way as other contractual terms, i.e. the rules will apply as they existed at the date of the contract, unaffected by any subsequent change in the law. On the other hand, where parties expressly choose the applicable law, that law and any subsequent changes to the applicable law will govern the contract and bind the parties. Although not common in practice, parties may expressly provide that certain provisions in the contract are to be regulated by specific rules of a foreign country.[138] These rules, however, will not inevitably amount to an express selection of the applicable law but will generally be regarded as incorporated terms of

---

be more readily used to determine its validity. But compare *Jan Kropholler*, Internationales Privatrecht, (2006) §40 III 1 and *Martiny*, in: MünchKomm (5th ed.) 497 marginal no. 44 and 105 who prefer the issue to be resolved according to the *lex fori*.

134 *Martiny*, in: MünchKomm (5th ed.) 497 marginal no. 43.

135 *ibid*; see also Judgment of the *OLG* Düsseldorf judgment of 16.7.2002 NJW-RR 2003, 1610.

136 Unless of course, one of the parties contests the choice in which case Article 10(2) may displace the alleged choice, see above Part 1/B. I.1.b.bb) *The exception*.

137 *Dicey & Morris* (15th ed.) Vol. II 1807–1809; *Christopher Clarkson/Jonathan Hill*, The Conflict of Laws (2011) 215.

138 *Jan Kropholler*, Internationales Privatrecht, (2006) § 52 II 3 462; *Martiny*, in: MünchKomm (5th ed.) Art. 3 Rom I-VO marginal no. 15.

the contract.[139] For example, although parties to a German contract provide that terms of performance are to be regulated by specific rules contained in the French Civil Code, German law will nevertheless be the applicable law to the contract into which the German rules have been incorporated.[140] The incorporation of foreign rules in this manner provides a convenient 'shorthand' alternative to a verbatim inclusion of the French articles. However, the reference to provisions of a legal system may justify that the law of that country was intended to govern the contract as a whole.[141] Thus, under the Rome I Regulation, the reference to foreign law and its incorporation into clauses of the contract may still provide courts with a source from which the governing law may be drawn.[142] The *Giuliano & Lagarde* Report states that the fact that parties have included specific provisions of a legal system "may leave the court in no doubt that the parties have deliberately chosen French law".[143] This would involve inferring the applicable choice of law as clearly demonstrated by the terms of the contract.

As already mentioned the determination of a choice of law clause as being an express choice will in most cases be relatively straightforward. However, problems surround clauses where the terms used fall short of an express choice. Such clauses may be unclearly formulated, contain contradictions or be inadmissible under the Rome I Regulation.[144] In such cases, courts will be required to ascertain the choice of law according to the rules in relation to an inferred choice of law.

### b. Inferred choice of law

aa) Clearly demonstrated by the terms of the contract

The Rome I Regulation does not require a choice of law by the parties to only be made expressly by including a choice of law clause in the contract. Instead of

---

139  See *Cheshire & North* (14th ed.) 701–702; *Dicey & Morris* (15th ed.) Vol. II 1807; *Martiny*, in: MünchKomm (5th ed.) Art. 3 Rom I-VO marginal no. 14–15.
140  This is the example given in the *Giuliano & Lagarde* Report 17. This concerns also the issue of splitting the applicable law, dealt with below. See Part 1/B.I.t.
141  *Dicey & Morris* (15th ed.) Vol. II 1813–1814; *Jan Kropholler*, Internationales Privatrecht, (2006) § 52 II 3 462; *Giuliano & Lagarde* Report 17.
142  Amin Rasheed Shipping Corp v Kuwait Insurance Co [1984] 1 AC 50 at 69 (per Lord Wilberforce).
143  Giuliano & Lagarde Report 17.
144  Such as the formulation "this law is to be governed according to British law." This problem is dealt with below under point II. 1. "The chosen law". Further on this see, *Peter Mankowski*, Überlegungen zur sach- und interessengerechten Rechtswahl für Verträge des internationalen Wirtschaftsverkehrs, RIW 2003 2–15.

adopting such a strict approach, the drafters of the Regulation acknowledged that a court may find that the parties have made a real choice of law, despite there being no express statement of the choice of law to that effect.[145] The Regulation thereby specifically recognises situations in which words in the contract do not amount to an express choice. Article 3(1) Rome I provides that the "choice shall be made expressly or clearly demonstrated by the terms of the contract or the circumstances of the case". Thus, if the parties have not expressed their choice in the contract an alleged choice may still be effective if it is *clearly demonstrable*. International contracts often do not include an express choice of law clause; by allowing courts the possibility to imply a choice of law agreement by reference to the circumstances of the case, the Regulation recognises commercial realities. In cases where parties are unable to establish that a choice of law has been made *either* expressly *or* clearly demonstrated by examination of all the circumstances of the case, Article 4 of Rome I will be applicable.

Although Article 3(1) allows for an implied choice of law agreement, a court may not impute a choice of law on the basis that had the parties chosen a law, it *would* be the law of a particular country.[146] Rather, it requires the courts to ascertain the true tacit will of the parties rather than a purely hypothetical will.[147] However, in practice the distinction between these two situations is not always clear and could result in differing approaches in interpreting a tacit choice of law by courts of Member States.[148] It has been suggested that the distinction between an implied choice of law (under Article 3(1)) and objectively ascertained choice of law (under Article 4) is that an implied choice of law must be based on the true tacit will of the parties (*realer Rechtswahlwille der Parteien*).[149] Where this is

---

145  Giuliano & Lagarde Report 16.

146  *Giuliano & Lagarde* Report 17. Such a situation would require courts to consider the determination of the applicable law according to Article 4.

147  Article commentary of *The Proposal*, 5.

148  For example, German courts have often held that an implied choice of law in the sense of Article 3(1) rather than Article 4 of the Rome Convention has been made by the parties. Compare the decisions of the *Bundesgerichtshof* of 28.1.1997, in RIW 1997, 426 and 14.1.1999, RIW 1999, 537. But see judgment of 25.2.1999, in NJW 1999, 2242, where similar factors were interpreted as objective factors indicating the applicable law by virtue of Article 4 of the Rome Convention. On this see also *Dicey & Morris* (15th ed.) Vol. II 1809.

149  *Martiny*, in: MünchKomm (5th ed.) marginal no. 46 (with further references): "Auf der Ebene der stillschweigenden Rechtswahl geht es daher (noch) nicht um die Anknüpfung des Art. 4".

unascertainable, Article 4 will apply. As will be discussed below, the court must examine all of the general circumstances of the case including the conduct of the parties and the nature and terms of the contract in order to establish a clearly demonstrated choice under Article 3(1) of the Rome I Regulation.

The approach taken in Article 3(1) Rome I is substantially the same as that taken in Article 3(1) of the Rome Convention. However, the Regulation contains one textual amendment. According to the wording under the earlier Rome Convention, a choice made by the parties must be express or "demonstrated with *reasonable certainty* by the terms of the contract or the circumstances of the case".[150] Under Rome I, the choice made "shall be expressly or *clearly demonstrated* by the terms of the contract or the circumstances of the case".[151] The vague wording *demonstrated with reasonable certainty* under the Rome Convention brought about significant criticism; in particular, that too much uncertainty was caused by the words *reasonable certainty*.[152] This is a flexible concept on which national standards differed. In addition, the various translations of the text produced further uncertainty through their choice of wording. So, for example, the German translation '*mit hinreichender Sicherheit*', corresponded to the expression 'with reasonable certainty' used in the English text. However, the French translation '*de façon certaine*' arguably implied a greater degree of certainty than the English text.[153] By substituting the words *reasonable certainty* with the words *clearly demonstrated* in Rome I, the uncertainty surrounding the word reasonable is removed.[154] It may also be viewed as a stricter approach than that taken under the Rome Convention.[155] It indicates a

---

150  Article 3(1), second sentence of the Rome Convention (emphasis added).

151  Article 3(1), second sentence of Rome I (emphasis added).

152  See e.g. *Andrea Bonomi*, Conversion of the Rome Convention on Contracts into an EC Instrument: Some Remarks on the Green Paper of the EC Commission', (2003) 5 YBPIL 53 at 67. The author considers two options. The first being to radically drop the possibility of a tacit choice of law. The second less radical option being to include more precise information stipulating that courts may only infer a choice of law if the circumstances clearly indicate that the parties were aware of the choice of law issue or to expressly specify circumstances which will not without further elements indicate a tacit choice of law by the parties, such as a choice of court clause.

153  See *Green Paper* 23, 24.

154  The German text of the Rome I Regulation now reads '*eindeutig aus den Bestimmungen des Vertrags*'. The French translation of clearly demonstrated is '*de façon certaine*'.

155  *Ole Lando/Peter Nielsen*, The Rome I Regulation, (2008) 45 CML Rev 1687–1725, 1698. Compare the even higher threshold provided in Article 2(2) of the Hague

preference for certainty over flexibility;[156] the words *clearly demonstrated* leaving less room for discretionary interpretation by the courts.[157]

But difficult questions may still arise in situations in which the words used in the contract may or may not amount to an implied choice of law by the parties. What are the other factors that courts may take into account in determining whether an implicit choice has been *clearly demonstrated*; and, how far may the courts discretion reach when interpreting the true tacit will of the parties? As mentioned above, although courts may be required to infer the parties' intention from the actual words used in the contract, the incorporation of specific foreign rules as terms of the contract may not automatically amount to an inferred choice of applicable law. The Explanatory Report on the Rome Convention by Giuliano and Lagarde provides guidance on some of the most common factors a court may take into account when interpreting the true tacit will of the parties.[158] These include: the choice of a particular forum or of a particular place of arbitration, the use of standard form governed by a particular system of law, previous course of dealings between the parties and references to specific provisions of a particular legal system. These factors will now be considered.

bb) Choice of a particular forum or of a particular place of arbitration

A vigorously debated issue concerns jurisdiction and arbitration clauses and to what extent these may imply a choice of law.[159] This is presumably due to the differing approaches taken in Member States to such agreements and their variable significance when determining an implied choice of law; some regarding such to clearly imply a choice of law, while others do not. According to the *Giuliano & Lagarde* Report, a choice of jurisdiction clause will not in itself imply a choice of law. The Report states that although the choice of a particular forum "may show in no uncertain manner that the parties intend the contract to be governed by the law of the forum", it is

---

Convention on the Law Applicable to International Sales of Goods of 15 June 1955 "[…] an express clause, or *unambiguously* result from the provisions of the contract." (emphasis added).

156  See Recital (16), Rome I.

157  See generally *Katharina Boele-Woelki/Vesna Lazic*, 'Where do we stand on the Rome I Regulation?' in *Katharina Boele-Woelki/W. Grosheide* (eds.), The Future of European Contract Law (2007).

158  Giuliano & Lagarde Report 17.

159  *Ole Lando/Peter Nielsen*, The Rome I Regulation, (2008) 45 CML Rev 1687, 1698. See also *Adrian Briggs* (ed.), Agreements on Jurisdiction and Choice of Law (2008); *idem*, On drafting agreements on choice of law, LMCLQ (2003) 389–395.

careful to specify that "this must always be subject to the other terms of the contract and all the circumstances of the case".[160] With regard to choice of arbitration clauses the Report continues that a court may conclude that the parties have made a real choice of law by "the choice of a place where disputes are to be settled by arbitration in circumstances indicating that the arbitrator shall apply the law of that place".[161]

Choice of forum clauses are commonplace in international contracts.[162] Such agreements may take either the form of a jurisdiction agreement that points exclusively to a particular forum (exclusive jurisdiction agreement) or a jurisdiction agreement that does not submit proceedings exclusively to a particular forum (non-exclusive or optional jurisdiction agreement).[163] An exclusive jurisdiction agreement is a clause in a contract, which imposes a mutual contractual obligation on the parties to litigate in a specified forum.[164] The parties thereby agree on trial in the chosen forum and implicitly agree not to object to the jurisdiction of that forum. On the other hand, a non-exclusive jurisdiction agreement is a clause in a contract, which allows parties the option to institute proceedings in one or more identified courts. A non-exclusive jurisdiction agreement does not create a contractual obligation on the parties to submit proceedings to a particular court.

---

160  *Giuliano & Lagarde* Report 16–17. See also *Marubeni Hong Kong and South China Ltd v Mongolian Government* [2002] 2 All ER (Comm) 873 at [35]. This case illustrates the potential width of an inquiry of "all the circumstances of the case"; the parties' negotiations were considered by the court in order to deduce the parties' intentions.

161  *Giuliano & Lagarde* Report 16. Further on arbitration clauses and specifically on the relationship between choice of law clauses and arbitration agreements, see *Klaus Peter Berger*, 'Re-examining the Arbitration Agreement – Applicable law: Consensus or Confusion?', in *Albert Jan van den Berg* (ed.), International Arbitration 2006: Back to Basics? (2007) 301–334; and generally, *idem*, International Economic Arbitration (1993).

162  A choice of jurisdiction clause may also be effective within the framework of Article 4, Rome I.

163  Such agreement clauses will not necessarily be referred to as exclusive or non-exclusive in the contract, adding to the uncertainty and thus requiring courts to interpret the meaning of the clause. There may also be a third type of jurisdiction clause which is exclusive for one party and optional for the other, *Adrian Briggs* (ed.), Agreements on Jurisdiction and Choice of Law (2008) 163–164.

164  Generally *Adrian Briggs* (ed.), Agreements on Jurisdiction and Choice of Law (2008) 163–167; *David Joseph*, Jurisdiction and Arbitration Agreements and their Enforcement (2005) Chapter 4; *James Fawcett*, Non-exclusive jurisdiction agreements in private international law, (2001) LMCLQ 234. This article is concerned with non-exclusive jurisdiction agreements but discusses jurisdictional choice in general. See also *Jonathan Harris*, Agreements on Jurisdiction and Choice of Law: Where Next? (2009) LMCLQ 537.

It has been suggested that in cases where parties to a contract include an exclusive jurisdiction clause it should also be presumed that the parties have chosen the law of that forum to govern their contract.[165] The European Commission also endorsed this approach. Initially, in its Green Paper, the Commission appeared to take the view that the existence of a jurisdiction clause without any corroborating factors should not be capable of conclusively inferring a tacit choice of law. However, *The Proposal* submitted a provision in which parties shall be presumed to have chosen the law of a Member State "if the parties have agreed to confer jurisdiction on one or more courts or tribunals of a Member State to hear and determine disputes that have arisen or may arise out of the contract".[166] In other words, the fact that parties have included a jurisdiction clause in their contract will be indicative of their intentions as to the choice of law. Apart from considerations that this presumption would reduce legal uncertainty by providing judges with guidance when determining the applicable law, the Commission gave no other justification for the inclusion of the provision.[167] As well as being contrary to the approaches taken in some Member States[168] the Commission's proposal was also contrary to

165 *Ole Lando/Peter Nielsen*, The Rome I Regulation, (2008) 45 CML Rev 1687, 1699. The authors criticise the approach taken in the Rome I Regulation as being inconsistent with the principle of party autonomy. Instead the authors justify the approach taken by the Commission in *The Proposal* on the following grounds: 1) that it is convenient for courts to be authorised to apply their own law instead of foreign law; 2) that the application of foreign law is often time-consuming and expensive; and 3) that such an approach is likely to be in accordance with the expectations of the parties. This is also the approach taken in Germany and England, see e.g. *Richard Plender/Michael Wilderspin*, The European Contracts Convention (2001); and see *Green Paper* paragraph 3.2.4.2.

166 *The Proposal* Article 3(1) second paragraph, 14. In effect, the Commission was proposing that even a non-exclusive jurisdiction agreement should be indicative of the parties' intentions as to choice of law.

167 *The Proposal* 5. See also *Francisco Alferez*, The Rome I Regulation: Much ado about nothing? (2/2008 EuL Forum) 61–79, 67. The solution laid down by the Proposal was welcomed by *Jürgen Basedow (et al.)*, Max Planck Institute for Comparative and International Private Law, Comments on the European Commission's Proposal for a Regulation of the European Parliament and the Council on the Law Applicable to Contractual Obligations (Rome I) 71 RabelsZ (2007) at 243: "synchronisation of forum and ius saves time and transaction costs."

168 Compare e.g. approach in England: *E.I. Du Pont de Nemours & Co v Agnew and others* [1987] 2 Lloyds Rep 585; *Travelers Casualty & Surety v Sun Life of Canada* [2004] EWHC 1704 (Comm) and Germany, see discussion with further references in *Martiny*, in: MünchKomm (5th ed.) marginal nos. 48–50: non-exclusive jurisdiction agreement by itself can only amount to a weak (or no) inference of choice of law.

the proposal by the European Group of Private International Law (*GEDIP*).[169] In this proposal the Group suggested that a "choice of a court or courts should not in itself be equivalent to a choice of the law of that State".[170] The rationale underlying the presumption of the Commission's Proposals received considerable criticism.[171] Hence, if the parties had wanted to make a choice as to the applicable law, they would have most likely included the corresponding clause and if not then either the parties only agreed on a choice of forum clause or they did not consider the applicable law problem. Assuming or automatically implying that the parties intended that the law of the chosen forum would also govern their contract may in some cases be tenuous. For example, parties may choose a jurisdiction in a neutral forum otherwise unrelated to the parties and their legal relationship.[172] However, it could equally be argued that the parties may have intended the application of a neutral law; or, that the synchronisation of forum and *ius* is cost saving and time efficient; or, that the parties expect the forum to be most familiar with their own law, an application of the *lex fori* thus indeed according with the parties' expectations.

However, following the responses to the Green Paper, the Commission Proposal presented a modified view of this issue and the final text of the Rome I Regulation did not adopt the Commission's proposal as a rule. Instead, Recital (12) to

---

169  *Groupe européen de droit international privé*. See also *Andrea Bonomi*, Rome I Regulation – Some general remarks, YBPIL 10 (2008) 171.

170  European Group of Private International Law, 'Second consolidated version of a proposal to amend Articles 1,3,4,5,6,7 and 9 of the Rome Convention of 19 June 1980 on the law applicable to contractual obligations, and Article 15 of the Regulation 44/2001/EC (Brussels I)' (2002) paragraph III, available at: http://www.gedip-egpil.eu/documents/gedip-documents-16pe.html.

171  *Franco Ferrari/Stefan Leible* (eds.), Ein neues Internationales Vertragsrecht für Europa – Der Vorschlag für eine Rom I-Verordnung (2007) 44; *Francisco Alferez*, The Rome I Regulation: Much ado about nothing? (2/2008 EuL Forum) 67; *Ulrich Magnus/Peter Mankowski*, Joint Response on the Green Paper on the Conversion of the Rome Convention on the Law Applicable to Contractual Obligations into a Community Instrument and its Modernisation, COM (2002) 654 final, at 17 (available at http://ec.europa.eu).

172  *Katharina Boele-Woelki/Vesna Lazic*, Where do we stand on the Rome I Regulation? in *Katharina Boele-Woelki/W. Grosheide* (eds.), The Future of European Contract Law (2007). The same applies to the choice by the parties of a neutral place of arbitration. Compare e.g. *Egon Oldendorff v Libera Corporation (No 1)* [1995] 2 Lloyd's Rep 64 where the arbitration clause in a contract between a Japanese defendant and German claimant provided for arbitration in London. In this case it was held to be indicative of an implied choice of law by the parties for English law.

the Regulation declares that "an agreement between the parties to confer on one or more courts or tribunals of a Member State exclusive jurisdiction to determine disputes under the contract should be *one* of the factors to be taken into account in determining whether a choice of law has been clearly demonstrated".[173] Although the wording of Recital (12) indicates that the choice of a particular forum should neither be conclusive nor peremptory, but rather one factor to be considered from the contract as a whole or the circumstances of the case, it falls short of ensuring certainty as to the law. As a result, there still remains scope for divergent interpretation, especially considering the differing approaches taken by Member States.[174] Additionally, the wording of the Recital contains a limitation to courts in 'Member States' only: "An agreement between the parties to confer on one or more courts or tribunals of a *Member* State exclusive jurisdiction [...]".[175] It is suggested that in practice a limitation to courts of Member States only is not warranted and is not in accordance with the underlying rationale of Article 3(1). There seems no apparent justification as to why an exclusive jurisdiction clause in favour of a non-Member State should be treated any differently.[176]

Similarly, as already mentioned, the inclusion of an arbitration clause providing for arbitration in a particular country may also serve as an indication of a tacit choice of law by the parties.[177] In the English Convention case *Egon Oldendorff v Libera Corporation*,[178] an arbitration clause providing for dispute resolution in London was treated as an inferred choice of English law by virtue of Article 3(1). The case involved a German commercial partnership (claimant) and a Japanese corporation (defendant). The claimant sought damages for breach of contract for a 10 year charter by them of two Panamax bulk carriers, which were to be built by the claimant. As there was no express choice of law, it was argued that Japanese law was the applicable law

---

173 Recital (12), emphasis added. See discussion in *Stefan Leible*, Rechtswahl, in: *Franco Ferrari/Stefan Leible* (ed.), Ein Neues Internationales Vertragsrecht für Europa (2007) 41, 44.

174 Courts in some Member States being more reluctant than English courts to draw an inference in such a case. See *Green Paper* 23–25; *Cheshire & North* (14th ed.) 707.

175 Recital (12) Rome I (emphasis added).

176 See also *David McCleen/Kisch Beevers*, The Conflict of Laws (2009), 361; *Jürgen Basedow et al.*, Max Planck Institute for Comparative and International Private Law, Comments on the European Commission's Proposal for a Regulation of the European Parliament and the Council on the Law Applicable to Contractual Obligations (Rome I), 71 RabelsZ (2007) 241 and 243–244.

177 *Peter Nygh*, Autonomy in International Contracts (1999) 117–118; *David Joseph*, Jurisdiction and Arbitration Agreements and their Enforcement (2005) 161.

178 [1995] 2 Lloyd's Rep 64.

as indicated by objective factors such as the fact that the defendant was a Japanese corporation, that a Japanese shipbroker acted as intermediary between the parties and that the ships chartered were to be delivered in Japan. Mance J rejected this argument, instead holding that the inclusion in the contract of an English arbitration clause showed with reasonable certainty that the parties had chosen English law as the applicable law for the purposes of Article 3 of the Convention.[179]

However, just as a choice of forum clause is to be treated as one of many factors to consider when inferring a choice of law, an arbitration clause also does not automatically suggest that the parties intended the law of that country to apply to their contract. Neither can it be said that the inference may be as easily drawn as in the case of a choice of forum clause. In the *Egon Oldendorff* case it was not only the existence of a clause providing for arbitration in England that was relevant when inferring the parties' intention but also the fact that the parties used a well-known English language form of charter party containing standard clauses based on well-known meanings of English law.[180] A further problematic issue concerning arbitration clauses is that parties often do not choose the place of arbitration directly. So, while a contract may include an arbitration clause, it may nevertheless fail to specifically identify the arbitrators and/or place of arbitration. For example, by providing in the arbitration clause that the arbitrators are to be appointed by an international arbitral body (such as the International Chamber of Commerce), the parties could not have contemplated the place of arbitration. Conversely, it could be argued that the parties could not have assumed that the arbitrator is competent to apply the law of another country and that therefore the parties assumed the arbitrator's law to apply. For that reason, where an arbitration clause clearly specifies that the arbitration will take place in a specified country and that the arbitrators will be of that nationality, an inference may easily be made that the parties intended that the law of that country shall apply.[181]

---

179   This decision was upheld in later proceedings by Clarke J in *Egon Oldendorff v Libera Corporation (No 2)* [1996] 1 Lloyd's Rep 380. Compare also *JSC Zestafoni v Ronly Holdings Ltd* [2004] EWHC 245 (Comm), [2004] 2 Lloyd's Rep 335.

180   [1996] 1 Lloyd's Rep 380. Holding that the contract was subject to Article 3(1) of the Convention, Clarke J (at 309) said: 'In short, having agreed English arbitration for the determination in London of disputes arising out of a well known English language form of charterparty which contains standard clauses with well known meanings of English law, it is in my judgment to be inferred that the parties intended that law to apply.'

181   Dicey & Morris (15th ed.) Vol. II 1813. Egon Oldendorff v Libera Corporation (No 2) [1996] 1 Lloyd's Rep 380.

Overall, the approach taken under Rome I to jurisdiction or arbitration agreements is similar to the approach taken at common law.[182] The existence of either a choice of forum clause or arbitration clause will be a strong indicator that the parties intended the contract to be governed by the law of that place.[183] But the determination of the parties' intention as to the applicable law is a question of fact, to be inferred from all of the circumstances of the case. Therefore, neither a choice of forum or arbitration clause will, without more, conclusively point to the chosen law. Indeed, such clauses may even be irrelevant when inferring a choice of law, e.g. situations where contractual terms or other relevant circumstances of the case contradict the alleged choice.[184] Thus, the issue remains unclear: how much weight should be attached to such clauses, particularly in the absence of any other factor indicating a choice of law by the parties as to the applicable law.

cc) Use of standard form governed by a particular system of law

Although jurisdiction clauses and arbitration agreements are treated as the clearest indications for inferring a choice of law,[185] these are not seen in isolation and difficulties surround the precise determination of other possible indications pointing to an implied choice of law. These difficulties surround claims that the parties have chosen a law by use of a certain standard form contract often governed by a particular system of law. The *Giuliano & Lagarde* Report cites such a situation as an example of a circumstance where a

---

182  Cf. The English pre-Convention case *Compagnie d'Armement Maritime v Compagnie Tunisienne de Navigation, SA* [1970] 3 ALL ER 71, at 84 (Lord Wilberforce) where the court held that the existence of an arbitration clause in the contract was merely one of the factors (albeit a 'weighty indication' or 'strong inference') to be taken into account when ascertaining the intention of the parties. It has also been suggested that Article 3 (of the Rome Convention) requires a stricter test when inferring the intention of the parties, see e.g. *C.G.J. Morse*, The EEC Convention on the Law Applicable to Contractual Obligations (1982) 2 YB Eur.L. 107, 117; *Volker Triebel*, The Choice of Law in Commercial Relations: A German Perspective, (1988) 37 ICLQ 935, 942; cf. *Richard Plender/Michael Wilderspin*, The European Contracts Convention (2001) 93.

183  *Ole Lando/Peter Nielsen*, The Rome I Regulation, (2008) 45 CML Rev. 1700. The authors regard the guidance provided by Recital (12) as 'giving courts a strong hint as how to treat such clauses when determining whether parties have made an implied choice of law.' See also *Peter Nygh*, Autonomy in International Contracts (1999) 116–118.

184  *Martiny*, in: MünchKomm (5th ed.) marginal no. 48.

185  *Jonathan Hill*, Choice of Law in Contract under the Rome Convention: The Approach of the UK Courts (2004) 53 ICLQ 325, 330.

choice of law by the parties may be inferred.[186] This is confirmed by English and German case law where courts have held that where parties contract on the basis of a form known in the trade as being founded on a particular law, that this was indicative of a tacit choice of law in favour of that law.[187] But the use of a standard form cannot by itself be taken as solely indicative of an intention of the parties. Thus, in the *Egon Oldendorff* case the existence of an English language form of charter party containing standard clauses based on well-known meanings of English law *and* the English arbitration clause were considered together as indicative of the parties' intention to have English law as the applicable law.[188]

Similarly, it has been held that where the terms of a reinsurance slip (i.e. a document setting out the main aspects of the risk requiring cover) referred to provisions of English law that this pointed to an implied choice of English law under Article 3 of the Convention. In the recent English case *Gard Marine & Energy Ltd (A company incorporated under the laws of Bermuda) v (1) Lloyd Tunnicliffe (2) Glacier Reinsurance AG (A company incorporated under the laws of Switzerland) (3) Agnew Higgins Pickering & Co Ltd*,[189] the court was first required to determine the applicable law of the Glacier Re Slip before being able to determine the issue of jurisdiction. The court held that although there was no express choice of law in the Glacier Re Slip that the circumstances of the placement and the use of the Lloyd's slip on the policy indicated a choice of English law. In addition, the slip included London market wordings and provisions associated with the laws of England, also pointing to English law.[190] Thus, the language used in contractual forms,

---

186  *Giuliano & Lagarde* Report 17. This was also the approach taken at common law in a case preceding the Rome Convention, see *Amin Rasheed Shipping Corp v Kuwait Insurance Co* [1984] 1 AC 50 (per Lord Diplock).

187  English case law see e.g. *Egon Oldendorff v Libera Corporation (No 2)* [1996] 1 Lloyd's Rep 380. See also *Tiernan v The Magen Insurance Co Ltd* [2000] IL Pr 517 at 522–523, where a reinsurance contract placed on the Lloyd's market in the normal way, which was in a Lloyd's form, containing London market clauses, was held sufficient to indicate a choice of English law under Article 3(1) of the Rome Convention. For German case law see e.g. Judgment of the *OLG* Karlsruhe 30.3.1979, RIW 1979, 642; Judgment of the *OLG* Hamburg 30.12.1985, RIW 1986, 462.

188  [1996] 1 Lloyd's Rep 380 (Clarke J) at 309.

189  [2009] EWHC 2388.

190  See also Gan Insurance Co Ltd v Tai Ping Insurance Co Ltd [1999] IL Pr 729, CA at [31] and [36]; Aegis Electrical and Gas International Services Co Ltd v Continental Casualty Co [2007] EWHC 1762 (Comm), [2008] Lloyd's Rep. IR 17; Tryg Baltica International (UK) Ltd v Boston Compania de Seguros SA [2004] EWHC

although by no means indicative on its own, may support together with other factors, a finding that a particular law was intended by the parties.[191] Particularly when used in a standard form known to be based on a particular system of law and incorporating provisions of that system of law.

dd) Other circumstances of the case

The examples given by the *Giuliano & Lagarde* Report are not exhaustive, but provide the most common situations from which a court may legitimately conclude that the parties have made a choice of law.[192] In order to establish an inferred choice under the Rome I Regulation the inference must be 'clearly demonstrated' and this must result in the real will or intention of the parties.[193] As discussed above, such a real intention has been established in cases involving a jurisdiction or arbitration clause, or a contract in a standard form known to be governed by the law of a particular country. The *Giuliano & Lagarde* Report provides two other examples from which a court may infer a real intention: first, where there is an express choice in a related transaction and secondly, where there is a previous course of dealing under contracts containing an express choice of the applicable law.[194]

---

1186 (Comm) at [8] (all the circumstances of the case, i.e. contracts, slips, certificates and all documentation issued in London in English, showed that the parties must have intended English law to apply); [2005] Lloyd's Rep IR 40; Markel International Insurance Co Ltd v La Compania Argentina de Seguros Generales SA [2004] EWHC 1826 (Comm) at [37], [2005] Lloyd's Rep IR 90; Dornoch Ltd v (1) Mauritius Union Assurance Co Ltd (2) Mauritius Commercial Bank Ltd [2006] EWCA Civ 389 at [43] Tuckey LJ stating: 'the Reinsurance was broked on the basis of a Lloyds proposal form by English brokers and written on a Lloyds slip in the London market on London market terms where it would be "surprising and improbable" (Hobhouse J. in Vesta v Butcher) that the contract was governed by anything other than English law' (Note here Tuckey LJ ascertained the proper law by virtue of Article 4 of the Rome Convention); [2006] 2 Lloyd's Rep 475. Contrast American Motorists Insurance Co v Cellstar Corp [2003] EWCA Civ 206, [2003] ILPr 370.

191 *Martiny*, in: MünchKomm (5th ed.) marginal no. 63.

192 *Peter Nygh*, Autonomy in International Contracts (1999) 113; *Jonathan Hill*, Choice of Law in Contract under the Rome Convention: The Approach of the UK Courts, (2004) 53 ICLQ 331 *Cheshire & North* (14th ed.) see considerations at 703–707.

193 As held in *Egon Oldendorff v Libera Corporation (No 2)* [1996] 1 Lloyd's Rep 380 (Clarke J) at 387–388.

194 Giuliano & Lagarde Report 17.

Regarding the express choice in a related transaction, the English Court of Appeal in the *Dornoch* case held that the applicable law of an excess reinsurance contract could be inferred from the law stipulated in the primary insurance policy.[195] Applying an express choice from a related transaction to a further contract between the parties may be substantiated by the fact that parties will often assume that the same terms and conditions will apply to the series of transactions between them, especially where they have specifically negotiated the choice of law clause in a related contract.[196] A sudden change of the governing law in a series of continued transactions between parties would need to be justified.[197] The second situation given by the Report is that: "a previous course of dealing between the parties under contracts containing an express choice of law may leave the court in no doubt that that contract in question is to be governed by the law previously chosen where the choice of law clause has been omitted in circumstances which do not indicate a deliberate change of policy by the parties".[198] Similar to the previous example of express choice of law in related transactions, this example also refers to different contracts between the same parties in which it would be not unreasonable to suppose that, if one of their contracts contains an express choice of law then the related or succeeding contract should also be governed by the same law.[199] The examples given in the Report reflect the approaches taken by English and German courts to related or previous transactions between the parties being indicative of the parties' intention when inferring a choice of law.[200]

---

195  *Dornoch Ltd & Ors v (1) Mauritius Union Assurance Co Ltd (2) Mauritius Commercial Bank Ltd* [2006] EWCA Civ 389 at [43]. Note, however, that the Court of Appeal determined this with reference to Article 4 of the Convention. Compare *ISS Machinery Services Ltd v Aeolian Shipping SA* [2001] EWCA Civ 1162 at [31] (per Mance LJ), [2001] 2 Lloyd's Rep 641, where the Court of Appeal that the law applicable to a counterclaim arising out of a supply contract (governed by Japanese law) could *not* be inferred by reference to an undertaking (governed by English law). See discussion of case in: *Jonathan Hill*, Choice of Law in Contract under the Rome Convention: The Approach of the UK Courts, (2004) 53 ICLQ 332–333.

196  *Peter Nygh*, Autonomy in International Contracts (1999) 116.

197  *Peter Mankowski*, Stillschweigende Rechtswahl und wählbares Recht in: *Stefan Leible* (ed.), Das Grünbuch zum Internationalen Vertragsrecht (2004) 80.

198  Giuliano & Lagarde Report 17.

199  *Dicey & Morris* (15th ed.) Vol. II 1810–1811.

200  See e.g. *Bundesgerichtshof* judgment of 14.11.1996 NJW 1997, 1150 and *Bundesgerichtshof* judgment of 7.12.2000 VII ZR 404/99, NJW 2001, 1936 where the choice of law for a building contract was indicative of the governing law for the architectural

But could a real intention be drawn, for example if there is a clause in the contract stipulating that payment is to be made in a specific currency,[201] or what about other objective connections of the contract with different countries such as the common residence or nationality of the parties, the place of business or the place of performance? Although it may be possible to connect objective factors with a particular law or country, it appears that cases where this will be sufficient to point to an inferred choice of law by the parties may be rare (unless it could be argued that an accumulation of objective connections points to a particular law or country). Thus in the *Egon Oldendorff* case, Mance J held that objective factors, including the place of delivery in Japan, were inadequate to lead him to conclude that the parties had intended Japanese law.[202] Under German law however, the specific nomination in the contract of the place of performance has been treated as an indication of the law intended by the parties.[203] Nonetheless, this is qualified by the requirement that there be a common place of performance of the parties (*gemeinsamer* or *einheitlicher Erfüllungsort*)[204] and it is submitted that under the Regulation, the (common) place of performance must not be taken by itself, but considered along with other circumstances of the case.[205] Another factor which German courts have taken as inferring a choice of law is the parties' conduct or attitude during legal proceedings.[206] However, as mentioned above, a choice of law inference may not be drawn unless the conduct points clearly and unequivocally to a choice of a particular law (i.e. the *lex fori*). Thus, courts may not infer a choice of law in cases where a choice of law is claimed through ignorance or the mistaken belief that the law of the forum is applicable. Generally, whenever the application of a law in such a situation is contested, this will be indicative of a lack of consent

---

contract; *Christoph Reithmann/Dieter Martiny* (eds.), Internationales Vertragsrecht (2010) marginal no. 129 n 4 with further references.

201   The authors in *Cheshire & North* (14th ed.) 703 say that this would not point to a real intention of the parties to choose the law of the currency.

202   [1996] 1 Lloyd's Rep 380, Clarke J at 387–388.

203   *Volker Triebel*, The Choice of Law in Commercial Relations: A German Perspective, (1988) 37 ICLQ 935, 942.

204   *Christoph Reithmann/Dieter Martiny* (eds.), Internationales Vertragsrecht (2010) marginal no. 124; *Cheshire & North* (14th ed.) marginal no. 65; *Jan Kropholler*, Internationales Privatrecht (2006) §52 II 1.

205   Note that the place of performance may be one of the factors to consider under Article 4 Rome I.

206   See also discussion with further references above at Part 1/B.1.c. *The problem of silent consent.*

and therefore lack of mutual choice of law by the parties. Courts should therefore cautiously approach situations in which an application of a law is argued for on the basis of the parties' conduct during legal proceedings, especially where the application of such is contested.

It is common in cases where there is dispute as to the applicable law that either party could equally argue for the application of a particular law based on various circumstances of the case. A conflict of connecting circumstances may in fact result. For example, a choice of jurisdiction or arbitration clause may point to an intention that the law of Country A shall apply, whereas a previous course of dealing may point to an intention that the law of Country B shall apply.[207] Where such conflicting inferences can be drawn from the circumstances of the case it cannot be said that the reliance on *one* of the inferences indicates a clearly demonstrated choice.[208] Courts are not permitted to infer the choice of law under Article 3(1) if no clear intention can be identified.[209] Under the Regulation, there is a rigid separation of demonstrable intention dealt with under Article 3(1) and when this cannot be established, other objective connections dealt with under Article 4 of the Regulation. Accordingly, in cases in which no clear intention can be demonstrated but other objective factors connect the contract to a specific law, courts should instead rely on the rules applicable in the absence of a choice of law by the parties; i.e. the default Article 4, in order to determine the governing law.[210] Tuckey LJ in the *Dornoch* case (when considering the argument that it was not open for the High Court Judge in the absence of sufficient indications under Article 3 to consider Article 4) firmly held: "If he could not determine the matter by reference to Article 3, I do not see how he had any other option but to go to

---

207 Example given in *Cheshire & North* (14th ed.) 705.

208 *ibid*, referring to the text of the former Article 3(1) Rome Convention: 'demonstrated with reasonable certainty'. A conflict of inferences will not be given in situations where an earlier draft of a contract contained an express choice of law clause that is subsequently deleted, see *Marubeni Hong Kong and South China Ltd v Mongolian Government* [2002] 2 All ER (Comm) 873 at [42]-[43].

209 Giuliano & Lagarde Report 17. See also Dornoch Ltd & Ors v (1) Mauritius Union Assurance Co Ltd (2) Mauritius Commercial Bank Ltd [2006] EWCA Civ 389 at [43].

210 E.g. *Dornoch Ltd & Ors v (1) Mauritius Union Assurance Co Ltd (2) Mauritius Commercial Bank Ltd* [2006] EWCA Civ 389 Tuckey LJ at [43] accepting the HC Judge's decision that there was a stalemate. In this case the conflicting inferences where: a) the excess reinsurance contract written on a Lloyd's slip in the London market on London market terms and b) the primary reinsurance that was governed by Mauritian law.

Article 4. Applying this Article he obviously reached the right conclusion".[211] Article 4 of the Rome I Regulation allows courts to determine the applicable law in the absence of choice through the identification of the law with which the contract is most closely connected. However, the distinction between determining the inferred intention of the parties according to Article 3(1) and identifying the law most closely connected with the contract under Article 4 appears unclear.[212]

## 3. Splitting the law applicable to contracts

Splitting the law applicable to contracts, also referred to as *dépeçage*, denotes the principle whereby the court will identify the law most appropriate to govern each particular issue or part of a contract.[213] In this context, the idea of not only allowing parties to choose the governing law but also to split the law applicable to their contract is a manifestation or logical conclusion of the principle of party autonomy.[214] Thus, in line with the broad approach taken to party autonomy by the Rome I Regulation, Article 3(1) Rome I provides for the severability of the parties' selection of law. The last sentence provides that: "By their choice the parties can select the law applicable to the whole or part only of the contract."[215] Although neither the Regulation nor the *Giuliano & Lagarde* Report actively address the point, it is generally accepted that the Regulation impliedly envisages that more

---

211 Dornoch Ltd & Ors v (1) Mauritius Union Assurance Co Ltd (2) Mauritius Commercial Bank Ltd [2006] EWCA Civ 389 at [43].

212 Also, *Dicey & Morris* (15th ed.) Vol. II 1809–1810. As mentioned above in Part 1/B.I. 2.b.aa) *Clearly demonstrated by the terms of the contract*, it has been suggested that the distinction between an implied choice of law (under Article 3(1)) and objectively ascertained choice of law (under Article 4) is that an implied choice of law must be based on the true tacit will of the parties (*realer Rechtswahlwille der Parteien*), see *Martiny*, in: MünchKomm (5th ed.) marginal no. 46.

213 For a comparative overview of contract splitting see *Peter Nygh*, Autonomy in International Contracts (1999) Chapter 6.

214 *Richard Plender/Michael Wilderspin*, The European Contracts Convention (2001) 100.

215 Compare also Article 4(1) second sentence of the Rome Convention, which provided that 'a severable part of the contract which has a closer connection with another country may by way of exception be governed by the law of that other country.' Similarly, the Hague Convention of December 22 1986 on the Law Applicable to Contracts for the International Sale of Goods, Article 7(1) states that 'such a choice may be limited to a part of the contract'.

than one law may be chosen by the parties to govern their contract.[216] The authors of Dicey and Morris point out that at first sight Article 3(1) appears to envisage an *either or* position excluding a multiple choice but go on to state that: "it is plainly intended in addition to allow the parties the choice of more than one law to govern different parts."[217] Thus, not only can the parties choose which law is to govern their contract, but they may make more than one choice, choosing different laws to apply to different parts of their contract. For example, parties may make an express choice of English law to govern one part and an express choice of French law to govern another part of the contract.

Other commentators have pointed out problems associated with splitting the applicable law.[218] Where rules of a legal system apply to one issue in a contract but the rules of a different legal system to another issue, the result may be that a decision is reached that is inconsistent and incompatible with the objectives of either legal system.[219] It is argued that the principle of unity should instead be given priority and that any split of the law be treated instead as an incorporation of the relevant rules of that law in the contract. In other words, provisions including more than one selection of foreign law should be treated as terms of the contract only.[220] A further argument put forward is that use of severability might be used to avoid mandatory rules.[221] Both of these arguments were rejected by the Working Party leading to the Rome Convention. The danger caused by the use of severance in order to avoid certain mandatory provisions was eliminated by the inclusion of Article 9 (Article 7 of the Rome Convention). Article 9 is one of the main concepts under the Rome I Regulation and ensures the application of mandatory provisions,

---

216 *Peter Nygh*, Autonomy in International Contracts (1999) 130; *Dicey & Morris* (15th ed.) Vol. II 1791; *Cheshire & North* (14th ed.) 691; *Andreas Heldrich*, in: Palandt Bürgerliches Gesetzbuch (2005) (hereinafter: *Heldrich*, in: Palandt) Art. 27 para. 9.

217 *Dicey & Morris* (15th ed.) Vol. II 1791.

218 See e.g. *Christopher Clarkson/Jonathan Hill*, The Conflict of Laws (2011) 217; *Campbell McLachlan*, Splitting the Proper Law in Private International Law, (1990) 61 BYIL 311; this also mentioned in *Giuliano & Lagarde* Report 17. See also *Jan Kropholler*, Internationales Privatrecht (2006) § 52 II 3 462.

219 *Christopher Clarkson/Jonathan Hill*, The Conflict of Laws (2011) 217.

220 See *Campbell McLachlan*, Splitting the Proper Law in Private International Law, (1990) 61 BYIL 311, 317. But see *Peter Nygh*, Autonomy in International Contracts (1999) 135–136 who maintains that as long as the parties have expressed their choices clearly that courts should recognise a split in the law and that anything less would be a denial of their autonomy.

221 Mentioned in *Giuliano & Lagarde* Report 17.

which cannot be opted out by selection of foreign law.[222] The *Giuliano & Lagarde* Report, when considering the arguments for and against severability, clearly support this solution and add that: "severability is directly linked with the principle of freedom of contract".[223] As a result, Article 3(1) of the Rome I Regulation allows parties to pick and choose more than one law to govern different 'parts of the contract' and thereby sever their contract, while Article 9 of the Regulation preserves the application of mandatory provisions.

However, the Regulation does not offer any guidance on what constitutes 'part only of a contract' and precisely what parts the parties may subject to different laws. Some commentators take the view that in principle a split choice of law should be permitted for separate clauses in a contract.[224] The *Giuliano & Lagarde* Report provides the example of an index-linking clause, which suggests that separate clauses may be made subject to a law different from the rest of contract. But no further guidance is offered on this point. According to this view 'part only' may also include a particular issue relating to the some or all parts of the contract.[225] Consequently, the interpretation of the contract, as an *issue* affecting all of its parts, may be governed by one law and a different law may govern the discharge of the contract.[226] Other commentators take the more narrow view, claiming that issues that affect all of the parts of the contract, such as construction, should not be governed by a different law to that which determines the substantive issues of the contract.[227] The argument is that it is not possible to clearly distinguish between questions of construction and questions relating to the substantial content of the contract. There does however, appear to be a common objection in principle to the general obligation[228] of a contract being governed by more than one law.[229] Based on the example given

---

222 See also Article 3(3) and (4) of the Rome I Regulation, which again emphasize that the choice of the parties shall not prejudice the application of provisions of law that cannot be derogated from by agreement.

223 Giuliano & Lagarde Report 17.

224 E.g. *Cheshire & North* (14th ed.) 691.

225 Giuliano & Lagarde Report 17.

226 *Cheshire & North* (14th ed.) 753.

227 *Peter Nygh*, Autonomy in International Contracts (1999) 132.

228 I.e. the obligations governing the core of the parties' relationship. The authors of *Dicey & Morris* (15th ed.) Vol. II 1792, give *frustration, illegality* or *repudiation* as examples of general obligations which affect the whole of the contract.

229 *Dicey & Morris* (15th ed.) Vol. II, 1790 *et seq.*; *Cheshire & North* (14th ed.) 691; *Centrax v Citibank NA* [1999] EWCA Civ 892 citing *Dicey & Morris* (12th ed.) Vol. II 1207.

in the *Giuliano & Lagarde* Report it seems that the authors of the Report also accept this. The example given in the Report relates to repudiation of a contract in which the authors mention that it would be unlikely that such an issue would be subjected to two different laws, one for the vendor and the other for the purchaser.[230]

Thus, it seems that part of a contract would cover separate clauses in a contract and that particular issues may also be severable.[231] The *Giuliano & Lagarde* Report only requires that the choices made are *logically consistent*. Provided this condition is met, the possibility of splitting the law applicable to a contract should not be prohibited. The laws expressed by the parties will be effective and govern the respective parts of the contract. But, what is meant by *logically consistent*? The Report stresses that the chosen laws will be logically consistent if the choices made relate to elements in the contract, which can be governed by different laws without giving, rise to contradictions.[232] So, if the parties wish to split the law applicable to their contract, the choices made must make sense and not conflict. Contradictions in the obligations accepted by the parties may not arise, i.e. parties may not choose a particular obligation and subject it to different laws depending on which party asserts it.[233] Such a situation would be regarded as involving two chosen laws, which cannot logically be reconciled. If the chosen laws cannot be logically reconciled the Report goes on to say that both choices of law fail. Recourse must then be had to Article 4 Rome I and the rules applicable in the absence of choice.[234]

National courts have been inclined to apply contract splitting rather restrictively. According to English case law, although a breach of an insurance policy can be severed from the insured's right under other parts of the policy, the definition of "insured" (i.e. the issue of construction of terms of the contract) under a policy cannot be severed and given variable meanings according to the law of the country in which the events giving rise to the claim arise.[235] Then again, it is possible for the general obligation under an agreement to be

---

230  Giuliano & Lagarde Report 17.
231  *ibid*; *Cheshire & North* (14th ed.) 691.
232  Giuliano & Lagarde Report 16–17.
233  This appears to be the approach to be taken to all general obligations; *Dicey & Morris* (15th ed.) Vol. II 1790 *et seq.*; *Cheshire & North* (14th ed.) 691.
234  Giuliano & Lagarde Report 17.
235  CGU International Insurance plc v Szabo [2002] 1 All ER (Comm) 83 at [39].

governed by New York law whilst payment instruments (i.e. cheques) and their validity to be governed by the drawee's law (potential drawees from many different countries).[236] The freedom to 'split' a contract therefore appears to be subject to restrictions, being admissible not as a rule but rather by way of exception only.[237]

Overall, the Regulation allows for a narrow application of the principle of *dépeçage*, whereby a court must identify the law which can most appropriately be applied to each particular clause or issue. The *Giuliano & Lagarde* Report rejects the presumption that the law chosen for one part of the contract should automatically govern the whole.[238] Therefore, as with the identification of choice of law generally, a court may also find that although the parties did not expressly provide for more than one law that they nevertheless intended to split the law applicable to their contract and infer a tacit choice.[239] In this situation, the identification of the applicable law will be subject to the general requirements of tacit choice. To conclude, the following four points may be made:

i. parties may choose different laws to apply to different parts of their contract;
ii. different laws may apply to different clauses;
iii. different laws may apply to different issues;
iv. the choices of law made by the parties must be logically consistent.

## 4. Changing the applicable law

Article 3(2) provides that the parties "may at any time agree to subject the contract to a law other than that which previously governed it." This applies irrespective of whether a choice of law was made at all, whether it was expressly

---

236  *Centrax v Citibank NA* [1999] EWCA Civ 892.
237  For further case law on this point see The Governor and Company of Bank of Scotland of the Mound v Butcher [1998] EWCA CIV 1306; American Motorists Insurance Co (AIMCO) v Cellstar Corp & Amor [2003] EWCA Civ 206, [2003] ILPr 370; also reference for preliminary ruling by the Hoge Raad (Netherlands) Case C-133/08 Intercontainer Interfrigo SC (ICF) v Balkenende Oosthuizen BV, MIC Operations BV ECR I-000 (6.10.2009). The German pre-Convention position has generally been that a 'core governing' law should principally be applicable, see e.g. Bundesgerichtshof judgment of 7.5.1969 (VIII ZR 142/68, DB 1969, 1053).
238  Giuliano & Lagarde Report 18.
239  *ibid*; *Cheshire & North* (14th ed.) 691; *Peter Nygh*, Autonomy in International Contracts (1999) 138.

or clearly demonstrated according to Article 3,[240] or determined through "other provisions of this Regulation".[241] In contrast with the position at common law,[242] the Regulation leaves parties maximum freedom as to the time at which the choice of law may be made. Under the Regulation, the change may be made before the contract is concluded, at the time the contract is concluded, or at a time subsequent to the conclusion of the contract. This may even include a change of the applicable law at a time when litigation is pending. The wording of the *Giuliano & Lagarde* Report on the change of law during proceedings is somewhat obscure, but it does appear that the approach to be taken under the Convention (i.e. Regulation) follows that taken in Germany and France.[243] This includes deducing the governing law from the parties' attitude when referring with clear agreement to a specific law during legal proceedings.[244] It is for the forum's law of procedure to decide the extent to which a change during proceedings is effective.[245] However, as mentioned above, it is suggested that courts approach such any inference in favour of forum law carefully and only apply it in situations where it can be clearly established that the parties were aware of the choice and not applying the law in the mistaken belief that that law is applicable. It is not entirely clear from the wording of the Article whether a change in the chosen law may only have prospective effect, or whether the change may also have retroactive effect. The *Giuliano & Lagarde* Report also does not clearly address this point, but appears to contemplate that a change may have retroactive effect.[246]

---

240 Courts will be slow to imply an agreement to change the applicable law, see *ISS Machinery Services Ltd v Aeolian Shipping SA* [2001] EWCA Civ 1162 at [15] (per Potter LJ) and [27] (per Mance LJ).

241 This is nearly a verbatim version of the corresponding Article 3(2) of the Rome Convention. The Regulation substitutes the word 'variation' with 'change'.

242 The authors of *Dicey & Morris* (15th ed.) Vol. II 1805 state that: "In England the parties were *probably* free to vary the proper law" [emphasis added]. See e.g. *Whitworth Street Estates (Manchester) Ltd v James Miller and Partners Ltd* [1970] AC 583, 603 (per Lord Reid); *El du Pont de Nemours v Agnew* [1987] 2 Lloyds Rep 585, 592 (CA). Compare *ISS Machinery Services Ltd v Aeolian Shipping SA* [2001] EWCA Civ 1162 at [31] (per Mance LJ), [2001] 2 Lloyd's Rep 641.

243 Cf. the approach of Italian courts on this issue; see *Giuliano & Lagarde* Report 17 with further references.

244 As mentioned above (with further references) under point I.2.a.dd) "Other circumstances of the case".

245 *Giuliano & Lagarde* Report 18; *Martiny*, in: MünchKomm (5th ed.) marginal no. 78.

246 Giuliano & Lagarde Report 18.

Four potential dangers in respect of a change of the applicable law have been identified: a) the new law may contain additional formal requirements; b) the contract may be invalid under the new law; c) the rights of third parties may be affected; and c) mandatory rules of the law of the originally applicable law may be evaded. The second sentence of Article 3(2) of the Regulation provides a safeguard in the following terms: "Any change in the law to be applied that is made after the conclusion of the contract shall not prejudice its formal validity under Article 11 or adversely affect the rights of third parties." The validity of the choice itself is always to be determined according to the chosen law.[247] The qualification concerning formal validity provides a solution to the potential problem whereby the new law chosen by the parties may contain formal requirements not required under the law originally applicable and thus create doubts as to the validity of the contract in the period preceding the new agreement between the parties.[248] Hence, a change in the law will not bring about the nullity of the contract and any additional formal requirements of the new law will be ignored. The existence and validity of consent of the parties as to the (new) choice of applicable law is to be determined according to Article 10(1) Rome I, i.e. the putative proper law. The problem of evasion of mandatory rules of the law originally applicable is to some extent dealt with by the limitations on choice discussed below.

## 5. The scope of the applicable law

When a choice of law reached by the parties by virtue of Article 3 of the Regulation (or as indicated under Article 4 in the absence of choice) is referred to as the "applicable law", this does not imply that the law so described necessarily governs all issues concerning the particular contract. Article 1(2) of the Regulation

---

247  This solution is also referred to as the "bootstrap rule", see e.g. *Richard Plender/ Michael Wilderspin*, The European Contracts Convention, (2001) 103. But this is not necessarily a strict 'bootstrap rule' as there is the possibility for a party to contest the validity under Article 10(2). On this, see, *Jan Kropholler*, Internationales Privatrecht, (2006) §40 III 1: "Die Prüfung dieser Erklärung [...] nach dem gewählten Recht bedeutet keine petition principia."; similar also *Martiny*, in: MünchKomm (5th ed.) 497 marginal no. 105.

248  *Giuliano & Lagarde* Report 18; *Dicey & Morris* (15th ed.) Vol. II 1806; *Cheshire & North* (14th ed.) 693; *Richard Plender/Michael Wilderspin*, The European Contracts Convention (2001) 102–103.

expressly excludes certain matters from the scope of the Regulation.[249] In a similar manner, the Regulation expressly leaves out capacity to contract[250] and manner of performance[251] from the scope of the applicable law.

As already mentioned, the applicable law or putatively applicable law will determine whether a contract has come into existence including the validity and consent of the parties as to choice of law.[252] Article 12 of the Regulation (Article 10 of the Rome Convention) provides a list of matters, which are governed "in particular" by the applicable law but is not intended to be an exhaustive list.[253] The matters include the interpretation of the contract,[254] performance,[255] consequences of breach,[256] various ways of extinguishing obligations, prescription and limitation of actions,[257] and consequences of nullity of the contract[258]. Under the Regulation, a contract must be construed according to the law applicable to the contract. Parties may, although this point is not generally accepted, subject different parts or specific issues of their contract (including interpretation) to different law under Article 3.[259] Whereas Article 12(1)(b) of the Regulation submits the issue of performance to the applicable law, the *manner* of performance is to be determined

---

249  These matters are not further dealt with here.

250  In general, questions of capacity are excluded from the Regulation (Article 1(2) (a) Rome I) and are therefore still an issue of national law. However, Article 13 Rome I, headed "Incapacity" provides one provision on this point. This provision is derived from the civil law and provides that where a contract is concluded between persons who are in the same country, a natural person who would have capacity under the law of that country may invoke his incapacity resulting from another law only if the other party to the contract was aware of this incapacity at the time of the conclusion of the contract or was not aware thereof as a result of negligence.

251  Article 12(2) Rome I provides that in relation to the manner of performance and the steps to be taken in the event of defective performance, regard shall be had to the law of the country in which performance takes place.

252  *Peter Nygh*, Autonomy in International Contracts (1999) 124. See above under Part 1/B.I.1. *The choice made by the parties.*

253  Giuliano & Lagarde 32.

254  Article 12(1)(a) Rome I.

255  Article 12(1)(b) Rome I.

256  Article 12(1)(c) Rome I.

257  Article 12(1)(d) Rome I.

258  Article 12(1)(e) Rome I.

259  *Cheshire & North* (14th ed.) 753; but compare *Peter Nygh*, Autonomy in International Contracts (1999) 132.

with regard to the law of the country in which performance takes place.[260] The Regulation does not offer criteria for distinguishing between "performance" and "manner of performance", but it appears settled that the distinction is to be drawn according to the law of the forum.[261] The reason for this distinction is explained in the Report as being necessary in order to allow the judge to "consider whether such a law has any relevance to the manner in which the contract should be performed and has discretion to apply it in whole or in part so as to do justice between the parties."[262] As well as providing various examples of issues coming within Article 12(1)(b),[263] the *Giuliano & Lagarde* Report provides that performance includes the totality of the conditions, resulting from the law or from the contract, in accordance with which the act is essential for the fulfilment of an obligation must be performed.[264]

According to the wording of Article 12 Rome I, the applicable law governs "within the limits of the powers conferred on the court by its procedural law, the consequences of a total or partial breach of obligations, including the assessment of damages in so far as it is governed by rules of law."[265] Thus, it appears that the applicable law will govern questions such as the heads of damages recoverable, remoteness of damage and monetary limits on recoverable amounts. However, the factual assessment of the quantum of damages is an issue left to the law of the forum to determine.[266] Article 12(1)(d) subjects two further issues to the applicable law: the first, concerning the ways in which obligations under the contract may be extinguished;[267] and the second, the prescription and limitation of actions. Finally, Article 12(1)(e) provides that the consequences of nullity of contract are governed by the law applicable to a contract.[268] Thus, an issue concerning the plea of *non est*

---

260 Article 12(2) Rome I. Compare also *Catalyst Recycling Ltd v Nickelhütte Aue GmbH* [2008] EWCA Civ 541, at [57].

261 This is suggested in the *Giuliano & Lagarde* Report 38 which states that the Group did not wish to give a strict definition of this concept; but see *Dicey & Morris* (15th ed.) Vol. II 1855, which suggest drawing a distinction in a uniform manner rather than by reference to the *lex fori*.

262 Giuliano & Lagarde Report 38.

263 Article 10(1)(b) of the Rome Convention.

264 Giuliano & Lagarde Report 37.

265 Article 12(1)(c) Rome I.

266 *Giuliano & Lagarde* Report 37; but see *Dicey & Morris* (15th ed.) Vol. II 1857.

267 E.g. by performance; by bankruptcy; by legislation; by novation, see *Dicey & Morris* (15th ed.) Vol. II 1858–1861.

268 The corresponding Article 10(1)(e) of the Rome Convention had been the subject of a reservation by the United Kingdom Contracts (Applicable Law) Act 1990, section 2(2)).

*factum* will be resolved according to the applicable law.[269] For example, the issue of whether money paid under a void contract is recoverable is subject to the law governing the contract.[270]

## II. Restrictions on Party Autonomy

As has been discussed above, the Rome I Regulation takes a wide approach to party autonomy. Thus, it is the choice of the parties that determines and gives the parties the power to select the law applicable to their contract. Accordingly, it should not be up to the forum to grant or withhold application of that law at its discretion. Article 3 Rome I does not stipulate a total restriction of the choice of law in order to protect the interests of a weaker party.[271] Instead the Regulation contains specific restrictions on a choice of law involving economically weaker parties, i.e. passengers (Article 5(2)), insurance policy holders (Article 7(3)), consumers (Article 6), and employees (Article 8). Consumer and individual employment contracts are widely recognised examples of situations in which limits on party autonomy are necessary in order to correct the imbalance of bargaining power. All provisions contain similar limitations on party autonomy in order to prevent the stronger party circumventing the protection afforded to the economically weaker party by the law of their home state. In other words, preventing a situation where the weaker party is required to pursue a complaint in a distant forum according to unfamiliar laws.[272]

In addition, the Rome I Regulation also restricts the extent of the parties' autonomy by placing general limits on the choice of law:[273] The choice of law must not contravene the application of the provisions which cannot be derogated from

---

269 Article 12(1)(e) Rome I. See also *Peter Nygh*, Autonomy in International Contracts (1999) 124. Note that under the common law, the issue of restitution of benefits under a void contract is considered to be a non-contractual issue relating to the law of restitution. See *Dicey & Morris* (15th ed.) Vol. II 1862 or generally *Cheshire & North* (14th ed.) Chapter 19.

270 *Giuliano & Lagarde* Report 37; *Cheshire & North* (14th ed.) 757.

271 *Martiny*, in: MünchKomm (5th ed.) Art. 3 Rom I-VO marginal no. 10; *Peter Nygh*, Autonomy in International Contracts (1999) Chapter 3, 7.

272 The limitations on choice of law clauses in consumer and employment contracts are complemented by the limitations on party autonomy to select the forum in the Brussels I Regulation. See Articles 15–17 (consumer contracts) and 18–21 (employment contracts).

273 See generally *Peter Nygh*, Autonomy in International Contracts (1999) Chapter 3, 7 and 9; *Martiny*, in: MünchKomm (5th ed.) Art. 3 Rom I-VO marginal no. 10 *et seq.*

by agreement in the event of a close connection with a single country,[274] imperative norms of Community law,[275] overriding mandatory provisions,[276] or the public policy of the forum[277]. Furthermore, the choice of law itself is restricted to State law only. These three restrictions will now be set out briefly.

## 1. The chosen law

Article 3(1) Rome I clearly states that the contract shall be governed by the law chosen by the parties. Thus, it is not possible to choose supranational or non-state rules of law as the law governing the contract.[278] The choice made must be of a law of a country, not a non-national system of law (e.g. Jewish law or the law of Sharia), or be expressed in formulations such as the law of Mars, the law of the United Kingdom, or of British law.[279] In the same way, parties may not choose customs of international trade (also referred to as *lex mercatoria*) or the rules of an international convention to govern their contract.[280] The absence of the possibility to choose a non-State law under the Rome Convention was criticised by some commentators.[281] In its Proposal, the European Commission included a

---

274 Article 3(3) Rome I. Compare Article 14(2) Rome II Regulation: "Where all the elements relevant to the situation at the time when the event giving rise to the damage occurs are located in a country other than the country whose law has been chosen, the choice of the parties shall not prejudice the application of provisions of the law of that other country which cannot be derogated from by agreement."

275 Article 3(4) Rome I. Compare Article 14(3) Rome II Regulation: "Where all the elements relevant to the situation at the time when the event giving rise to the damage occurs are located in one or more of the Member States, the parties' choice of the law applicable other than that of a Member State shall not prejudice the application of provisions of Community law, where appropriate as implemented in the Member State of the forum, which cannot be derogated from by agreement."

276 Article 9 Rome I; Article 16 Rome II.

277 Article 21, Rome I; Article 26 Rome II.

278 *Dicey & Morris* (15th ed.) Vol. II 1803.

279 *Adrian Briggs*, The Conflict of Laws (2002) 159. See e.g., *Shamil Bank of Bahrain v Beximco Pharmaceuticals Ltd* [2004] EWCA Civ 19 at [48], [2004] 1 WLR 1784 (concerning the law of Sharia); *Halpern v Halpern* [2007] EWCA Civ 291 at [19] *et seq.*, [2007] Lloyd's Rep 56 (concerning Jewish law).

280 Generally, *Peter Nygh*, Autonomy in International Contracts (1999) Chapter 8; *Wulf-Henning Roth*, Zur Wählbarkeit nichstaatlichen Rechts, FS Jayme (Vol. 1 2004) 757, 768 *et seq.*

281 *Andrea Bonomi*, Conversion of the Rome Convention into an EX Instrument: Some Remarks on the Green Paper of the EC Commission, YBPIL (2003) 53, 66; *Ole*

compromise, the purpose of which was to extend the classical limits on choice of law by permitting the choice of a law other than national law.[282] It provided that: "the parties may also choose as the applicable law the principles and rules of the substantive law of contract recognised internationally or in the Community".[283] The final version of the Rome I Regulation does not reflect the original proposal of the Commission. But Recital (13) clarifies that although parties are not authorised to choose a non-state body of law as the applicable law in a conflicts sense (*kollisionsrechtliche Rechtswahl*), the Regulation does not preclude parties from incorporating into their contract a non-State body of law or an international convention.[284] Hence, the parties can refer to a non-State law as part of the *lex contractus*,[285] i.e. law applicable to their contract (*materiellrechtliche Rechtswahl*), but only to the extent that they do not violate mandatory provisions of the State law, as determined as the applicable law under the Regulation.[286] Moreover,

---

    *Lando/Peter Nielsen*, The Rome I Regulation, (2008) 45 CML Rev 1695–1696. Compare, *Peter Nygh*, Autonomy in International Contracts (1999) 182–185.

282  *Peter Mankowski*, Der Vorschlag für die Rom I-Verordnung (2006) IPRax 101, 102; *Ulrich Magnus/Peter Mankowski*, Joint Response on the Green Paper on the Conversion of the Rome Convention on the Law Applicable to Contractual Obligations into a Community Instrument and its Modernisation, COM (2002) 654.

283  *The Proposal* Article 3(2). *The Proposal*, at 5 explains: "The form of words used would authorise the choice of the UNIDROIT Principles, the Principles of European Contract Law (PECL) or a possible future optional Community instrument, while excluding the *lex mercatoria*, which is not precise enough, or private codifications not adequately recognised by the international community". Cf. *Ole Lando/Peter Nielsen*, The Rome I Regulation, (2008) 45 CML Rev 1696–1698, who state that as it is also accepted in international arbitration, it would have been an improvement to also authorise the choice of that part of the *lex mercatoria* which is codified and internationally recognised. Further, if parties wish for their entire contract to be governed by the *lex mercatoria* that they would have to agree to arbitration and a tribunal which recognises such. See e.g. Arbitration Act 1996 (UK) Section 46(1)(b).

284  *Martiny*, in: MünchKomm (5th ed.) Art. 3 Rom I-VO, marginal no. 14–15.

285  Compare *lex loci contractus* – the law of a place where the contract is made.

286  This distinction between "conflictual choice or *materiellrechtliche Verweisung*" tends to be marginal, see *Ulrich Magnus/Peter Mankowski*, Joint Response on the Green Paper on the Conversion of the Rome Convention on the Law Applicable to Contractual Obligations into a Community Instrument and its Modernisation, COM (2002) 654; *Francisco Alferez*, The Rome I Regulation: Much ado about nothing? (2/2008 EuL Forum) 61–79, 67. Also, *Ole Lando/Peter Nielsen*, The Rome I Regulation, (2008) 45 CML Rev 1698. Compare also *Gerhard Kegel/Klaus Schurig*, Internationales Privatrecht, (2004) §18 I c).

Recital (14) provides that parties may choose to apply "rules of substantive contract law, including standard terms and conditions", should the Community adopt such an appropriate legal instrument.[287]

## 2. The effect of mandatory laws on the autonomy of the parties

The parties' freedom to choose the applicable law is restricted, in particular, by a number of Articles dealing with mandatory provisions.[288] The provisions contained in Article 3 of the Regulation must be distinguished from the provisions contained in Article 9 of the Regulation.[289] Article 3 provides for the application of imperative norms or *ius cogens*, i.e. rules which cannot be derogated from by agreement. Article 9, relates to the application of "overriding mandatory provisions".[290]

Article 3 contains two restrictions in the form of imperative norms. Article 3(3) is concerned with cases where a foreign law has been chosen by the parties in a

---

287 *Cheshire & North* (14th ed.) 699; *Ole Lando/Peter Nielsen*, The Rome I Regulation, (2008) 45 CML Rev 1698.

288 On overriding mandatory provisions in the Rome I Regulation see e.g. *Felix Maultzsch*, Rechtswahl und ius cogens im Internationalen Schuldvertragsrecht, RabelsZ Vol. 75 (2011) 60, 65 *et seq.*; *Andrea Bonomi*, Overriding Mandatory Provisions in the Rome I Regulation on the Law Applicable to Contracts, (2008) 10 YPIL 285–300; *Karsten Thorn*, Eingriffsnormen, in *Franco Ferrari/Stefan Leible* (eds.), Ein neues Internationales Vertragsrecht für Europa – Der Vorschlag für eine Rom I-Verordnung (2007) 129 *et seq.*; *Robert Freitag*, Einfach und international zwingende Normen, in *Stefan Leible* (ed.), Das Grünbuch zum internationalen Vertragsrecht (2004) 167 *et seq.* For the Rome Convention see e.g., *Richard Plender/Michael Wilderspin*, The European Contracts Convention (2001) Chapter 9; *Abbo Junker*, Empfiehlt es sich, Art. 7 EVÜ zu revidieren oder aufgrund der bisherigen Erfahrungen zu präzisieren? (2000) IPRax 65–73.

289 Note there are additional limitations on choice, that is provisions that cannot be derogated from by contract, specifically set out in the Regulation itself, see: Art. 6(2) (compare Art. 5(2) Rome Convention; Art. 8(1) (compare Art. 6(1) Rome Convention); and Art. 11(5) (compare Art. 9(6) Rome Convention). These are not dealt with further here. For an in-depth and critical analysis of party autonomy and Articles 3(3), 6(2) and 9 Rome I see *Felix Maultzsch*, Rechtswahl und ius cogens im Internationalen Schuldvertragsrecht, RabelsZ Vol. 75 (2011) 60, 65 *et seq.* See also *Cheshire & North* (14th ed.) Chapter 18; *Andrea Bonomi*, Overriding Mandatory Provisions in the Rome I Regulation on the Law Applicable to Contracts, (2008) 10 YPIL 285–300.

290 In the Rome Convention text both Article 3(3) and Article 7 confusingly refer to 'mandatory rules', in German *zwingende Vorschriften* and French *dispositions imperatives*.

purely internal or 'domestic' contractual relationship,[291] i.e. a situation where the parties and their contractual relationship are connected to one country only. Although there is no requirement that the law chosen by the parties have any relevant connection with the parties or their legal relationship, Article 3(3) provides that:[292]

> Where all other elements relevant to the situation at the time of the choice are located in a country other than the country whose law has been chosen, the choice of the parties shall not prejudice the application of provisions of the law of that other county which cannot be derogated from by agreement.

Recital (15) reflects the position under the Rome Convention and provides that this rule applies whether or not the choice of law was accompanied by a choice of court or tribunal. This means that although all relevant factual connections are situated in Country A, parties may still choose the law of Country B to govern their contractual relationship. In such a situation, Article 3(3) preserves the parties' choice of applicable law but provides that the mandatory rules of Country A will still be applicable and will override any different rules in the law of Country B.[293]

Article 3(4) provides an additional restriction:

> Where all other elements relevant to the situation at the time of the choice are located in one or more Member States, the parties' choice of applicable law other than that of a Member State shall not prejudice the application of provisions of Community law, where appropriate as implemented in the Member State of the forum, which cannot be derogated from by agreement.

---

291 According to Article 3(1) or (2) Rome I.

292 Article 3(3) Rome I, presents no substantial change to the corresponding Article 3(3) of the Rome Convention but adopts slightly different wording in order to align the provision with the Rome II Regulation (Article 14(2)).

293 On this see e.g. *Felix Maultzsch*, Rechtswahl und ius cogens im Internationalen Schuldvertragsrecht, RabelsZ Vol. 75 (2011) 60, 65 *et seq*. The author criticises this approach and instead suggests that any choice of foreign law should be incorporated as terms of the contract only. See also *Jörg Köndring*, Flucht vor deutschem AGB-Recht bei Inlandsverträgen: Gedanken zu Art. 3 Abs. 3 Rom I-VO und § 1051 ZPO, RIW 2010, 184–191, 185; *Rolf Wagner*, Der Grundsatz der Rechtswahl und das mangels Rechtswahl anwendbare Recht (Rom I-Verordnung), Ein Bericht über die Entstehungsgeschichte und den Inhalt der Artikel 3 und 4 Rom I-Verordnung (2008) IPRax 377–386, 380; *Thomas Rauscher*, Internationales Privatrecht, mit internationalen und europäischen Verfahrensrecht (2009) marginal no. 1198. Compare *Stefan Leible/Matthias Lehmann*, Die Verordnung über das auf vertragliche Schuldverhältnisse anzuwendende Recht (Rom I), RIW 2008 528–543, 534 and *Peter Mankowski*, Die Rom I-Verordnung, Änderungen im europäischen IPR für Schuldverträge, Internationales Handelsrecht 2008 133–152, 134.

Thus, this provision explicitly provides that where all elements of a particular relationship are located in one or more Member State,[294] and the parties choose the law of a non-Member State, that choice shall not prejudice the application of mandatory rules of Community law. Both provisions are concerned with situations in which a choice of foreign law is the only international element in an otherwise purely domestic relationship.

The "overriding mandatory provisions" contained in Article 9 of the Regulation[295] are different in nature to the imperative norms provided for in Article 3 paragraphs (3) and (4).[296] The content of Article 9 is narrower and Article 9(1) provides a definition:

> Overriding mandatory provisions are provisions the respect for which is regarded as crucial by a country for safeguarding its public interests, such as its political, social or economic organisation, to such an extent that they are applicable to any situation falling within their scope, irrespective of the law otherwise applicable to the contract under this Regulation.

Nothing in the Regulation is to restrict the application of such mandatory provisions. The court will not be required to assess which law would be applicable but will automatically apply mandatory provisions of the law of the forum.[297]

---

294 Note that Article 1(4) second sentence Rome I states that the term Member State shall mean all the Member States for the purposes of Article 3(4) and 7 of the Regulation. Cf. Article 1(4) Rome II: "For the purposes of this Regulation, 'Member State' shall mean any Member State other than Denmark."

295 Article 7 of the Rome Convention. The United Kingdom, Luxemburg, Germany and Ireland entered reservations to this part of the provision (Article 22 Rome Convention). On this and the addition of Article 9(3) (the application of overriding mandatory provisions of a foreign State), see *Dicey & Morris* (14th ed.) 2nd suppl. 2008, 227–228; Ministry of Justice, Rome I – Should the UK Opt in? Consultation Paper CP05/08, April 2, 2008 paras. 79–81, available at: http://www.justice.gov.uk/docs/cp0508.pdf. Further on Article 9 Rome I and party autonomy, see *Felix Maultzsch*, Rechtswahl und ius cogens im Internationalen Schuldvertragsrecht, RabelsZ Vol. 75 (2011) 60, 81 *et seq.*

296 See Recital (37) Rome I Regulation: "The concept of 'overriding mandatory provisions' should be distinguished from the expression 'provisions which cannot be derogated from by agreement' and should be construed more restrictively."

297 *Green Paper*, para. 3.2.8.1. An English example is the Unfair Contract Terms Act 1977, the provisions of which are mandatory and cannot be contracted out of (but see section 26, unless a contract is an "international supply contract"). *Andrea Bonomi*, Overriding Mandatory Provisions in the Rome I Regulation on the Law Applicable to Contracts, (2008) 10 YPIL 285–300; for the Rome Convention,

However, where a mandatory rule of a law other than the applicable law is applied, this will not mean that the parties' choice of law is invalid. The parties' choice remains effective for all substantive issues, except for those issues covered by the mandatory laws.

Where overriding mandatory provisions of a foreign state are concerned, the limitation to party autonomy is narrowly drawn.[298] The parties' choice of law may only be displaced in favour of the law of the state of performance or the contractual obligation, in so far as the mandatory provisions of that state render performance of the contract unlawful. Even then, a court is not obliged to give effect to the foreign mandatory rules.[299] The distinction in Article 9 between mandatory law of the forum or of a foreign state recognises that while a court is obliged to give effect to imperative rules of the forum, it has no obligation to enforce public interests of other states.

## 3. Public policy

In addition to the imperative norms in Article 3 and the overriding mandatory provisions applicable under Article 9, the public policy of the forum may also be relevant Regulation.[300] Article 21 (in substance the same as Article 16 of the Rome Convention), provides national courts with another route to apply the law of the forum rather than the law applicable as identified by the Regulation.[301] The law as specified under the Regulation can only be denied in situations where its application would lead to consequences contrary to or "manifestly incompatible" with the public policy (*ordre public*) of the forum.

---

see *Andrea Bonomi*, Mandatory Rules in Private International Law – The quest for uniformity of decision in a global environment, (1999) YPIL 215 *et seq*. Compare also ECJ *Case C-381/98 Ingmar GB Ltd v Eaton Leonard Technologies Inc [2000] ECR I-9305*; *H. Verhagen*, The Tension between Party Autonomy and European Union Law: Some observations on *Ingmar GB Ltd v Eaton Leonard Technologies Inc*, (2002) 51 ICLQ, 135–154.

298  Article 9(3) Rome I. See further *Felix Maultzsch*, Rechtswahl und ius cogens im Internationalen Schuldvertragsrecht, RabelsZ Vol. 75 (2011) 60, 92 *et seq*.

299  When considering whether to give effect to those foreign provisions, a court shall have regard to their nature and purpose and the consequences of their application or non-application; Article 9(3) Rome I.

300  Public policy includes Community public policy; see *Giuliano & Lagarde* Report 44.

301  *David McClean/Kisch Beevers* (eds.), The Conflict of Laws (2009) 391.

# C. Summary

The Rome I Regulation provides a systematic conflict-of-laws system, designating the applicable law to contractual obligations in civil and commercial matters. It supplements the Brussels I Regulation and Rome II Regulation and forms an integral part facilitating the unification of the rules of private international law within the European Union. It has made the doctrine of party autonomy the general choice of law rule and thereby reaffirms the approach embodied in the private international law of all of the Member States of the community, and indeed most other countries.[302] The Regulation presents a revised version of the Rome Convention of 1980, and in Article 3 Rome I reaffirms the prominence to be given to freedom of choice of the applicable law by the parties. The rule provided in Article 3(1) Rome I is considered to be the most central of the choice of law rules in the Regulation. Parties may make a choice as to the applicable law, they may choose whichever law they wish, they may choose different laws for different parts of the contract, exercise their choice at any time, and change their choice. The parties' choice should be decisive and only in clearly specified situations or where no choice is made, should a court displace it, restrict it, or resort to determining the applicable law objectively.

The power of parties to specify the law applicable to their contract had been established by case law and following the adoption of the Rome Convention, was firmly recognised by pre-Regulation conflict-of-law rules in both Germany and England.[303] Nevertheless, issues concerning the effect and validity of a choice of law were not resolved consistently. In particular, the approach to be taken to the problem of silent consent differed under pre-Regulation German and English law. The Rome I Regulation does not explicitly address the issue of silent consent; however, as has been discussed above, it is accepted that the effect of silence is regulated in Article 10. It provides for the putative proper law to be displaced in situations where it would be unreasonable to apply it, i.e. where a choice of law is based on the silent acceptance of the law during proceedings or negotiations. The result of the approach to be taken according to Article 10 Rome

---

302 See *Giuliano & Lagarde* Report 14–16.
303 *Christoph Reithmann/Dieter Martiny* (eds.), Internationales Vertragsrecht (2010) marginal no. 87 with further references; *Martiny* in: MünchKomm (5th ed.) 461; and English case law established by *Vita Food Products Inc v Unus Shipping Company Ltd* [1939] AC 277, 289–290 (PC); *R v International Trustee for the Protection of Bondholders Aktiengesellschaft* [1937] AC 500, 530.

I is that although the pre-Regulation approach in Germany considered it sufficient to infer a silent consent of German law as evidenced by the parties conduct during legal proceedings, such an approach can no longer be maintained under the Rome I Regulation.

Overall, due to the adoption of the Rome Covention the recognition of party autonomy in the Regulation does not present any significant changes to the pre-Regulation approaches taken in both Germany and England. However, it does promote a more uniform approach to issues of formation, formal validity, inferring a choice of law and restrictions placed on party autonomy.

# Part 2: Freedom of choice of law under the Rome II Regulation on the law applicable to non-contractual obligations

In 2007 the European Union adopted the Regulation on the Law Applicable to Non-Contractual Obligations, known as Rome II, in order to provide for the unification of choice of law for non-contractual obligations in the European Community. The most innovative rule to be introduced into choice of law for non-contractual obligations in the Rome II Regulation is the principle of party autonomy. It is innovative because it is a principle long established in contract, but is considerably less well developed in the area of non-contractual obligations; for a long time this principle had nothing to do with non-consensual obligations. The inclusion of it in the Rome II Regulation reflects a gradually increasing trend in contemporary conflict of laws to extend the principle from contract to torts, succession,[304] matrimonial property[305] and even divorce[306] and maintenance[307]. A brief summary of the history of the Rome II Regulation will be followed by a detailed analysis of the principle of party autonomy established in Article 14 of the Rome II Regulation.

---

304 See e.g. Article 5 Hague Convention of 1 August 1989 on the Law Applicable to Succession to the Estates of Deceased Persons: "(1) A person may designate the law of a particular State to govern the succession to the whole of his estate"; and Article 22 of Council Regulation No 650/2012 of the European Parliament and of the Council of 4 July 2012 on jurisdiction, applicable law, recognition and enforcement of decisions and acceptance and enforcement of authentic instruments in matters of succession and on the creation of a European Certificate of Succession, OJ L201, 107 ff.

305 See e.g. Articles 3 and 6 Hague Convention of 14 March 1978 on the Law Applicable to Matrimonial Property Regimes; Article 15 German *EGBGB*; Green Paper on Conflict of Laws in Matters Concerning Matrimonial Property Regimes, including the question of jurisdiction and mutual recognition COM (2006) 400 final [17.7.2006], at 2.2.2.

306 See e.g. Article 5 of Council Regulation No 1259/2010 of 20 December 2010 implementing enhanced cooperation in the area of the law applicable to divorce and legal separation, OJ L343 [29.12.10] 10–16.

307 E.g. Articles 7–8 of the Hague Protocol of 23 November 2007 on the law applicable to maintenance obligations; Council Regulation (EC) No 4/2009 of 18 December 2008 on jurisdiction, applicable law, recognition and enforcement of decisions and cooperation in matters relating to maintenance obligations, Article 15 (incorporating the Hague Protocol) and Article 4 (freedom to choose the competent court by agreement).

# A. Overview of the Rome II Regulation

The EC Regulation on the law applicable to non-contractual obligations (hereafter referred to as the Rome II Regulation or Rome II)[308] should be understood in light of the historical developments that have taken place within the Community.[309] The Regulation belongs to a series of European regulations in private international law, established according to the competence provided for in Article 61 and 65 EC Treaty, with the view towards the unification of private international choice of law rules for different areas of law.[310] The Rome II Regulation was adopted on 11 July 2007. As of 11 January 2009, the Regulation will be applicable in all European Member States,[311] with the exception of Denmark.[312] According to Article 249 of the EC Treaty, the Regulation "shall have general application" and "shall be binding and directly applicable in all Member States." This entails that pursuant to

---

308  Regulation (EC) no 864/2007, OJ L299, 40 [31.7.2007].
309  General background of codifications at the Member State level, see amongst others *Symeon Symeonides*, Rome II and Tort Conflicts: A Missed Opportunity (2008) 56 Am. J. Comp. L. 471; *Jan Von Hein*, Something Old and Something Borrowed, But Nothing New? Rome II and the European Choice-of-Law Evolution (2008) 82 Tul. L. Rev. 1663; *Xandra Kramer*, The Rome II Regulation on the Law Applicable to Non-Contractual Obligations: The European private international law tradition continued (2008) NIPR 4 414–424; *Cheshire & North* (14th ed.) 770 *et seq*. For a chronology of key developments in the process leading to the adoption of the Rome II Regulation, see *Andrew Dickinson*, The Rome II Regulation: The Law Applicable to Non-Contractual Obligations (2008) (hereafter: *Andrew Dickinson*, The Rome II Regulation) Appendix 5.
310  The Explanatory Memorandum to the Commission Proposal of 22 July 2003, COM (2003) 427 final (hereafter the *Explanatory Memorandum*), makes clear at page 8 that: "Brussels I Regulation, the Rome Convention and the Regulation proposed here constitute a coherent set of instruments covering the general field of private international law in matters of civil and commercial obligations."
311  The United Kingdom and Ireland have opted into the Rome II Regulation according to Art. 3 of the Protocol on the position of the United Kingdom and Ireland annexed to the Treaty on European Union and to the Treaty establishing the European Community, see Recital (39) to the Rome II Regulation. For a criticism of the United Kingdom Government's decision to opt in see House of Lords European Union Committee, 8th Report of Session 2003–4, HL Paper 66, paragraphs 80–82, available at http://www.publications.parliament.uk/pa/ld200304/ldselect/ldeucom/66/66.pdf.
312  According to Recital (40) to the Rome II Regulation and the Protocol on the position of Denmark annexed to the Treaty on European Union and to the Treaty establishing the European Community.

Section 2(1) of the European Communities Act 1972, the Rome II Regulation has direct effect in the United Kingdom[313] and Germany without the need to implement specific legislation. The Regulation effectively replaces the existing statutory basis for the determination of foreign torts in the United Kingdom laid down in the Private International Law (Miscellaneous Provisions) Act 1995 (UK)[314] and the relevant choice of law rules[315] laid down in the German Introductory Act to the Civil Code (*Einführungsgesetz zum Bürgerlichen Gesetzbuch*)[316].

# I. Before Rome II

Attempts towards establishing uniform European rules for non-contractual obligations go back to the establishment of the Rome Convention.[317] In 1972, the original six Member States of the European Community presented a first preliminary E.E.C. Draft Convention on Contractual and Non-Contractual Obligations.[318] However, in 1978 the decision was made to abandon the non-contractual provisions of the draft convention and to rather focus attention only on contractual

---

313   R v Secretary of State for Transport, ex p Factortame (No. 2) [1991] 1 AC 603 (UKHL).

314   Hereafter abbreviated 'UK PIL Act 1995'. See Part III of the UK PIL Act 1995.

315   Articles 38–46 *EGBGB*.

316   (*EGBGB*). This law was the product of major statutory reforms introduced in 1986 and 1999 respectively; see Gesetz zur Neuregelung des IPR vom 25.7.1986, BGBl. I/1986, 1142; Gesetz zum IPR für außervertragliche Schuldverhältnisse und das Sachenrecht vom 21.5.1999, BGBl. I 1026. For comments in English on the changes brought about by the 1986 reform see *Rainer Gildeggen/Jochen Langkeit*, The new Conflict of Laws Code Provisions of the Federal Republic of Germany: Introductory Comment and Translation (1986) 17 Ga J Int'l & Comp L 229–259. For the 1999 reform see generally *Andreas Spickhoff*, Die Restkodifikation des Internationalen Privatrechts: Außervertragliche Schuldverhältnisse und Sachenrecht, (1999) NJW 2209; *Rolf Wagner*, Zum Inkrafttreten des Gesetzes zum Internationalen Privatrecht für außervertragliche Schuldverhältnisse und für Sachen (1999) IPRax 210; for English commentary see *Peter Hay*, From Rule-Orientation to 'Approach' in German Conflicts Law – The Effect of the 1986 and 1999 Codifications (1999) 47 Am. J. Comp. L. 633; *Matthias Reimann*, Codifying torts Conflicts: The German Legislation in Comparative Perspective (2000) 60 La L Rev 1297.

317   Convention on the Law applicable to Contractual Obligations, OJ L 266, 1. See the *Explanatory Memorandum* 3.

318   For comments on the draft see amongst others *Ole Lando*, The EC-Draft Convention on the Law Applicable to Contractual and Non-Contractual Obligations, (1974) RabelsZ 6–55.

obligations. In 1980, the Convention on the Law Applicable to Contractual Obligations, known as the "Rome Convention" was opened for signature, and entered into force in 1991.[319]

## II. The path to Rome II

Work on a draft Convention on the law applicable to non-contractual obligations was resumed only in 1996.[320] Preparatory work was carried out by the European Council's working group, *Groupe européen de droit international privé* (*GEDIP*).[321] A further impetus was gained with the Treaty of Amsterdam[322] that entered into force on 1 May 1999. For the first time, the European Community was expressly empowered to deal with matters of private international law, so that in 1999, the Council's working group prepared a further preliminary draft on the law applicable to non-contractual obligations.[323] This internal draft, served as a basis for the European Commission's preliminary draft proposal, for the purpose of consulting interested parties, which was submitted to a round of public consultations in 2002.[324] Written contributions were received from Member States, trade and

---

319 The consolidated text of the Convention is published in OJ C 27 [26.01.1998] 0034 – 0046 (English text). See also Rome I Regulation (EC) No 593/2008 on the law applicable to contractual obligations (Rome I) OJ L 177, 6 [4.7.2008], which replaces the Rome Convention. For text of Rome Convention in various languages, see http://eurlex.europa.eu/LexUriServ/LexUriServ.do?uri=CELEX:41998A0126(02):EN:NOT.

320 For the relevant documents, see the public register of the Council of the European Union, available at: http://register.consilium.europa.eu.

321 A proposal for a European Convention on the law applicable to non-contractual obligations was produced by *GEDIP* and adopted at the meeting of 25–27 September 1998, *see*: http://www.gedip-egpil.eu/documents/gedip-documents-8pe.html. Professor Symeonides described the *GEDIP* proposal as 'an elegant, sophisticated, and flexible document which has influenced the general content and coverage of Rome II, although not where it matters most' in *Symeon Symeonides*, Rome II and Tort Conflicts: A Missed Opportunity (2008) 56 Am. J. Comp. L. 173 177 and see *idem*, Tort Conflicts and Rome II: A View from Across (2004) FS Jayme 935–954. For a different view, see *Andrew Dickinson*, The Rome II Regulation 31–32.

322 Treaty of Amsterdam Amending the Treaty on European Union, the Treaties Establishing the European Communities and Certain Related Acts of 10 November 1997, OJ C 340/01.

323 For a discussion, see *Andrew Dickinson*, The Rome II Regulation 32–40.

324 See Preliminary Draft Proposal for a European Council Regulation on the Law Applicable to Non-Contractual Obligations, available at http://ec.europa.eu/justice_home/news/consulting_public/rome_ii/news_hearing_rome2_en.htm.

industry groups, academics and practitioners, which culminated in a public hearing in 2003.[325] Following these consultations, the European Commission finalised its first proposal for a Rome II Regulation in 2003 (hereafter referred to as 'Commission Proposal').[326] The Commission Proposal was accompanied by a detailed Explanatory Report (hereafter: Explanatory Memorandum), including article commentaries and differed considerably from the preliminary draft proposal.[327]

The reaction to the Commission Proposal following its publication in 2003 was generally hostile,[328] and the process then shifted to the European Parliament. By June 2005, a Report[329] produced by the European Parliament's Committee on Legal Affairs was adopted by the JURI Committee (European Parliament Committee on Legal Affairs and the Internal Market), a standing committee of

---

325  For the contributions received, see http://ec.europa.eu/justice_home/news/consulting_public/rome_ii/news_summary_rome2_en.htm. For a detailed proposal, see *Hamburg Group for Private International Law*, Comments on the European Commission's Draft Proposal for a Council Regulation on the Law Applicable to Non-Contractual Obligations (2003) RabelsZ 67 1–56.

326  Proposal for a Regulation of the European Council on the Law Applicable to Non-Contractual Obligations ("Rome II") COM (2003) 427 final, 22 July 2003. For a critique of the Commission Proposal, see *Symeon Symeonides*, Tort Conflicts and Rome II: A view from Across (2004) FS Jayme 935 *et seq.*

327  For a discussion, see *Andrew Dickinson*, The Rome II Regulation 40–43.

328  For international reactions to the Commission Proposal, cf. e.g. *Martina Benecke*, Auf dem Weg zu "Rom II" – Der Vorschlag für eine Verordnung zur Angleichung des IPR der außerverträglichen Schuldverhältnisse RIW 2003 830; *Jan von Hein*, Die Kodifikation des europäischen Internationalen Deliktsrecht – Zur geplanten EU-Verordnung über das außervertragliche Schuldverhältnisse anzuwendende Recht, ZVglRWiss. 102 (2003) 528; *Angelika Fuchs*, Zum Kommissionsvorschlag einer „Rom II"-Verordnung GPR 2003–04 100; House of Lords European Union Committee, 8th Report of Session 2003-4, HL Paper 66; *Peter Huber/Ivo Bach*, Die Rom-II VO: Kommissionsentwurf und aktuelle Entwicklungen (2005) IPRax 73; *Stefan Leible/Andreas Engel*, Der Vorschlag der EG-Kommission für eine "Rom II"-Verordnung' EuZW 2004 4; *Dorothea Lück*, Neuere Entwicklungen des deutschen und europäischen internationalen Deliktsrecht (2006) 161; *Symeon Symeonides*, Tort Conflicts and Rome II: A View from Across (2004) FS Jayme 935–954 and see also contributions by *Borchers, Glenn, Symeonides, Watt, Weintraub* available at http://www.dianawallismep.org.uk/pages/Rome-II-seminars.html.

329  Report on the proposal for a regulation of the European Parliament and of the Council on the law applicable to non-contractual obligations (Rome II) (COM (2003)0427 – C5–0338/2003 – 2003/0168(COD)) (Rapporteur: Diana Wallis). Document EP A6-0211/2005 [27.6.2005] available with votes and amendments at: http://www.europarl.europa.eu/oeil/file.jsp?id=235142.

the European Parliament that focuses on the interpretation and application of European law.[330] This report formed the basis for the position of the European Parliament's published in July 2005.[331] At its first hearing before the European Parliament, the report met with significant criticism resulting in the proposal of various amendments, most of which promoted more flexibility in the conflict-of-law rules.[332] As a result, the European Commission presented an amended proposal in February 2006 (Commission Amended Proposal).[333] In September 2006, the Council of the European Union adopted its version of the Amended Proposal, the Common Position,[334] which largely followed the approach of the Commission, rather than that of the European Parliament.[335] In December 2006, the JURI Committee adopted its Recommendation for the second reading.[336] At the second reading, most of the amendments proposed by JURI were approved by the European Parliament. However, the Commission did not support the further amendments proposed by the Parliament.[337] Following a series of trilogues[338] between

---

330  The Commission focuses particularly on the fields of civil, commercial and company law, intellectual property legislation and procedural law and is competent to provide opinions on proposed Regulations. For more information see http://www.europarl. europa.eu/committees/juri_home_en.htm.

331  OJ C 157/06, 0098–0370.

332  See Proposal for a Regulation of the European Parliament and of the Council on the law applicable to non-contractual obligations (ROME II) – Outcome of the European Parliament's first reading (Strasbourg, 4 to 7 July 2005), available at http://register. consilium.europa.eu/pdf/en/05/st10/st10812.en05.pdf.

333  Amended Proposal for a European Parliament and Council Regulation on the Law Applicable to Non-Contractual Obligations ("Rome II") COM (2006) 83 final, 21 February 2006 (*Commission Amended Proposal*).

334  Council Common Position OJ C 289/68, [28.11.2006]. See also Communication from the Commission concerning the Council's Common Position (COM (2006) 566 final [27.9.2006].

335  See Statement of the Councils Reasons (accompanying the Council's Common Position) OJ C 289E, [28.11.2006], at 76.

336  Recommendation for Second Reading on the Council common position for adopting a regulation of the European Parliament and of the Council on the law applicable to non-contractual obligations (Rome II) <DocRef>(9751/7/2006 – C60317/2006 – 2003/0168(COD)) [22.12.2006] (Rapporteur: Diana Wallis) available at http://www. dianawallis.org.uk/pages/rome2.html.</DocRef>

337  See Commission Opinion on the European Parliament's amendments to the Council Common Position (COM (2007) 126 final [14.3.2007]) available at http://www.europarl. europa.eu/oeil/file.jsp?id=235142.

338  *Andrew Dickinson*, The Rome II Regulation 58 at n 394.

the representatives of the Council, Commission and Parliament, an agreement was finally reached on a provisional joint text in May 2007.[339] The European Parliament formally adopted the Regulation on 11 July 2007 as the final text, which is hereafter referred to as the Rome II Regulation.

## III. Justifying party autonomy in the conflict of laws

Over the course of the previous decades, the concept of party autonomy has gained more and more recognition in contemporary conflict of laws and it now appears to be generally accepted that parties should be free to determine the applicable law to govern their relations. For a long time, party autonomy had nothing to do with non-consensual obligations but was instead confined to consensual obligations.[340] However, a gradual increasing expansion of the principle from the field of contracts to torts and other fields including succession,[341] matrimonial property,[342]

---

339 Parliament Council Conciliation Committee: Agreement on regulation on the law applicable to non-contractual obligations (Rome II) 16 May 2007, 9713/07 (Presse 111) available at: http://register.consilium.europa.eu/pdf/en/07/st09/st09713.en07.pdf.

340 See e.g. on the history of the concept of autonomy in contract *Peter Nygh*, Autonomy in International Contracts (1999) 3–14; *Kurt Siehr*, Die Parteiautonomie im Internationalen Privatrecht FS Keller 1989 485–510. See also *Russel J. Weintraub*, Functional Developments in Choice of Law for Contracts 187 Recueil des Cours 1984, 239; *Patrick Joseph Borchers*, Categorical Exceptions to Party Autonomy in Private International Law 82 Tul. L. Rev. (2008) 1645, 1646 and n 4; see comparative analysis in *Gisela Rühl*, Party Autonomy in the Private International Law of Contracts: Transatlantic Convergence and Economic Efficiency CLPE Research Paper 4/2007 Vol. 03 No. 01 (2007) available at: http://ssrn.com/abstract=921842; *William J. Woodward*, Contractual Choice of Law: Legislative Choice in an Era of Party Autonomy 54 SMU Law Rev. (2001) 697 available at: http://ssrn.com/abstract=1005412.

341 See e.g. Article 5 Hague Convention of 1 August 1989 on the Law Applicable to Succession to the Estates of Deceased Persons: "(1) A person may designate the law of a particular State to govern the succession to the whole of his estate"; and Article 22 of Regulation No 650/2012 of the European Parliament and of the Council of 4 July 2012 on jurisdiction, applicable law, recognition and enforcement of decisions and acceptance and enforcement of authentic instruments in matters of succession and on the creation of a European Certificate of Succession, OJ L201, 107 ff.

342 See e.g. Articles 3 and 6 Hague Convention of 14 March 1978 on the Law Applicable to Matrimonial Property Regimes; Article 15 German *EGBGB*; Green Paper on Conflict of Laws in Matters Concerning Matrimonial Property Regimes, including the question of jurisdiction and mutual recognition COM (2006) 400 final [17.7.2006] at 2.2.2.

divorce[343] and maintenance[344], was substantiated when in 2007, party autonomy was included as a central choice of law rule of the Rome II Regulation on the law applicable to non-contractual obligations. But on what rationale does the increasing importance of the role of party autonomy lie? Are economic considerations requiring foreseeability and certainty of the applicable law in cross-border commerce; or, are considerations of individual liberty, self-determination and the protection of interests at the forefront? In particular, on what rationale does the acceptance of party autonomy within the field of non-consensual obligations lie?

## 1. General justification of party autonomy in the conflict of laws

The freedom of parties to choose the applicable law is a principle that forms an integral part in the private international law of not only European but the majority of legal systems worldwide including the USA, Canada, Australia, New Zealand, Singapore and Hong Kong. But although party autonomy as a fundamental principle in the conflict of laws appears to be generally accepted in practice, global recognition does not justify its prevalence. Moreover, in theory the principle is often neglected. There is a surprisingly sparse academic examination of and theoretical explanation *why* parties should be allowed to choose the applicable law in the conflict of laws.[345] Noticeably, in contract law the right to choose the applicable

---

343 E.g. Article 22 of Council Regulation No 1259/2010 of 20 December 2010 implementing enhanced cooperation in the area of the law applicable to divorce and legal separation, OJ L343 [29.12.10] 10–16.

344 E.g. Council Regulation (EC) No 4/2009 of 18 December 2008 on jurisdiction, applicable law, recognition and enforcement of decisions and cooperation in matters relating to maintenance obligations (OJ L 7/1 [10.1.2009] Article 4 (freedom to choose the competent court by agreement); and the effect of Article 15 is that the law applicable to maintenance obligations is to be determined according to the 2007 Hague Protocol on the law applicable to maintenance obligations (see Article 8). Compare also the recent decision of the UK Supreme Court *Radmacher (formerly Granatino) v Granatino* [2010] UKSC 42, in which the Supreme Court upheld an ante-nuptial agreement that included a choice of law clause providing for the application of German law, even though the issues that arose in the case were held to be governed exclusively by English law.

345 *Matthias Lehmann*, Liberating the individual from battles between states: justifying party autonomy in conflict of laws Vanderbilt Journal of Transnational Law Vol. 41 2008 381, 383. See generally *Jürgen Basedow*, Theorie der Rechtswahl oder Parteiautonomie als Grundlage des Internationalen Privatrechts RabelsZ Vol. 75 (2011) 32–59; *Peter Nygh*, Autonomy in International Contracts (1999); *Stefan Leible*, Parteiautonomie im

law is essentially accepted and not much consideration is given to the rationale underlying the freedom to choose.

Under English law, the possibility of parties to make an express and implied choice of law for contractual obligations is well established.[346] German law also provides the option for the parties to choose the governing law. Similar to English law developments, the principle is founded on case law and has emerged as a fundamental principle, supported by present day theorists.[347] This general acceptance of party autonomy within the field of contract peaked in Europe, when in 1980 the principle of party autonomy was incorporated as the general choice of law rule in the Rome Convention on the law applicable to contractual obligations. Unfortunately, a precise explanation of the rationale underpinning the inclusion of party autonomy as a principle choice of law rule in the Convention, or later the Rome I Regulation, was omitted. The *Giuliano & Lagarde* Report merely states that the inclusion of such a rule reaffirms a rule already embodied in the private international law of Member States and most other countries, without any further discussion.[348] Mirroring the Rome I Regulation, the Rome II Regulation on the law applicable to non-contractual obligations also includes party autonomy as a central choice of law rule.

But why should parties be given the right to choose the applicable law to govern their relationship? A tempting way to answer the question may be simply with "why not" and thereby ignore any theoretical explanation of the rationale underpinning party autonomy as a choice of law rule. Another simple way to bypass

---

IPR – Allgemeines Anknüpfungsprinzip oder Verlegenheitslösung? FS Jayme (2004) 485; *Axel Flessner*, Interessenjurisprudenz im IPR (1990) 98–111.

346 For a recognition of the autonomy principle in the common law, see the classic formulation by Lord Atkin in the English case *R v International Trustee for the Protection of Bondholders Aktiengesellschaft* [1937] AC 500, [1937] 2 ALL ER 164. For an express choice for contracts under English law see the landmark case *Vita Food Products Inc. v Unus Shipping Co Ltd* [1939] AC 277 (PC) where it was decided that an express choice would be upheld "provided the intention expressed is *bona fide* and legal and there is no reason for avoiding the choice on the grounds of public policy". For an implied choice see *Egon Oldendorff v Liberia Corporation (No 1)* [1995] 2 Lloyds Rep. 64; *(No 2)* [1996] 2 Lloyds Rep. 380, in which the choice of a particular place of arbitration was taken as an implied choice of law. Also discussed in *Abla Mayss/John O'Brian*, Principles of Conflict of Laws (1999) 112 *et seq*.

347 Compare Article 27 *EGBGB*. For case references see *Christoph Reithmann*, Internationales Vertragsrecht. Das internationale Privatrecht der Schuldverträge (1980) marginal no. 6. See also *Jan Kropholler*, Internationales Privatrecht, (2006) 459 *et seq*.

348 Giuliano & Lagarde Report 13.

theoretical justification of party autonomy in is with the "killer argument" that parties are allowed to choose the applicable law because the legislator has provided conflict-of-law rules that allow this.[349] Nevertheless, this argument is able to offer an "external justification" (äußere Legitimation); in other words, an argument to justify the procedural validity of a rule, as opposed to the "internal justification" (*innere Legitimation*), explaining the theoretical validity of a rule.[350]

There are numerous ways in which the theoretical validity or internal justification of party autonomy in contract is explained: the rationale of freedom of contract and individual liberty (the principle of *in dubio libertas*),[351] from an economic point of view with the commercial convenience and legal certainty argument,[352] or simply that

---

349 As stated in *Matthias Lehmann*, Liberating the individual from battles between states: justifying party autonomy in conflict of laws (2008) Vanderbilt Journal of Transnational Law Vol. 41 381, 383–4. See also *Jan Kropholler*, Internationales Privatrecht (2006) §40 III (*aüßere positivrechtliche Legitimation*); *Jens Köthe*, Schranken der Parteiautonomie im internationalen Deliktsrecht (2008) 39.

350 See e.g. also *Jan Kropholler*, Internationales Privatrecht (2006) §40 III; *Felix Maultzsch*, Rechtswahl und ius cogens im Internationalen Schuldvertragsrecht RabelsZ Vol. 75 (2011) 60, 63 *et seq*; *Kathrin Kroll-Ludwig*, Die Rolle der Parteiautonomie im europäischen Kollisionsrecht (2013) 148–171.

351 E.g. *Matthias Lehmann*, Liberating the individual from battles between states: justifying party autonomy in conflict of laws (2008) Vanderbilt Journal of Transnational Law Vol. 41 381; *Jan Kropholler*, Internationales Privatrecht (2006) §40 III. But compare *Gerhard Kühne*, Die Parteiautonomie im internationalen Erbrecht Schriften zum deutschen und europäischen Zivil-, Handels-, und Prozessrecht, Vol. 75 (1973) 23 *et seq*. 61 *et seq*.

352 For further discussion on the economic basis see e.g., *Jürgen Basedow*, Lex Mercatoria und Internationales Schuldvertragsrecht, Eine rechtsökonomische Skizze, in: Zivil- und Wirtschaftsrecht im europäischen und globalen Kontext FS Horn (2006) 229, 242; *Jürgen Basedow*, Lex Mercatoria and the Private International Law of Contracts in Economic Perspective, in: *Jürgen Basedow/Toshiyuki Kono* (eds.) An Economic Analysis of Private International Law (2006) 57, 66–67; *Ralf Michaels*, Two Economists, Three Opinions? Economic Models for Private International law – Cross Border Torts as Example, in: *Jürgen Basedow/Toshiyuki Kono* (eds.), An Economic Analysis of Private International Law (2006) 143 *et seq*.; *Gisela Rühl*, Die Kosten der Rechtswahlfreiheit: Zur Anwendung ausländischen Rechts durch deutsche Gerichte RabelsZ Vol. 71 (2007) 559–596; *Gisela Rühl*, Party Autonomy in the Private International Law of Contracts: Transatlantic Convergence and Economic Efficiency CLPE Research Paper 4/2007 Vol. 03 No. 01 (2007) 33. See also *Kurt Siehr*, Ökonomische Analyse des internationalen Privatrechts FS Firsching (1985) 269, 280; *Stefan Leible*, Außenhandel und Rechtssicherheit ZVglRWiss 97 (1998) 286; *John Prebble*, Choice of Law to Determine the Validity and Effect of Contracts: A Comparison of English and American Approaches to Conflict of Laws (1973) Cornell Law Rev. Vo. 58 No. 3 433, 496.

it provides a "stopgap"[353]. The latter argument maintains that the supremacy of party autonomy within the law of obligations is merely a makeshift or anomalous rule of last resort to account for the lack of other more appropriate conflict-of-law rules.[354] Proponents of this view argue that parties are only allowed to choose the applicable law because in many cases a general balance of competing party interests is not possible.[355] According to the principle of freedom of contract, it is believed that where parties are given the freedom to enter into any contract they wish that they should, as a matter of course, also have the liberty to choose the law by reference to which their contract will be construed. This is partially based on the principle *in dubio libertas*: where the legislator has not or cannot provide an objectively determinable choice of law rule, the parties should be given the liberty to choose the applicable law.[356] A more functional argument provides that party autonomy protects the legitimate expectations of the parties, promotes legal certainty and thus advances economic efficiency – all achieved by enabling the parties to know their rights and liabilities under the contract in advance.[357] The question that remains is whether the theoretical underpinnings justifying party autonomy generally can apply to freedom of choice in non-contractual obligations.

## 2. Specific justification of party autonomy in non-contractual obligations

Article 14 of the Rome II Regulation permits parties to select the law applicable to most non-contractual obligations. Up until now, differing approaches had been

---

353  E.g. *Gerhard Kegel/Klaus Schurig*, Internationales Privatrecht (2004) 653 §18 I c).

354  See critically *Matthias Lehmann*, Liberating the individual from battles between states: justifying party autonomy in conflict of laws (2008) Vanderbilt Journal of Transnational Law Vol. 41 381, 387; *Stefan Leible*, Parteiautonomie im IPR – Allgemeines Anknüpfungsprinzip oder Verlegenheitslösung? FS Jayme (2004) 485; *Jan Kropholler*, Internationales Privatrecht (2006) §40 III 2.

355  *Gerhard Kegel/Klaus Schurig*, Internationales Privatrecht (2004) 653 §18 I c).

356  *Jan Kropholler*, Internationales Privatrecht (2006) §40 III; *Paul Neuhaus*, Die Grundbegriffe des internationalen Privatrechts (1976) 257.

357  Professor *C.G.J. Morse*, The EEC Convention on the Law Applicable to Contractual Obligations' (1982) 2 YB Eur.L. 107, 116 maintains that the justification for the principle is found in international commercial convenience. See also *Gisela Rühl*, Party Autonomy in the Private International Law of Contracts: Transatlantic Convergence and Economic Efficiency CLPE Research Paper 4/2007 Vol. 03 No. 01 (2007). See also *Peter Nygh*, Autonomy in International Contracts (1999) 2–3; *Stefan Leible*, Außenhandel und Rechtssicherheit ZVglRWiss 97 (1998) 286, 288; *Jan Jan Kropholler*, Internationales Privatrecht (2006) 295 *et seq.*

taken towards the significance of party autonomy in non-contractual obligations within Europe.[358] While partially recognised under German law, English law neglected to entertain the practical importance of the principle outside of contractual obligations.[359] The recognition of party autonomy and importance attached to it in the Rome II Regulation, clarifies the up to now unclear position under English law, follows a recent trend in several European states,[360] and represents an innovative evolution in choice of law on a European level.[361]

However, while the acceptance of the freedom to choose the applicable law for contractual obligations is generally derived from the principle of freedom of contract and substantiated by recognition of the need for legal certainty and economic efficiency, on what rationale does the general acceptance of party autonomy within the area of non-contractual obligations rest?[362] Similar advantages can be cited in support of providing for party autonomy in non-contractual obligations. A starting point may be that if it is accepted that in accordance with the principle of freedom of contract parties should have the freedom to choose the law applicable to their contract, then parties should also be guaranteed the freedom to choose the applicable law to govern any non-contractual obligations related to their contractual relationship. However, the rationale for choice of law

---

358 See e.g. unlimited party autonomy provided for in § 35 I of the Austrian and Article 39 I of the Lichtenstein *IPRG*, and Article 6 of the Dutch Act *Wet conflictenrecht onrechtmatige daad* of 11 April 2001. Limited party autonomy restricted to *ex post* agreements only in Article 42 of the German *EGBGB*; in Article 132 of the Swiss *IPRG* and Article 101 of the Belgium *Wetboek van International Privaatrecht*.

359 See e.g. no right to choose in: *Morin v Bonhams & Brooks Ltd* [2003] IL Pr 25 at [33]; [2003] EWCA Civ 1802, [2004] 1 Lloyd's Rep 702; *Cheshire & North* (14th ed.) 838.

360 *Explanatory Memorandum* 22 (referring to Article 10 Commission Proposal).

361 *Mo Zhang*, Party Autonomy in Non-Contractual Obligations: Rome II and its Impacts on Choice of Law 39 Seton Hall Review (2009) 4; *Ralf Michaels*, The New European Choice-of-Law Revolution 82 Tul. L. Rev. (2008) 1607; critically see *Symeon Symeonides*, The American Revolution and the European Evolution in Choice of Law: Reciprocal Lessons 82 Tul LRev (2008) 1741, available at: http://ssrn.com/abstract=1104284; *idem*, Rome II and Tort Conflicts: A Missed Opportunity (2008) 56 Am. J. Comp. L. 303.

362 See e.g. thorough discussion of this issue by *Matthias Lehmann*, Liberating the individual from battles between states: justifying party autonomy in conflict of laws (2008) Vanderbilt Journal of Transnational Law Vol. 41 381, 383. The author attempts to demonstrate that current conflicts theory is unable to account for party autonomy; *Jan von Hein*, Rechtswahl im internationalen Deliktsrecht RabelsZ 64 (2000) 595, 598 *et seq.*; *Jens Köthe*, Schranken der Parteiautonomie im internationalen Deliktsrecht (2008).

for non-contractual obligations is inevitably less clear-cut. Non-contractual obligations are much more of an unknown. Even for contractual relations it will at first be unclear, which party will be in breach or in what respect, but at least the relevant obligations will be known. On the other hand, non-contractual obligations are by their nature more unpredictable and it is not possible to specifically provide for them in advance. It will be particularly difficult to select an appropriate law *ex ante*, especially if parties are to act in numerous countries.

Any theoretical explanation of party autonomy for non-contractual obligations could easily be side-stepped with reference to the legal framework with its abstract rules permitting the parties to choose the law to govern their relations.[363] Party autonomy, according to this view, is justified simply by the fact that the legal framework of the Rome II Regulation provides for it under Article 14. However, rather than merely relying on abstract rules, theoretical considerations may be able to provide a more 'human' touch to the dilemma. These will now be briefly considered in relation to the provision guaranteeing party autonomy under Article 14 Rome II.

*a. Theoretical analysis of party autonomy in non-contractual obligations*

Historically, the will of the parties as a means to determine the applicable law in tort was considered to be functionally unworkable.[364] The widespread opinion was that party autonomy in the field of torts would probably not be desirable.[365] Nowadays, some commentators suggest that freedom of choice for non-contractual obligations largely remains dormant in practice, while others suggest that the inclusion of party autonomy in the Rome II Regulation signifies the important role the principle now plays in the area of non-contractual obligations.[366]

---

363  See e.g. *Christian v. Bar/Peter Mankowski*, Internationales Privatrecht Band 1: Allgemeine Lehren (2003).

364  *Matthias Lehmann*, Liberating the individual from battles between states: justifying party autonomy in conflict of laws, (2008) Vanderbilt Journal of Transnational Law Vol. 41 381, 387.

365  See *Leo Raape*, Nachträgliche Vereinbarung des Schuldstatuts, in: FS Boehmer (1954) 110–123, 122. The author categorically dismissed party autonomy in the area of non-contractual obligations, but supported the possibility to choose the applicable law (*lex fori*) *ex post*. More recently see e.g. *Peter Huber/Ivo Bach*, Die Rom II-VO. Kommissionsentwurf und aktuelle Entwicklungen (2005) IPRax 73, 75.

366  See comprehensive analysis of the development party autonomy for non-contractual obligations in *Jens Köthe*, Schranken der Parteiautonomie im internationalen Deliktsrecht (2008) 17–39.

Similar to the Rome I Regulation, the Rome II Regulation omits to include any explanation of the rationale underpinning the inclusion of party autonomy as a principle choice of law rule for non-contractual obligations. According to Recital (31) of the Rome II Regulation, the inclusion of party autonomy under Article 14 Rome II is substantiated by two objectives: in order to respect the principle of party autonomy and to enhance legal certainty. The Regulation does not provide any further guidance why party autonomy should be respected or why a choice by the parties would lead to greater legal certainty; nor does it explain why the parties should be free to choose a law that is unconnected to the non-contractual obligation.[367] The only other guidance that can be deduced from reading the various draft documents and the final version of the Rome II Regulation, is that the inclusion of party autonomy appears to be based on disparate objectives: the need for uniformity, forseeability and legal certainty,[368] the protection of public interests[369], the concern for weaker parties[370] and the rights of third parties[371], respect of the parties' intentions and freedom of will[372], and ensuring a balance between the interests of the person claimed to be liable and the person who has sustained damage[373].

Although it is not the aim of this contribution to offer a detailed examination of the various approaches to party autonomy in conflicts theory,[374] these objectives, although

---

367 *Th. M. de Boer,* Party Autonomy and its Limitations in the Rome II Regulation YPIL (2007) Vol. 9 19, 22.
368 Recital (16), (31) Rome II.
369 Recital (32) Rome II.
370 Recital (31) Rome II.
371 Article 14(1) Rome II.
372 Recital (31) Rome II; see also paragraph (28) of *Common Position*; Amendment 17, Chapter II Section 1, Article 2a (new) Draft Report on the proposal for a regulation of the European Parliament and of the Council on the law applicable to non-contractual obligations ("Rome II") (COM(2003)0427 – C5–0338/2003 – 2003/0168(COD)) of 11.11.2004 (Rapporteur: Diana Wallis); and paragraph (16) of the European Parliament's Position 2005.
373 Recital (16) Rome II.
374 For further analysis see e.g. *Jürgen Basedow,* Theorie der Rechtswahl oder Parteiautonomie als Grundlage des Internationalen Privatrechts RabelsZ Vol. 75 (2011) 32 *et seq.* with further references; *Jörg G. A. Schmeding,* Zur Bedeutung der Rechtswahl im Kollisionsrecht, Ein Beitrag zur funktionalen Methode nach von Mehren/Trautmann RabelsZ Vol. 41 (1977) 299–331, 305 *et seq.*; *Erik Jayme,* Die Parteiautonomie im internationalen Vertragsrecht auf dem Prüfstand, 65. Sitzung des Institut de Droit International in Basel (1991) IPRax 429–430; *Rudolf Moser,* Vertragsabschluß, Vertragsgültigkeit und Parteiwille im internationalen Obligationenrecht (1948) 190.

unsystematically expressed in the Rome II Regulation can be broadly categorised as falling under either economic considerations,[375] or considerations focusing on individual "interests"[376]. These two broad categories offering an internal justification for party autonomy in non-contractual obligations will now be briefly set out.

aa) Economic rationale

The explanation of party autonomy from an economic perspective starts from the premise that the freedom to choose the applicable law is correlative to the freedom to enter into contracts. Where parties are given the freedom to enter into any contract they wish, they should, as a matter of course, also have the liberty to choose the applicable law. As a result, granting parties the freedom to choose the applicable law to govern their relations will promote legal certainty and the legitimate expectations of the parties will be protected.[377] The idea behind this rationale is that economic efficiency is advanced because individuals will usually enter into a choice of law agreement that will maximise their own welfare while not reducing the welfare of third parties.[378] The subjective determination of the law will not

---

375  See e.g. *Gisela Rühl*, Party Autonomy in the Private International Law of Contracts: Transatlantic Convergence and Economic Efficiency CLPE Research Paper 4/2007 Vol. 03 No. 01 (2007); also considered by *Stefan Leible*, Parteiautonomie im IPR – Allgemeines Anknüpfungsprinzip oder Verlegenheitslösung? FS Jayme (2004) 485.

376  *Axel Flessner*, Interessenjurisprudenz im internationalen Privatrecht (1990)117 *et seq.*; *idem*; Privatautonomie und Interessen im internationalen Privatrecht, am Beispiel der Forderungsabtretung Festschrift für Canaris 2007 545; *Thomas Kadner Graziano*, Freedom to Choose the Applicable Law in Tort, in: *John Ahern/William Binchy* (eds.), The Rome II Regulation on the Law Applicable to Non-Contractual Obligations (2009) 126.

377  Professor *C.G.J. Morse*, The EEC Convention on the Law Applicable to Contractual Obligations (1982) 2 YB Eur.L. 107, 116 maintains that the justification for the principle is found in international commercial convenience. See also *Gisela Rühl*, Party Autonomy in the Private International Law of Contracts: Transatlantic Convergence and Economic Efficiency CLPE Research Paper 4/2007 Vol. 03 No. 01 (2007); *Felix Maultzsch*, Rechtswahl und ius cogens im Internationalen Schuldvertragsrecht RabelsZ Vol. 75 (2011) 60, 63 *et seq.*; *Peter Nygh*, Autonomy in International Contracts (1999) 2–3; *Stefan Leible*, Außenhandel und Rechtssicherheit ZVglRWiss 97 (1998) 286, 288; *Jan Kropholler*, Internationales Privatrecht (2006) 295 *et seq.*; *David Mc-Clean/Kisch Beevers*, The Conflict of Laws (2009) para. 13–003.

378  The so-called "Pareto effect" discussed in *Gisela Rühl*, Party Autonomy in the Private International Law of Contracts: Transatlantic Convergence and Economic Efficiency CLPE Research Paper 4/2007 Vol. 03 No. 01 (2007) 33; *Hans-Bernd Schäfer/Katrin*

(or should not) put the parties in a worse position than they would be where the law is ascertained on an objective basis.[379]

Applying this rationale to the freedom to choose the law applicable to non-contractual obligations, parties involved in non-contractual disputes will be in a better position to respond to their own needs and protect their best interests than any external third party.[380] In doing so, the parties maximise their welfare and reduce costs through exercising the freedom to choose the applicable law. Party autonomy, when exercised in an informed and rational manner by the parties, presents a Pareto efficient answer to the choice of law question.

bb) Interest analysis

An alternative approach, propounded by a German conflicts scholar that similarly considers the best interests of the parties, advances that party autonomy can be theoretically explained by the consideration or analysis of the various "party interests" involved (*Interessenjurisprudenz*).[381] Instead of focusing analysis on the interests of the states involved,[382] this approach holds that choice of law rules should intend to maximise individual interests.[383] The central element, according to this theory, is respect for the individual interests of the parties expressed by their choice of law. In this way, justification for party autonomy simply becomes that because the parties and their interests are at the centre of the conflicts problem, they should

---

*Lantermann*, Choice of Law from an Economic Perspective, in: *Jürgen Basedow/Toshiyuki Kono* (eds.), An Economic Analysis of Private International Law (2006) 92 *et seq.*

379 It may even put the parties in a better position (Pareto *improvement*), see *Felix Maultzsch*, Rechtswahl und ius cogens im Internationalen Schuldvertragsrecht RabelsZ Vol. 75 (2011) 60, 63 *et seq.*

380 *Stefan Leible*, Parteiautonomie im IPR – Allgemeines Anknüpfungsprinzip oder Verlegenheitslösung? FS Jayme (2004) 485, 487.

381 *Axel Flessner*, Interessenjurisprudenz im internationalen Privatrecht (1990) 117 *et seq.*; *idem*, Privatautonomie und Interessen im internationalen Privatrecht, am Beispiel der Forderungsabtretung Festschrift für Canaris 2007 545.

382 See proponent of the American conflicts theory of "governmental interest analysis" *Brainerd Currie*, Selected Essays on the Conflict of Laws (1963) 190. Critically see *Friedrich Juenger*, Conflict of Laws: A Critique of Interest Analysis Am J Comp Law 32 (1984) 1–50; *Axel Flessner*, Interessenjurisprudenz im internationalen Privatrecht (1990).

383 *Axel Flessner*, Interessenjurisprudenz im internationalen Privatrecht (1990) 102 *et seq.*; *Abbo Junker*, Die freie Rechtswahl und ihre Grenzen (1993) IPRax 1; *Stefan Leible*, Parteiautonomie im IPR – Allgemeines Anknüpfungsprinzip oder Verlegenheitslösung? FS Jayme (2004) 485, 488.

be allowed to choose the applicable law to govern their dispute.[384] Thus, party autonomy allows individuals to take care of their own affairs and choose the law that best serves their interests, because after all, it is their interests that will be directly affected by the outcome of their dispute.[385] According to this reasoning, party autonomy in the conflict of laws becomes private autonomy (*privatautonomie*); the power of self-determination allowing the individuals involved to choose the applicable law autonomously.[386] In other words, the basis of this approach is to give effect to the natural freedom and will of the individual, by providing for the recognition of party autonomy within conflict of laws legislation.[387] This interest analysis not only focuses on the interests that would be served by allowing the parties involved to choose the applicable law, but also the competing interests which may require protection. Competing interests may be the need to protect public interests (of both national and foreign law),[388] weaker parties,[389] and third parties[390].

Similar to the economic rationale, allowing parties to choose the law respects and maximises the parties' interests. Accordingly, if competing interests are adequately protected, party autonomy necessarily becomes a legitimate choice of law rule.[391] This reasoning can also extend to party autonomy for non-contractual obligations. Based on the above considerations, it may be concluded that party autonomy for non-contractual obligations can be justified if two key criteria are met: 1) respect for the parties' interests; and, 2) protection of weaker parties and the rights of third parties.

---

384 *Matthias Lehmann*, Liberating the individual from battles between states: justifying party autonomy in conflict of laws (2008) Vanderbilt Journal of Transnational Law Vol. 41 381, 398.

385 *ibid*, 397.

386 *Axel Flessner*, Privatautonomie und Interessen im internationalen Privatrecht, am Beispiel der Forderungsabtretung, Festschrift für Canaris 2007 551.

387 *Jürgen Basedow*, Theorie der Rechtswahl oder Parteiautonomie als Grundlage des Internationalen Privatrechts RabelsZ Vol. 75 (2011) 32, 52.

388 See Recital (32) Rome II and Article 6; 14(2), (3); 16; and 26 Rome II. Compare Recital (37) Rome I and Articles 3(3), (4); 9 and 21 Rome I.

389 See Articles 6(4) (unfair competition, a restriction of competition); 8(3) (infringement of intellectual property rights) Rome II. Compare Rome I which also contains specific restrictions on the choice of law involving economically weaker parties. See Articles Article 5(2) (passengers), Article 7(3) (insurance policy holders), Article 6 (consumers), and Article 8 (employees) Rome I.

390 Article 14(1) Rome II. Compare Article 3(2) Rome I.

391 See *Stefan Leible*, Parteiautonomie im IPR – Allgemeines Anknüpfungsprinzip oder Verlegenheitslösung? FS Jayme (2004) 485; *Jan Kropholler*, Internationales Privatrecht (2006) §40 III 2.

## b. Application to Article 14 Rome II

### aa) Respect for the parties' interests

This criterion considers the respect for the parties' interests as central to the justification of party autonomy. It encompasses the respect for the parties' freedom of will, self-determination and intent, evidenced by their choice of a particular law. A further interest served by the provision of party autonomy in either contractual or non-contractual obligations is legal certainty. To be able to know and agree on the applicable law serves individual interests and interests of a more general nature within the conflict of laws, namely, uniformity and predictability of results. It is in the interest of the parties involved, as well as in the interest of third parties, to have legal certainty as to the law that will be applicable to their legal relations. Permitting the parties to signal their agreed intent to have a particular law apply to their relationship, rather than await the often uncertain ascertainment of applicable law based on objective connecting factors (such as country in which damage occurred, habitual residence or other objective factors indicating a manifestly closer connection), promotes legal certainty. Keeping costs to a minimum is also a key party interest. Knowing in advance which law will be applicable avoids the need to litigate choice of law and thereby reduces added costs. However, parties should bear in mind that a choice of foreign law can also mean added costs.[392]

Article 14 Rome II provides for a choice of law agreement *ex ante* (freely negotiated by parties pursuing a commercial activity) and *ex post* (for all parties). For agreements reached *ex ante*, it will be in the interest of commercial parties to be able to submit all obligations (contractual or non-contractual) to the same law. It will also be in their interest to be able to know in advance which law will govern any possible non-contractual liability arising from the relationship. Where an agreement is made *ex post*, it will be in the parties' interest to have the possibility to agree on a choice of law in situations where the objectively ascertained law is unfavourable or inapt.

### bb) Protection of weaker parties and the rights of third parties

Unlike in contractual obligations, where it can be assumed that in most cases the parties to the dispute will be dealing at arm's-length, a specific difficulty that arises in relation to non-contractual obligations is that generally speaking, the parties will not have an equal bargaining position. The concern becomes how best to protect

---

392 See *Gisela Rühl*, Die Kosten der Rechtswahlfreiheit: Zur Anwendung ausländischen Rechts durch deutsche Gerichte RabelsZ Vol. 71 (2007) 559, 560 *et seq.*

the weaker party to the dispute, normally the victim of the tort. In particular, there is a need to ensure that an informed, conscious choice of law is made, free from undue pressure or carelessness. Regardless of whether the choice of law is made before or after the occurrence of the tort, both parties must be aware of all the legal consequences arising from the choice in order for there to be an effective choice of law.[393] The Rome II Regulation makes provision for the concern of the weaker party by either excluding a choice of law in particular cases, or by distinguishing between *ex post* and *ex ante* agreements.

According to Article 14(1)(b) Rome II, non-commercial parties may only enter into choice of law agreements *following* the occurrence of the event. The concern to protect the weaker party to the dispute, normally the victim of the tort, becomes less crucial in *ex post* agreements. This is because after the occurrence of the tort parties are usually in a position to know of their rights and obligations.[394] The parties will in most cases seek legal advice on the consequences of a particular choice of law following the event and it may be assumed that a weaker party would not agree to the application of a law that is unfavourable to him. In addition, it may be assumed that parties will usually only agree on a choice of law *ex post*, if the application of the objectively determined law is unfavourable.

However, a choice of law agreed to by the parties *before* the event giving rise to non-contractual liability, may still indirectly assume significance via the secondary connection provided for in Article 4(3) Rome II ("manifestly more closely connected"). As a result, a pre-tort choice of law could be applicable even in cases where at the time of the occurrence of the event giving rise to the damage the parties are no longer in a commercial relationship. Nevertheless, the Rome II Regulation still requires the protection of the weaker party in such a situation and the Explanatory Memorandum stresses that an application of that law, chosen before the event, may not harm weaker parties.[395] Accordingly, where the pre-existing relationship consists of a non-commercial contract, such as a B2C or employment contract, the secondary connection provided for in

---

393 *Axel Flessner*, Interessenjurisprudenz im internationalen Privatrecht (1990) 109–110.

394 *Peter Mankowski*, Ausgewählte Einzelfragen zur Rom II-VO: Internationales Umwelthaftungsrecht, internationales Kartellrecht, renvoi, Parteiautonomie (2010) IP-Rax 389, 399. Similar approach taken in Art. 13 No. 1; 17 No. 1; 21 No. 1 of the Council Regulation (EC) No 44/2001 of 22 December 2000 on jurisdiction and the recognition and enforcement of judgments in civil and commercial matters (OJ L/12 [16.1.2001]).

395 Explanatory Memorandum 13.

Article 4(3) "cannot have the effect of depriving the weaker party of the protection of the law otherwise applicable."[396]

Where a choice of law agreement is made *before* the occurrence of the event the parties must already be pursuing a commercial activity and the agreement must have been freely negotiated.[397] The rationale behind the imposed restriction of *ex ante* agreements to parties pursuing a commercial activity only, is protection of the weaker party. Recital (31) of Rome II emphasises that while parties should be allowed to make a choice as to the applicable law to a non-contractual obligation that "protection should be given to weaker parties by imposing certain conditions on the choice."[398] The additional requirement of "free negotiation" contained in Article 14(1)(b) is intended to support this concern. It implies that even in B2B relationships commercial parties may not have equal bargaining power and that they should therefore be assured a reasonable opportunity to negotiate the terms of the choice of law.[399] The effect of this added requirement is that a weak commercial party may be able to challenge the validity of an *ex ante* choice of law agreement where it is maintained that the agreement is not the result of free negotiation.

In addition to the distinction between agreements *ex ante* and *ex post* in Article 14 Rome II, the mandatory rules contained in the Regulation also provide weaker parties with protection. Article 14(2) provides that the mandatory laws of a country, which is solely connected to the dispute at the time when the event giving rise to the damage occurs, must be adhered to. Article 14(3) further provides that the mandatory EC laws of a Member State whose forum is determining the dispute must be adhered to if one or more Member States are solely connected to the dispute at the time when the event giving rise to the damage occurs.[400]

---

396 *Explanatory Memorandum* 13. On this issue see, *Jan von Hein*, Rechtswahlfreiheit im Internationalen Deliktsrecht RabelsZ 64 (2000) 595, 600 *et seq.*; *Thomas Kadner Graziano*, Freedom to Choose the Applicable Law in Tort, in: *John Ahern/William Binchy* (eds.), The Rome II Regulation on the Law Applicable to Non-Contractual Obligations (2009) 126 *et seq.*

397 Article 14(1)(b) Rome II.

398 See also Report of the EP JURI Committee, *EP 1st Reading Report*, justification of Article 2a (new) available at http://www.europarl.europa.eu/oeil/file.jsp?id=235142.

399 *EP 1st Reading Report*, justification of Article 2a (new).

400 E.g. Council Directive 85/374/EEC of 25 July 1985 on the approximation of the laws, regulations and administrative provisions of the Member States concerning liability for defective products (OJ L/210 [7.08.1995]).

# B. The Applicable Law and Freedom of Choice under the Rome II Regulation

Like the Rome I Regulation, the Rome II Regulation is also divided into Chapters. The Chapters are further divided into Articles, each addressing specific issues applicable to non-contractual obligations. The central provisions of the Regulation are the conflict-of-law rules set out in Chapters II–IV (Articles 4 to 14) of the Rome II Regulation. Chapter II (Articles 4 to 9) of the Regulation contains the rules for all torts other than those specifically covered in Chapter III of the Regulation.[401] Chapter II is intended to provide a "flexible framework of conflict-of-law rules" that provide legal certainty while enabling courts to respond to the individual need of cases.[402] This rationale is reflected in Article 4 of the Regulation, which provides the central provision applicable to all torts. According to the general rule in Article 4(1) Rome II, the applicable law shall be the law of the country in which the damage occurs[403] – the *lex loci delicti*.[404] However, the general rule will be displaced in situations where a special rule is provided for in the Regulation[405] and where the parties have made a choice of law.[406]

Chapter III deals with obligations, referred to as "quasi-*delict*" or "quasi-contract",[407] that neither properly fall under contract, because there is no agreement, nor under tort within the meaning of Chapter II of the Regulation, because there is no wrongful act. Because of the wide divergences between the categorisation of these types of non-contractual obligations between national systems, it was decided to segregate them from Chapter II of the Regulation. Chapter III thus provides a special section dealing only with discrete choice of law rules for obligations arising out of an act other than a tort or *delict*.[408] More specifically this

---

401 Chapter III Rome II deals separately with unjust enrichment, *negotiorum gestio* and *culpa in contrahendo*.
402 Recital (14) Rome II.
403 References in the Regulation to damage includes damage that is likely to occur, see Article 2(3)(b).
404 While Article 4 offers a general rule it can be further divided into three separate rules. Paragraph (1) states the general principle; paragraph (2) the exception to the principle; and paragraph (3) provides an escape clause. These will not be further considered here.
405 See Articles 5–12 Rome II.
406 Pursuant to Article 14 Rome II.
407 The Rome II Regulation does not expressly refer to these obligations as 'quasi-*delict*' or 'quasi-contract'. C.f. *Explanatory Memorandum* 8.
408 Recital (29) Rome II.

Chapter sets out choice of law rules for unjust enrichment (Article 10), *negotiorum gestio* (Article 11) and *culpa in contrahendo* (Article 12).[409]

Chapter IV of the Regulation is headed 'Freedom of Choice' and contains only one article, Article 14. Whereas under Articles 4–12 the determination of the applicable law is based on objective connections, Article 14 allows for the determination of the applicable law based on a subjective connection, namely through a choice reached autonomously by the parties.[410] Under Article 14, the parties are given the freedom to pick and choose the law to govern the non-contractual obligations between them. It provides: "The parties may agree to submit non-contractual obligations to the law of their choice".[411] The fact that Chapter IV of the Regulation only includes one Article exclusively dealing with party autonomy draws attention to the prominence of the freedom of choice within the Regulation and highlights that parties may choose the applicable law for all non-contractual obligations.[412]

As mentioned above, under the Regulation, the law applicable to a non-contractual obligation shall be *first* governed by the law that is agreed to by the parties.[413] Thus, only where there is no choice made by the parties, the law applicable to a non-contractual obligation arising out of tort/*delict* shall be the law of the country in which the damage occurs, i.e. the *lex loci delicti*.[414] In this sense, the rule in Article 14 should be viewed as the central choice of law rule in the Regulation,[415]

---

409 These are not dealt with further in this paper.

410 The identified law being referred to in German as *objektives* and *subjektives Statut*. See *Abbo Junker*, in: Münchener Kommentar zum Bürgerlichen Gesetzbuche (2010) (hereafter: *Junker*, in: MünchKomm (5th ed.)) Art.14 marginal no. 1.

411 Article 14(1) Rome II.

412 *Junker*, in: MünchKomm (5th ed.) Art.14 marginal no. 1. But where the non-contractual obligation arises from an act of unfair competition, a restriction of competition or an infringement of intellectual property rights, the Regulation does not allow the parties to agree to a law of their choice.

413 According to Article 14 Rome II. Compare *EP 1st Reading Report* at justification of Article 2a, proposing – moving the former Article 10 (Freedom of Choice) to the beginning of the Rome II Regulation.

414 Article 4(1) Rome II, subject to Article 4(2) (common habitual residence) and Article 4(3) (tort manifestly closer connection with another country).

415 Compare Rome I Regulation Article 3 under the same title "Freedom of Choice" and Recital (11) that states: "The parties' freedom to choose the applicable law should be one of the cornerstones of the system of conflict-of-law rules in matters of contractual obligations." Note however, that the Rome II Regulation does not expressly permit *dépeçage*. On this issue, see *Andrew Dickinson*, The Rome II Regulation 333–335 and 552; *Symeon Symeonides*, Rome II and Tort Conflicts: A Missed Opportunity (2008)

even if a choice of law by parties to govern a non-contractual obligation is not as common as it is in contractual obligations. Hence, methodically speaking, Article 14 precedes the general rule in Article 4: where parties have reached a valid agreement as to the applicable law this choice will displace any other objective connection established by the Rome II Regulation.[416] The ordering of the provisions, i.e. placing party autonomy (Article 14) after the *lex loci delicti* rule (Article 4), perhaps is intended to reflect actual practice whereby courts commonly identify the law applicable to non-contractual obligations objectively.[417]

# I. Principle of Party Autonomy under Article 14 Rome II Regulation

Article 14 of the Regulation permits parties to select the law applicable to most non-contractual obligations. This freedom of will encompasses unjust enrichment, *negotiorum gestio* and *culpa in contrahendo*. In cases where the non-contractual obligation arises from an act of unfair competition, a restriction of competition[418] or an infringement of intellectual property rights,[419] the Regulation explicitly does not allow the parties to agree to a law of their choice.[420]

---

56 Am. J. Comp. L. 184 *et seq.*; compare *Phaedon John Kozyris* Rome II: Tort Conflicts on the Right Track! A Postscript to Symeon Symeonides' "Missed Opportunity" 56 Am. J. Comp. L. (2008) 481.

416 Subject to Article 14(2) and (3) and Article 16 Rome II, which cannot be derogated from by agreement (discussed below under Part 2/B.II.2. *Mandatory provisions*). On this also *Stefan Leible/Matthias Lehmann*, Die neue EG-Verordnung über das auf außervertragliche Schuldverhältnisse anzuwendende Recht ("Rom II") RIW 10 2007 721–727, 726; *Junker*, in: MünchKomm (5th ed.) Art.14 marginal no. 38.

417 Cf. European Commission, Amended proposal for a Regulation on the law applicable to non-contractual obligations (Rome II) (COM (2006) 83 final) [21.2.2006]), Article 4. *Junker*, in: MünchKomm (5th ed.) Art.14 marginal no. 38; *Jan von Hein*, Die Kodifikation des europäischen Internationalen Deliktsrecht ZVglRWiss 102 (2003) 528, 547.

418 Article 6(4) Rome II.

419 Article 8(3) Rome II.

420 See further, *Th. M. de Boer*, Party Autonomy and its Limitations in the Rome II Regulation (2007) YBPIL Vol. 9 19–29; and general overview of Article 14 and Rome II by *Paolo Bertoli*, Choice of Law by the Parties in the Rome II Regulation (2009) Rivista di Diritto Internazionale 697–716; *Peter Huber* (ed.) Rome II Regulation, Pocket Commentary (2011).

The parties may choose any law, including the law of the habitual residence of the parties or an otherwise unrelated law of a third party state. Generally speaking, a choice by the parties of the *lex fori* as the governing law may be preferable, presenting a cost and time efficient choice.[421] Moreover, in many legal systems a decision that is based on the application of foreign law is not appealable.[422] But according to Article 14, parties may choose any law to govern their non-contractual obligations regardless of relevant connection, provided that the mandatory provisions are not derogated from.

The right to choose the applicable law according to Article 14 Rome II can be summarised into three main rules: The first rule relates to the timing for making the choice of law (Article 14(1)(a) and (b)); the second rule concerns the way in which a choice may be made (Article 14(1) second sentence); and the third rule concerns mandatory provisions (Article 14(2) and (3))[423]. These conditions are imposed on a choice of law with the intention of protecting weaker parties.[424] They can be further broken down into the following six points:

**Timing for making the choice**

(1) a choice of law agreement may be entered into *after* the event giving rise to the damage occurred;[425]

(2) a choice of law agreement may be entered into *before* the event giving rise to the damage occurred, provided that the choice is freely negotiated by parties that are engaged in commercial activities;[426]

---

421 *Thomas Kadner Graziano*, Das auf außervertragliche Schuldverhältnisse anzuwendende Recht nach Inkrafttreten der Rom II-Verordnung RabelsZ 73 (2009) 1, 6; *Stefan Leible*, Rechtswahl im IPR der außervertraglichen Schuldverhältnisse nach der Rom II-Verordnung RIW 2008 257; *Junker*, in: MünchKomm (5th ed.) Art. 14 marginal no. 6.

422 *Thomas Kadner Graziano*, Das auf außervertragliche Schuldverhältnisse anzuwendende Recht nach Inkrafttreten der Rom II-Verordnung RabelsZ 73 (2009) 1, 6. See also *idem*, Europäisches Internationales Deliktsrecht (2003) 31–32, with further references to case law under n 161, and the discussion of the *Case C-21/76 Handelskwekerij G. J. Bier BV v Mines de potasse d'Alsace SA NJ [1976] ECR I-1735,* No. 113, 313–320. The case, although based on the application of the Brussels Convention on jurisdiction and the enforcement of Judgment (Article 5(3) (liability in tort, *delict* or quasi-*delict*)), is an example of the preference of the *lex fori* under consideration of the possibility of appeal.

423 To which Articles 16 and 26 Rome II are also relevant.

424 Recital (31) Rome II.

425 Article 14(1)(a) Rome II.

426 Article 14(1)(b) Rome II.

| | |
|---|---|
| **The way in which the choice may be made** | (3) the choice must be express, or demonstrated with reasonable certainty by the circumstances of the case,[427] and it shall not prejudice the rights of third parties;[428] |
| **Mandatory provisions** | (4) in domestic cases, a choice of foreign law cannot prejudice the application of provisions of the law that would apply without the choice;[429]

(5) in intra-Community cases, the parties' choice of law cannot displace mandatory provisions of Community law;[430]

(6) the parties' choice of foreign law cannot displace mandatory provisions of the law of the forum[431] and may not be manifestly incompatible with the public policy of the forum[432] |

These six conditions will now be discussed respectively.

# 1. The timing of the choice made by the parties (Article 14(1) Rome II)

The first requirement under Article 14 is the rule concerning the timing of the agreement. Article 14(1) distinguishes between agreements entered into after the tort (*ex post* agreement, also referred to as *post eventum* agreement, or more specifically *post delictum* agreement[433]) and agreements entered into before the tort (*ex ante* agreement, also referred to as *ante eventum* agreement, or *ante delictum* agreement[434]). In accordance with Article 14(1) the parties may choose a governing law:

---

427  Article 14(1) and Recital (31) Rome II; cf. Article 3(1) Rome I.

428  Article 14(1) Rome II; cf. Article 3 Rome I; Article 42, second sentence EGBGB.

429  Article 14(2) Rome II; cf. Article 3(3) Rome I.

430  Article 14(3) Rome II; cf. Article 3(4) Rome I.

431  Article 16 Rome II; cf. Article 9(2) and (3) Rome I.

432  Article 26 Rome II; cf. Article 21 Rome I.

433  *Junker*, in: MünchKomm (5th ed.) Art.14 marginal no. 16.

434  *Junker*, in: MünchKomm (5th ed.) Art.14 marginal no. 16; *Stefan Leible*, Rechtswahl im IPR der außervertraglichen Schuldverhältnisse nach der Rom II-Verordnung RIW 2008 257, 258.

(a) by an agreement entered into after the event giving rise to the damage occurred;

or

(b) where all the parties are pursuing a commercial activity, also by an agreement freely negotiated before the event giving rise to the damage occurred.[435]

A limitation to freedom of choice, stipulating the time that a choice of law may be made, is also found in German law, which indeed provided the inspiration for the present Article 14. The principle of *Parteiautonomie* contained in Article 42 *EG-BGB*[436] only allows the parties subsequently, i.e. after the occurrence of the tort, to choose the applicable law.[437] However, where the parties have stipulated the application of a law before the occurrence of the tort, it may influence the operation of art 41 I and II *EGBGB*, which provides for the application of law with a manifestly closer connection (*wesentlich engere Verbindung*).[438] However, the practical need to provide for the possibility to reach *ex ante* agreements was also greatly advocated.[439]

---

435 The freedom to choose the applicable law is not permitted in the matters governed by Articles 6 and 8, neither *ex ante* nor *ex post*.

436 German *EGBGB* (of 1.6.1999). Article 42 *EGBGB* provides: "Nach Eintritt des Ereignisses, durch das ein außervertragliches Schuldverhältnis entstanden ist, können die Parteien das Recht wählen dem es unterliegen soll. Rechte Dritter bleiben unberührt." *Jan Kropholler*, Internationales Privatrecht (2006) 294 and 519; *Robert Freitag/Stefan Leible*, Das Bestimmungsrecht des Art. 40 Abs. 1 *EGBGB* im Gefüge der Parteiautonomie im Internationalen Deliktsrecht ZVglRWiss 99 (2000) 101, 103 *et seq.*

437 This should be read together with § 32 of the German Code of Civil Procedure *Zivilprozessordnung* (ZPO), *Jan Kropholler*, Internationales Privatrecht (2006) §58 II; *Robert Freitag/Stefan Leible*, Das Bestimmungsrecht des Art. 40 Abs. 1 EGBGB im Gefüge der Parteiautonomie im Internationalen Deliktsrecht ZVglRWiss 99 (2000) 101, 118 *et seq.*

438 The so-called "escape clause", whereby only Article 41 II (1) provides for an "accessory connection" in cases involving non-contractual obligations, see *Jan Kropholler*, Internationales Privatrecht (2006) §53 IV 4; *R. Robert Freitag/Stefan Leible*, Das Bestimmungsrecht des Art. 40 Abs. 1 EGBGB im Gefüge der Parteiautonomie im Internationalen Deliktsrecht ZVglRWiss 99 (2000) 101, 109 *et seq.*

439 See e.g. *Jan von Hein*, Rechtswahl im internationalen Deliktsrecht RabelsZ 64 (2000) 595, 598; *Gerhard Hohloch*, Rechtswahl im internationalen Deliktsrecht Neue ZVerkehrsR 1988 161–168, 164; *Jan Kropholler*, Ein Anknüpfungssystem für das Deliktstatut RabelsZ Vol. 33 (1969) 601–653, 635 *et seq.*; *Dorothee Einsele*, Rechtswahlfreiheit im IPR RabelsZ 60 (1996) 417–447, 427. Compare also the *OLG* München judgment from 9.8.1995, RIW 1996, 955 (956) = IPRax 1997, 38 (40) = IPRspr. 1995 Nr. 38 (68). The court described an ex ante choice of law agreement for non-contractual obligations as possible in principle.

Partly, it was argued that an *ex ante* choice of law should be limited to the choice of a law connected with the facts.[440]

But while German law provides for the option to choose the law applicable to non-contractual obligations, English law has never made any specific provision allowing freedom of choice for non-contractual obligations.[441] The traditional common law double-limbed choice of law rule applicable to foreign torts was first formulated in the well-known case of *Phillips v Eyre* (1870).[442] Known as the double actionability rule, the approach amounted to the strict application of the *lex fori* subject to civil actionability in the *lex loci delicti*.[443] Although the problems associated with the forum-centric and strict requirement of double actionability[444] were subsequently mitigated by the addition of a flexible exception to the rule by the House of Lords and the Privy Council,[445] it nevertheless continued to be subject to much academic debate and adverse comment.[446] The Private International Law (Miscellaneous Provisions) Act 1995 introduced a statutory basis for the determination of foreign torts abolishing the double actionability rule.[447] But although

---

440  Critically on this see *Jan von Hein*, Rechtswahl im internationalen Deliktsrecht RabelsZ 64 (2000) 595, 612.

441  Compare though, the Law Commission (Working Paper No. 87) Private International Law: Choice of Law in Tort and Delict (Joint Working Paper – Scottish Law Commission Consultative Memorandum No. 62), in which the inclusion of a choice of law by the parties' clause in the PIL Act 1995 was recommended. See also *Pippa Rogerson*, Choice of Law in Tort: A Missed Opportunity? ICLQ 44 (1995) 650–658, 657.

442  LR 6 QB 1, at 28–29 per Willes J citing *Liverpool, Brazil and River Plate Steam Navigation Co Ltd v Benham, 'The Halley'* (1868) LR 2 PC 193 as authority for the first part of the rule.

443  For a summary of the rule see *Dicey & Morris* (12th ed.) Vol. II 1487–1488; *Cheshire & North* (14th ed.) 766–768.

444  The effect of the first limb can be seen in *Metall und Rohstoff AG v Donaldson Lufkin & Jenrette Inc* [1990] 1 QB 391, 446; the effect of the second limb in *Boys v Chaplin* [1971] AC 356 (HL).

445  *Boys v Chaplin* [1971] AC 356 (HL); Red Sea Insurance Co Ltd v Bouygues SA [1995] 1 AC 190 (PC). See also Coupland v Arabian Gulf Petroleum Co [1983] 2 All ER 434.

446  See e.g. *Christopher Morse*, Torts in Private International Law: A New Statutory Framework (1996) 45 Int. Comp. L. Q. 888, 1002; *Elsabe Schoeman*, Tort Choice of Law in New Zealand: Recommendations for Reform [2004] NZ L Rev 537–561. The Scottish case of *M'Elroy v M'Allister* (1949) SC 110 (especially at 132 per Lord Keith's dissent) also serves as an example of the difficulty in application of the rule and the potential for grave injustice it presented.

447  The Act expressly abolished the application of the common law rules in the United Kingdom (see Section 10(a) of the PIL Act 1995). For a commentary on the common

the 1995 UK PIL Act brought a radical change to the English choice of law rules for foreign torts,[448] it still did not provide for a freedom for parties to choose the applicable law to govern their non-contractual obligations.[449] But similar to the German Article 41 II No. 1 *EGBGB*, the parties presumed intention may be recognised by the application of Section 12(2) of the Act, whereby "factors relating to the parties" may be considered when determining the closest connection. Relevant factors include "the fact that there is some pre-tort relationship between them" and "the fact that a contract exists between them".[450]

*a.* Ex post *agreement (Article 14(1)(a) Rome II)*

Of the two alternatives provided for in Article 14(1), it seems that the least problematic is where the parties choose to reach an agreement as to the applicable law *after* the event giving rise to the damage occurred. Article 14(1)(a) expressly allows all parties to reach such an *ex post* agreement. In most cases this alternative will prove sufficient for claims involving non-contractual obligations as a relationship between the parties will only arise following the occurrence of the event.[451] In contrast to paragraph 14(1)(b) that requires all parties to be

---

law and the statutory reform see *Abla Mayss*, Statutory Reform of Choice of Law in Tort and Delict: A Bitter Pill or a Cure for the Ill? [1996] 2 Web JCLI available at: http://webjcli.ncl.ac.uk/1996/issue2mayss2.html.

448 The Act contains a two-stage process for the determination of the applicable law. The first stage, contained in Section 11 of the 1995 Act that the prima facie applicable law will be the *lex loci delicti* subject to the law of the country in which the "most significant element or elements of those events occurred" as formulated in Section 11(1)(c) PIL Act 1995. See further *Morin v Bonhams & Brooks Ltd* [2004] EWCA Civ 1802; [2004] 1 Lloyd's Rep 702. This residual rule under the Act is reminiscent of the 'substance' test used at common law for the determination of the location of a tort. See e.g. *Distillers Co (Biochemicals Ltd v Thomson* [1971] AC 458 (PC); *Metall und Rohstoff AG v Donaldson Lufkin & Jenrette Inc* [1990] 1 QB 391, 446; *James Hardie & Co Pty Ltd and Another v Hall as administrator of Estate of Putt* [1998] 43 NSWLR 554.

449 Compare though the Law Commission (Working Paper No. 87) Private International Law: Choice of Law in Tort and Delict (Joint Working Paper – Scottish Law Commission Consultative Memorandum No. 62), in which the inclusion of a choice of law by the parties' clause in the PIL Act 1995 was recommended but subsequently not adopted.

450 *Christopher Morse*, Torts in Private International Law: A New Statutory Framework (1996) 45 Int. Comp. L. Q. 888, 899; *Peter Nygh*, Autonomy in International Contracts (1999) 245.

451 *Stefan Leible*, Rechtswahl im IPR der außervertraglichen Schuldverhältnisse nach der Rom II-Verordnung RIW 2008 257, 258.

"pursuing a commercial activity",[452] paragraph (a) does not stipulate conditions for the choice of law. In other words, all parties, whether commercial or non-commercial may enter into an *ex post* agreement, provided that the event giving rise to the damage has occurred. In order to determine the relevant point in time when the event giving rise to the damage *occurred* (i.e. either the point in time of conduct or the point in time of injury/damage), it is necessary to distinguish between torts and other non-contractual obligations.[453] For torts (as defined in Articles 4–9 Rome II), the relevant time will be when the "event" occurred (the point in time of the defendant's conduct giving rise to tortious liability) and not when the damage resulted.[454] This will also be the relevant interpretation for acts arising from *cupla in contrahendo*. But for other non-contractual obligations, in particular claims arising from *negotiorum gestio* or unjustified enrichment, the relevant point in time will be when the event giving rise to the enrichment occurs (Article 10), or when the intervener's act is performed (Article 11).[455]

The *ex post* alternative follows the trend of developments in national private international law[456] that all appear to rest on the same rationale, which is: to encourage a greater freedom of will, while at the same time preventing abuse of choice of law agreements where parties do not have equal bargaining power.[457] Concern for protecting the weaker party to the dispute, i.e. normally the victim of the tort, is less crucial in *ex post* agreements, because after the occurrence of the tort parties are usually in a position to know of their rights and obligations. The parties will in most cases seek legal advice on the consequences of a particular choice of law following the event. Thus, where an *ex post* agreement is reached between the parties it may be assumed that a weaker party would not agree to the application of a law that is unfavourable to him.[458] Even so, this is not necessarily unproblematic – surely neither of the parties would agree to a choice of law unfavourable to them.[459]

---

452 Discussed further below under Part 2/B.I.1.a.aa) *Pursuing a commercial activity*.

453 *Junker*, in: MünchKomm (5th ed.) Art.14 marginal no. 17.

454 *Junker*, in: MünchKomm (5th ed.) Art.14 marginal no. 18; *Gerhard Wagner*, Die neue Rom-II-Verordnung (2008) IPRax 1, 17.

455 *Junker*, in: MünchKomm (5th ed.) Art.14 marginal no. 19; *Gerhard Wagner* Die neue Rom-II-Verordnung (2008) IPRax 14.

456 See e.g. above n 358.

457 *Explanatory Memorandum* 22 referring to Article 10 of the original proposal.

458 *Cheshire & North* (14th ed.) 838; *Symeon Symeonides*, Rome II and Tort Conflicts: A Missed Opportunity (2008) 56 Am. J. Comp. L. 173, 303.

459 See e.g. *Peter Hay*, Contemporary Approaches to Non-Contractual Obligations in Private International Law (Conflict of Laws) and the European Community's

Nevertheless, even though according to Article 14(1) Rome II non-commercial parties may only enter into *ex post* agreements, Article 4(3) of the Rome II Regulation (the escape clause), may still provide for the application of a law that is connected to a *pre-existing* relationship between the parties, such as contract, by way of "accessory connection".[460] In other words, it may be established that according to the circumstances of the case that the tort is manifestly more closely connected to the parties existing contractual relationship (see Article 4(3), second sentence; Article 5(2), second sentence; Article 10(1); Article 11(1) and Article 12(1) Rome II Regulation). Article 4(3) of the Rome II Regulation expressly provides that where the tort is manifestly more closely connected with a country, i.e. based on a pre-existing contractual relationship, then the law of that country shall apply. Thus, where parties are, or were, in an existing contractual relationship before the occurrence of the tort and have chosen a law to govern their contract (according to Article 3(1) Rome I Regulation), that law may be indirectly applicable to the tortious claim, by way of accessory connection. The following example further clarifies such a case.[461] Where a transport contract contains a clause stipulating: "Any claims arising out of this contract shall be governed by German law", a court may be able to apply the law chosen under the contract by way of accessory connection to govern the tortious claim.[462] In this way, the contractual choice indirectly assumes significance for any non-contractual obligations arising between the parties. As a result, a choice of law agreed to *before* the occurrence of the tort, could be applicable even in cases where at the time of the occurrence of the event giving rise to the damage, the parties are no longer in a commercial relationship.

---

'Rome II' Regulation 4 EuLF (2007) I-149, who notes: "And how realistic is it anyway that parties to a traffic accident will subsequently agree on the applicable law over a cup of tea?"

460 Also possible under German law through the application of 41 II *EGBGB*; see, *Junker*, in: MünchKomm (5th ed.) Art.14 marginal no. 3, 9; *Karsten Thorn*, in: Palandt Bürgerliches Gesetzbuch (2005) (hereinafter: *Thorn*, in Palandt) Art. 14 marginal no. 7; *Jan von Hein*, Something Old and Something Borrowed, but Nothing New? – Rome II and the European Choice of Law Revolution (2008) 82 Tul.L.Rev. 1663, 1694; *idem,* Rechtswahl im internationalen Deliktsrecht, RabelsZ 64 (2000) 595, 602.

461 Based on the example given by *Abbo Junker*, Das Internationale Privatrecht der Straßenverkehrsunfälle nach der Rom II-Verordnung JZ 2008 169, 173; *Junker*, in: MünchKomm (5th ed.) Art.14 marginal no. 9.

462 See *Abbo Junker*, in: Münchener Kommentar zum Bürgerlichen Gesetzbuche (2006) (hereafter: *Junker*, in: MünchKomm (4th ed.)) Article 42 *EGBGB* marginal no. 18, 21.

Yet, the Explanatory Memorandum stresses that an application of that law may not harm weaker parties.[463] Accordingly, where the pre-existing relationship consists of a non-commercial contract, such as a consumer or employment contract, the secondary connection provided for in Article 4(3) "cannot have the effect of depriving the weaker party of the protection of the law otherwise applicable."[464] Consequently, an accessory connection under Article 4(3) of the Rome II Regulation should, in principle, be excluded where in a consumer or employment contract the applicable law has been determined according to the Rome I Regulation.[465] Strictly speaking, it is possible to apply the law agreed to by a consumer and professional according to Articles 3 and 6(2) Rome I Regulation to the non-contractual obligation by way of accessory connection through Article 4(3) Rome II Regulation, even if a direct choice of law reached *ex ante* between the parties is ineffective under Article 14(1)(b) Rome II Regulation. However, an accessory connection may not necessarily correspond to the will of the parties. For example, a German manufacturer may be prepared to agree to the application of Californian law to govern the contractual relationship with the Californian consumer, but not be prepared to submit to the exorbitant sanctions under Californian tort law.[466] Therefore, as Article 4(3) Rome II is (only) an escape clause courts should exercise their judicial discretion bearing in mind the need give effect to the parties' intention and to protect parties that do not have equal bargaining power.[467]

---

463 Explanatory Memorandum 13.

464 *Explanatory Memorandum* 13. On this issue see, *Jan von Hein*, Rechtswahl im internationalen Deliktsrecht RabelsZ 64 (2000) 595, 600 *et seq.*; *Thomas Kadner Graziano*, The Application of Multiple Laws Under the Rome II Regulation, in: *John Ahern/William Binchy* (eds.), The Rome II Regulation on the Law Applicable to Non-Contractual Obligations (2009) 126 *et seq.*

465 See *Thomas Kadner Graziano*, The Application of Multiple Laws Under the Rome II Regulation, in: *John Ahern/William Binchy* (eds.), The Rome II Regulation on the Law Applicable to Non-Contractual Obligations (2009) 126.

466 Example from *Jan von Hein*, Rechtswahl im internationalen Deliktsrecht RabelsZ 64 (2000) 595, 602.

467 See *Thomas Kadner Graziano*, The Application of Multiple Laws Under the Rome II Regulation, in: *John Ahern/William Binchy* (eds.), The Rome II Regulation on the Law Applicable to Non-Contractual Obligations (2009) 128 *et seq.*; *Jan von Hein*, Europäisches Internationales Deliktsrecht nach der Rom II-Verordnung ZeuP 2009 21. Compare also *Gerhard Wagner*, Ein neuer Anlauf zur Vereinheitlichung des IPR für außervertragliche Schulverhältnisse auf EU-Ebene EuZW 1999 709, 713.

## b. Ex ante *agreement (Article 14(1)(b))*

Whereas *ex post* agreements are permitted between all parties (commercial and non-commercial), *ex ante* agreements are allowed only if all the parties are "pursuing a commercial activity".[468] Particularly in B2C contracts, such a choice will not be permissible. In general, parties do not and should not contemplate a future tort and for a long time the practical need for *ex ante* choice of law for non-contractual obligations was debated.[469] However, it now appears generally accepted that parties may have a legitimate interest in ascertaining in advance the law governing any issues of non-contractual or contractual liability in order to assure legal certainty.[470] Its inclusion in the Rome II Regulation has been described as innovative, liberal and progressive.[471] Indeed, without the possibility to stipulate in advance the applicable law, any issues of liability between the parties would be subject to the general rule identifying the law applicable to non-contractual obligations and its many exceptions.

---

468 Article 14(1)(b) of the Regulation. Such an agreement was not included in the Commission Proposal, see *Explanatory Memorandum*, 22. See detailed discussion in, *Stefan Leible*, Rechtswahl im IPR der außervertraglichen Schuldverhältnisse nach der Rom II-Verordnung RIW 2008 257; *Sven Rugullis*, Die antizipierte Rechtswahl in außervertraglichen Schuldverhältnissen (2008) IPRax 319; *Paolo Bertoli*, Choice of Law by the Parties in the Rome II Regulation Riv. dir. int. 2009 697; *Peter Mankowski*, Ausgewählte Einzelfragen zur Rom II-VO: Internationales Umwelthaftungsrecht internationales Kartellrecht, renvoi, Parteiautonomie (2010) 389–492, 399.

469 *Symeon Symeonides*, Rome II and Tort Conflicts: A Missed Opportunity (2008) 56 Am. J. Comp. L. 173, 215.

470 For example for insurance reasons, or in cases involving complex international industrial projects with numerous subcontractors. See *Thorn*, in: Palandt Art. 14 marginal no. 7; Recital 31 Rome II. *Ex ante* agreements may raise the additional "thorny issue" of concurrent liability in contract and tort and whether the issue in dispute should be classified non-contractual or contractual, see *Cheshire & North* (14th ed.) 838; see also *Paolo Bertoli*, Choice of Law by the Parties in the Rome II Regulation Riv. dir. int. 2009 697, 706; *Peter Mankowski*, Ausgewählte Einzelfragen zur Rom II-VO: Internationales Umwelthaftungsrecht, internationales Kartellrecht, renvoi, Parteiautonomie (2010) IPRax Vol. 5 389–492, 399.

471 *Peter Mankowski*, Ausgewählte Einzelfragen zur Rom II-VO: Internationales Umwelthaftungsrecht, internationales Kartellrecht, renvoi, Parteiautonomie (2010) IPRax 389–492, 399; also *Karsten Thorn*, Der Unternehmer im Kollisionsrecht FS Karsten Schmidt 2009 1561, 1566; *Paolo Bertoli*, Choice of Law by the Parties in the Rome II Regulation Riv. dir. int. 2009 697, 703; *Jan von Hein*, Europäisches Internationales Deliktsrecht nach der Rom II-Verordnung ZEuP 2009 6, 20; *Adrian Briggs*, When in Rome, chose as the Romans chose (2009) 125 LQR 191, 193.

A choice of law to cover an anticipatory tort made by the parties in advance will principally arise in situations where there is a pre-existing contractual relationship and the parties have a strong interest in determining in advance the law applicable to all their relationships including non-contractual liability arising from the contract.[472] For example, a transport contract may include an agreement as to the law governing liability of the transport provider in case of an accident caused by the transport provider causing injury to the guest passenger.[473] Similarly, complex construction projects may also stipulate by *ex ante* agreement the law applicable to govern any claims and liability arising out of non-contractual obligations, even though not all of the parties involved will be in a direct contractual relationship with each other. Further, participating teams of certain competitive sports (e.g. motorsports), will often enter into an agreement settling in advance any dispute concerning the law governing liability in the case of an accident.[474] Or, a contract may simply state that the specified law covers both contractual and tort liability.[475] It is difficult to imagine cases where parties that are not bound by a pre-existing commercial relationship agree on a choice of law covering an anticipated tort and such cases are unlikely to arise in actual practice.[476]

Before considering the requirements for *ex ante* agreements it is appropriate to briefly consider the legislative developments preceding the present Article 14(1)(b) of the Rome II Regulation, which highlight the sensitivity taken to the risks involved in permitting an *ex ante* choice of law for non-contractual obligations.[477] On 3 May 2002, the European Commission launched a consultation process with interested parties on a preliminary draft proposal for a Rome

---

472  For example, the Loan Market Association has made amendments to governing law clauses in its recommended forms of documents, see http://www.loan-market-assoc. com/documents.

473  Compare e.g. *Babcock v Jackson* [1963] 2 Lloyd's Rep 286, 12 NY 2d 473, 240 NYS 2d 743, New York Court of Appeals.

474  *Thorn*, in: Palandt Art. 14 marginal no. 7.

475  For example: "This agreement and any non-contractual obligations arising out of or in connection with it are governed by English law."

476  *Th. M. de Boer*, Party Autonomy and its Limitations in the Rome II Regulation 9 YB-PIL (2007) 19, 23; *Francisco Alférez*, The Rome II Regulation: On the way towards a European Private International Law Code 3 EuLF (2007) I-82.

477  See generally *Richard Plender/Michael Wilderspin*, The European Private International law of Obligations (2009) 765–766; *Andrew Dickinson*, The Rome II Regulation 540–541; *Cheshire & North* (14th ed.) 770–772; *Stefan Leible*, Rechtswahl im IPR der außervertraglichen Schuldverhältnisse nach der Rom II-Verordnung RIW 2008 257, 258.

II Regulation,[478] which culminated in a public hearing in 2003.[479] Following these consultations, the Commission finalised its first proposal in 2003 (hereafter referred to as 'Commission Proposal').[480] The Commission Proposal of 2003, unlike the preliminary draft proposal of 2002 which contained no time restriction for a choice of law agreement,[481] took a more restrictive approach to freedom of choice for non-contractual obligations. Like Article 42 of the German *EGBGB*, it placed a general limitation on party autonomy allowing parties

---

478 See Preliminary Draft Proposal for a European Council Regulation on the Law Applicable to Non-Contractual Obligations, available at http://ec.europa.eu/justice_home/news/consulting_public/rome_ii/news_hearing_rome2_en.htm. For an overview of the legislative developments, see generally *Sven Rugullis*, Die antizipierte Rechtswahl in außervertraglichen Schuldverhältnissen (2008) IPRax 319–323, 322; *Richard Plender/Michael Wilderspin*, The European Private International law of Obligations (2009) Chapter 17.

479 For the contributions received, see http://ec.europa.eu/justice_home/news/consulting_public/rome_ii/news_summary_rome2_en.htm. For a detailed proposal, see *Hamburg Group for Private International Law* Comments on the European Commission's Draft Proposal for a Council Regulation on the Law Applicable to Non-Contractual Obligations RabelsZ (2003) 1–56

480 COM (2003) 427 final, 22 July 2003. See e.g. discussion of Proposal in *Hamburg Group for Private International Law* Comments on the European Commission's Draft Proposal for a Council Regulation on the Law Applicable to Non-Contractual Obligations RabelsZ (2003) 1; *Martina Benecke*, Auf dem Weg zu Rom II – Der Vorschlag für eine Verordnung zur Angleichung des IPR der außervertraglichen Schuldverhältnisse RIW 2003 830; *Stefan Leible/Andreas Engel*, Der Vorschlag der EG-Kommission für eine Rom II-Verordnung – Auf dem Weg zu einheitlichen Anknüpfungsregeln für außervertragliche Schuldverhältnisse in Europa EuZW 2004 7; *Michael Sonnentag*, Zur Europäisierung des Internationalen außervertraglichen Schuldrechts durch die geplante Rom II-Verordnung ZVglRWiss 105 (2006) 256; *Jan von Hein*, Die Kodifikation des europäischen Internationalen Deliktsrecht ZVglRWiss 102 (2003) 528; *Peter Stone*, The Rome II Proposal on the Law Applicable to Non-Contractual Obligations EuLF 2004 213; *Gerhard Wagner*, Internationales Deliktsrecht, die Arbeiten an der Rom II-Verordnung und der Europäische Deliktsgerichtsstand (2006) IPRax 372. Critical of Proposal, see *Symeon Symeonides*, Tort Conflicts and Rome II: A view from Across (2004) FS Jayme 935 *et seq.*

481 See Article 11 of the Preliminary Draft Proposal. Some commentators argued that the law should only be determinable after the event, whereas others welcomed the broad approach to freedom of choice, see e.g *Hamburg Group for Private International Law* Comments on the European Commission's Draft Proposal for a Council Regulation on the Law Applicable to Non-Contractual Obligations RabelsZ (2003).

only to agree "by an agreement entered into *after* their dispute arose".[482] According to this approach it may still have been possible to find an *ex ante* choice of law reached for contractual claims, indirectly applicable to non-contractual claims by way of an "accessory connection".[483] In this way, Rome I (Article 3) indirectly governs the law applicable to the tortious claim.[484] In 2005, the European Parliament proposed extending the right to choose the applicable law by granting parties the right to also enter into a choice of law agreement *ex ante*.[485] However, the right to agree on a choice of law covering an anticipated tort was ineptly formulated, only permitting the freedom to choose before the event where there is a "pre-existing arms-length commercial relationship between

---

482 Article 10(1) of the Commission's Proposal 2003 (emphasis added), in this regard following several other European codifications, e.g. the Article 42 of the German *EGBGB* of 1.6.1999. Compare supra n 358. See also the draft regulation (unpublished) proposed by the Groupe Européen de Droit International Privé (GEDIP) Proposition pour une convention européenne sur la loi applicable aux obligations non contractuelles (Texte adopté lors de la réunion de Luxembourg du 25–27 septembre 1998) available at: http://www.gedip-egpil.eu/documents/gedip-documents-9pf.html. Article 8 ("Liberté de choix) only provides for an *ex post* choice of law: "*Les parties pouvent choisir la loi applicable à l'obligation non contractuelle par une convention postérieure à la naissance du différend. Ce choix doit être exprès. Il ne peut pas porter atteinte aux droits des tiers.*" See also *Erik Jayme*, Entwurf eines EU-Übereinkommens über das außervertragliche Schuldverhältnisse anwendbare Recht (1999) IPRax 298; *Gerhard Wagner*, Ein neuer Anlauf zur Vereinheitlichung des IPR für außervetragliche Schulverhältnisse auf EU-Ebene EuZW 1999 709; *Junker*, in: MünchKomm (5th ed.) Art. 14 marginal no. 2; *Junker*, in: MünchKomm (4th ed.) Art. 42 *EGBGB* marginal no. 18, 21; *Stefan Leible/Andreas Engel*, Der Vorschlag der EG-Kommission für eine Rom II-Verordnung – Auf dem Weg zu einheitlichen Anknüpfungsregeln für außervertragliche Schuldverhältnisse in Europa EuZW 2004 11–12.

483 Also possible under German law through the application of 41 II *EGBGB*; see, *Junker*, in: MünchKomm (5th ed.) Art. 14 marginal no. 3, 9; *Thorn*, in: Palandt Art. 14 marginal no. 7.

484 See Article 4(3) second sentence; Article 5(2) second sentence; Article 10(1); Article 11(1) and Article 12(1) Rome II.

485 European Parliament legislative resolution on the proposal for a regulation of the European Parliament and of the Council on the law applicable to non-contractual obligations ("Rome II") COM (2003) 0427 [06.07.2005], OJ C157E Vol. 49, also available at: http://www.europarl.europa.eu/oeil/file.jsp?id=235142. See critically *Jan von Hein*, Die Kodifikation des europäischen Internationalen Deliktsrechts, ZVglRWiss 102 (2003) 528, 548.

traders of equal bargaining power".[486] The latter, imprecise requirement was subsequently dropped and the wording of the provision in the final Regulation now simply provides for "parties pursuing a commercial activity". The present Article 14(1)(b) of the Rome II Regulation now sets out two conditions for *ex ante* agreements, in addition to those that apply to *ex post* choices of law. These are: (1) all the parties must be "pursuing a commercial activity"; and, (2) the agreement must be "freely negotiated".

aa) Pursuing a commercial activity

Article 14(1) draws a distinction between professional or commercial parties and other parties (such as consumers, employees, insured persons etc):[487] An *ex post* agreement under paragraph (a) being possible for all parties whether consumers or professionals; an *ex ante* agreement under paragraph (b) only for professionals "pursuing a commercial activity". While Article 14(1)(b) does not expressly stipulate whether and to what extent the commercial activity being pursued and the non-contractual obligation should be connected, it has been submitted that the agreement must be made while the parties are in exercise of their commercial activities.[488] Therefore, the facts giving rise to the tortious liability should have a connection to the commercial activities being pursued by the parties.

It is presumed that parties pursuing a commercial activity will be in an arms-length commercial relationship, ensuring that the parties will act in their own self-interest and free from pressure by the other party.[489] Allowing parties[490] that

---

486 *Junker*, in: MünchKomm (5th ed.) Art.14 marginal no. 4; *Jan v Hein*, Die Kodifikation des europäischen IPR vor dem Abschluss? VersR 2007 440, 445.

487 *Jan von Hein*, Of Older Siblings and Distant Cousins: The Contribution of the Rome II Regulation to the Communitarisation of Private International Law RabelsZ 73 (2009) 486.

488 *Stefan Leible/Matthias Lehmann*, Die neue EG-Verordnung über das auf außervertragliche Schuld-verhältnisse anzuwendende Recht ("Rom II") RIW 2007 721, 727; *Stefan Leible*, Rechtswahl im IPR der außervertraglichen Schuldverhältnisse nach der Rom II-Verordnung RIW 2008 257, 260; *Peter Mankowski*, Ausgewählte Einzelfragen zur Rom II-VO: Internationales Umwelthaftungsrecht, internationales Kartellrecht, renvoi, Parteiautonomie (2010) IPRax 389, 400.

489 *EP 1st Reading Report*, justification of Article 2a (new). However, under Article 4(3) of the Regulation, a law agreed to before the tort to govern contractual obligations could be applied indirectly, conceivably even if this was not 'freely negotiated'. See *Cheshire & North* (14th ed.) 838.

490 Note that relevant are the parties to the agreement. See *Peter Mankowski*, Ausgewählte Einzelfragen zur Rom II-VO: Internationales Umwelthaftungsrecht, internationales Kartellrecht, renvoi, Parteiautonomie (2010) IPRax 389–492, 399.

are in on-going commercial relationships to choose the law governing anticipatory tort claims supports the legitimate expectations of the parties and provides certainty both as to the law applicable to their contracts and tort claims arising out of their commercial B2B relationship.[491] However, if the exclusion of *ex ante* agreements for non-commercial parties is justified by the concern for the protection of the weaker party then it could be argued that there should be an exception, allowing the weaker party to rely on such an agreement if that party wishes to do so.[492]

Nevertheless, the requirement "pursuing a commercial activity" is not further defined.[493] It has been noticed that this has the potential of creating added definitional problems, inviting divergent interpretations.[494] On the one hand, a narrow interpretation of the term "commercial activity" may refer only to professional parties pursuing a business activity, and on the other hand, a broad

---

491  *Peter Hay*, Contemporary Approaches to Non-Contractual Obligations in Private International Law (Conflict of Laws) and the European Community's "Rome II" Regulation 3 EuLF (2007) I-151.

492  *Th. M. de Boer*, Party Autonomy and its Limitations in the Rome II Regulation 9 YBPIL (2007) 19, 29. However, in such a case, the parties may still enter into an *ex post* agreement stipulating the application of that law. On this see also *Kathrin Kroll-Ludwig*, Die Rolle der Parteiautonomie im europäischen Kollisionsrecht (2013) 448–462.

493  *Gerhard Wagner*, Die neue Rom II-Verordnung (2008) IPRax 1, 13; *Helmut Ofner*, Die Rom II-Verordnung – Neues Internationales Privatrecht für außervertragliche Schuldverhältnisse in der Europäischen Union ZfRV 2008 13, 21; Die Rom II-Verordnung – Neues Internationales Privatrecht für außervertragliche Schuldverhältnisse in der Europäischen Union, 400; *Stefan Leible*, Rechtswahl im IPR der außervertraglichen Schuldverhältnisse nach der Rom II-Verordnung RIW 2008 257, 259; *Jan von Hein*, Of Older Siblings and Distant Cousins: The Contribution of the Rome II Regulation to the Communitarisation of Private International Law RabelsZ 73 (2009) 461, 489.

494  Critical of the wording of Article 14(1)(b), see *Gerhard Wagner*, Die neue Rom II-Verordnung (2008) IPRax 1, 13; *Helmut Ofner*, Die Rom II-Verordnung – Neues Internationales Privatrecht für außervertragliche Schuldverhältnisse in der Europäischen Union ZfRV 2008 13, 21; *Peter Mankowski*, Ausgewählte Einzelfragen zur Rom II-VO: Internationales Umwelthaftungsrecht, internationales Kartellrecht, renvoi, Parteiautonomie (2010) IPRax 389–492; *Junker*, in: MünchKomm (5th ed.) Art.14 marginal no. 5, 21; *Abbo Junker*, Reformbedarf der Rom II-Verordnung RIW 2010 Heft 5 257, 267; *Karsten Thorn*, Der Unternehmer im Kollisionsrecht FS Karsten Schmidt 2009 1561, 1566; *Symeon Symenoides*, The American Revolution and the European Evolution in Choice of Law: Reciprocal Lessons Tul LRev (2008) 27–28 available at: http//ssrn.com/abstract=1104284; *idem*, Rome II and Tort Conflicts: A Missed Opportunity (2008) 56 Am. J. Comp. L. 301–302.

interpretation may extend the term to include any party involved in a commercial transaction. In addition, the terminology of Article 14(1)(b) is not consistent with Article 23(1) Rome II where reference is made to business activities.[495] Hence, the requirement "pursuing a commercial activity" could include one-sided relationships (e.g. those arising from franchising or licensing contracts), where one of the parties (franchisee or licensee) is in a very weak position without equal bargaining power.[496] Based on Recital 7 of the Rome II Regulation in the interest of consistency, it is argued that "commercial activity" should be construed in accordance with the term "professional" used in Article 6(1) Rome I Regulation, i.e. pursuing a "trade or profession".[497] Without any further guidance provided in the Regulation it will be necessary to await judgments of the European court to further define this term.

bb) Freely negotiated

Whereas the Rome I Regulation merely requires "agreement" (see Article 3(2) Rome I) and "consent" of the parties as to the choice of the applicable law (see Article 3(5) Rome I),[498] Article 14(1)(b) Rome II includes the condition that the *ex ante* choice of law must be "freely negotiated". Thus, in addition to the requirement that all parties pursue a commercial activity, an *ex ante* choice of law clause must also have been "freely negotiated". However, three issues arise under Article 14(1)(b): the first relating to the scope of the requirement in relation to *ex post* agreements; the second, regarding the construction of the phrase "freely negotiated"; and the third, the indirect application of Article 3 Rome I via 'accessory connection'.

---

495 *Junker*, in: MünchKomm (5th ed.) Art.14 marginal no. 5.
496 *Symeon Symenoides*, The American Revolution and the European Evolution in Choice of Law: Reciprocal Lessons Tul LRev (2008) 27–28 available at: http//ssrn. com/abstract=1104284; *idem*, Rome II and Tort Conflicts: A Missed Opportunity (2008) 56 Am. J. Comp. L. 301–302.
497 See *Jan von Hein*, Europäisches Internationales Deliktsrecht nach der Rom II-Verordnung ZEuP 2009 20; *Abbo Junker*, Reformbedarf der Rom II-Verordnung RIW 2010 Heft 5 257, 267; *Peter Mankowski*, Ausgewählte Einzelfragen zur Rom II-VO: Internationales Umwelthaftungsrecht, internationales Kartellrecht, renvoi, Parteiautonomie (2010) IPRax 389, 400.
498 It is submitted that the same approach taken to the issue of consent as to the choice of law under the Rome I Regulation should be taken (see comments made under Part 1/B.I.1. *The choice made by the parties*).

## i. Scope

The first issue is whether the requirement of free negotiation applies only to *ex ante* agreements or whether the requirement is also applicable to *ex post* agreements. The prevailing academic assumption appears to be that only *ex ante* agreements need be "freely negotiated".[499] This view is simply based on the wording of Article 14(1)(a) and that there is no mention of free negotiation for agreements entered into after the event giving rise to the damage occurred.[500] However, other opinions suggest that such a view is irreconcilable with teleological reasoning.[501] In other words, the reason behind the inclusion of this requirement must be to ensure a fair agreement between the parties when agreeing on a choice of law; the drafters thus recognising the value of including such a requirement. Based on this, it remains hard to understand why a choice of law must be freely negotiated where all the parties are pursuing a commercial activity but no such requirement being necessary in cases where not all of the parties are professionals. It does appear tenable, especially in cases involving non-commercial parties such as consumers or employees for example, that a fair process whereby each party has the chance to negotiate the choice of law should be guaranteed. In addition, it has been suggested that the word order of Article 14(1)(b) indicates that the requirement of free negotiation is to be applied to both *ex ante* and *ex post* agreements because the words "also by an agreement freely negotiated [...]" precede the *ex ante* option.[502] Thus, had the drafters wanted to limit the requirement of free negotiation to *ex ante* agreements only paragraph (b) should have been phrased "before the event giving rise to the damage occurred also by an agreement freely negotiated."[503] When reading Article 14(1)(a) and (b) together the scope of the requirement of free negotiation remains unclear and further guidance through case law development will be required.

---

499  *Stefan Leible*, Rechtswahl im IPR der außervertraglichen Schuldverhältnisse nach der Rom II-Verordnung RIW 2008 257, 260; *Gerhard Wagner*, Die neue Rom II-Verordnung (2008) IPRax 1, 13; *Helmut Heiss/Leander Loacker*, Die Vergemeinschaftung des Kollisionsrechts der außervertraglichen Schuldverhältnisse durch Rom II JBl 2007 613, 623; *Thorn*, in: Palandt Art. 14 marginal no. 9; *Cheshire & North* (14th ed.) 838; *Richard Plender/Michael Wilderspin*, The European Private International law of Obligations (2009) 764, 769 *et seq.*

500  *Helmut Heiss/Leander Loacker*, Die Vergemeinschaftung des Kollisionsrechts der außervertraglichen Schuldverhältnisse durch Rom II JBl 2007 613 623, critical of this view see *Junker*, in: MünchKomm (5th ed.) Art.14 marginal no. 34 n 78.

501  *Junker*, in: MünchKomm (5th ed.) Art.14 marginal no. 34.

502  *Junker*, in: MünchKomm (5th ed.) Art. 14 marginal no. 35.

503  As suggested by *Junker*, in: MünchKomm (5th ed.) Art. 14 marginal no.35.

## ii. Construction

The second issue concerns the definition of the phrase "freely negotiated" and its legal significance. Recital (31) emphasises that while parties should be allowed to make a choice as to the applicable law to a non-contractual obligation, "protection should be given to weaker parties by imposing certain conditions on the choice."[504] Thus, the requirement of free negotiation is intended to support this concern, implying that in order to protect parties who may not have equal bargaining power they should be assured a reasonable opportunity to negotiate the terms of the choice of law.[505] It in effect provides a party in a weaker position with an opportunity to challenge the validity of an *ex ante* choice of law agreement where it is maintained that the agreement is not the result of free negotiation.[506] However, the fact that *ex ante* agreements can only be made by professional parties "pursuing a commercial activity" already prevents taking advantage of weaker parties, so the addition of the phrase "freely negotiated" arguably does not provide any significant further protection to weaker parties.[507]

But inherent in the requirement that the agreement is "freely negotiated", is the possibility of divergent interpretation of the phrase.[508] In particular, Article 14(1)

---

504  See also Report of the EP JURI Committee, EP 1st Reading Report, justification of Article 2a (new) available at http://www.europarl.europa.eu/oeil/file.jsp?id=235142.

505  *EP 1st Reading Report*, justification of Article 2a (new).

506  *Mo Zhang*, Party Autonomy in Non-Contractual Obligations: Rome II and its Impacts on Choice of Law 39 Seton Hall Review (2009) 43.

507  *Junker*, in: MünchKomm (5th ed.) Art.14 marginal no. 36; *Abbo Junker*, Der Reformbedarf im Internationalen Deliktsrecht der Rom II-Verordnung drei Jahre nach ihrer Verabschiedung RIW 5/2010 257, 267. The author suggests deleting this phrase upon review. Instead the following formulation of Article 14(1) Rome II is proffered (here: English translation, amendments italicised): Art. 14. Freedom of choice (1) The parties may agree to submit non-contractual obligations to a law of their choice: a) by an agreement entered into after the event giving rise to the damage occurred; or b) *by an agreement before the event giving rise to the damage occurred, entered into by parties acting in the exercise of their trade or profession*. The choice shall be expressed or demonstrated with reasonable certainty by the circumstances of the case and shall not prejudice the rights of third parties.

508  *Junker*, in: MünchKomm (5th ed.) Art.14 marginal no. 5, 34 *et seq.*; *Stefan Leible*, Rechtswahl im IPR der außervertraglichen Schuldverhältnisse nach der Rom II-Verordnung RIW 2008 257, 260; *Peter Mankowski*, Ausgewählte Einzelfragen zur Rom II-VO: Internationales Umwelthaftungsrecht, internationales Kartellrecht, renvoi, Parteiautonomie (2010) IPRax 389, 401. The latter author suggests that both terms "commercial activity" and "freely negotiated" should be aligned with European

(b) fails to address whether a choice of law clause commonly found in a standard form agreement can said to be freely negotiated, leaving the issue debatable. This raises the point of debate concerning the control of the terms included in standard form contracts (*Inhaltskontrolle von AGB-Rechtswahlklauseln*); or more specifically, whether or not Article 14 Rome II permits the scrutiny of a choice of law clause contained in a standard form contract according to the *lex causae*, over and above the control mechanisms provided for within the Regulation.[509] The Rome II Regulation provides control mechanisms for issues of formation and validity of a choice of law clause, however it does not provide for any specific control of choice of law clauses contained within standard form contracts. In principle, an agreement based on the free negotiation of the parties would exclude choice of law clauses (often found together with choice of court clauses) in pre-formulated standard contracts. Several commentators suggest that the formulation "freely negotiated" implies such a control, some going as far to argue that the formulation excludes the freedom to choose the applicable law within standard form contracts.[510] A widespread academic opinion appears to be that free negotiation cannot encompass cases involving the usage of pre-formulated contracts and that a choice of law clause found therein is not sufficient.[511] In agreement with this opinion, the

---

consumer law, in particular with the Council Directive 93/13/EEC of 5 April 1993 on unfair terms in consumer contracts.

509  On this further *Andreas Vogeler*, Die freie Rechtswahl im Kollisionsrecht der ausservertraglichen Schuldverhaeltnisse (2012) 274 *et seq.*

510  *Helmut Heiss/Leander Loacker*, Die Vergemeinschaftung des Kollisionsrechts der außervertraglichen Schuldverhältnisse durch Rom II JBl 2007 613, 623; *Helmut Heiss*, Inhaltskontrolle von Rechtswahlklauseln in AGB nach europäischem Internationalen Privatrecht? RabelsZ 65 (2001) 636 *et seq.*; *Stefan Leible*, Rechtswahl im IPR der außervertraglichen Schuldverhältnisse nach der Rom II-Verordnung RIW 2008 257, 260; *Jan von Hein*, Of Older Siblings and Distant Cousins: The Contribution of the Rome II Regulation to the Communitarisation of Private International Law RabelsZ 73 (2009) 487; *Jan von Hein*, Europäisches Internationales Deliktsrecht nach der Rom II-Verordnung ZEuP 2009 20; *Andreas Spickhoff*, Die Produkthaftung im Europäischen Kollisions- und Zivilverfahrensrecht Festschrift für Kropholler 2008 671, 682.

511  See e.g. *Helmut Heiss/Leander Loacker*, Die Vergemeinschaftung des Kollisionsrechts der außervertraglichen Schuldverhältnisse durch Rom II JBl 2007 613, 623; *Helmut Heiss*, Inhaltskontrolle von Rechtswahlklauseln in AGB nach europäischem Internationalen Privatrecht? RabelsZ 65 (2001) 635; *Richard Plender/Michael Wilderspin*, The European Private International law of Obligations (2009) 764; *Thorn*, in: Palandt Art. 14 marginal no. 9; *Gerhard Wagner*, Die neue Rom II-Verordnung (2008) IPRax 1, 14; *Stefan Leible*, Rechtswahl im IPR der außervertraglichen Schuldverhältnisse

European Parliament's tabled legislative resolution of 2005, adopted at first reading on 6 July 2005,[512] cited standard form contracts – *contrats d'adhésion* as an example of agreements not freely negotiated.[513]

Others commentators take an opposing view, arguing that a specific control or exclusion of choice of law clauses within standard form contracts would curtail party autonomy in commercial dealings and that it would be inconsistent to require a specific control of such clauses for *ex ante* agreements, but not for *ex post* agreements.[514] It is recognised that to exclude choice of law clauses found in standard form contracts would deprive Article 14(1)(b) of all its value

---

nach der Rom II-Verordnung RIW 2008 257, 260; *Jan von Hein*, Of Older Siblings and Distant Cousins: The Contribution of the Rome II Regulation to the Communitarisation of Private International Law RabelsZ 73 (2009) 487; *Jan von Hein*, Europäisches Internationales Deliktsrecht nach der Rom II-Verordnung ZEuP 2009 20; *Francisco Alférez*, The Rome II Regulation: On the way towards a European Private International Law Code EuLF 2007 I-82; *Sven Rugullis*, Die antizipierte Rechtswahl in außervertraglichen Schuldverhältnisse (2008) IPRax 319, 322; *Andrew Rushworth/ Adam Scott*, Rome II: Choice of Law for Non-Contractual Obligations (2008) LM-CLQ 274, 293; *John Phaedon Kozyris*, Rome II: Tort Conflicts on the Right Track! A Postscript to Symeon Symeonides' "Missed Opportunity" 56 AmJCompL (2008) 471, 484. But compare *Abbo Junker*, Der Reformbedarf im Internationalen Deliktsrecht der Rom II-Verordnung drei Jahre nach ihrer Verabschiedung RIW 2010 257, 267; *Andreas Vogeler*, Die freie Rechtswahl im Kollisionsrecht der ausservertraglichen Schuldverhaeltnisse (2012) 275 *et seq.*

512 European Parliament legislative resolution on the proposal for a regulation of the European Parliament and of the Council on the law applicable to non-contractual obligations ("Rome II") COM (2003) 0427 [06.07.2005], OJ C157E Vol. 49, also available at: http://www.europarl.europa.eu/oeil/file.jsp?id=235142.

513 See Justification following Article 2a(1) Amendment 25: "...the wording of this amendment is designed to exclude consumer contracts and agreements not freely negotiated (such as standard-form contracts – *contrats d'adhésion*) where the contracting parties do not have equal bargaining power (e.g. insurance, franchise and licensing contracts)", Report on the proposal for a regulation of the European Parliament and of the Council on the law applicable to non-contractual obligations ("Rome II"), COM(2003) 0427 – C5–0338/2003 – 2003/0168(COD) of 27 June 2005.

514 *Abbo Junker*, Der Reformbedarf im Internationalen Deliktsrecht der Rom II-Verordnung drei Jahre nach ihrer Verabschiedung RIW 2010 257, 267; *Gerhard Wagner*, Die neue Rom II-Verordnung (2008) IPRax 1, 14; *Erik Jayme*, Inhaltskontrolle von Rechtswahlklauseln in Allgemeinen Geschäftsbedingungen FS Werner Lorenz (1991) 435.

in practice.[515] In other words, carefully drafted *ex ante* choice of law agreements are seldom individually negotiated in practice. There appears no reason why choice of law clauses found in standard form contracts should automatically fall outside of Article 14(1)(b) – provided that the terms imposed by one party are expressly accepted by the other party.[516] It should depend on the consideration of the individual circumstances surrounding the agreement between the parties whether a choice of law in a standard form will fall outside of Article 14(1)(b). Situations where the choice of law clause is considered by the imposing party to be "non-negotiable" or where a party is induced by misrepresentation should be excluded.[517] But, where it can be established that each party had the opportunity (but need not have taken up the opportunity) to inspect and influence the terms of the contract, the choice of law should be effective in terms of Article 14(1)(b).[518] Any additional scrutiny of a choice of law clause found within a standard form contract would devalue the place of party autonomy within commercial dealings and increase uncertainty as it would be unclear according to which standards such a clause would be scrutinised.

---

515  *Gerhard Wagner*, Die neue Rom II-Verordnung (2008) IPRax 1, 13–14: "seiner praktischen Bedeutung weitgehend beraubt"; see also *Junker*, in: MünchKomm (5th ed.) Art.14 marginal no. 36; *Abbo Junker*, Der Reformbedarf im Internationalen Deliktsrecht der Rom II-Verordnung drei Jahre nach ihrer Verabschiedung RIW 2010 257, 267; *Thomas Kadner Graziano*, The Application of Multiple Laws Under the Rome II Regulation, in: *John Ahern/William Binchy* (eds.), The Rome II Regulation on the Law Applicable to Non-Contractual Obligations (2009) 121 at n 26.

516  *Thomas Kadner Graziano*, The Application of Multiple Laws Under the Rome II Regulation, in: *John Ahern/William Binchy* (eds.), The Rome II Regulation on the Law Applicable to Non-Contractual Obligations (2009) 121; *idem*, Das auf außervertragliche Schuldverhältnisse anzuwendende Recht nach Inkrafttreten der Rom II-Verordnung (2009) RabelsZ 73 8; *Gerhard Wagner*, Die neue Rom II-Verordnung (2008) IPRax 1, 13–14; *Andrew Dickinson*, The Rome II Regulation 563. Compare *Peter Mankowski*, Ausgewählte Einzelfragen zur Rom II-VO: Internationales Umwelthaftungsrecht internationales Kartellrecht, renvoi, Parteiautonomie (2010) IPRax 389, 400.

517  See also *Gerhard Wagner*, Die neue Rom II-Verordnung (2008) IPRax 1, 13.

518  See *Andrew Dickinson*, The Rome II Regulation 563 who draws support for this argument from the approach taken by the Article 3(2) of the Directive (EC) No 93/13 on unfair terms in consumer contracts (OJ L95, 29 [21.4.1993]): Article 3(2) "A term shall always be regarded as not individually negotiated where it has been drafted in advance and the consumer has therefore not been able to influence the substance of the term, particularly in the context of a pre-formulated standard contract." See also *Helmut Ofner*, Die Rom II-Verordnung – Neues Internationales Privatrecht für außervertragliche Schuldverhältnisse in der Europäischen Union ZfRV 2008 13, 22.

### iii. Accessory connection of Article 3 Rome I

As mentioned above, it may still be possible to find a previously agreed to choice of law for contractual claims, indirectly applicable to non-contractual claims, through the "backdoor", by way of an accessory connection.[519] This is because normally, parties will agree to an *ex ante* choice of law in conjunction with their choice of law for contract. Accordingly, even if parties have not agreed to a non-contractual choice of law or have agreed to the applicable law to govern their contract using a standard form agreement under Article 3(1) Rome I Regulation, the choice may still satisfy the requirements of Article 4(3) Rome II Regulation and be 'indirectly' applicable.[520] On this basis, the need for permitting *ex ante* agreements under the Rome II Regulation only between commercial parties, in other words between parties who are more than likely in a contractual relationship anyway, arguably becomes redundant – although there may be certain situations where commercial parties are not in a direct contractual relationship, such as parties working on the same project under a complex construction contract.[521] Another point of difference between the application of a law previously agreed to by way of accessory connection and an *ex ante* agreement reached in accordance with Article 14(1)(b) is that for the latter agreement the parties are free to choose

---

519 *Thomas Kadner Graziano*, The Application of Multiple Laws Under the Rome II Regulation, in: *John Ahern/William Binchy* (eds.), The Rome II Regulation on the Law Applicable to Non-Contractual Obligations (2009) 117, 125–131. Accessory connection exception also found in Article 41 II (1) *EGBGB*; Article 133 III Swiss PIL Act; Article 5 Dutch Act *Wet conflictenrecht onrechtmatige daad* of 11 April 2001.

520 *Jan von Hein*, Of Older Siblings and Distant Cousins: The Contribution of the Rome II Regulation to the Communitarisation of Private International Law RabelsZ 73 (2009) 487; cf. *Th. M. de Boer*, Party Autonomy and its Limitations in the Rome II Regulation 9 YBPIL (2007) 19, 27 who argues that an accessory connection will still be possible even where an invalid choice of law under Article 14(1) Rome II is made; this also noted in *Cheshire & North* (14th ed.) 838.

521 As observed by *Thomas Kadner Graziano*, The Application of Multiple Laws Under the Rome II Regulation, in: *John Ahern/William Binchy* (eds.), The Rome II Regulation on the Law Applicable to Non-Contractual Obligations (2009) 117; e.g. there may be no contractual basis for an accessory connection in cases involving complex construction contracts. See also examples in *Jan von Hein*, Rechtswahl im internationalen Deliktsrecht RabelsZ 64 (2000) 595, 601; and *Peter Mankowski*, Ausgewählte Einzelfragen zur Rom II-VO: Internationales Umwelthaftungsrecht, internationales Kartellrecht, renvoi, Parteiautonomie (2010) IPRax 389, 401.

any law without having to additionally establish a close connection.[522] This allows parties to be certain that the law applicable to their contract will govern any non-contractual obligations.[523] In addition, Article 14(1)(b) offers commercial parties the possibility to choose a different law to cover liability in tort and thereby avoid an accessory connection through Article 4(3) Rome II Regulation.[524]

The extension of party autonomy to include *ex ante* choice of law agreements quite clearly has the possibility of contributing to legal certainty. Where the limits of such a choice are clearly defined, it may provide parties with an incentive to settle in advance the law applicable to non-contractual obligations, rather than relying on a "backdoor" method of applying a law already connected to their relationship.[525] However, the requirements stipulated in Article 14(1)(b) are neither sufficiently defined in the Regulation, nor uniformly interpreted throughout the European-Union. In particular, the requirement of free negotiation does not have a counterpart in the Rome I Regulation. But because in practice choice of law clauses for non-contractual obligations will almost always be agreed upon in conjunction with a choice of law for contract (more often than not in the same clause, stipulating one law to govern both contractual and non-contractual obligations), it seems inconsistent to impose a stricter process requiring free negotiation for the pre-tort choice of law but not for the contractual choice of law.[526] Hence, it remains to be seen to what

---

522 Compare Article 4(3) Rome II that invites a degree of judicial discretion: "A manifestly closer connection [...] *might be* based in particular on a pre-existing relationship between the parties, such as a contract" (emphasis added). On this see *Jan von Hein*, Of Older Siblings and Distant Cousins: The Contribution of the Rome II Regulation to the Communitarisation of Private International Law RabelsZ 73 (2009) 487; *Stefan Leible*, Rechtswahl im IPR der außervertraglichen Schuldverhältnisse nach der Rom II-Verordnung RIW 2008 257, 258; *Stefan Leible/Andreas Engel*, Der Vorschlag der EG-Kommission für eine Rom II-Verordnung – Auf dem Weg zu einheitlichen Anknüpfungsregeln für außervertragliche Schuldverhältnisse in Europa EuZW 2004 15.

523 *Stefan Leible*, Rechtswahl im IPR der außervertraglichen Schuldverhältnisse nach der Rom II-Verordnung RIW 2008 257, 258.

524 *Thorn*, in: Palandt Art. 14 marginal no. 7.

525 *Thomas Kadner Graziano*, The Application of Multiple Laws Under the Rome II Regulation, in: *John Ahern/William Binchy* (eds.), The Rome II Regulation on the Law Applicable to Non-Contractual Obligations (2009) 117.

526 *Peter Mankowski*, Ausgewählte Einzelfragen zur Rom II-VO: Internationales Umwelthaftungsrecht, internationales Kartellrecht, renvoi, Parteiautonomie (2010) IPRax 389, 401.

extent Article 14 will be practically relevant and how far courts will allow Article 14 to be used as a vehicle for taking advantage of weak "commercial" parties.[527]

## 2. The way in which the choice may be made (Article 14(1) second sentence)

The first sentence of Article 14(1) requires that the parties "agree" to the choice of law.[528] The second sentence provides two alternatives from which an agreement may be drawn. Both *ex post* and *ex ante* agreements may be reached either: by an express choice of law, and in the absence of such, according to the wording "demonstrated with reasonable certainty by the circumstances of the case", by an implied choice of law.[529] Accordingly, a choice of law reached either expressly or tacitly, must be substantiated by the existence of agreement as to that choice.[530] The ensuing question therefore is: how, i.e. according to which criteria, the existence of *consensus ad idem* or agreement between the parties is to be determined. For instance, the relevant criteria could be derived from the *lex fori*, the putative applicable law or *lex contractus* (identified in accordance with the rules contained in the Rome I Regulation)[531], or be given an autonomous meaning under European Community law.[532] Recital 6 of the Rome II Regulation identifies the objective to ensure predictability

---

527 For a very critical stance on Article 14 Rome II and the need to protect all weaker parties, see *Symeon Symenoides*, The American Revolution and the European Evolution in Choice of Law: Reciprocal Lessons Tul LRev (2008) 27–28 available at: http//ssrn.com/abstract=1104284; *idem*, Rome II and Tort Conflicts: A Missed Opportunity (2008) 56 Am. J. Comp. L. 301–302.

528 Article 14(1) first sentence Rome II.

529 Article 14(1) second sentence Rome II. Compare Article 3(1) of the Rome I Regulation that broadly corresponds with the requirements established in Article 14(1) Rome II.

530 *Adrian Briggs* (ed.), Agreements on Jurisdiction and Choice of Law (2008) 37.

531 Either through direct application of Article 8 of the Rome Convention, Article 10 of the Rome I Regulation, or by analogy. This option is favoured by *Thomas Kadner Graziano*, The Application of Multiple Laws Under the Rome II Regulation, in: *John Ahern/William Binchy* (eds.), The Rome II Regulation on the Law Applicable to Non-Contractual Obligations (2009) 123; *idem*, Das auf außervertragliche Schuldverhältnisse anzuwendende Recht nach Inkrafttreten der Rom II-Verordnung RabelsZ 73 (2009) 1, 13; *Andrew Rushworth/Adam Scott*, Rome II: Choice of Law for Non-Contractual Obligations (2008) LMCLQ 274, 292.

532 *Richard Plender/Michael Wilderspin*, The European Private International law of Obligations (2009) 767.

of the outcome of litigation and certainty as to the law applicable. It further emphasises the need to "designate the same national law irrespective of the country of the court in which an action is brought." Consequently, the existence of agreement between the parties must be interpreted consistently with the principles established in EU doctrine and case law, in particular on the corresponding application of Article 10 Rome I, and not according to the national approach of the *lex fori*.[533]

In addition, Article 14(1) second sentence also includes the condition that the choice "shall not adversely affect the rights of third parties."[534] The same condition can be found in Article 3(2) of Rome I and is included in Article 42 *EGBGB*.[535] This requirement protects insurance contracts in particular from unfavourable choice of law agreements between a tortfeasor and the insured victim.[536]

---

533 *Junker*, in: MünchKomm (5th ed.) Art.14 marginal no. 27; *Stefan Leible*, Rechtswahl im IPR der außervertraglichen Schuldverhältnisse nach der Rom II-Verordnung RIW 2008 257, 260. This also appears to be the English court's current approach to the corresponding issue under the Rome I Regime, see e.g. *Dicey & Morris* (15th ed.) Vol. II 1802. The authors state that as to matters of interpretation of contractual provisions, Article 3 of the preceding Rome Convention "should be looked at from a broad Regulation-based approach, not constrained by national rules of construction". This statement was approved by Clarke J in *Egon Oldendorff v Libera Corporation (No 2)* [1996] 1 Lloyd's Rep 380, 387 (EWHC) and by the Court of Appeal in *Samcrete Egypt Engineers and Contractors SAE v Land Rover Exports Ltd* [2002] EWCA Civ 2019 [26]-[27] (Potter LJ). But see *Helmut Heiss/Leander Loaker*, Die Vergemeinschaftung des Kollisionsrechts der außervertraglichen Schuldverhältnisse durch Rom II, JBl 2007 at 623 or *Andrew Dickinson*, The Rome II Regulation 542–550 who presents a choice between giving the term "agreement" an autonomous meaning under EC law, or the law applicable to that agreement under the Rome I Regulation, preferring the latter. Compare also *Richard Plender/Michael Wilderspin*, The European Private International law of Obligations (2009) 767–768, who prefer a practical, objective approach: where agreement is *in fact* present, this should be sufficient.

534 Further, *Thomas Kadner Graziano*, Das auf außervertragliche Schuldverhältnisse anzuwendende Recht nach Inkrafttreten der Rom II-Verordnung RabelsZ 73 (2009) 1, 11–12.

535 Article 42 second sentence *EGBGB*, "Rechte Dritter bleiben unberührt."

536 *Stefan Leible/Matthias Lehmann*, Die neue EG-Verordnung über das auf außervertragliche Schuld-verhältnisse anzuwendende Recht ("Rom II") RIW 2007 727; *Jan von Hein*, Die Kodifikation des europäischen IPR vor dem Abschluss? VersR 2007 440, 445; *Junker*, in: MünchKomm (5th ed.) Art.14 marginal no. 49–50.

## a. Express choice of law

An express choice includes a choice by way of a contractual clause.[537] For example, a choice of law clause may stipulate that the chosen law is to govern "all relations between the parties". Or, an agreement may be reached where the parties specifically agree to the application of a legal system to govern any non-contractual disputes between them. Generally, express agreements should be easily applicable under Article 14(1) Rome II. However, as discussed above, an express choice of law clause found in a standard form agreement may lead to problems of admissibility, specifically for *ex ante* agreements.[538] The safest option for *ex ante* agreements is therefore, for commercial parties to formulate an express choice of law widely so as to include all substantive obligations arising out of contract and tort.[539]

## b. Inferred choice of law

### aa) Demonstrated with reasonable certainty by the circumstances of the case

An implied choice of law requires a court to determine whether a choice of law in the parties' agreement can be inferred by taking account of the "circumstances of the case". No further guidance is given as to how an implied choice of law may be inferred or what circumstances should be taken into account. The wording of the last sentence of Article 14(1) of the Regulation follows closely the wording of Article 3(1) of the Rome I Regulation. Article 3(1) Rome I, requires that the choice of law between the parties "shall be made expressly or clearly demonstrated by the terms of the contract or the circumstances of the case". Problematic is the flexible concept of "reasonable certainty" in Article 14(1) Rome II, which potentially provides room for discretionary interpretation by the courts. The various translations of the text generate further uncertainty through their choice of wording. So, for example, although the German translation '*mit hinreichender Sicherheit*', corresponds to the expression 'with reasonable certainty' used in the English, the French translation '*de façon certaine*' arguably implies a greater degree of certainty than the English text. This was precisely a point of criticism of the wording of Article 3(1) of the Rome Convention, which led to substituting the words *reasonable certainty*

---

537 Another example may be a choice of jurisdiction clause and arbitration clause, see *Cheshire & North* (14th ed.) 839 and 700–701.
538 *Junker*, in: MünchKomm (5th ed.) Art.14 marginal no. 28, 34 *et seq.*
539 Compare examples given in *Adrian Briggs* (ed.), Agreements on Jurisdiction and Choice of Law (2008) 158 and *Andrew Dickinson*, The Rome II Regulation 555.

with the words *clearly demonstrated* in the Rome I Regulation.[540] This may suggest that the wording under the Rome I Regulation requires a stricter approach than that taken under the Rome Convention and indeed the Rome II Regulation.[541] Yet, although the wording in Article 14(1) Rome II differs from Article 3(1) Rome I, there appears nothing to suggest that the drafters intended the requirements in either Regulation to differ.[542] Accordingly, courts may seek guidance from the interpretation of inferred choices of law in contract under Rome I,[543] in particular considering that the principle of party autonomy for non-contractual obligations is currently less well developed than for contractual obligations.[544]

In addition, further guidance on the circumstances that may indicate an implied choice of law by the parties may be drawn from commentaries on the Rome I provision. Such a commentary, namely the *Giuliano & Lagarde* Report, provides examples of factors that may assist a court when inferring a choice of law for contract. The examples given by the Report are not intended to be exhaustive, but provide the most common situations from which a court may legitimately conclude that the parties have made a choice of law. Among the factors given are: the choice of a jurisdiction or arbitration clause; the reference to a particular system

---

540  See *The Green Paper* 23 and 24. The German text of the *Rome I Regulation* now reads *'eindeutig aus den Bestimmungen des Vertrags'*. The French translation of clearly demonstrated is *'de façon certaine'*.

541  *Ole Lando/Peter Nielsen*, The Rome I Regulation (2008) 45 CML Rev. 1687, 1698. Compare the even higher threshold provided in Article 2(2) of the Hague Convention on the Law Applicable to International Sales of Goods of 15 June 1955 "[...] an express clause, or *unambiguously* result from the provisions of the contract." (emphasis added).

542  On this see *Helmut Heiss/Leander Loacker*, Die Vergemeinschaftung des Kollisionsrechts der außervertraglichen Schuldverhältnisse durch Rom II JBl 2007 613, 623; *Stefan Leible/Matthias Lehmann*, Die neue EG-Verordnung über das auf außervetragliche Schuldverhältnisse anzuwendende Recht ("Rom II") RIW 10 2007 721, 727; *Gisela Rühl*, Rechtswahlfreiheit im europäischen Kollisionsrecht, FS Jan Kropholler zum 70. Geburtstag 2008 187, 197 n 46; *Stefan Leible*, Rechtswahl im IPR der außervertraglichen Schuldverhältnisse nach der Rom II-Verordnung RIW 2008 257, 260; Symeon *Symeonides*, Rome II and Tort Conflicts: A Missed Opportunity (2008) 56 Am. J. Comp. L. 173, 215. But see *Junker*, in: MünchKomm (5th ed.) Art.14 at marginal no. 29, who states that it should not be assumed that the requirements for an implied choice of law in contract under Rome I should necessarily be applicable to implied choices of law for non-contractual obligations under Rome II.

543  *Helmut Heiss/Leander Loacker*, Die Vergemeinschaftung des Kollisionsrechts der außervertraglichen Schuldverhältnisse durch Rom II JBl 2007 613, 623.

544  *Andrew Dickinson*, The Rome II Regulation 554.

of law in the contract; an express choice of law in a related transaction; and, the use of a standard form, known to be governed by a particular system of law. The authors conclude that courts may not infer a choice of law where the parties had no clear intention of making a choice. The concern to respect and give effect only to the manifest intention of the parties is also evident in the Rome II Regulation. Recital 31 of the Rome II Regulation repeats the requirement that a choice should be expressed or demonstrated with reasonable certainty by the circumstances of the case and further adds "[w]here establishing the existence of the agreement, the court has to respect the intentions of the parties." Thus, although like Article 4(3) Rome I, Article 14(1) Rome II also allows for an implied choice of law agreement, a court may not impute a choice of law on the basis that had the parties chosen a law, it *would* be the law of a particular country.[545] It requires the courts to ascertain the true will of the parties (*realer Rechtswahlwille der Parteien*), identifying facts that indicate a will and intention to have a particular law applicable, rather than impute a purely hypothetical will (*hypothetischer Rechtswahlwille der Parteien*).[546] Problematic is identifying the distinction between an implied choice of law (Article 14(1) Rome II)[547] and a choice of law "manifestly more closely connected" ascertained according to the escape clause (Article 4(3) Rome II)[548]. A distinction can be drawn whereby a choice according to Article 14(1) Rome II requires that both parties were actively aware or conscious of the choice of law (*Erklärungsbewusstsein* or *Rechtswahlbewusstsein beider Parteien*), whereas under Article 4(3) Rome II a choice of law is to be objectively ascertained, without the additional requirement of 'awareness' of both parties.[549]

---

545 *Junker*, in: MünchKomm (5th ed.) Art.14 marginal no. 29. See also *Giuliano & Lagarde* Report 17. Such a situation would require courts to consider the determination of the applicable law according to Article 4.

546 *Junker*, in: MünchKomm (5th ed.) Art.14 marginal no. 29; *Thorn*, in: Palandt Art. 14 marginal no. 6.

547 The same difficulty arises under the Rome I Regulation. Compare Articles 3(1) and 4 Rome I.

548 Where it is clear from all the circumstances of the case that the tort/delict is manifestly more closely connected with a country other than that indicated in paragraphs 1 or 2, the law of that other country shall apply." Compare the almost identical wording of Article 4(3) Rome I: "Where it is clear from all the circumstances of the case that the contract is manifestly more closely connected with a country other than that indicated in paragraphs 1 or 2, the law of that other country shall apply."

549 *Junker*, in: MünchKomm (5th ed.) Art.14 marginal no. 29 and 32–33; *Thorn*, in: Palandt Art. 14 marginal no. 6; *Michael Sonnentag*, Zur Europäisierung des Internationalen außervertraglichen Schuldrechts durch die geplante Rom II-Verordnung,

Under the common law neither an express nor an implied choice of law by the parties for non-contractual obligations was possible. Rather, the choice of law in tort was a choice of law by the court.[550] A law impliedly 'chosen' by the parties was only possible through the device of not pleading and proving foreign law. Or, a law impliedly 'chosen' by the parties could be relevant when considering the 'flexible exception' of the rule of 'double actionability'.[551] Reliance on the so called 'flexible exception' resulted in the unsatisfactory position of distinguishing between tort claims on the basis of the location of the tort. In other words, the otherwise applicable law under the rule of double actionability could be set aside where another law is substantially more appropriate for application. It has been noted that although there were several objections to the common law rule and set of sub rules for choice of law in tort claims, the lack of a role for the law chosen by the parties was not considered to be principal motive for reform of English law.[552] Instead objections focused on the need to prove that a claimant could succeed under the *lex fori* and the unfairness of a rule which required a claimant to prove actionability under two legal systems.[553] The English regime of statutory choice of law rules contained in Part III of the Private International Law (Miscellaneous Provisions) Act 1995 therefore does not include any reference to the concept of party autonomy in tort.[554] On the other hand, the possibility of an implied choice of law for *contractual* obligations is well established in the common law.[555] In particular, arbitration and choice of

---

ZVglRWiss 105 (2006) 278. See further discussion of Article 4 Rome II in *Richard Fentiman*, The Significance of Close Connection, in: *John Ahern/William Binchy* (eds.), The Rome II Regulation on the Law Applicable to Non-Contractual Obligations (2009) 85–112.

550 See *Adrian Briggs* (ed.), Agreements on Jurisdiction and Choice of Law (2008) 403–404; *Dicey & Morris* (13th ed.) Vol. II 2000.

551 See further below, Part 4/B.I. Common law choice of law in non-contractual obligations.

552 *Adrian Briggs* (ed.), Agreements on Jurisdiction and Choice of Law (2008) 404.

553 ibid.

554 Although the Law Commission's Working Paper No 87 (1984) at para 4.21 did propose that it should be possible, before or after a *delict* occurred, to agree by means of contract what law should govern the parties mutual liability in tort or *delict*. Compare also the English case *Morin v Bonhams & Brooks Ltd* [2003] EWCA Civ 1802, [2004] 1 Lloyd's Rep 702, at [23] (per Mance LJ), where it was considered that "it would seem odd, if an express choice of law were not at least relevant to the law governing a tort".

555 *Dicey & Morris* (15th ed.) Vol. II 1802; *Andrew Dickinson*, The Rome II Regulation 554. See discussion of inferred choice of law under the Rome I Regulation above, Part 1/B.I.2.b. *Inferred choice of law*. For specific discussion of common law position in contract law, see below Part 4/A.I.2. *Implied choice of law*.

forum clauses may imply a contractual choice of law.[556] The now applicable Rome I Regulation also specifically provides in Recital (12) that exclusive jurisdiction clauses should be one of the factors to be taken into account in determining whether a choice of law has been clearly demonstrated in terms of Article 3(1) Rome I.

Could therefore the inclusion of an exclusive jurisdiction clause in a contract signify the parties' intention to have all obligations arising between them to be governed by that law? Surely, it cannot be assumed or inferred with 'reasonable certainty' that where commercial parties state in their contract that it shall be governed exclusively by the law of 'X' that the chosen law is to apply not only to contractual but *also* to non-contractual obligations. Unless such an agreement expressly includes that the clause applies also to all obligations (e.g. all obligations whether contractual or non-contractual, or all contractual and non-contractual obligations), a more cautious approach seems required under Article 14(1) of the Rome II Regulation, it being necessary to distinguish between *ex ante* and *ex post* agreements and perhaps also between the different non-contractual obligations.[557] As a result, an exclusive jurisdiction clause agreed to by the parties indicating an implied choice of law for non-contractual obligations, should only be contemplated where the agreement is reached *following* the event giving rise to the damage, or *before* the event where all the parties are pursuing a commercial activity (Article 14(1) (b) Rome II).[558] But perhaps more importantly, where parties have entered into a choice of jurisdiction agreement after being aware of the non-contractual obligations arising between them, it should be considered why then the parties did not expressly stipulate that non-contractual obligations are to be subject to that choice of forum, or indeed reach an express agreement stipulating the applicable law.[559]

---

556  See e.g. *Egon Oldendorff v Libera Corporation (No 1)* [1995] 2 Lloyd's Rep 64 and (No. 2) [1996] 1 Lloyd's Rep 380; *JSC Zestafoni v Ronly Holdings Ltd* [2004] EWHC 245 (Comm), [2004] 2 Lloyd's Rep 335. But compare the English pre-Convention case *Compagnie d'Armement Maritime v Compagnie Tunisienne de Navigation, SA* [1970] 3 ALL ER 71, at 84.

557  *Junker*, in: MünchKomm (5th ed.) Art.14 marginal no. 30–31; *Andrew Dickinson*, The Rome II Regulation 554.

558  *Junker*, in: MünchKomm (5th ed.) Art.14 marginal no. 30; *Helmut Heiss/Leander Loacker*, Die Vergemeinschaftung des Kollisionsrechts der außervertraglichen Schuldverhältnisse durch Rom II JBl 2007 613, 623. A non-exclusive jurisdiction agreement will not have the same effect; see *Stefan Leible*, Rechtswahl im IPR der außervertraglichen Schuldverhältnisse nach der Rom II-Verordnung RIW 2008 257, 261 with further references.

559  *Junker*, in: MünchKomm (5th ed.) Art.14 marginal no. 31.

Under German law, the parties have the right to choose the law applicable to contractual *and* non-contractual obligations according to Article 42 *EGBGB*, either expressly or tacitly, but the agreement may only be made *after* the event giving rise to the dispute.[560] Where a choice of law is reached between the parties, it will pertain exclusively to the internal law, i.e. excluding the application of *renvoi*.[561] Implied choice of law agreements have principally been considered by German courts in cases involving a so-called "*Rechtswahl im Prozess*", or tacit choice of law in proceedings.[562]

bb) Tacit choice of law in proceedings

This issue involves asking the question whether a choice of law can be inferred by the parties' general silence as to the choice of law during legal proceedings. German courts have regularly inferred a choice of law from the parties' conduct or attitude during legal proceedings.[563] For example, agreeing to initiate proceedings (suing and defending) in a German court has been held to be an agreement to apply the *lex fori* (German law) by implication.[564] The same issue arises under the Rome I Regulation and it is submitted that the same cautious approach should be taken when inferring a choice of law for non-contractual obligations based on the parties' conduct during proceedings.[565] This is substantiated by Recital (31) of Rome II, which explicitly requires

---

560 *Jan Kropholler*, Internationales Privatrecht (2006) §40 IV 4; *Mathias Reimann*, Codifying Tort Conflicts, The 1999 German Legislation in Comparative Perspective (2000) 60 La. L. Rev. 1297, 1302–1303.

561 Article 4(2) *EGBGB*.

562 *Junker*, in: MünchKomm (4th ed.) Art. 42 *EGBGB* marginal no. 12, 13 with further references; *Abbo Junker*, Das Internationale Unfallrecht nach der IPR-Reform von 1999 JZ 2000 477, 478.

563 See *Christoph Reithmann/Dieter Martiny* (eds.), Internationales Vertragsrecht (2010) 111–128; *Stefan Leible*, Rechtswahl im IPR der außervertraglichen Schuldverhältnisse nach der Rom II-Verordnung RIW 2008 257, 261; *Bundesgerichtshof* judgment of 20.9.1995 – VIII 52/94, WM 1995, 2073, 2074; *Bundesgerichtshof* judgment of 21.10.1992 – XII ZR 182/90, BGHZ 119, 392, 396; *Bundesgerichtshof* judgment of 12.12.1990 – VIII ZR 332/89, WM 1991, 464, 465; *Bundesgerichtshof* judgment of 30.9.1987 – Iva ZR 22/86, WM 1987, 1501, 1502; *Bundesgerichtshof* judgment of 15.1.1986 – VIII ZR 6/85, WM 1986, 527, 528. See also discussion with further references above, Part 1/B.I.1.c. *The problem of silent consent*.

564 Critically *Jan von Hein*, Die Kodifikation des europäischen Internationalen Deliktsrechts ZVglRWiss 102 (2003) 528, 545, n 126; compare also *Heldrich*, in: Palandt Art. 42 *EGBGB* marginal no. 1

565 *Stefan Leible*, Rechtswahl im IPR der außervertraglichen Schuldverhältnisse nach der Rom II-Verordnung RIW 2008, 257, 261 at n 57. Compare discussion of the issue in contract law above in Part 1/B.I.1.c. *The problem of silent consent*.

the court to respect the intention of the parties when establishing the existence of the agreement. The conduct of the parties needs to clearly evidence an awareness and intention to have the particular law (i.e. *lex fori*) apply to the dispute. It will not be enough if the parties were unaware of the choice, if they were under the mistaken belief that the law of the forum is applicable, or to base the inference on the consideration of objective connecting factors.[566] The court will need to be convinced that the parties were *aware* of the right to choose the applicable law and that through their silent acceptance of the law of the forum they consciously intended to affirm that choice.[567] Inferring a choice of law without an active awareness by both parties would be a mere fictitious application and recognition of party autonomy.[568] Awareness by the parties as to the choice of law may possibly be inferred in situations where both parties assume a foreign law as applicable.[569] But the parties should take especial care in cases where the inference leads to the application of the lex fori without the prior direction of the court or consideration of the issue of applicable law.[570] Based on this, the approach of the German *Bundesgerichtshof*,[571] for example inferring German law as the choice of law where the parties merely relied on particular legal provisions during proceedings, is no longer reconcilable with Recital (31), Article 14(1) Rome II.[572] A cautious approach

---

566  The Rome II Regulation requires the separation of demonstrable intention (Article 14(1)) and objective factors connecting the tort/*delict* with another country (Article 4(3)). This is also found in the Rome I Regulation, compare Article 3(1) and 4 Rome I.

567  *Junker*, in: MünchKomm (5th ed.) Art.14 marginal no. 32; *Stefan Leible*, Rechtswahl im IPR der außervertraglichen Schuldverhältnisse nach der Rom II-Verordnung RIW 2008 257, 261.

568  *Thomas Kadner Graziano*, The Application of Multiple Laws Under the Rome II Regulation, in: *John Ahern/William Binchy* (eds.), The Rome II Regulation on the Law Applicable to Non-Contractual Obligations (2009) 120; *Hamburg Group for Private International Law* 'Comments on the European Commission's Draft Proposal for a Council Regulation on the Law Applicable to Non-Contractual Obligations' (2003) RabelsZ 67 1, 4.

569  Too far *Stefan Leible*, Rechtswahl im IPR der außervertraglichen Schuldverhältnisse nach der Rom II-Verordnung RIW 2008 257 at 261, who states that this will *generally* indicate awareness.

570  *Stefan Leible*, Rechtswahl im IPR der außervertraglichen Schuldverhältnisse nach der Rom II-Verordnung RIW 2008 257, 261.

571  Compare for example, *Bundesgerichtshof* judgment of 19.1.2000 – VIII ZR 275/98, NJW-RR 2000, 1002, 1004.

572  See *Junker*, in: MünchKomm (5th ed.) Art.14 marginal no. 33; *Jan von Hein*, Die Kodifikation des europäischen Internationalen Deliktsrechts ZVglRWiss 102 (2003) 528, 548; *Michael Sonnentag*, Zur Europäisierung des Internationalen außervertraglichen Schuldrechts durch die geplante Rom II-Verordnung ZVglRWiss 105 (2006) 256, 278.

is preferable, especially when considering that private legal practice and in particular lower courts are not practised in the impact of private international law and possible application of foreign law and for obvious reasons prefer the convenient application of familiar national law.[573] The safer option would be that parties make an express choice of law in such a way as to put it beyond doubt that they intended the choice to apply to non-contractual obligations arising out of their relationship.[574]

# II. Other restrictions on Party Autonomy

Several restrictions in addition to those already discussed are imposed on the autonomy of the parties to choose the governing law under the Regulation. These restrictions mirror those set out in the Rome I Regulation: The chosen law is restricted to State law only[575] and the choice of law must not prejudice the application of provisions of the law with which the non-contractual obligation has a close connection,[576] imperative norms of Community law,[577] overriding mandatory provisions,[578] or public policy of the forum[579].

---

573 *Stefan Leible*, Rechtswahl im IPR der außervertraglichen Schuldverhältnisse nach der Rom II-Verordnung RIW 2008 257, 261.
574 Compare suggested clauses given in *Adrian Briggs* (ed.), Agreements on Jurisdiction and Choice of Law (2008) 158 and *Andrew Dickinson*, The Rome II Regulation 555: "This Agreement and all matters (including, without limitation, any contractual or non-contractual obligation) arising from or connected with it are governed by English law".
575 Compare Article 3(1) Rome I.
576 Article 14(2) Rome II; compare Article 3(3) Rome I: "Where all other elements relevant to the situation at the time of the choice are located in a country other than the country whose law has been chosen, the choice of the parties shall not prejudice the application of provisions of the law of that other country which cannot be derogated from by agreement."
577 Article 14(3) Rome II; compare Article 3(4) Rome I: "Where all other elements relevant to the situation at the time of the choice are located in one or more Member States, the parties' choice of applicable law other than that of a Member State shall not prejudice the application of provisions of Community law, where appropriate as implemented in the Member State of the forum, which cannot be derogated from by agreement."
578 Article 16 Rome II; compare Article 9 Rome I.
579 Article 26 Rome II; compare Article 21 Rome I.

## 1. The chosen law

Article 14 simply states that the "parties may agree to submit non-contractual obligations to the law of their choice." The provision does not require that a factual or physical connection exist between the legal system and their relationship or the event giving rise to the damage, leaving parties the freedom to choose any law.[580] Like Article 3(1) of the Rome I Regulation, Article 14(1) Rome II presupposes that the law chosen by the parties will be the law of a country.[581] This interpretation of Article 14 is consistent with Article 4 of the Rome II Regulation which provides: "the law applicable to a non-contractual obligation arising out of a tort/delict shall be the *law of the country*".[582] Thus, like under the Rome I Regulation, parties are not authorised to choose supranational, non-state or non-national (religious) rules of law to govern their non-contractual obligations.[583] The Regulation does not expressly preclude the choice of non-state rules, but the general view is that rules such as those published in the Draft Common Frame of Reference (DCFR)[584] are excluded.[585]

---

580  *Stefan Leible*, Rechtswahl im IPR der außervertraglichen Schuldverhältnisse nach der Rom II-Verordnung RIW 2008 257, 261.

581  Compare also Article 14(2) Rome II: "*the country* whose law has been chosen" [emphasis added]. *Richard Plender/Michael Wilderspin*, The European Private International law of Obligations (2009) 768; *Stefan Leible*, Rechtswahl im IPR der außervertraglichen Schuldverhältnisse nach der Rom II-Verordnung RIW 2008 257, 261; *Gisela Rühl*, Rechtswahlfreiheit im europäischen Kollisionsrecht FS Jan Kropholler zum 70. Geburtstag 2008 187, 190; *Jan von Hein*, Of Older Siblings and Distant Cousins: The Contribution of the Rome II Regulation to the Communitarisation of Private International Law RabelsZ 73 (2009) 461, 490.

582  Article 4(1) Rome II [emphasis added]; compare also Article 24 Rome II: "the *law of any country* specified by this Regulation" [emphasis added].

583  Compare the Rome Convention case *Shamil Bank of Bahrain v Beximco Pharmaceuticals Ltd* [2004] EWCA Civ 19 at [48], [2004] 1 WLR 1784 (concerning a choice of Sharia law). Different *Jan von Hein*, Of Older Siblings and Distant Cousins: The Contribution of the Rome II Regulation to the Communitarisation of Private International Law, RabelsZ 73 (2009), 461, at 491 who argues in favour of a more liberal approach to the choice of non-state law under the Rome I than under the Rome II Regulation. He states that soft law instruments such as the UNIDROIT Principles or the Principles of European Contract Law have gained increasing importance and acceptance in international arbitration.

584  Study Group on a European Civil Code/Research Group on EC Private Law (Acquis Group) (eds.), Principles, Definitions and Model Rules of European Private Law. Draft Common Frame of Reference (DCFR), Interim Outline Edition, 2008.

585  *Thorn*, in: Palandt Art. 14 marginal no. 5; *Stefan Leible*, Rechtswahl im IPR der außervertraglichen Schuldverhältnisse nach der Rom II-Verordnung RIW 2008 257,

## 2. Mandatory provisions

The third rule applicable to Article 14 Rome II is that concerning mandatory rules. Article 14 includes two imperative norms: the first (Article 14(2)), concerns provisions of law that cannot be derogated from by agreement; the second (Article 14(3)), provisions of Community law that cannot be derogated from by agreement. Both Articles 16 and 26 Rome II further provide that the chosen law may not derogate from overriding mandatory provisions of the law of the forum or hinder the operation of public policy of the forum. According to Article 14, parties may choose any law to govern their non-contractual obligations regardless of relevant connection, provided that the mandatory provisions are not derogated from.

*a. All relevant elements in a single country (Article 14(2))*

Article 14(2) Rome II provides that:

> Where all the elements relevant to the situation at the time when the event giving rise to the damage occurs are located in a country other than the country whose law has been chosen, the choice of the parties shall not prejudice the application of provisions of the law of that other country which cannot be derogated from by agreement.

Such a situation is referred to as internal or domestic,[586] where all the relevant elements apart from choice of law are connected to a law other than the one chosen. In such a situation the mandatory provisions of that other law may not be prejudiced.[587] This limitation copies Article 3(3) Rome Convention and Article 3(3) Rome I Regulation. Article 14(2) should therefore be interpreted in light of the interpretation of Article 3(3) of the Rome I Regulation.[588] The objective of both provisions is to ensure that a choice of law made by the parties does not have the effect of displacing mandatory rules that would otherwise apply in a purely internal situation. The restriction is qualified in that it requires *all* of the elements relevant to the situation to be located in some

---

261; *Jan von Hein*, Of Older Siblings and Distant Cousins: The Contribution of the Rome II Regulation to the Communitarisation of Private International Law RabelsZ 73 (2009) 461, 491.

586   *Dicey & Morris* (14th ed.) Vol. I, 320.

587   An English example is to be found in the Unfair Contract Terms Act 1977, section 2 provides that: "a person cannot by reference to any contract term or to a notice [...] exclude or restrict his liability for death or personal injury resulting from negligence".

588   According to Recital (7) Rome II and Recital (15) Rome I. Compare Article 3(3) Rome Convention that uses the term 'mandatory rules' to describe the provisions that may not be derogated from by agreement.

other country.[589] Accordingly, all elements relevant to the situation giving rise to the damage or non-contractual liability must be identified.[590] The objective of both Article 3(3) Rome I and Article 14(2) Rome II is however, not to entirely disapply the law chosen by the parties.[591] It will only be disapplied or limited to the extent to which the law chosen by the parties is inconsistent with the mandatory rule of the country in which all the elements are located. The result is a "law-mix" consisting of the *ius cogens* of the country with which the elements relevant to the non-contractual liability are located and the law chosen by the parties, i.e. to the extent that the chosen law is consistent *ius cogens*.[592]

German law did not explicitly address the effectiveness of a choice of law in situations where the elements giving rise to non-contractual obligations where connected with a different country.[593] According to Article 42 *EGBGB* the mandatory provisions of the chosen law are also applicable. Where all the elements are connected with a different country, the prevailing academic opinion was that Article 27 III *EGBGB* was to be drawn upon by analogy.[594] Accordingly, only the mandatory provisions of that law remain applicable.[595]

---

589  *Richard Plender/Michael Wilderspin*, The European Private International law of Obligations (2009) 776.

590  *ibid*, The European Private International law of Obligations (2009) 776–777. See also in relation to Article 3(3) Rome Convention *Caterpillar Financial Services v Passion* [2004] EWHC 569, Cook J holding: "elements 'relevant to the situation' which is wider than 'elements relevant to the contract' which again is different from and much wider than 'elements relevant to the "mandatory rules" of the law of any once country'".

591  *Richard Plender/Michael Wilderspin*, The European Private International law of Obligations (2009) 777.

592  *Stefan Leible*, Rechtswahl im IPR der außervertraglichen Schuldverhältnisse nach der Rom II-Verordnung RIW 2008 257, 262; *Helmut Heiss/Leander Loacker*, Die Vergemeinschaftung des Kollisionsrechts der außervertraglichen Schuldverhältnisse durch Rom II JBl 2007 613, 623.

593  *Junker*, in: MünchKomm (5th ed.) Art.14 marginal no. 7 and 39. See also *Junker*, in: MünchKomm (4th ed.) Art. 42 *EGBGB* marginal no. 26.

594  *Junker*, in: MünchKomm (5th ed.) Art.14 marginal no. 39

595  *Junker*, in: MünchKomm (4th ed.) Art. 27 *EGBGB* Article 42 *EGBGB* marginal no. 26; *Robert Freitag/Stefan Leible*, Das Bestimmungsrecht des Art. 40 Abs. 1 EGBGB im Gefüge der Parteiautonomie im Internationalen Deliktsrecht ZVglRWiss 99 (2000) 101, 106.

*b. All relevant elements in Member States (Article 14(3))*

Article 14(3) Rome II provides that:

> Where all the elements relevant to the situation at the time when the event giving rise to the damage occurs are located in one or more of the Member States, the parties' choice of the law applicable other than that of a Member State shall not prejudice the application of provisions of Community law, where appropriate as implemented in the Member State of the forum, which cannot be derogated from by agreement.

This restriction is reproduced in Article 3(4) of the Rome I Regulation.[596] The objective of this limitation is to ensure that in cases where the damage occurs in a Member State that the application of non-EC country's law may not prejudice the application of provisions of Community law.[597] Like the limitation found in Article 14(2) Rome II, the effect of the provision is not a total disregard for the law chosen

---

596 This situation was not expressly covered in the Rome Convention. However, Article 7(2) Rome Convention provided: "Nothing in this Convention shall restrict the application of the law of the forum in a situation where they are mandatory irrespective of the law otherwise applicable to the contract." Article 16 Rome II Regulation repeats this limitation, Article 14(3) is therefore arguably redundant, see *Peter Hay*, Contemporary Approaches to Non-Contractual Obligations in Private International Law (Conflict of Laws) and the European Community's 'Rome II' Regulation 4 EuLF (2007) I-149, 151 n 142; but cf. *Jan von Hein*, Of Older Siblings and Distant Cousins: The Contribution of the Rome II Regulation to the Communitarisation of Private International Law RabelsZ 73 (2009) 461, 488 n 151.

597 The reference to "Member State" is problematic. Article 1(4) of the Rome II Regulation merely states that "'Member State' shall mean any Member State other than Denmark." A literal interpretation of Article 14(3) and 1(4) of the Rome II Regulation would lead to the conclusion that Article 14(3) is not applicable where the relevant elements are connected to Denmark. However, the second sentence of Article 1(4) Rome I adds: "However, in Article 3(4) and Article 7 the term shall mean all the Member States." It has therefore been suggested that based on the principle of consistency enunciated in Recital (7) of Rome II together with Article 1(4) Rome I that Denmark is to be classified as Member State for the purposes of Article 14(3) Rome II. On this see *Helmut Heiss/Leander Loacker*, Die Vergemeinschaftung des Kollisionsrechts der außervertraglichen Schuldverhältnisse durch Rom II JBl 2007 613, 623; *Stefan Leible*, Rechtswahl im IPR der außervertraglichen Schuldverhältnisse nach der Rom II-Verordnung RIW 2008 257, 263; *Gisela Rühl*, Rechtswahlfreiheit im europäischen Kollisionsrecht, FS Jan Kropholler zum 70. Geburtstag 2008 187, 204 n 70.

by the parties but a law mix consisting of the chosen law and the internally mandatory rules[598] of community law.[599]

## c. Overriding mandatory provisions (Article 16) and public policy (Article 26)

Both Article 16 and 26 of the Rome II Regulation prescribe that the application of the law applicable to non-contractual obligations is subject to overriding mandatory provisions of the law of the forum and to the operation of public policy of the forum. Recital (32) to the Rome II Regulation envisages that these two restrictions will only apply in "exceptional circumstances".

Article 16 of the Regulation states that nothing "shall restrict the application of the provisions of the law of the forum in a situation where they are mandatory irrespective of the law otherwise applicable to the non-contractual obligation."[600] Again, like in the Rome I Regulation, a distinction can be drawn between the imperative norms provided for in Article 14(2) Rome II and overriding mandatory rules provided for in Article 16 Rome II.[601] In English law, the statutory choice of law rules also expressly provided for the application for the mandatory rules of the forum.[602] Article 9(1) of the Rome I Regulation is also headed "overriding

---

598    An example of mandatory provision might be Council Directive 85/374/EEC of 25 July 1985 on the approximation of the laws, regulations and administrative provisions of the Member States concerning liability for defective products, implemented in the United Kingdom by the Consumer Protection Act 1987; in Germany by the *Produkthaftungsgesetz* of 15 December 1989.

599    This solution is criticised as being "doctrinally unsound" by *Jan von Hein*, Of Older Siblings and Distant Cousins: The Contribution of the Rome II Regulation to the Communitarisation of Private International Law RabelsZ 73 (2009) 461 at 488. The author suggests that it would be more coherent to apply the law designated by the objective conflicts rules in the Rome II Regulation (i.e. Article 4(3) Rome II, Article 4(4) Rome I). Yet the author continues that for practical reasons it is preferable to apply the *lex fori* in this specific context. Cf. *Stefan Leible*, Rechtswahl im IPR der außervertraglichen Schuldverhältnisse nach der Rom II-Verordnung RIW 2008 257, 263. Different *Cheshire & North* (14th ed.) at 840 who suggest that since national law includes Community law that Article 14(3) may not add anything to what is already provided for in Article 14(2) Rome II; also *Andrew Dickinson*, The Rome II Regulation 558.

600    Compare Article 9 Rome I Regulation; Article 7(2) Rome Convention.

601    *Cheshire & North* (14th ed.) 849; see also Recital (37) Rome I Regulation that emphasises that the expression 'overriding mandatory provisions' should be construed more restrictively.

602    See s 14(4) of the PIL Act 1995; exception also found at common law, see further *Cheshire & North* (14th ed.) 849–851.

mandatory provisions" and provides a precise definition of overriding mandatory provisions. It may be assumed that the same definition of such provisions is applicable under Article 16 Rome II Regulation.[603] The exception in Article 16 Rome II only provides for the application of the mandatory rules of the *lex fori* and it remains unclear to what extent foreign mandatory rules should be taken into consideration.[604]

The public policy of the forum may restrict the parties' choice of law in addition to the mandatory provisions applicable under Article 16. Article 26 Rome II provides that the otherwise applicable law may be refused only if such application is manifestly incompatible with the public policy (*ordre public*) of the forum. This restriction is repeated verbatim in Article 21 of the Rome I Regulation. Under German law Article 40 III *EGBGB* provides a specific provision on public policy, expressly excluding punitive or exemplary damages of an excessive nature.[605] The Rome II Regulation does not expressly mention these restrictions;[606] however, Recital (32) of the Rome II Regulation emphasises that provisions of the applicable law that have the effect of causing non-compensatory exemplary or punitive damages of an excessive nature may be regarded by the court seised as being contrary to the public policy of the forum. The use of the words 'excessive nature' and the discretion to be exercised by the court seised suggests that exemplary damages or punitive damages will not be *ipso facto* excessive.[607]

---

603 *Helmut Heiss/Leander Loacker*, Die Vergemeinschaftung des Kollisionsrechts der außervertraglichen Schuldverhältnisse durch Rom II JBl 2007 613, 644.

604 Compare *Commission Proposal* of 2003 Article 12(1); *Commission Amended Proposal* of 2006 Article 13(2). There is nothing in the current version of the Rome II Regulation to suggest that such norms should not be considered, see *Stefan Leible*, Rechtswahl im IPR der außervertraglichen Schuldverhältnisse nach der Rom II-Verordnung RIW 2008 257, 263; *Stefan Leible/Mathias Lehmann*, Die neue EG-Verordnung über das auf außervertragliche Schuldverhältnisse anzuwendende Recht ("Rom II") RIW 2007 721, 726. But cf. *Gerhard Wagner*, Die neue Rom II-Verordnung (2008) IPRax 1, 15.

605 Different to the position under the common law where exemplary or punitive damages may well be applicable and not necessarily regarded as penal or excessive in nature. On the German law see e.g. *Jan Kropholler*, Internationales Privatrecht (2006) § 53 IV 6; *Stefan Leible*, Rechtswahl im IPR der außervertraglichen Schuldverhältnisse nach der Rom II-Verordnung RIW 2008 257, 263. Section 14(3)(a)(i) of the PIL Act 1995 sets out a public policy exception to the statutory tort choice of law rules, see e.g. *Cheshire & North* (14th ed.) 854 and 139–150.

606 Compare the earlier *Commission Proposal* of 2003 Article 24; *Commission Amended Proposal* of 2006 Article 23.

607 Presumably why the final version of the Rome II Regulation only mentioned this category of damages in Recital (32) as an example, see the *EP 1st Reading Report* 33.

# C. Summary

The Rome II Regulation takes an important further step towards unifying the Member States' laws on this difficult subject. Considering the variable nature of torts and connecting factors available in the field of non-consensual obligations, the Rome II Regulation is able to provide a set of uniform, rational, comprehensive and balanced rules for choice of law for torts. The legislative confirmation of party autonomy it offers in Article 14 Rome II has been largely welcomed as innovative, signifying a European revolution within the conflict of laws.[608] It reflects the gradual trend in favour of putting the will of the parties at the forefront of choice of law rules and has made the task of ascertaining the applicable law for non non-contractual obligations methodologically similar to contractual obligations.

Following the above exposition of the Article 14 Rome II, it is suggested that the two key reforms achieved by the inclusion of party autonomy in the Rome II Regulation are: the confirmation of party autonomy for non-contractual obligations; and, the possibility to reach a choice of law to cover anticipatory torts. Whereas pre-Regulation German law already recognised the option to choose the law applicable to non-contractual obligations, English law failed to recognise the freedom of choice for non-contractual obligations. Any reference to the parties presumed intentions as to the choice of law was restricted to the application of Section 12(2) of the 1995 UK PIL Act when determining the "closest connection".[609] In this respect, the inclusion of the principle of party autonomy in the Rome II Regulation represents a dramatic change to the pre-Regulation common law rules and as will be seen below (Part 4/B. IV.) offers a great opportunity to rethink traditional common law tort choice of law approaches. The second most innovative change brought about by Article 14 Rome II is the possibility to reach *ex ante* agreements. Article 14 distinguishes between choice of law agreements reached before and after the tort. *Ex post* agreements are permitted between all parties while *ex ante* agreements only if all the parties are "pursuing a commercial activity". An additional restriction placed on pre-tort agreements is that it must be "freely negotiated". It is apparent from the above analysis of the restrictions placed on *ex ante* agreements that neither restriction is free of problems. Both phrases are not further defined in the Regulation. As a result, definitional problems

---

608 Compare *Symeon Symeonides*, The American Revolution and the European Evolution in Choice of Law: Reciprocal Lessons 82 Tul LRev (2008) 28.

609 Similar to Article 41 II No. 1 German *EGBGB*.

arise and possibilities for divergent interpretations of the restrictions become inevitable. It will be necessary to await further clarification through case law or the review of Article 14(1) Rome II to further define the restrictions.

Overall, the Rome II Regulation presents a significant additional move towards the unification of private international law within the European Community. It primarily seeks to maintain the status quo in relation to the approach taken to choice of law rules for non-contractual obligations, but in regards to party autonomy takes a dramatic innovative step: It has elevated the parties' free will to choose the applicable law to become a central conflict-of-law rule in non-contractual obligations. By doing so it has clarified the previously unclear approach under English law. Although not entirely free from criticism, the inclusion of party autonomy in the Rome II Regulation recognises the practical importance of the principle outside of contractual obligations, in particular, by permitting commercial parties to be able to submit all obligations to their chosen law in advance.

# Part 3: Rome I and Rome II and the Procedural Treatment and Application of Foreign Law

Traditionally, national courts were primarily concerned with applying national law in order to resolve national disputes. However, thriving international trade, increasing cross-border transactions and the ensuing path towards the European harmonisation and unification of private international law has changed the traditional approach towards the status of foreign law in national courts. In particular, the unification of choice of law rules in the Rome I and Rome II Regulation further paves the way for an ever-increasing application of foreign law in national courts. The result is the growing need to give effect to foreign law where even in purely domestic cases foreign law may be applicable when parties have agreed on that law to govern their contractual or non-contractual obligations. Delicate issues arise concerning the pleading and ascertainment of foreign law, the most frequent questions being:[610] How does foreign law enter the court? Once it is in court, what is the relationship between the law of the forum and the chosen foreign law? How is its substance and meaning determined and proved?

Part A will briefly address these questions exclusively in light of the operation of the parties' choice of foreign law according to Rome I and Rome II. Part B will focus more specifically on the national procedural approaches taken to these issues in German and English courts. The comparative consideration of these questions will highlight that the procedural treatment of foreign law by English and German courts is inconsistent and inadequate and as a result has the potential to undermine the effect of party autonomy. In addition, such discrepancy constitutes an obstacle to the underlying aims of the Rome I and II Regulations, namely of legal certainty, uniformity, and satisfaction of expectations. As such, a uniform approach to the procedural treatment and application of foreign law is required.

---

610 *Sofie Geeroms*, Foreign Law in Civil Litigation. A comparative and functional analysis (2004) 1–2; *Maarit Jänterä-Jareborg*, Foreign Law in National Courts (2003) Recueil des cours Vol. 304 181.

# A. Choice of foreign law

## I. The introduction of the chosen foreign law in court

Generally speaking, foreign law will enter the court via the operation of choice of law rules, which operate where there is a conflict of different laws in the same case. The importance given to the principle of party autonomy in the Rome I and II Regulations now means that even cases concerning little or no international elements may be subject to foreign law where the parties have agreed to the application of that law. Even so, where parties agree on a foreign choice of law to govern their relations, it will often also coincide with a choice of a foreign tribunal in order to ensure the simultaneous application of choice of law and international jurisdiction.[611]

In the past, the general consensus appeared to be that the chosen law should have some connection with the matter before court.[612] The repeated opinion in common law courts and academic commentary was that parties should only be permitted to choose a law, which had a *substantial* connection to the issue in dispute.[613] In the civil law a similar objective connection was considered necessary.[614] Today, it is generally accepted that parties can select an unconnected 'neutral' law to govern their relations.[615] For contractual and non-contractual obligations it has been settled by both

---

611 Also noted by *Gisela Rühl*, Die Kosten der Rechtswahlfreiheit: Zur Anwendung ausländischen Rechts durch deutsche Gerichte RabelsZ Vol. 71 (2007) 559–596, 567.

612 *Peter Nygh*, Autonomy in International Contracts (1999) 55.

613 *ibid*, 55–56. See e.g. *Re Helbert Wagg & Co Ltd* [1956] Ch 323, 341 (per Upjohn J.); *Kay's Leasing Corp v Fletcher* (1964) 64 SR (NSW) 195, 205 (per Walsh J.); *Queensland Estates Pty Ltd v Collas* [1971] Qd R 75, 80–81 (per D.M. Campbell J.) (albeit obiter support). Compare *Vita Food Products Inc v Unus Shipping Co* [1939] AC 277 at 290 in which Lord Wright declared that a connection with the chosen system of law is not as a matter of principle essential. For academic opinion compare: *Frederick A. Mann*, The Proper Law of the Contract (1950) 3 ILQ 60 at 67 who although accepting Lord Wrights statement thought that a 'capricious' choice of law should not be permissible; and see *Peter North/James Fawcett*, Cheshire & North's Private International Law (1987) 454–455.

614 See e.g. *Gerhard Kegel/Klaus Schurig*, Internationales Privatrecht (2004) 653. The authors refer to the need for "some recognisable interest" in the application of the law (*irgendein anerkennenswertes Interesse*), which would be missing in cases involving a purely domestic or national situation.

615 *Gerhard Kegel/Klaus Schurig*, Internationales Privatrecht (2004) 653; *Peter Nygh*, Autonomy in International Contracts (1999) 57. See also *Gisela Rühl*, Die Kosten der Rechtswahlfreiheit: Zur Anwendung ausländischen Rechts durch deutsche Gerichte

the Rome I and Rome II Regulations, which permit the parties to choose whichever law they wish, whether or not it has a connection to their relations. Neither Regulation requires that any factual or physical connection exist between the legal system and their relationship. They clearly allow for the determination of the applicable law based solely on the subjective connection, namely through a choice reached autonomously by the parties pursuant to Article 3 Rome I or Article 14 Rome II.

Article 3(1) of the Rome I Regulation simply states: A contract shall be governed by the law chosen by the parties. There is no requirement that the law chosen have any relevant connection with the parties, their legal relationship or the forum. Although not directly expressed in the Regulation, Article 3(3) Rome I implies that no "other elements relevant to the situation at the time of the choice" need to be located in the country whose law has been chosen. Simply stated, where all other relevant factors except the choice of law are located in another country, the choice of law made by the parties will still be effective, albeit subject to mandatory laws.[616] The Regulation reaches a compromise between the need to protect the principle of party autonomy on the one hand, and on the other, the recognition of those mandatory laws connected to the parties' relationship. In sum, parties may choose any law provided that it does not contravene the application of the provisions, which cannot be derogated from by agreement in the event of a close connection with a single country,[617] imperative norms of Community law,[618] overriding mandatory provisions,[619] or the public policy of the forum[620].

---

RabelsZ Vol. 71 (2007) 559, 567 who notes that German courts are often confronted with the application of a foreign law, particularly in cases concerning contract, marriage or issues concerning names; see examples given at n 30.

616  *Peter Nygh*, Autonomy in International Contracts (1999) 58. According to the *Giuliano & Lagarde* Report the provision is a compromise presenting the least departure from the principle of the parties' freedom of choice, see 18.

617  Article 3(3) Rome I: "Where all other elements relevant to the situation at the time of the choice are located in a country other than the country whose law has been chosen, the choice of the parties shall not prejudice the application of provisions of the law of that other country which cannot be derogated from by agreement." Compare Article 14(2) Rome II Regulation.

618  Article 3(4) Rome I: "Where all other elements relevant to the situation at the time of the choice are located in one or more Member States, the parties' choice of applicable law other than that of a Member State shall not prejudice the application of provisions of Community law, where appropriate as implemented in the Member State of the forum, which cannot be derogated from by agreement." Compare Article 14(3) Rome II Regulation.

619  Article 9 Rome I; compare Article 16 Rome II.

620  Article 21, Rome I; compare Article 26 Rome II.

Similarly, the Rome II Regulation allows parties the freedom to choose any law to govern their non-contractual obligations regardless of relevant connection. Article 14 Rome II states: "The parties may agree to submit non-contractual obligations to the law of their choice". It does not require that a factual or physical connection exist between the legal system and their relationship or the event giving rise to the damage, leaving parties the freedom to choose any law, provided that the mandatory provisions are not derogated from.[621] Mirroring the Rome I Regulation, the choice of law reached by the parties under the Rome II Regulation must not prejudice the application of provisions of the law with which the non-contractual obligation has a close connection,[622] imperative norms of Community law,[623] overriding mandatory provisions,[624] or public policy of the forum[625].

Assuming then that foreign law has entered the court through the parties' choice of law, according to either the Rome I or the Rome II Regulation, the next question is: what is the relevance of the law of the forum?

## II. The significance of the *lex fori*

The law of the judicial forum will not automatically become redundant once it is determined that foreign law is the applicable law. In view of this, to what extent should the forum influence the chosen law and what issues must the *lex fori* determine? According to the Rome Regulations, the identified foreign law will generally govern all substantive issues arising in relation to the contractual or

---

621 *Stefan Leible*, Rechtswahl im IPR der außervertraglichen Schuldverhältnisse nach der Rom II-Verordnung RIW 2008 257, 261.

622 Article 14(2) Rome II: "Where all the elements relevant to the situation at the time when the event giving rise to the damage occurs are located in a country other than the country whose law has been chosen, the choice of the parties shall not prejudice the application of provisions of the law of that other country which cannot be derogated from by agreement.". Compare Article 3(3) Rome I.

623 Article 14(3) Rome II: "Where all the elements relevant to the situation at the time when the event giving rise to the damage occurs are located in one or more of the Member States, the parties' choice of the law applicable other than that of a Member State shall not prejudice the application of provisions of Community law, where appropriate as implemented in the Member State of the forum, which cannot be derogated from by agreement." Compare Article 3(4) Rome I.

624 Article 16 Rome II; compare Article 9 Rome I.

625 Article 26 Rome II; compare Article 21 Rome I.

non-contractual issue before court.[626] However, both Regulations expressly exclude matters of evidence and procedure from their scope and such issues will be required to be determined by the law of the forum.[627] Although matters of evidence and procedure lying outside of the Rome I and Rome II Regulations will not be further dealt with here, it is considered appropriate to examine further issues in relation to the exercise of party autonomy and the significance of the forum.[628]

The preliminary issues that may arise when a court is asked to apply foreign law in accordance with either the Rome I or Rome II Regulation are:

1. whether the parties are permitted to choose a law;
2. issues of interpretation;

---

626 See Article 12 Rome I and Article 15 Rome II. However, neither Regulation characterises issues covered as 'substantive'. On this point in regard to the Rome II Regulation see *Elsabe Schoeman*, Rome II and the substance–procedure dichotomy: crossing the Rubicon [2010] LMCLQ 81.

627 See Articles 1 of both Rome I and Rome II. According to Article 1(3) Rome I, "without prejudice to Article 18" (burden of proof); Article 1(3) Rome II "without prejudice to Articles 21 (formal validity) and 22 (burden of proof)". The excluded matters will not be dealt with further here. For further commentary on these issues, see generally *James Cheshire & North* (14th ed.) 677 *et seq.*; 775 *et seq.*; *Andrew Dickinson*, The Rome II Regulation 156 *et seq.* and *Elsabe Schoeman*, Rome II and the substance–procedure dichotomy: crossing the Rubicon [2010] LMCLQ 81.

628 It is noted that the judicial forum may also be required to consider questions of characterization, in particular: whether the situation is a conflict of laws involving civil and commercial matters (in terms of Articles 1(1) Rome I and 1(1) Rome II); whether the obligation in question arises out of tort/*delict*, unjust enrichment, *negotiorum gestio, culpa in contrahendo* (Article 2(1) Rome II) or contract (Article 1(1) Rome I); whether the case falls within a particular category of non-contractual obligation under Rome II e.g. product liability (Article 5 Rome II), unfair competition (Article 6 Rome II), environmental damage (Article 7 Rome II), infringement of intellectual property rights (Article 8 Rome II), industrial action (Article 9 Rome II), or that the obligation has arisen out of dealings prior to the conclusion of a contract (Article 12 Rome II). Under Rome I, a court may, in the absence of a choice by the parties, be required to categorise the particular type of contract according to Article 4(1) a-h Rome I. It is submitted that issues of characterization should be considered taking account of Recitals (7) of both Regulations, including ECJ rulings, e.g. on Article 5 (1) and (3) *Brussels I* and the Rome Regulations. For more on this, see e.g. *Andrew Dickinson*, The Rome II Regulation Chapter 3 147 *et seq.*; *Janeen Carruthers*, Has the Forum Lost Its Grip? in: *John Ahern/William Binchy* (eds.), The Rome II Regulation on the Law Applicable to Non-Contractual Obligations (2009) 25–46.

3. the extent to which mandatory laws are applicable; and
4. whether or to what extent the public policy of the forum will affect the choice made by the parties (Article 21 Rome I; Article 26 Rome II).

These issues will now be considered in turn.

## 1. Whether the parties are permitted to choose a law

Both Regulations clearly permit parties to choose the applicable law. Therefore, since the Rome I and II Regulations are directly applicable in all Member States,[629] no consent to the choice of applicable law, neither by the judicial forum nor the chosen legal system, is required. As a result, the parties can, once it is established that the specific Regulation is applicable to the dispute, count on their choice of law to be given effect by the forum.

Although the Rome I and II Regulations endeavour to clearly identify the applicable law, both Regulations permit a degree of forum control to displace the prima facie applicable law in cases where the parties' choice may not be permitted. Due to the variable nature and breadth of circumstances that may give rise to both contractual and non-contractual liability, it has been generally accepted that providing for such displacement is inevitable.[630] A mixture of specific rules, coupled with rules of displacement or rules excluding choice of law by the parties, strikes an appropriate and reasonably predictable balance between the competing objectives of certainty and flexibility. As a result, the forum may either be required to displace (not simply in favour of the *lex fori*) the law applicable law in the absence of choice, or, displace the law chosen by the parties.

Where parties have not made a choice, the law applicable in the absence of such may still be displaced through general rules of displacement. The various instances allowing the forum discretion to displace are found, for example, in: Articles 4(3);[631] 5(3);[632] 7(2), second paragraph;[633] and, 8(4)[634] of the Rome I

---

629  Except Denmark, see Recital (46) Rome I and Recital (40) Rome II.
630  *Janeen Carruthers*, Has the Forum Lost Its Grip? in: *John Ahern/William Binchy* (eds.), The Rome II Regulation on the Law Applicable to Non-Contractual Obligations (2009) 2009, 31–32.
631  Applicable law in the absence of choice.
632  Contracts of carriage.
633  Insurance contracts.
634  Individual employment contracts. ("Where it appears from the circumstances as a whole[…]").

Regulation and Articles 4(3);[635] 5(2);[636] 10(4);[637] 11(4);[638] and, 12(2)(c)[639] of the Rome II Regulation. But these provisions do not invariably provide for displacement in favour of the *lex fori*. Instead the provisions use the same formula, namely: "Where it is clear from all the circumstances of the case that the [contract/tort/ *delict*] is manifestly more closely connected with a country other than that indicated in [...], the law of that other country shall apply". Considering that all rules of displacement found in the Rome Regulations are all similarly formulated, it is suggested that all should be applied in a like manner. Commentary on the general escape clause in Article 4(3) Rome II, suggests that such a rule of displacement should be considered as exceptional, requiring strong and clear reasons for displacing the law otherwise applicable.[640] The purpose of these provisions is not to permit recourse to the application of the *lex fori*, but to create the necessary degree of flexibility for situations where the application of one of the specific choice of law rules would not produce an appropriate result[641].

Similarly, where parties *have* made a choice in accordance with Article 3 Rome I or Article 14 Rome II, the forum may also be required to displace the law. The Rome I Regulation carefully regulates the parties' freedom to choose the applicable law for certain contracts. For example, whereas Article 5(1) Rome I grants parties the freedom to choose the applicable law for a contract for the carriage of goods, Article 5(2) stipulates that for contracts for the carriage of passengers, parties may only choose the law of the country listed in points (a) – (e).[642] Article 6(2) Rome I

---

635　'Escape clause' of general rule for torts/*delicts* (Article 4(2) Rome II also provides for displacement in favour of the country of common habitual residence).

636　Product liability (Article 5(1) Rome II also provides for displacement in favour of country of habitual residence of person claimed to be liable or of common habitual residence).

637　Unjust enrichment. (Article 5(1) Rome II also provides for displacement in favour of country of habitual residence of person claimed to be liable or of common habitual residence).

638　Negotiorum gestio.

639　Culpa in contrahendo.

640　*Andrew Dickinson*, The Rome II Regulation, 340 *et seq*. See also *Commission Proposal* 12 (referring to Articles 3(3) of *The Proposal* and 4(5) of the Rome Convention), which states that it should be understood as a "general exception clause which aims to bring a degree of flexibility, enabling the court to adapt the rigid rule to an individual case so as to apply the law that reflect the centre of gravity of the situation."

641　Ministry of Justice (UK), Guidance on the law applicable to contractual obligations (Rome I), of February 2010 at page 6, available at: http://www.justice.gov.uk/publications/contractual-obligations-rome.htm.

642　Article 5(2) Rome I: The parties may choose as the law applicable to a contract for the carriage of passengers in accordance with Article 3 only the law of the country

also limits the parties' choice of law in regards to consumer contracts whereby their choice of law must fulfil the requirements set out in Article 6(1).[643] Article 7 Rome I is a consolidation of the rules contained in the Rome Convention and the Insurance Directive,[644] and includes in Article 7(3) Rome I a list of permissible choices of law aimed at protecting the weaker party to the contract, here the policy holder.[645] Article 8(1) Rome I also regulates a choice of law made by the parties in favour of the employee.[646]

---

where: (a) the passenger has his habitual residence; or (b) the carrier has his habitual residence; or (c) the carrier has his place of central administration; or (d) the place of departure is situated; or (e) the place of destination is situated.

643 Article 6(1) Rome I which states that the contract shall be governed by the law of the country where the consumer has his habitual residence, provided that the professional: (a) pursues his commercial or professional activities in the country where the consumer has his habitual residence, or (b) by any means, directs such activities to that country or to several countries including that country, and the contract falls within the scope of such activities.

644 First Council Directive 73/239/EEC of 24 July 1973 on the coordination of laws, regulations and administrative provisions relating to the taking-up and pursuit of the business of direct insurance other than life assurance (OJ L 228, [16.8.1973]) 3. Directive as last amended by Directive 2005/68/EC of the European Parliament and of the Council (OJ L 323 [9.12.2005]) 1.

645 Article 7(3) Rome I: In the case of an insurance contract other than a contract falling within paragraph 2, only the following laws may be chosen by the parties in accordance with Article 3: (a) the law of any Member State where the risk is situated at the time of conclusion of the contract; (b) the law of the country where the policy holder has his habitual residence; (c) in case of life assurance, the law of the Member State of which the policy holder is a national; (d) for insurance contracts covering risks limited to events occurring in one Member State other than the Member State where the risk is situated, the law of that Member State; (e) where the policy holder of a contract falling under this paragraph pursues a commercial or industrial activity or a liberal profession and the insurance contract covers two or more risks which relate to those activities and are situated in different Member States, the law of any of the Member States concerned or the law of the country of habitual residence of the policy holder. Where in cases set out in points (a), (b) or (e), the Member States referred to grant greater freedom of choice of the law applicable to the insurance contract, the parties may take advantage of that freedom.

646 Article 8(1) Rome I: An individual employment contract shall be governed by the law chosen by the parties in accordance with Article 3. Such a choice of law may not, however, have the result of depriving the employee of the protection afforded to him by provisions that cannot be derogated from by agreement under the law that, in the absence of choice, would have been applicable pursuant to paragraphs 2, 3 and 4 of this Article.

The Rome II Regulation similarly restricts party choice of law for non-contractual obligations and specifically excludes party autonomy for certain non-contractual obligations. Both Articles 6(4) (unfair competition and acts restricting free competition) and 8(3) (infringement of intellectual property rights) of Rome II explicitly state that the law applicable under the Articles may not be derogated from by an agreement pursuant to Article 14. This suggests that parties may choose the law applicable to all other non-contractual obligations covered by the Regulation.[647] In a case where parties have chosen a law derogating from the law applicable under either Article 6 or 8 Rome II, the forum will be required to declare such a choice as invalid.

Any role of the forum is restricted to the consideration of the validity of a choice of law. Any declaration of invalidity or displacement of the chosen law is carefully regulated in both Rome I and Rome II and should not automatically result in the application of the *lex fori*.

## 2. Issues of interpretation

The forum may be required to interpret particular concepts or phrases used in the Rome Regulations. For example, the court may need to resolve whether the parties in fact reached an agreement as to the choice of law. More specifically, in the context of the Rome II Regulation, a court may be required to determine whether according to Article 14(1)(b) Rome II the agreement was 'freely negotiated'. It has already been suggested that issues relating to the parties' consent to the choice of law should be resolved according to the putative proper law,[648] i.e., that the issue should not be resolved according to the requirements under the *lex fori* but rather according to the *lex causae*. This is the approach to be taken under the Rome I Regulation. In Rome I, the forum may be required to determine whether a choice of law has been 'clearly demonstrated' in terms of Article 3(1) Rome I and could include the examination of the extent a jurisdiction clause may be indicative of the parties' choice. Although Recital (12) Rome I attempts to delineate the effect of such a clause,[649] there remains a potential scope for divergent interpretation by the

---

647 Note however, that Article 7 Rome II (Environmental damage) states that the law applicable shall be determined pursuant to Article 4(1) but includes the proviso: "unless the person seeking compensation for damage chooses to base his or her claim on the law of the country in which the event giving rise to the damage occurred."

648 See above under Part 1/B.I.1.b.aa) *The general rule under the Regulation*.

649 See e.g. *Stefan Leible*, Rechtswahl, in: *Franco Ferrari/Stefan Leible* (eds.), Ein neues Internationales Vertragsrecht für Europa – Der Vorschlag für eine Rom I-Verordnung (2007) 41, 44.

forum, especially considering the differing approaches taken by Member States to this issue.[650] However, Article 12(1)(a) Rome I clearly provides that the law applicable to the contract shall govern issues of interpretation. This plainly indicates that the *lex causae* and not the *lex fori* is to govern interpretation. Thus, even where a court is faced with the interpretion or determination of the existence of terms of the contract (e.g in a situation involving a battle of the forms), the application of the *lex causae* should prevail over the *lex fori*. Indeed, no express guidance is given in the Rome I Regulation to this issue specifically and courts have tended to apply the *lex fori* to resolve such issues.[651] But without an autonomous interpretation and strict adherence by courts to the application of the *lex causae* to issues of interpretation, the possibility of a discretionary application of the *lex fori* and its influence on the scope of the parties' choice of law remains.

Recitals (7) of both the Rome I and Rome II Regulations further reference the need to adhere to the principle of an autonomous interpretation of EC law. The recitals instruct that the substantive scope and the provisions of the Regulations should be considered consistent with the Brussels I Regulation and with each other. Therefore, it is submitted that when considering issues of interpretation, the forum should as a matter of course take into account ECJ rulings on interpretation (of e.g. Article 5(1) or (3) Brussels I) as well as relevant rulings on both Rome Regulations.[652] A forum should not confine itself to the ambit of its own law. An approach, ensuring an autonomous interpretation of concepts used within EC Regulations must be taken, particularly when considering the objectives of both Regulations – legal certainty in the European judicial area.[653] Recitals to both Regulations[654]

---

650 Courts in some Member States being more reluctant than English courts to draw an inference in such a case. See *Green Paper* 23–25; *Cheshire & North* (14th ed.) 707.

651 See discussion of this point under Part 1/B.I.1.b.bb) *The exception* and accompanying references.

652 I.e. the decision of courts in Member States, which have applied the Regulations. See, e.g. *Janeen Carruthers*, Has the Forum Lost Its Grip? in: *John Ahern/William Binchy* (eds.), The Rome II Regulation on the Law Applicable to Non-Contractual Obligations (2009) 34; *Cheshire & North* (14th ed.) 675 *et seq.*

653 E.g. Recital (16) Rome I; Recitals (6) and (14) Rome II.

654 E.g. Recitals (11) and (30) Rome II (dealing with the concepts 'non-contractual obligation' and '*culpa in contrahendo*') both recognise that these concepts vary from one Member State to another and instruct that these be interpreted autonomously (but compare Recital (27) Rome II which refers the concept of industrial action to be governed by each Member State's internal rules). Recital (17) and (24) Rome I expressly refer the interpretation of certain concepts to be carried out autonomously with the concepts used in the Brussels I Regulation (but compare Recital (8) Rome I which

similarly support the approach that the concepts used should be interpreted autonomously and not be left to individual treatment by Member States.[655] In sum, courts should not resort to *lex forism* when interpreting the Regulations. Instead courts should consider the three additional factors: First, any relevant decisions of, or opinions of the ECJ on the Rome Regulations and the Brussels Convention and subsequent Brussels I Regulation; secondly, any relevant decisions of courts of other Member States on the Rome Regulations and the Brussels Convention and subsequent Brussels I Regulation;[656] thirdly, the court may consider and rely on commentary (i.e. *Giuliano & Lagarde* Report) and recitals to the Regulations[657] when considering the meaning or effect of any of the provisions. Rather than leaving issues of interpretation open to discretionary treatment by the national rules of Member States, a broad Regulation-based approach promotes legal certainty and uniformity of interpretation of European Community law.[658]

## 3. Whether or to what extent mandatory laws are applicable

It will be for the forum hearing the case to decide whether it must give effect to the mandatory laws or imperative norms provided for in Regulations. These provisions

---

refers relationships having comparable effects to marriage and other family relationships to be interpreted in accordance with the law of the Member State in which the court is seised).

655 See e.g. *Andreas Vogeler*, Die freie Rechtswahl im Kollisionsrecht der ausservertraglichen Schuldverhaeltnisse (2012) 45–51; *Hugh Beale* (ed.), Chitty on Contracts (2012) Vol. 1 30–133; *Andrew Dickinson*, The Rome II Regulation, 122 and at 676 regarded by the authors "as not usually justified" and "a dangerous habit to get into". Compare Article 18 Rome Convention (headed "Uniform interpretation") subsequently dropped; *Giuliano & Lagarde* Report 38.

656 Such decisions (even where appropriate, based on other language versions) will be of persuasive authority.

657 Recitals to the Rome I and II Regulations contain explanations, amplifications (e.g. Recitals (13) Rome I; (8) Rome II) and definitions (e.g. Recitals (8) and (9) Rome I; (9) and (10) Rome II).

658 An autonomous interpretation of concepts to be used in the Regulations is also advocated in *Dicey & Morris* (14th ed.) Vol. II 1803, 1854; and has been approved in *Egon Oldendorff v Libera Corporation (No 2)* [1996] 1 Lloyd's Rep 380, 387 (EWHC) and by the Court of Appeal in *Samcrete Egypt Engineers and Contractors SAE v Land Rover Exports Ltd* [2002] EWCA Civ 2019 [26]-[27] (Potter LJ). See further *Andreas Vogeler*, Die freie Rechtswahl im Kollisionsrecht der ausservertraglichen Schuldverhaeltnisse (2012) 45–51.

expect the forum to interpret: whether a rule of a country in which elements relevant to the situation are located, is mandatory and thus applicable;[659] whether imperative norms of community law require application;[660] and whether the mandatory laws of the forum are applicable[661]. Whether a rule is non-mandatory, mandatory or imperative is a question of interpretation to be resolved by the law of the country of which the rule forms a part.[662] National courts should exercise their discretion so as to give the same effect to the mandatory or imperative rules as the courts of that country would give.[663] Courts should take a restrictive view when considering displacing the rules on applicable law by virtue of the choice of the parties or otherwise prescribed by the Regulations. Recitals (37) Rome I and (32) Rome II both emphasize that provisions providing for the consideration of public interest should provide courts the possibility to apply qualifications to the otherwise applicable law only in "*exceptional circumstances*".[664] Courts may be faced with situations where contradictory mandatory rules of two different countries both purport to be applicable to the parties' relationship, and be required to exercise discretion when making the necessary choice between them.[665]

## 4. Whether or to what extent the public policy of the forum will affect the choice made by the parties be imposed (Article 21 Rome I; Article 26 Rome II)

In addition to the principle that national courts can give effect to mandatory provisions provided for in the Rome Regulations, the forum retains a further power of discretion; namely, the power to displace or limit the effect of a choice of foreign law in order to give effect to the public policy of the forum. The common law doctrine of public policy, or in civil law countries *ordre public*, is considered a

---

659 Articles 3(3) Rome I; 14(2) Rome II. Article 3(3) Rome I was at issue in the case *Caterpillar Financial Services v SNC Passion* [2004] EWHC 569, but held by Cooke J to be inapplicable.

660 Articles 3(4) Rome I; 14(3) Rome II, cf. Case C-381/98 *Ingmar GB Ltd v Eaton Leonard Technologies Inc* [2000] ECR I-9305.

661 Articles 9 Rome I; 16 Rome II.

662 *Christopher Clarkson/Jonathan Hill*, The Conflict of Laws (2011) 231. See further *Christopher Tillman*, The Relationship Between Party Autonomy and the Mandatory Rules in the Rome Convention JBL 2002 45–77, at 49.

663 *Richard Plender/Michael Wilderspin*, The European Contracts Convention (2001) 107.

664 See also *Giuliano & Lagarde* Report 28–30.

665 *ibid*, 30.

well-established familiar exception to choice of law, although reluctantly made use of in English law.[666] Similarly, under the Rome Regulations, the exception of public policy is intended to be of very limited scope and its provisions are to be narrowly construed. Objection cannot be taken to the foreign law as such, but only to its application by the forum in the particular case.[667] In other words, the foreign law chosen by the parties will not be rendered ineffective, but will be displaced to the extent that it conflicts with the forums' *ordre public*.[668]

The use of the words "manifestly incompatible" in both Articles 21 Rome I and 26 Rome II, read together with the words "exceptional circumstances" in Recitals (37) Rome I and (32) Rome II,[669] clearly indicate that use of public policy to displace the foreign law should be rare. However, precisely what will fall under the concept public policy will be determined according to the law of the forum and not according to European Community law.[670] Although this undoubtedly leaves national courts a significant amount of scope when determining the meaning of the concept, the ECJ retains full jurisdiction to control the application of the notion

---

666  See *Cheshire & North* (14th ed.) 741, 852, 1018–1023; *Richard Fentiman*, Foreign Law in English Courts (1998) 108–109. See e.g. *Ralli Bros. v Compania Naviera Sota y Aznar* [1920] 2 KB 287 (CA); *Rossano v Manufacturers' Life Insurance Co* [1963] 2 QB 352 (QBD). But compare more recently *Duarte v Black and Decker Corp* [2007] EWHC 2720 (QB), [2008] 1 All ER (Comm) 401, at [56]-[63]. The case is an example of English courts not enforcing a restrictive covenant that is contrary to the English doctrine of restraint of trade even when the parties have made an express choice of foreign law.

667  *David McCleen/Kish Beevers*, The Conflict of Laws (2009) 391; *Cheshire & North* (14th ed.) 741, 852.

668  *Christoph Reithmann/Dieter Martiny* (eds.), Internationales Vertragsrecht (2010) 132; *Martiny*, in: MünchKomm (5th ed.) Vol. 10 Art. 3 Rom I-VO, IX marginal no. 2. Compare Judgment of *LG* Berlin 9.11.1994, NJW-RR 1995, 754 = IPRspr. 1994 Nr. 42.

669  Recital (32) Rome II provides an example of public policy in relation to non-contractual obligations: "[…] In particular, the application of a provision of the law designated by the Regulation which would have the effect of causing non-compensatory exemplary or punitive damages of an excessive nature to be awarded may, depending on the circumstances of the case and the legal order of the Member State of the court seised, be regarded as being contrary to the public policy (*ordre public*) of the forum."

670  *Stefan Leible/Matthias Lehmann*, Die Verordnung über das auf vertragliche Schuldverhältnisse anzuwendende Recht (Rom I), RIW 2008, 543. However, it would appear to defeat the purpose of the Regulations to invoke public policy on the basis that there is so equivalent cause of action under the *lex fori*: *Cheshire & North* (14th ed.) 854. See e.g. English authority *Phrantzes v Argenti* [1960] 2 QB 19.

of public policy in any particular case where it was invoked.[671] Presumably, the forum may also invoke public policy in order to override provisions that cannot be derogated from by agreement under Article 3(3) Rome I and 14(2) Rome II.[672] As a result, a minimal amount of discretion by the forum is retained to enable the court to refuse application of objectionable mandatory rules of a foreign country on the basis that the application of the mandatory rule would be against the public policy of the forum.

# B. Introduction and ascertainment of foreign law in national courts

It is apparent from the previous sections that according to the Rome I and Rome II Regulation parties may choose any foreign law to govern their dispute. It has also been established that the national court, in applying the foreign law may potentially influence the extent to which the *lex causae* is applied. Assuming then, that foreign law is in issue in court, how is its substance and meaning to be determined? More specifically, who may establish and prove the parties' choice of foreign law; and, are the parties required to introduce (plead) foreign law? These issues are not easily resolved and are exacerbated by the fact that neither Rome Regulations expressly address any of these issues.[673] Moreover, the legal systems of the Member States follow widely differing practices in relation to the classification of issues

---

671 *Case C-7/98 Krombach v Bamberski* [2000] ECR I-1935; [2001] QB 709 at [22] (recourse to the public policy exception could be envisaged only if recognition or enforcement constitutes a manifest breach of a rule of law regarded as essential or as a fundamental right in the legal forum; Case C-38/98 *Régie Nationale des Usines Renault SA v Maxicar SpA* [2000] ECR I-2973 at [27] (equality of national and Community law). The forum may also be guided by the case law of the European Court of Human Rights.

672 *Cheshire & North* (14th ed.) 741, 852 *et seq.*

673 Compare Articles 12 and 13 and Recital (20) of the European Parliament's Position 2005 proposing a partial harmonisation of the Member States' rules for pleading and proof of the applicable law under the Regulation. These proposals were subsequently rejected by the Commission in its Amended Proposal. Instead, following the insertion and deletion of several other Articles and Recitals dealing with introduction and ascertainment, the conciliation process resulted in the insertion of Article 30 (Review clause) in the Rome II Regulation with the specific requirement that the Commission consider the treatment of foreign law. Accordingly, see project JLS/CJ/2007-I/03, Principles for a Future EU Regulation on the Application of Foreign Law (Madrid Principles).

such as the introduction and proof (ascertainment) of foreign law as substantive or procedural.[674] It is questionable then, to which extent the EC conflict-of-laws regulations can provide complete uniformity in practice.[675] A uniform approach to the application of foreign law in the form of a European Regulation is advocated.

# I. Germany

## 1. General

Unlike in many other legal systems, in Germany the ascertainment and application of foreign law is principally the same as the ascertainment and application of the *lex fori*. The starting point is that the ascertainment of foreign law is considered to be a question of 'law' as opposed to 'fact'.[676] This means that the parties are neither

---

674 See generally, *Richard Fentiman*, Foreign Law in English Courts (1998); *Thomas Rogoz*, Ausländisches Recht im deutschen und englischen Zivilprozess (2008); *Rainer Hausmann*, Pleading and Proof of Foreign Law – A Comparative Analysis, EuL Forum (1/2008); *Trevor Hartley*, Pleading and Proof of Foreign Law: The Major European Systems Compared 45 ICLQ (1996) 271; *Andrew Dickinson*, The Rome II Regulation 598–600; *Hartmut Ost*, EVÜ und Fact Doctrine: Konflikte zwischen europäischer IPR-Vereinheitlichung und der Stellung ausländischen Rechts im angelsächsischen Zivilprozess (1996) 41–113; *Maarit Jänterä-Jareborg*, Foreign Law in National Courts Recueil des cours (2003) Vol. 304, 181. Differences exist not only between common law and civil law, but also within civil law approaches, see *Sofie Geeroms*, Foreign Law in Civil Litigation. A comparative and functional analysis (2004) 389 *et seq.* (not further expounded here).

675 *Urs Peter Gruber/Ivo Bach*, The Application of Foreign Law: A progress report on a new European project (2009) YBPIL Vol. 11 157–169, 158.

676 *Christian v. Bar/Peter Mankowski*, Internationales Privatrecht Band 1: Allgemeine Lehren (2003) § 5, marginal no. 96; *Reinhold Geimer*, Internationales Zivilprozessrecht (2009) marginal no. 2577; *Richard Zöller/Reinhold Geimer*, Zivilprozessordnung (30th ed.) § 293 marginal no. 14; *Bernd v. Hoffmann/Karsten Thorn*, Internationales Privatrecht (2007) § 3 marginal no. 134; *Jan Kropholler*, Internationales Privatrecht (2006) 644; *Joachim Gruber*, Die Anwendung ausländischen Rechts durch deutsche Gerichte ZRPol 1992, 6; *Gerhard Kegel/Klaus Schurig*, Internationales Privatrecht (2004) 500 *et seq.*; *Hanns Prütting*, in: MünchKomm-ZPO Vol. 1 3rd ed. 2008 § 293 marginal no. 1 14; *Eberhard Schilken*, Zur Rechtsnatur der Ermittlung ausländischen Rechts nach § 293 ZPO FS Schumann 2001 373, 374 *et seq.*; *Gisela Rühl*, Die Kosten der Rechtswahlfreiheit: Zur Anwendung ausländischen Rechts durch deutsche Gerichte RabelsZ Vol. 71 (2007) 559, 568; *Andreas Spickhoff*, Fremdes Recht vor inländischen Gerichten: Rechts- oder Tatfrage? ZZP 112 (1999) 265; *Johann Kindl*,

obliged to introduce nor prove the applicable foreign law.[677] The general opinion is that courts must apply foreign law *ex officio*, i.e. by their own motion (*Grundsatz der Amtsermittlung*).[678] In other words, because foreign law is a question of law,

Ausländisches Recht vor deutschen Gerichten ZZP 111 (1998) 177, 179. This is also the approach taken in Austria, Switzerland and Italy, see *Andreas Spickhoff*, Fremdes Recht vor inländischen Gerichten: Rechts- oder Tatfrage? ZZP 112 (1999) 265, 284 *et seq*. See also other civil law countries that classify foreign law as law: Austria (§ 3 PILA); Belgium (Art. 15 § 1 PILA); Czech Republic (Art. 53 PILA); Estonia (Art. 2 Code of PIL); Greece (Art. 337 Code of civil procedure); the Netherlands (Art. 25 Code of civil procedure); Romania (Art. 7 Law No 105/1992); Slovakia (Art. 53 PILA); Slovenia (Art. 12(1) PILA).

677 See e.g. *Bundesgerichtshof* judgment of 23.12.1981, NJW 1982, 1215, 1216; *Bundesgerichtshof* judgment of 24.11.1960, NJW 1961, 410; *Reinhold Geimer*, Internationales Zivilprozessrecht (2009) marginal no. 2588; *Andreas Heldrich*, Probleme bei der Ermittlung ausländischen Rechts in der gerichtlichen Praxis FS Nakamura (1996) 243, 244; *Johann Kindl*, Ausländisches Recht vor deutschen Gerichten ZZP 111 (1998) 177, 180; *Christian v. Bar/Peter Mankowski*, Internationales Privatrecht Band 1: Allgemeine Lehren (2003) § 5.

678 *Jan Kropholler*, Internationales Privatrecht (2006) 212 *et seq.*, and 45–46. See *Fritz Sturm*, Fakultatives Kollisionsrecht: Notwendigkeit und Grenzen in FS Zweigert 1981 329; *Peter-Christian Müller-Graf*, Fakultatives Kollisionsrecht im Internationalen Wettbewerbsrecht? 48 RabelsZ (1984) 289; *Th. de Boer*, Facultative Choice of Law, The Procedural Status of Choice of Law Rules and Foreign Law Rec. des Cours (1996-I) 223, 303–385; *Lorenz Fastrich*, Revisibilität der Ermittlung ausländischen Rechts ZZP 97 (1984) 423, 425; *Johann Kindl*, Ausländisches Recht vor deutschen Gerichten ZZP 111 (1998) 177, 179; *Andreas Spickhoff*, Fremdes Recht vor inländischen Gerichten: Rechts- oder Tatfrage? ZZP 112 (1999) 265, 272; *Clemens Trautmann*, Ausländisches Recht vor deutschen und englischen Gerichten ZEuP 2006 283, 287; *Utz Küster*, Zur richterlichen Ermessensausübung bei der Ermittlung ausländischen Rechts RIW 1998 275; *Peter Mankowski/Ralf Kerfack*, Arrest, Einstweilige Verfügung und die Anwendung ausländsichen Rechts (1990) IPRax 372. Also established in case law, see e.g.: *Bundesgerichtshof* judgments of 23.6.2003, NJW 2003, 2685, 2686; 30.1.2001, WM 2001, 502, 503; 19.9.2001, NJW 2002, 1209; 15.12.1986, WM 1987, 273, 274; 20.3.1980, BGHZ 77, 32, 38; 30.3.1976, NJW 1976, 1581, 1583; 23.6.1964, NJW, 2012. But compare the opposing opinions, similar to the English approach, advocating a 'facultative' application of choice of law rules – i.e. courts should apply foreign law only if and when the parties choose to do so. Instead courts should prefer the application of the *lex fori*, which furthers the parties' interest and provides a more effective form of judicial litigation. See in particular, *Axel Flessner*, Fakultatives Kollisionsrecht 34 RabelsZ (1970) 547, 581 *et seq.*; *Axel Flessner*, Interessenjurisprudenz im IPR (1990) 119 *et seq.*; critically *Klaus Schurig*, Interessenjurisprudenz contra Interessenjurisprudenz im IPR – Anmerkungen zu Flessners Thesen

a court must apply it even if the parties have failed to raise its application.[679] This approach is an expression of the recognition that a foreign legal system, and those foreign laws, are on par with the court's national laws. The only provision in the German Civil Procedure Code (*Zivilprozessordnung* – "ZPO") dealing with foreign law and its application in German courts is paragraph 293 ZPO.[680] Although a literal reading of paragraph 293 ZPO does not impose an express duty on the judge to ascertain the content of the law *ex officio*, the prevailing opinion both in practice[681] and theory[682] appears to assume such. Such a duty is instead deduced from the civil law maxims *iura novit curia* (the judge knows the law) and *da mihi factum dabo tibi ius* (give me the facts; I will give you the law).[683]

---

RabelsZ 59 (1995) 229, 243; also discussed in *Thomas Rogoz*, Ausländisches Recht im deutschen und englischen Zivilprozess (2008) 71–74.

679 *Dieter Leipold*, in: *Christian Berger* (et al.), Stein & Jonas, Kommentar zur Zivilprozessordnung Vol. 4 (2008) § 293 marginal no. 31. Compare the German law traditional approach where omission to plead a law amounts to the choice of German law as the applicable law. See e.g. *Bundesgerichtshof* judgment of 15.1.1986 (1986) IPRax 292; *Bundesgerichtshof* judgment of 18.1.1988, NJW 1988, 1592. Critically *Haimo Schack*, Keine stillschweigende Rechtswahl im Prozeß! (1986) IPRax 272, 292; *Christian von Bar*, Internationales Privatrecht Vol. II (1991).

680 See also paragraph 545 ZPO, which provides that an appeal to the German *BGH* on questions of law can only be based on federal law, i.e. not foreign law (principle of irrevisibility of foreign law). See *Bundesgerichtshof* judgments of 14.12.1958, ZZP 71 1958, 363; 14.4.1969, WM 1969, 858; 27.4.1976, NJW 1976, 1588, 1589; 30.4.1992, NJW 1992, 2026, 2029; 23.6.2003, NJW 2003, 2685, 2686.

681 See the stance taken in the *Bundesgerichtshof* judgment of 7.4.1993, NJW 1993, 2305. Also *Bundesgerichtshof* judgment of 13.12.2005, NJW 2006, 762, 764; 25.1.2005, NJW-RR 2005, 1071, 1072; 23.6.2003, NJW 2003, 2685, 2686, referring to the earlier judgments from 21.2.1962, NJW 1962, 961 and 20.3.1980, BGHZ 77, 32 = NJW 1980, 2022.

682 *Reinhold Geimer*, Internationales Zivilprozessrecht (2009) marginal no. 2577; *Gerhard Kegel/Klaus Schurig*, Internationales Privatrecht (2004) §15 II; *Richard Zöller/ Reinhold Geimer*, Zivilprozessordnung (30th ed.) §293 marginal no. 9a; *Jan Kropholler*, Internationales Privatrecht (2006) § 59 I 1 626; *Johann Kindl*, Ausländisches Recht vor deutschen Gerichten ZZP 111 (1998) 177, 179; *Lorenz Fastrich*, Revisibilität der Ermittlung ausländischen Rechts ZZP 97 (1984) 423, 425; *Günter Otto*, Der verunglückte §293 ZPO und die Ermittlung ausländischen Rechts durch „Beweiserhebung" (1995) IPRax 299, 301.

683 These maxims have been incorporated into the German Constitution (*Grundgesetz/ GG*); see Section 20(3) GG, '*Bindung an Recht und Gesetz*' (Courts are bound to decide according to the law and statutes). See *Bundesgerichtshof* judgment of 23.6.2003, NJW 2003, 2685, 2686; 19.9.2001, NJW 2002, 1209. Further, *Winfried Kralik*, Iura Novit

This approach requires courts to take judicial notice of foreign law. This means that the court has or is deemed to have knowledge of foreign law. To say that a court has judicial notice does not impute actual or presumed knowledge of its content, but instead it is assumed that once the court acknowledges the applicability of foreign law, the court has the *capacity and means* to know its content.[684] Not only is a German judge required to ascertain the relevant foreign laws, but also to apply it the same way as it is in its country of origin.[685] According to paragraph 293 ZPO, in order to establish the content of foreign law a court is not required to carry out the taking of evidence in a strict sense. This assessment corresponds to the application of foreign law as 'law' as opposed to 'fact'. Instead, paragraph 293 ZPO provides that foreign law must only be evidenced to the extent that it is unknown to the court. But paragraph 293 ZPO does not stipulate the manner in which this is to be done. The provision merely provides that in ascertaining the foreign law, the court is authorised to consult all available sources and is not confined to information provided by the parties or strict rules of formal proof.[686] Available sources

---

Curia und das ausländische Recht, 3 ZfRV 75 (1962) 75; *Lorenz Fastrich*, Revisibilität der Ermittlung ausländischen Rechts ZZP 97 (1984) 423; *Utz Küster*, Zur richterlichen Ermessensausübung bei der Ermittlung ausländischen Rechts RIW 1998 275; *Reinhold Geimer*, Internationales Zivilprozessrecht (2009) marginal no. 2577; *Richard Zöller/Reinhold Geimer*, Zivilprozessordnung (30th ed.) §293 marginal no. 10; *Gisela Rühl*, Die Kosten der Rechtswahlfreiheit: Zur Anwendung ausländischen Rechts durch deutsche Gerichte RabelsZ Vol. 71 (2007) 559, 568–569; *Ulrich Drobnig*, The use of foreign law by German Courts, in: *Erik Jayme* (ed.), German National Reports in Civil Matters for the XIVth Congress of Comparative Law, Athens, 1994, 5 *et seq.*; *Axel Flessner*, Diskriminierung von grenzübergreifenden Rechtsverhältnissen im europäischen Zivilprozess ZeuP 14 (2006) 737 *et seq.*; *Hilmar Krüger*, Zur Ermittlung ausländischen Rechts in Deutschland: Ein Bericht aus der Praxis FS Nomer 2003 357 *et seq.*

684 § 293 ZPO. See also *Hanns Prütting*, in: MünchKomm-ZPO Vol. 1 § 293 marginal no. 3 *et seq.*; *Dieter Leipold*, in: *Christian Berger* (et al.), Stein & Jonas, Kommentar zur Zivilprozessordnung Vol. 4 (2008) § 293 ZPO; *Sofie Geerooms*, Foreign Law in Civil Litigation. A comparative and functional analysis (2004) 92–99; *Thomas Rogoz*, Ausländisches Recht im deutschen und englischen Zivilprozess (2008) 69 *et seq.*

685 Having regard to foreign judicial interpretations or rulings; *Richard Zöller/Reinhold Geimer*, Zivilprozessordnung (30th ed.) §293 marginal no. 24. See *Bundesgerichtshof* judgments of 27.4.1976, 1588, 1589; 24.3.1987, NJW 1988, 648; 21.1.1991, NJW 1991, 1418, 1419; 8.5.1992, NJW 1992, 3106; 30.1.2001, WM 2001, 502, 503 = IPRax 2002, 302; 23.6.2003, NJW 2003, 2685, 2686.

686 According to § 293 ZPO, second sentence: "[…] Bei Ermittlung dieser Rechtsnormen ist das Gericht auf die von den Parteien beigebrachten Nachweise nicht beschränkt; es ist befugt, auch andere Erkenntnisquellen zu benutzen und zum Zwecke einer solchen

may include: available literature on that foreign law; academics or professionals; informal advice (e.g. from embassies, consulates or ministries); expert advisory opinions; or, requiring the parties to assist.[687] In practice therefore, it will be within the judge's discretionary power to decide what method of procedural inquiry into the foreign law will be carried out, but only to the extent that the foreign law is unknown to the court.[688]

---

Benutzung das Erforderliche anzuordnen." *Rainer Hüßtege*, Zur Ermittlung ausländischen Rechts: Wie man in den Wald hineinruft, so hallt es auch zurück (2002) IPRax 292, 293; *Erhard Huzel*, Zur Zulässigkeit eines „Auflagenbeschlusses" im Rahmen des §293 ZPO (1990) IPRax 77, 78–79; Utz Küster, Zur richterlichen Ermessensausübung bei der Ermittlung ausländischen Rechts RIW 1998 275; *Hanns Prütting*, in: MünchKomm-ZPO, Vol. 1, 2008 § 293 marginal no. 3; *Günter Otto*, Der verunglückte §293 ZPO und die Ermittlung ausländischen Rechts durch „Beweiserhebung" (1995) IPRax 299.

687  For more on the specific sources used see, *Richard Zöller/Reinhold Geimer*, Zivilprozessordnung (30th ed.) § 293 marginal nos. 15, 20; *Rainer Hüßtege*, Zur Ermittlung ausländischen Rechts: Wie man in den Wald hineinruft, so hallt es auch zurück (2002) IPRax 292, 293; *Hanns Prütting* in: MünchKomm-ZPO Vol. 10 2007 § 293 marginal no. 4, 23, *et seq.*; *Heinz-Peter Mansel*, Vollstreckung eines französischen Garantieurteils (1995) IPRax 362, 365; *Eberhard Schilken*, Zur Rechtsnatur der Ermittlung ausländischen Rechts nach § 293 ZPO FS Schumann 2001 373, 376; *Gisela Rühl*, Die Kosten der Rechtswahlfreiheit: Zur Anwendung ausländischen Rechts durch deutsche Gerichte RabelsZ Vol. 71 (2007) 559, 569–570. Advisory opinions (*Rechtsgutachten*) are provided on foreign legal issues, one of the main suppliers of such opinions being the Max Plank Institute for Comparative and International Law in Hamburg. Critically *Paul Heinrich Neuhaus/Jan Kropholler*, Entwurf eines Gesetzes über Internationales Privat- und Verfahrensrecht RabelsZ 44 (1980) 340; *Jürgen Samtleben*, Der unfähige Gutachter und die ausländische Rechtspraxis NJW 1992 3057, 3058; *Angelika Fuchs*, Die Ermittlung ausländischen Rechts durch Sachverständige RIW 1995 807 *et seq.*; *Johann Kindl*, Ausländisches Recht vor deutschen Gerichten ZZP 111 (1998) 177, 187. See also *Bundesgerichtshof* judgments of 21.01.1991 – II ZR 50/90, NJW 1991 1418. Compare the European Convention on Information on Foreign law from 7 June 1968, entered into effect in Germany 19 March 1975, BGBl. 1975 II, 300 (see *Auslands-Rechtsauskunftsgesetz*: AuRAG from 5 July 1974, BGBl. 1974 I, 1433). On this Convention see: *Serge-Daniel Jastrow*, Zur Ermittlung ausländischen Rechts: Was leistet das Londoner Auskunftsübereinkommen in der Praxis (2004) IPRax 402 *et seq.*; *Dirk Schellack*, Selbstermittlung oder ausländische Auskunft unter dem europäischen Rechtsauskunftsübereinkommen (1998) 136–164.

688  See first sentence of § 293 ZPO: "Das in einem anderen Staat geltende Recht, die Gewohnheitsrechte und Statuten bedürfen des Beweises nur insofern, als sie dem Gericht unbekannt sind."Compare Bundesgerichtshof judgments of 30.3.1976, IPRspr 1976 No 2, p 8 = NJW 1976, 1581; 30.4.1992, BGHZ 118, 151, 163; 8.11.1994, NJW 1995,

## 2. Failure to plead or prove the content of foreign law

It is disputed whether an implied choice of law can be inferred from the fact that neither party pleads foreign law but instead relies on German substantive law despite strong foreign elements. In such cases, German courts have tended to infer an implied choice of German law,[689] an approach that has been largely criticised in German literature.[690] Instead it has been advocated that it should be the duty of the judge according to paragraph 139 ZPO to draw the parties' attention to the assumed inferred intention to choose German law as the *lex causae*.[691]

A subsequent problem is what will happen in a situation where despite exhausting all possible sources the content of foreign law is unascertainable. In fact, it will almost always be practically possible to determine the content of foreign law. Thus, although this issue may seem purely theoretical in nature, courts may still in practice hold for reasons of complexity, disproportionate cost or unreasonable delay that a foreign law is unascertainable.[692] Neither the German conflict-of-law

---

1032; 23.4.2002, BGH NJW-RR 2002, 1359, 1360. German courts are supported by an established infrastructure offering opinions on foreign legal laws. See further *Jan Kropholler*, Internationales Privatrecht (2006) 645–646; *Klaus Sommerlad/ Joachim Schrey*, Die Ermittlung ausländischen Rechts im Zivilprozeß und die Folgen der Nichtermittlung NJW 1991 1377, 1378 *et seq.*, *Johann Kindl*, Ausländisches Recht vor deutschen Gerichten ZZP 111 (1998) 177, 182 *et seq.*; *Gisela Rühl*, Die Kosten der Rechtswahlfreiheit: Zur Anwendung ausländischen Rechts durch deutsche Gerichte RabelsZ Vol. 71 (2007) 559, 569; *Peter Mankowski/Ralf Kerfack*, Arrest, Einstweilige Verfügung und die Anwendung ausländischen Rechts (1990) IPRax 372; *Hanns Prütting* in: MünchKomm-ZPO Vol. 10 2007 § 293 marginal no. 16.

689 *Bundesgerichtshof* judgments of 28.11.1963, BGHZ 40, 320, 323; 27.3.1968, BGHZ 50, 32, 33; 23.10.1970, NJW 1971, 30.9.1987, NJW-RR 1988, 159, 160; 323, 324; 12.12.1990, NJW 1991, 1292, 1293; 28.1.1992, NJW 1992, 1380; 21.10.1992, NJW, 1993, 385, 386; 12.5.1993, NJW 1993, 2753; 20.9.1995, BGHZ 130, 371. Also judgments from the German *Oberlandesgericht* Hamm from 9.6.1995, NJW-RR 1996, 179; Düsseldorf 19.12.1997, NJW-RR 1998, 1716.

690 See e.g. *Haimo Schack*, Rechtswahl im Prozeß? NJW 1984 2737, 2738; *Axel Steiner*, Die Stillschweigende Rechtswahl im Prozess im System der subjektiven Anknüpfungen im deutschen internationalen Privatrecht (1988); *Heinz-Peter Mansel*, Kollisions- und zuständigkeitsrechtlicher Gleichlauf der vertraglichen und deliktischen Haftung – zugleich ein Beitrag zur Rechtswahl durch Prozessverhalten ZVglRWiss 86 (1987) 12.

691 *Gerhard Wagner*, Fakultatives Kollisionsrecht und prozessuale Parteiautonomie ZEuP 1999 6, 44.

692 See principle pronounced in the Bundesgerichtshof judgment of 26.10.1977, BGHZ 69, 387 = NJW 1978, 496: Wenn das ausländische Recht "nicht oder nur

rules, nor the German ZPO regulate this matter. Instead, a myriad of views have developed in practice and theory as to the best way to resolve such a situation.[693] Of these views, two contrasting views have crystallised in case law and literature. According to the German BGH, courts may apply the *lex fori* as "*Ersatzrecht*" (substitute law) in cases where there are significant national connections and no objection from the parties involved. This is based on the view that it is better to correctly apply the law of the forum than to wrongly apply foreign law. The majority of academic opinion doubts an approach where courts simply resort to the familiar *lex fori*.[694] Instead, the "*nächstverwandte Recht*" (most closely related law), most likely applicable law, or general comparative law or conflict-of-law principles should be applied.[695] It has also been suggested, in order to promote

---

mit unverhältnismäßigem Aufwand und erheblicher Verfahrensverzögerung feststellbar" ist. Confirmed by Bundesgerichtshof judgment of 23.12.1981, NJW 1982, 1215, 1216. Foreign law may also be unascertainable for reasons such as contrary to ordre public or when a situation involving limping legal relations would arise, for exceptions to this general rule see further Jan Kropholler, Internationales Privatrecht (2006) 215–221.

693 *Johann Kindl*, Ausländisches Recht vor deutschen Gerichten ZZP 111 (1998) 177, 196; *Karl Kreuzer*, Einheitsrecht als Ersatzrecht: Zur Frage der Nichtermittelbarkeit fremden Rechts, in NJW 1983 1943, *Dirk Schellack*, Selbstermittlung oder ausländische Auskunft unter dem europäischen Rechtsauskunftsübereinkommen (1998) 236; *Nils Jansen/Ralf Michaels*, Die Auslegung und Fortbildung ausändischen Rechts ZZP 116 (2003) 3; *Jürgen Samtleben*, Der unfähige Gutachter und die ausländische Rechtspraxis NJW 1992 3057, 3062.

694 *Gerhard Kegel/Klaus Schurig*, Internationales Privatrecht (2004) §15 V 2 512; *Karl Kreuzer*: Einheitsrecht als Ersatzrecht: Zur Frage der Nichtermittelbarkeit fremden Rechts, in NJW 1983 1943, 1946. However, approval of the approach of the *BGH* can also be found in the literature. See e.g. *Christian v. Bar/Peter Mankowski*, Internationales Privatrecht Band 1: Allgemeine Lehren (2003) § 5, marginal no. 104; *Jan Kropholler*, Internationales Privatrecht (2006) 216 *et seq.*; *Axel Flessner*, Interessenjurisprudenz im IPR (1990) 119, 125.

695 See e.g. *Gerhard Kegel/Klaus Schurig*, Internationales Privatrecht (2004) §15 V 2 512; *Karl Kreuzer*, Einheitsrecht als Ersatzrecht: Zur Frage der Nichtermittelbarkeit fremden Rechts, in NJW 1983 1943, 1946; *Reinhold Geimer*, Internationales Zivilprozessrecht (2009) marginal n. 2600; *Karl Kreuzer*, Einheitsrecht als Ersatzrecht: Zur Frage der Nichtermittelbarkeit fremden Rechts, in NJW 1983 1943, 1946; *Johann Kindl*, Ausländisches Recht vor deutschen Gerichten ZZP 111 (1998) 177, 200; *Dirk Schellack*, Selbstermittlung oder ausländische Auskunft unter dem europäischen Rechtsauskunftsübereinkommen (1998) 242; *Hein Kötz*, Allgemeine Rechtsgrundsätze als Ersatzrecht RabelsZ 34 (1970) 663, 671; approaches also summarised in *Thomas Rogoz*, Ausländisches Recht im deutschen und englischen Zivilprozess (2008) 96–100.

legal certainty, that the process of ascertaining a substitute law, in cases where the foreign law is not sufficiently ascertainable, should be defined by law in accordance with German conflict-of-law rules and only where this is not possible, resort to the *lex fori*.[696]

## 3. Foreign law chosen in accordance with Rome I or Rome II

A mandatory *ex officio* approach to the application of a law chosen by the parties assumes that a German court will know, or have the means to know the content of national law, including private international law and civil procedure; European law; public international law and foreign laws. As a result, where parties have made a choice of foreign law according to either the Rome I or Rome II Regulation, the court will be required to take notice of the Regulations and apply the applicable law in accordance with them. However, where parties have not made an express choice of law, German courts tend to infer a choice of German law based on the parties' reliance on the *lex fori* during proceedings. In view of this approach taken by the courts, where the parties have not made an express choice according to Article 3(1) Rome I or Article 14(1) Rome II, German courts are likely to apply German law under the guise of an implied choice of law.

# II. England

## 1. General

Embedded in the English common law adversarial system, is the rule that the parties control and shape the nature of disputes.[697] It is traditionally for parties to establish the facts and provide the evidence to prove those facts. The English approach starts from the assumption that 'foreign laws are facts'. The traditional justification for such an approach starts from the premise that an English court knows nothing of foreign law and so must be informed of its content. In order to be informed, a court requires the parties to lead evidence of foreign law. Because foreign law is established according to the rules of evidence and parties must

---

696  See e.g. suggestion made in *Paul Heinrich Neuhaus/Jan Kropholler*, Entwurf eines Gesetzes über Internationales Privat- und Verfahrensrecht RabelsZ 44 (1980) 340.

697  *Richard Fentiman*, Foreign Law in English Courts (1998) 266; see generally *Sofie Geeroms*, Foreign Law in Civil Litigation. A comparative and functional analysis (2004) 14–25.

164

plead[698] it in the same way as any other fact, it therefore becomes a matter of fact.[699] What follows from this is that foreign law can only enter the court if at least one party raises its applicability.[700] Once raised, establishing foreign law is a matter of evidence and a party wishing to rely on the choice of foreign law is required to not only plead but also to prove foreign law, generally by expert evidence.[701] In contrast to German law, an English judge has neither the power nor the duty to

---

698    The term 'pleading' has been replaced by the term 'statement of case' and is regulated by Part 16 of the Civil Procedure Rules 1998 (CPR) and its accompanying Practice Direction (CPR PD 16).

699    English courts have upheld the fact doctrine as reliable and convincing, see e.g. *Mostyn v Fabrigas* (1774) 1 Cowp 161, 174, (per Lord Mansfield); compare, *Bumper Development Corp v Commissioner of Police* [1991] 1 WLR 1362, 1368; *MCC Proceeds Inc v Bishopsgate Investment Trust plc* [1999] CLC 417 (CA); *Morgan Grenfell & Co Ltd v SACE – Istituto per I Servici Assicurativi del Commercio* [2001] EWCA Civ 1932, at [45]-[52]. See also *Albert V. Dicey*, Conflict of Laws (1908) 23 in which Dicey presents the 'vested rights theory', offering a new justification for the qualification of foreign law as fact. But although English courts have sometimes taken a strict view of the fact doctrine it has also been recognised that the legal character of foreign laws makes them different from normal facts, see e.g. *Dicey & Morris* (15th ed.) Vol. I, 318 and authorities at n 4. See also *Richard Fentiman*, Laws, Foreign Laws, and Facts Current Legal Problems 2006 Vol. 59 391, 396; *Richard Fentiman*, Foreign Law in English Courts (1998) 173, and authorities at fn 1; *Andrew Dickinson*, The Rome II Regulation 598–599.

700    *Ascherberg, Hopwood & Crew Limited v Casa Musicale Sonzogno* [1971] WLR 173, 178; *Dicey & Morris* (15th ed.) Vol. I, 319; *Richard Fentiman*, Foreign Law in English Courts (1998) 3–4; *Trevor Hartley*, Pleading and Proof of Foreign Law: The Major European Systems Compared 45 ICLQ (1996) 271, 282–289. Also *Cheshire & North* (14th ed.) 111 *et seq.*; *Dicey & Morris* (15th ed.) Chapter 9; *Richard Fentiman*, Foreign Law in English Courts (1998) 3–6.

701    King of Spain v Machado (1827) 4 Russ 225, 239; Ascherberg, Hopwood & Crew Ltd v Casa Musicale Sonzogno [1971] 1 WLR 173, 1128 (CA); Morgan Grenfell & Co Ltd v SACE – Istituto per I Servici Assicurativi del Commercio [2001] EWCA Civ 1932, at [45]-[52]. But note that a more flexible 'legalist' approach has acknowledged the special status of foreign law as facts of a special sort and has elusively suggested that courts may be permitted to take judicial notice of foreign law, see MCC Proceeds Inc v Bishopsgate Investment Trust plc [1999] CLC 417 (CA); Morgan Grenfell & Co Ltd v SACE – Istituto per I Servici Assicurativi del Commercio [2001] EWCA Civ 1932, at [45]-[52]. See also Section 4(2) of the Civil Evidence Act 1972, which provides that where an English court has previously determined a question on foreign law that such a decision shall be admissible as evidence in proving that foreign law and will be regarded conclusive unless the contrary is proved.

introduce and apply foreign law *ex officio*.[702] What follows from this is that if the parties fail to plead or sufficiently prove the content of foreign law according to the rules of evidence, the court will resort to English law by default, as though the case was wholly domestic.[703]

## 2. Failure to plead or prove the content of foreign law

Because foreign law is considered fact, and must be proven according to the normal rules of evidence, the evidential presumption is that in the absence of any or satisfactory evidence, foreign law is the same as English law. This so called 'presumption of identity' between English and foreign law traditionally was considered to justify applying English law where either foreign law is pleaded, but no evidence of the content has been established, or where neither party has relied upon foreign law.[704] Indeed, in the prominent case *Aluminium Industrie Vaasen BV* v *Romalpa Aluminium Ltd,*[705] the Court of Appeal held English law as the applicable law because neither party pleaded foreign law. This was despite the fact that the contract in question contained an express choice of law clause in favour of Dutch law. It has been maintained that this approach is a simple and pragmatic approach, preserved by Article 1(3) of Rome I and Rome II.[706]

The principle of presumption of identity was comprehensively reviewed by the Court of Appeal in *Shaker* v *Al-Bedrawi*.[707] The court adopted a broad and flexible view of the treatment of foreign law and concluded that there cannot be a presumption of identity between English and foreign law. Denying that English law can apply on the basis that it has the content of English law, it was instead held that English law was the *lex causae* in cases where foreign law is not proved. The approach taken by the Court of Appeal has changed the default rule in favour of

---

702 Ascherberg, Hopwood & Crew Ltd v Casa Musicale Sonzogno [1971] 1 WLR 173, 1128 (CA).

703 *Bundesgerichtshof* judgment of 23.12.1981, NJW 1982, 1215, 1216. Further, *Dicey & Morris* (15th ed.) Vol. I, 322–323; *Richard Fentiman*, Foreign Law in English Courts (1998) 281; *Trevor Hartley*, Pleading and Proof of Foreign Law: The Major European Systems Compared, 45 ICLQ (1996) 271, 285.

704 Critically, *Richard Fentiman*, Laws, Foreign Laws, and Facts Current Legal Problems 2006 Vol. 59 391, 406.

705 [1976], 1 WLR 676 (CA).

706 *Cheshire & North* (14th ed.) 694 and 839.

707 [2002] EWCA Civ 1452; [2003] Ch 350 (CA); discussed in *Richard Fentiman*, Laws, Foreign Laws, and Facts Current Legal Problems 2006 Vol. 59 391, 419 *et seq.*

English law where it is not pleaded, into a choice of law rule. Similar to the German approach, a failure to raise the application of foreign law has the same effect as an implied choice of the *lex fori* during proceedings.

## 3. Foreign law chosen in accordance with Rome I or Rome II

A choice of law clause agreed to between the parties according to either Rome I or Rome II will not by itself be enough to ensure the applicability of the chosen foreign law. According to English law, rules on pleading and proof of foreign law are considered to be part of evidence and procedure. Since both the Rome I and Rome II Regulations omit evidence and procedure from their scope (Article 1(3) Rome I; Article 1(3) Rome II), it follows that such issues will be resolved according to English law and an English judge will not be required to apply foreign law *ex officio*.

According to English evidence and procedure, in order to ensure the application of a chosen foreign law, at least one party would be required to raise its application during proceedings.[708] As a result, where neither party pleads foreign law, English law will apply by default. Whether this English approach and the presumption of identity can be reconciled with the mandatory nature of the choice of law rules contained in the Rome I and Rome II Regulations, is controversial. Such an approach would allow parties to evade application of the Regulations merely because the pleading and proof of foreign law is a voluntary matter for the parties.

# III. Analysis

The objective behind including choice of law rules in a Community instrument is to ensure that the same law will be applied irrespective of the country of the court in which an action is brought. Accordingly, since the same law *should* be applied, the problem of forum shopping is removed and predictability of the outcome of litigation and certainty as to the law applicable is promoted.[709] Resorting to the familiar law of the forum in cases where the parties omit to plead foreign law, or where the content of foreign law cannot be established, may present a practical and efficient solution. Doing so will reduce costs, court time and allow a judge to apply a familiar law. As noted above, German and English national courts attitudes

---

708   Critically *Gisela Rühl*, Die Kosten der Rechtswahlfreiheit: Zur Anwendung ausländischen Rechts durch deutsche Gerichte RabelsZ Vol. 71 (2007) 559, 577.

709   Recital (6) Rome I; Recital (6) Rome II.

towards the application of foreign law are similar. Both are inclined to relapse into *lex forism* in cases where foreign law is either not raised or proven. But a court's inclination to apply the *lex fori* in disregard of the applicable foreign law does not advance the underlying objectives of the Rome I and II Regulations. Requiring parties to plead foreign law, especially in consumer or employment cases would defy the rationale underlying those conflict-of-law rules, namely protection of the weaker party.[710] More specifically, an undue preference for the law of the forum undermines the status given to party autonomy in the Regulations. One of the key objectives in both Regulations is that parties should have the freedom to choose the applicable law. It should then logically follow that their choice of law be applied irrespective of which Member State forum is hearing the dispute and irrespective of the national rules of procedure concerning the application of foreign law. In other words, the Rome Regulations require the introduction and application of that chosen foreign law and courts should resort to the *lex fori* with restraint only.[711]

In Germany, it is settled that where a rule of private international law refers to foreign law such law must be applied by the judge *ex officio*. An *ex officio* approach to the introduction of foreign law to the proceedings is easier to reconcile with the mandatory nature of the Rome Regulations. The rules concerning the applicable law contained in the Regulations are all expressed in mandatory terms (e.g. "A contract shall be governed": Article 3(1) Rome I; "the law applicable … shall be": Article 4(1) Rome II). The use of this language places the court under a positive obligation to apply the law applicable under the Regulations.[712] On the other hand, English law requires foreign law to be raised by the parties. Such an approach has the potential to exclude party autonomy and prevents the enforcement of the substantive choice of law rules, depriving EC law of its 'useful effect' (*effet utile*). The principle of *effet utile* obliges national courts to give effect to the European choice of law rules contained in Rome I and Rome II, including the parties' right to choose the applicable law.[713]

---

710 *Gisela Rühl*, Die Kosten der Rechtswahlfreiheit: Zur Anwendung ausländischen Rechts durch deutsche Gerichte RabelsZ Vol. 71 (2007) 559, 577–578.

711 Note the examination of the very limited signifiance of the *lex fori*, above under Part 3/A.II.2.*The role of the* lex fori.

712 Compare the parallel arguments of the debate between the compatibility of the Brussels Convention and the common law doctrine of *forum non conveniens*, discussed in *Andrew Dickinson*, The Rome II Regulation 603–606.

713 The English Court of Appeal has signalled a change of approach to the principle that English law will be applied where foreign law is not pleaded or proved, see e.g. *Shaker v Al-Bedrawi* [2002] EWCA Civ 1452; [2003] Ch 350, [64]-[72] (CA) (English law as *lex causae*); *Morgan Grenfell & Co Ltd v SACE – Istituto per I*

Following this reasoning what it comes down to is: Should the introduction or pleading of foreign law be a substantive or procedural matter?[714] If it is considered procedural, the matter would remain unaffected by both Rome Regulations[715] and be determined according to the procedural rules of the forum. As seen from the discussion above, this would unavoidably result in the possibility to undermine the effectiveness of the rules laid down in the Rome Regulations simply by omission to plead, or as a result of insufficient proof of foreign law.[716]

In order to avoid this, it has been suggested that a more legitimate approach would be to split the issue of pleading foreign law by classifying the question *whether* foreign law must be introduced and applied as substantive, and *how* it should be pleaded as procedural.[717] This approach, similar to the approach taken by German courts, recognises the legal character of foreign law, rather than it being merely a question of fact to be dealt with by the relevant rules of evidence. In practice, parties would therefore not be able to argue that because pleading of foreign law is procedural it is voluntary, and when not raised invite the application of the *lex fori*. In other words, whether foreign law or the *lex fori* is relied upon should be a choice of law matter. Rome I and Rome II are European Regulations with direct effect, which require mandatory application. In other words, national courts are bound to recognise and enforce the rules contained therein including the application of any foreign law chosen by the parties.

---

*Servici Assicurativi del Commercio* [2001] EWCA Civ 1932, at [53] both discussed in *Richard Fentiman*, Laws, Foreign Laws, and Facts Current Legal Problems 2006 Vol. 59 391, 419 *et seq.*

714   See generally *Rainer Hausmann*, Pleading and Proof of Foreign Law – A Comparative Analysis, EuL Forum (1/2008); *Hartmut Ost*, EVÜ und Fact Doctrine: Konflikte zwischen europäischer IPR-Vereinheitlichung und der Stellung ausländischen Rechts im angelsächsischen Zivilprozess (1996); and *Richard Fentiman*, Foreign Law in English Courts (1998) 295–296.

715   Both Articles 1(3) the Rome I, 1(3) Rome II expressly exclude procedural matters from their scope.

716   *Richard Fentiman*, Foreign Law in English Courts (1998) 296; *Hartmut Ost*, EVÜ und Fact Doctrine: Konflikte zwischen europäischer IPR-Vereinheitlichung und der Stellung ausländischen Rechts im angelsächsischen Zivilprozess (1996) 243 *et seq.* Consider also the view expressed by the ECJ in relation to the Brussels Convention that "the national procedural rules may not impair the effectiveness of the Convention". See, e.g. European Court of Justice Case C-159/02 *Turner v Grovit* [2004] ECR I-3565, para. 29.

717   *Richard Fentiman*, Foreign Law in English Courts (1998) 70–74. Compare also suggestions made by *Urs Peter Gruber/Ivo Bach*, The Application of Foreign Law: A progress report on a new European project (2009) YBPIL Vol. 11 157–169, 166.

Generally speaking, any omission to plead (or insufficient proof of foreign law) must then result in the failure of the claim or defence rather than application of the *lex fori*.[718] Such an approach makes issues concerning pleading of foreign law more than a matter of fact and evidence and would promote the underlying objectives of the Rome Regulations – consistency, uniformity, and satisfaction of expectations.[719] Considering that judges are expected to be familiar with the provisions of the Rome I and Rome II Regulations, it may be more efficient to require judges to raise with the parties the possibility of application of a foreign law *or* of the *lex fori*.[720] This would allow parties at this stage the possibility to agree on the application of a different law (i.e. the *lex fori*) during proceedings, even if a foreign law previously governed their relationship.[721] However, in the absence of a clear express choice of law by the parties, it may be doubted whether a choice of the *lex fori* is clearly demonstrated or demonstrated with reasonably certainty merely by the conduct of the parties during proceedings.[722] In such a situation, the applicable rules in the absence of choice, regardless of whether they lead to the application of the *lex fori* or a foreign law must be applied. Thus, in accordance with the primacy of European law and in the context of the Rome Regulations, it will never be maintainable for the forum to interpret silence as to the applicable law by the parties as a choice of the *lex fori*, since in the absence of a choice of law both Regulations provide clear rules for ascertaining the otherwise applicable law.

## C. Summary

The importance given to the principle of party autonomy in both the Rome I and Rome II Regulations has paved the way for an increasing application of foreign law in national courts. Even in purely domestic cases, parties may still agree on the application of a foreign law to govern their contractual or non-contractual

---

718  *Richard Fentiman*, Foreign Law in English Courts (1998) 68 *et seq.*
719  *idem*, Laws, Foreign Laws, and Facts Current Legal Problems 2006 Vol. 59 391, 422 and 425.
720  *Andrew Dickinson*, The Rome II Regulation 605; *Rainer Hausmann*, Pleading and Proof of Foreign Law – A Comparative Analysis EuL Forum (1/2008) I-3. Compare § 139 ZPO, which requires the court to ask parties if they intend to choose German law as the *lex causae*; *Gerhard Wagner*, Fakultatives Kollisionsrecht und prozessuale Parteiautonomie ZEuP 1999 6, 44. Compare also § 139 ZPO.
721  Articles 3(2) Rome I; 14(1)(a) Rome II.
722  See discussion under Part 2/B.I.2.b.bb) *Tacit choice of law in proceedings*.

obligations. Parties may choose whichever law they wish, whether or not it has a connection to their legal relationship, forum, or the event giving rise to the non-contractual obligation. The chosen foreign law will generally govern all substantive issues, whereas matters of evidence and procedure are excluded from the Rome I and Rome II Regulations and thus must be determined according to the law of the forum. It has been seen that any significance of the *lex fori* (apart from matters of evidence and procedure) is restricted to the consideration of the validity of a choice of law, which will not automatically result in the application of the *lex fori*. In addition, the forum may be required to determine the scope and effect of mandatory laws or imperative norms on the parties' chosen law. However, where a national court is required to determine whether or not the parties are permitted to choose the applicable law, it will effectively only be monitoring and enforcing the provisions of the Rome Regulations. The starting point is that parties are permitted to choose the applicable law, but because both Regulations also carefully regulate the parties' freedom to choose the applicable law for certain contracts and certain non-contractual obligations, a court may be required to displace the chosen law. Nevertheless, this law is specifically regulated in the Regulations and therefore any substantive significance of the *lex fori* is displaced by the *lex causae*.

In a case that calls for the interpretation of certain terms used within the Regulations the role of the *lex fori* will also be displaced by the application of the *lex causae* to resolve any interpretive issues. Where terms are vaguely formulated and not adequately explained in the Regulations, a court must strive to give effect to an autonomous interpretation of all concepts used in the EC Regulations. A broad Regulation-based approach will require national courts to also consider: 1) relevant decisions or opinions of the ECJ on EC Regulations; 2) relevant decisions of courts of other Member States on EC Regulations; and, 3) commentary and recitals to EC Regulations. Such an approach, together with the mandatory application of the *lex causae* to resolve these issues, promotes legal certainty and the uniform application of a law chosen in accordance with Article 3 of Rome I and Article 14 of Rome II.

Because of the importance given to party autonomy in both Rome Regulations and the objectives underlying its inclusion, national courts are required to apply the foreign law and should resort to the *lex fori* with restraint only. Any omission to plead or insufficient proof of foreign law should not be interpreted as a choice of the *lex fori*, since in the absence of a choice of law the Rome Regulations clearly provide rules ascertaining the otherwise applicable law. As of yet, neither Rome Regulation deals explicitly with the introduction and ascertainment of the foreign law chosen or otherwise determined applicable by the Regulations. In 2005, the European Parliament proposed an amendment to the Rome II Regulation to ensure a more uniform approach to the application of foreign law by courts throughout the EU, requiring the court seised to establish the content of foreign law of its own motion.[723] This amendment was dropped and as a compromise the Rome II Regulation now included a review clause in Article 30 requiring the Commission to submit to the European Parliament, the Council and the European Economic and Social Committee a report on the application of the Regulation, including a study on the "effects of the way in which foreign law is treated in the different jurisdictions and on the extent to which courts in the Member States apply foreign law in practice" pursuant the Regulation.[724] The inconsistent national practices in relation to the treatment of foreign law constitute an obstacle to the underlying aims of the Regulations of legal certainty and uniformity of result. This is a long-standing issue and if left disregarded, leaves too much scope for disparate application of the choice of law rules in the Regulations. In order to reach the objectives of both Regulations, the uniform choice of law rules provided for in Rome I and Rome II need to be supplemented by uniform procedural rules governing the introduction and ascertainment of foreign law in court. The legal basis for taking action is grounded in Article 65 c) EC Treaty[725] and now provided for in Article 81 of the TFEU[726]. In 2010, several European Scholars and Professionals drafted the so-called Madrid Principles. The goal of this undertaking was to highlight some basic principles for acceptance by the EU Member States and foster the adoption of a common approach in the form of a Regulation in this area. Principle IV states that the application of foreign law should be made *ex officio* by the national authority, which must use its best endeavours to ascertain the content of foreign law.[727] This prospective regulation-based approach would be fully in line with that embodied in the Rome Regulations, further promoting the unification of private international law in Europe.

---

723  *EP Report* A6–0211/2005 of 27 June 2005 (Wallis Report) Amendment 43, Art. 11 b (new) para. 1: 1."The court seised shall establish the content of the foreign law of its own motion. To this end, the parties' collaboration may be required. 2. If it is impossible to establish the content of the foreign law and the parties agree, the law of the court seised shall be applied."

724  Article 30(1)(i) Rome II.

725  *Maarit Jänterä-Jareborg*, Foreign Law in National Courts Recueil des cours (2003) Vol. 304 181, 370; generally: *Ansgar Staudinger/Stefan Leible*, Article 65 of the EC Treaty in the EC System of Competencies EuL Forum (4/2001) 225.

726  *Heinz-Peter Mansel/KarstenThorn/ Rolf Wagner*, Europäisches Kollisionsrecht 2009: Hoffnungen durch den Vertrag von Lissabon (2010) IPRax 1 *et seq*.

727  See project JLS/CJ/2007-I/03, Principles for a Future EU Regulation on the Application of Foreign Law (Madrid Principles).

# Part 4: Party Autonomy in the Common Law: A Cross-National Comparison with the Rome I and Rome II Regulations

## A. Party autonomy in contractual obligations

At common law, the rules of private international law to determine the law to be applied to an international contract were developed by judges.[728] Two connecting factors were considered appropriate to govern the law of a contract: the *lex loci contractus* (the law of the place where the contract was made) and the *lex loci solutionis* (the law of the place where performance of the contract was due). However, both formulations were unable to resolve difficult issues. Not only would it be difficult to identify the *lex loci contractus* in cases where negotiations are carried out across international borders, it could have also been fraudulently chosen or have little connection with the substance of the contract. The *lex loci solutionis* could cause difficulty if the place of performance was not known at the time of contracting or, if the contract was bilateral and performance was to be carried out in more than one country. It would be highly impractical to have the parties' rights and obligations governed by different laws.

These rules underwent a process of continual development and refinement through case law; and, from as early as the 18th Century, English common law courts sought to move away from rigid criteria and recognised party autonomy as a general principle in contract choice of law.[729] Early decisions referred to the law to which "the parties had a view",[730] or the law "the parties intended that the transaction should be governed...that they have submitted themselves in the matter"[731]. The general trend

---

728  *Dicey & Morris* (15th ed.) Vol. II 1776, see also n 4 where the authors provide a list of the leading cases in the development of the rules. For a full account of the English common law approach prior to 1990, see *Lawrence Collins et al.* (eds.), Dicey and Morris on the Conflict of Laws (1987) (hereafter: *Dicey & Morris*, (11th ed.)) Vol. II Chapter 32.

729  *Dicey & Morris* (15th ed.) Vol. II 1777. Also *Gienar v Meyer* (1796) 2 Hy Bl 603; *P & O Steam Navigation Co v Shand* (1865) 3 Moo PC (NS) 272.

730  *Robinson v Bland* (1760) 1 Bl.W. 257, 259.

731  *Lloyd v Guibert* (1865) LR 1 QB 115, 120–121. See also *P & O Steam Navigation Co v Shand* (1865) 3 Moo PC (NS) 272.

taken by English courts was explained by Lord Wright in *Mount Albert Borough Council v Australasian Temperance and General Assurance Society*:[732]

> English law, in deciding these matters, has refused to treat as conclusive rigid or arbitrary criteria such as *lex loci celebrationis* or *lex loci solutionis* and has treated the matter as depending on the intention of the parties to be ascertained in each case on a consideration of the terms of the contract, the situation of the parties and generally on all the surrounding facts.

This flexible approach taken by the courts to choice of law was notably influenced by the laissez-faire traditions in domestic law of this time period. According to this philosophy, where an agreement is freely negotiated between economic equals it should be honoured and upheld by the courts and the intention of the parties should be given effect to.[733] In the United States, party autonomy (then referred to as 'the doctrine of the parties' intention') was also accepted by the judiciary in the early 19th Century.[734] In 1882 in *Pritchard v Norton*,[735] the US Supreme Court made it clear that "the law we are in search of ... is that which the parties have, either expressly or presumptively, incorporated into their contract as constituting its obligation." However, despite the Supreme Court's clear recognition of the parties' choice of law, party autonomy received considerable opposition from scholars, and under the influence of Joseph Beale, party autonomy did not find its place in the first Restatement of Conflict of Laws.[736] Professor Beale's view was

---

732 [1938] AC 224, 240.

733 See e.g. the approach as expressed by Jessel MR in *Printing and Numerical Registering Co v Sampson* (1875) LR 19 Eq 462, 465: "if there is one thing more than another which public policy requires, it is that men of full age and competent understanding shall have the utmost liberty in contracting, and that their contracts, when entered into freely and voluntarily shall be held sacred and shall be enforced by Courts of Justice."

734 See *Wayman v Southard* 23 US (10 Wheat.) 1 (1825) in which the US Supreme Court stated that "in every forum, the contract is governed by the law with a view to which it was made". See further on the US development of party autonomy, *Symeon Symeonides*, American Private International Law (2008) 197 *et seq.*; *David Frisch*, Contractual Choice of Law and the Prudential Foundations of Appellate Review (2003) Vanderbilt Law Review 57–112.

735 106 US 124 (1882).

736 See Restatement of the Law, Conflict of Laws (1933) as adopted and promulgated by the American Law Institute at Washington, D.C., May 1934, §332, which specified the *lex loci contractus* rule – i.e. the application of the law of the State in which the contract was made. Joseph Beale's objection to party autonomy was based on the vested rights theory. Further on this position see *Joseph Beale*, A Treatise on the Conflict of Laws Vol. 2 1080 (1935); also generally, *Ernest Lorenzen*, Validity and Effect

that giving parties the freedom to choose the applicable law would be tantamount to giving parties the power to legislate.[737] Following the adoption of the Second Restatement in 1971,[738] and the inclusion of the principle of party autonomy in § 187, the prevailing view came to be that parties should be given the freedom to choose the applicable law.[739] In the absence of a choice, the applicable law is the law which has "the most significant relationship to the transaction and the parties".[740] This approach has brought US choice of law rules in contract very close to the Anglo-Saxon common law rules. Nevertheless, although the principle of party autonomy is generally accepted it presents only one of several approaches employed by US courts[741] and as a result remains unsettled.[742] An examination of

---

of Contracts in the Conflict of Laws 30 Yale LJ (1921) 655, 658. See generally on the First Restatement *Symeon Symeonides*, The American Choice of Law Revolution in the Courts: Today and Tomorrow 298 Recueil des Cours 9, 34 (2002); *idem*, The First Conflicts Restatement Through the Eyes of Old: As Bad as Its Reputation? 32 So Ill ULJ (2007) 39; *Patrick Borchers*, Categorical Exceptions to Party Autonomy in Private International Law (2008) 82 Tul L Rev 1645–1661.

737   *Joseph Beale*, A Treatise on the Conflict of Laws Vol. 2 1080 (1935).

738   Restatement of the Law (Second): Conflict of Laws (1971) as adopted and promulgated by the American Law Institute at Washington, D.C., May 1969.

739   For a comparative view of the US position and the Rome I and Rome II Regulations, see *Symeon Symeonides*, Party Autonomy in Rome I and Rome II From a Comparative Perspective, in: *Katharina Boele-Woelki/Talia Einhorn/ Daniel Girsberger/ Symeon Symeonides* (eds.), Convergence and Divergence in Private International Law – Liber Amicorum Kurt Siehr (2010) 513–550.

740   Restatement of the Law (Second) § 188. Special rules are further provided for particular kind of contracts. See further, *Symeon Symeonides*, Party Autonomy in Rome I and Rome II From a Comparative Perspective, in: *Katharina Boele-Woelki/Talia Einhorn/ Daniel Girsberger/Symeon Symeonides* (eds.), Convergence and Divergence in Private International Law – Liber Amicorum Kurt Siehr (2010) 513–550; *Mo Zhang*, Party Autonomy and Beyond: An International Perspective of Contractual Choice of Law Emory International Law Review (2006) Vol. 20 511–562 at 529 *et seq.*

741   The position in the US is more complex as choice of law is a state and not federal matter. See specific discussion of the differing treatment throughout the US in *Symeon Symeonides*, Choice of Law in the American Courts in 2009: Twenty-Third Annual Survey 58 Am J Comp L 221 231–232 (2010).

742   This is mainly due to the inconsistent acceptance of the Restatement by courts throughout the United States. Although largely accepted, they are still considered secondary authority. Further see, *Mo Zhang*, Party Autonomy and Beyond: An International Perspective of Contractual Choice of Law Emory International Law Review (2006) Vol. 20 511. For discussion of the application of § 187 Restatement of

the English doctrine of the proper law and its reception and development in the common law countries Australia, New Zealand, Canada and Singapore follows.

# I. The English doctrine of the proper law

The significant feature underpinning the English common law rules on choice of law in contract is that the parties have had substantial autonomy.[743] From the middle of the 19th Century, developments made in English courts, centred on the "proper law" of the contract as the law to govern contracts with a foreign element.[744] According to this doctrine, when the parties had expressed their intention as to the law governing the contract, their expressed intention would determine the proper law of the contract. The doctrine is best explained with a view to freedom of contract; because parties are permitted to create rights and duties between themselves, they should be given the freedom to choose the law to govern those rights and duties. Over the course of the 19th and 20th centuries, the proper law doctrine developed into a system of three hierarchical rules used to determine the applicable law. First, the parties may make an express choice of law. Secondly, where there is no express choice, the proper law of the contract may be implied. Thirdly, and similar to the approach taken in § 188 of the US Restatement of the Law (Second), if the parties fail to make a choice of law, the proper law of the contract may be the law with which the contract had the closest and most real connection.

## 1. Express choice of law

At common law, the right of parties to expressly select the law to govern their contract was recognised from as early as the 18th century.[745] Allowing parties to expressly choose the applicable law, was consistent with the theory that parties are free to enter into contractual bargains and courts should therefore recognise the intention of the

---

the Law (Second), see *Peter Hay/Patrick Borchers/Symeon Symeonides*, Conflict of Laws (2010) §§ 18.4–18.7.

743 *Peter Nygh*, Autonomy in International Contracts (1999).

744 The term "proper law of the contract" was first coined by *John Westlake* in A Treatise on Private International Law (1858). See also, *Frederick Alexander Mann*, The proper law in the conflict of laws (1986) 36 ICLQ 437; *idem*, The proper law of the contract – an obituary (1991) 107 LQR 353.

745 *John O'Brien* (ed.), Conflict of Laws (1999) Chapter 16 309–310.

parties as manifested by the terms of the contract.[746] The principle issue that arose was whether there were any limits to the parties' unrestricted freedom to choose the applicable law.

In the landmark case *Vita Food Products Inc v Unus Shipping Company Ltd*,[747] the Privy Council firmly established that the law chosen by the parties should be honoured provided that the agreement was *bona fide*, legal and not against public policy. The claim arose from damage to a shipment of fish on a Canadian ship, from Newfoundland to New York, under bills of lading issued in Newfoundland. According to Newfoundland law, all bills of lading were required to expressly incorporate the Hague Rules.[748] The bill of lading contained a clause exempting the carrier from liability for the master's negligence. It did not contain the required express statement incorporating the Hague Rules (paramount clause), but merely stated: "This contract shall be governed by English law." Under the Hague rules, such clauses exempting liability were considered void. Due to negligence, the ship sank off the coast of Nova Scotia. The consignees of the fish brought an action against the carrier. The issue before the court was which law applied to the bills of lading. The Privy Council held that the requirement under Newfoundland law to incorporate the Hague Rules was directory and not mandatory. The bills of lading were therefore not illegal. When addressing the argument that there were limits upon the parties' freedom to choose the applicable law, Lord Wright began by clearly stating that the proper law of the contract, or governing law is the law, which the parties intended to apply.[749] According to

---

746 Mount Albert BC v Australasian Temperance and General Assurance Society [1938] AC 224. Compare also Whitworth Street Estates (Manchester) Ltd v James Miller and Partners Ltd [1970] AC 583 where Lord Reid stated at 603: "Parties are entitled to agree what is to be the proper law of their contract…There have been from time to time suggestions that parties ought not to be so entitled, but in my view there is no doubt that they are entitled to make such an agreement, and I see no good reason why, subject maybe to some limitations, they should not be so entitled." However, as the legal issue in the case did not concern express choice of law the statement made by Lord Reid is obiter dicta only.

747 [1939] 3 All ER 589; AC 277 (PC Nova Scotia).

748 Newfoundland Carriage of Goods by Sea Act 1932, section 3: "Every bill of lading, or similar document of title, issued in this Dominion which contains or is evidence of any contract to which the rules apply shall contain an express statement that is to have effect subject to provisions of the said Rules as applied by this Act."

749 *Vita Food Products Inc v Unus Shipping Company Ltd* [1939] AC 277 at 289–290; see *R v International Trustee for the Bondholders Aktiengesellschaft* [1937] AC 500 (HL), in which Lord Atkin stated: "The proper law of the contract…is the law which the parties intended to apply."

the parties' expressed intention, English law was to apply and not the Newfoundland Act. He then observed:[750]

> ...where the English rule that intention is the test applies, and where there is an express statement by the parties of their intention to select the law of the contract, it is difficult to see what qualifications are possible, provided the intention expressed is *bona fide* and legal, and provided there is no reason for avoiding the choice on the ground of public policy.

Courts would respect an express choice of law, selected at the time of contracting,[751] irrespective of any connection with the contract,[752] provided that it was *bona fide* and legal and not against public policy.[753] If the choice of law was made for the specific purpose of avoiding the consequence of the illegality, then it is not *bona fide* and legal. A foreign law will not be applied if it contravened the public policy of the forum or the mandatory provisions of the proper law.[754] Subsequent case law concerning express selection of the proper law further made clear that in accordance with the domestic rules on certainty of contractual terms, an express choice must clearly formulated.[755] However, there has been no subsequent judicial elaboration of the reasoning or formulation given by Lord Wright of the approach taken in *Vita Foods*, or any later decision implementing it,[756] and the

---

750 Vita Food Products Inc v Unus Shipping Company Ltd [1939] AC 277 at 290.

751 It will not be possible to leave it to one of the parties to nominate the governing law at a later date, see *Dubai Electricity Company v Islamic Republic of Iran Shipping Lines (The Iran Vojdan)* [1984] 2 Lloyd's Rep 380 at 385.

752 Although there is some authority in support of the view that the parties can only select a system that has a substantial connection with the contract: *Re Helbert Wagg & Co* [1956] Ch 323 at 341; but compare more recently *Beximco Pharmaceuticals Ltd v Shamil Bank of Bahrain* [2004] 1 WLR 1784 at [54] where Potter LJ stated that English law is a law commonly adopted internationally as the governing law for banking and commercial contracts.

753 An example of the use of the power to disregard law offending public policy is discussed in *Kuwait Airways Corporation v Iraqi Airways Company and others* [2002] UKHL 19 at [15]-[18].

754 As suggested in *Dicey & Morris* (11th ed.) Vol. II 1172.

755 See e.g. Compagnie d'Armement Maritime SA v Compagnie Tunisienne de Navigation SA [1969] 3 All ER 589; 1 WLR 1338.

756 But see the Australian cases *Golden Acres Ltd v Queensland Estates Pty Ltd* [1969] Qd R 378; and, *Queensland Estates Pty Ltd v Collas* [1971] Qd R 75, 80–81 (Supreme Court of Queensland), both discussed below at Part 4/A.II.1. *Australia*. Compare also *R v International Trustee for the Protection of Bondholders Aktiengesellschaft* [1937] AC 500, 530 (HL).

position taken in the case has been subject to vigorous criticism.[757] In particular, criticism focused on preferring a contractual choice of law over The Hague Rules and thereby frustrating the unification of legislation among shipping nations.

## 2. Implied choice of law

The second rule, where there is no express choice, permits courts to identify the proper law of the contract by inferring a choice of law by the parties. Case law has established that where parties have not made an express selection of the law, an intention with regard to the law to govern their contract could be inferred from the particular terms and nature of the contract and from the general circumstances of the case.[758] Courts will not determine the proper law retrospectively and circumstances not existing at the time of the formation of the contract will not be relevant.[759] Often, a clause indicating that disputes were to be submitted to the courts of, or arbitration in, a particular forum was considered to be a strong indication or "conclusive presumption" that the parties intended the law of that forum to govern their contract.[760] This presumption in turn pointed to the English *lex fori*

---

757 See e.g. Denning LJ in *Boissevain v Weil* [1968] 1 KB 482 at 491; Upjohn J in *Re Helbert Wagg and Co* [1956] 1 All ER 129 at 136; Diplock LJ in *Owners of Cargo on Board the Morviken v Owners of the Hollandia* [1983] 1 Lloyd's Rep 1, 9 (HL); not followed by the Canada Supreme Court in *Dominion Glass Co v The Ship Anglo Indian* [1944] SCR 409; [1944] 4 DLR 721. For academic criticism, see e.g. *Harold Cooke Gutteridge* Case Comment on Vita Food (1939) 55 LQR 323; *Otto Kahn-Freud*, Case Comment on Vita Food (1939) 3 Modern LR 61; *J.H.C. Morris/G.G. Cheshire*, The Proper Law of a Contract in the Conflict of Laws (1940) 56 LQR 320; *William Tetley*, Vita Food Products Revisited (1992) 37 RD McGill LJ 292; *Walter W. Cook*, The Logical and Legal Bases of the Conflict of Laws (1942) 426; *Raoul Colinvaux* (ed.), Carver's Carriage by Sea, Vol. 1, (1982) 573; *Cheshire & North* (11th ed.) 453; *Dicey & Morris* (11th ed.) Vol. II 1284–1285. Nevertheless, the proposition in the *Unus Shipping* case on the effect of a choice of law by the parties was reaffirmed in *The Komninos S* [1991] 1 Lloyds Rep 370 (CA) at 373 and other commentators were in support of the decision, see e.g. *Frederick Alexander Mann*, The Proper Law of the Contract (1950) 3 ILQ 60; *Martin Wolff*, Private International Law (1950) 418; *Jean Gabriel Castel*, Canadian Conflict of Laws (1986) 542.

758 *Dicey & Morris* (15th ed.) Vol. II 1777.

759 Armar Shipping Co Ltd v Caisee Algérienne d'Assurance et de Réassurance [1981] 1 All ER 498 (CA); Amin Rasheed Shipping Corp v Kuwait Insurance Co [1984] AC 50 (HL).

760 The rationale being based on the principle qui elegit iudicium elegit ius. See also Hamlyn and Co v Talisker Distillery [1894] AC 202; NV Kwik Hoo Tong Handel Maatschappij v James Findlay and Co [1927] AC 604; Makender v Feldia AG [1967]

as the applicable law. Thus, in *Tzortzis v Monark Line A/B*,[761] the court identified English law as the proper law by virtue of the inclusion in the contract of an arbitration clause, subjecting the parties to arbitration in London, despite all the indications pointing to the law of Sweden.[762] In the later case *Compagnie D'Armement Maritime SA v Compagnie Tunisienne de Navigation SA*,[763] the House of Lords disagreed with the approach taken by the Court of Appeal in the *Tzortzis* case. The contract concerned a contract between French ship-owners and a Tunisian company involving the shipment of oil between Tunisian ports. Clause 13 of the contract declared that the contract was to be governed "by the laws of the flag of the vessel carrying the goods". However, the parties had omitted to fill in the names of the ships and flags involved. Clause 18 of the contract provided for the settlement of disputes by arbitration in London. It further provided in Clause 28 that shipments were to be made in "tonnage owned or controlled or chartered by French ship-owners".[764] The House of Lords by majority concluded that clauses 13 and 28 together sufficiently indicated a choice of French law, reversing a unanimous Court of Appeal. Lord Wilberforce stated that:

> …an arbitration clause must be treated as an indication, to be considered together with the rest of the contract and relevant surrounding facts. Always, it will be a strong indication…but in some cases it must give way where other indications are clear.

There was a clear balance in favour of French law: the contract was made in France, freight was payable in French francs in Paris, the contract was to be performed in Tunisia, and French commercial law was applicable in Tunisia. The only connection with England was in terms of the arbitration clause. However, although the House of Lords were unanimous in their application of French law as the

---

  2 QB 590; James Miller and Partners Ltd v Whitworth Street Estates (Manchester) Ltd [1970] AC 583.

761 [1968] 1 All ER 949; 1 WLR 406 (CA).

762 The case concerned a contract to be made and performed in Sweden for the sale of a ship by Swedish sellers to Greek buyers and had no other connection with England apart from the arbitration clause. Similarly, in *Whitworth Street Estates (Manchester) Ltd v James Miller and Partners Ltd* [1970] AC 583 the House of Lords deduced the proper law from a contract which had significant connections with Scotland but was concluded using a standard Lloyd's policy of marine insurance and providing for arbitration in England.

763 [1971] AC 572.

764 Although it may have been contemplated that vessels flying the French flag would be employed, in fact, shipments were made in French, Norwegian, Swiss, Bulgarian and Liberian ships.

proper law of the contract, all five law lords gave divergent reasons, disagreeing on whether Clause 13 identified French law.[765] Lord Wilberforce concluded that Clause 13 was not sufficient to identify the proper law and inferred the intention of the parties from the nature of the contract and the circumstances of the case. Lord Reid, agreeing with Lord Wilberforce that Clause 13 was on its own not a basis to upon which to determine the proper law, preferred an objective identification of the country or system of law with which the contract was most closely associated. Lord Diplock held that Clause 13 was sufficient to indicate a choice of French law and could be relied upon to show the intention of the parties by inference but that the implication arising from such a clause might be rebutted by other indications of intention. Lord Morris concluded that Clause 13 sufficiently expressed an intention that the parties intended French law to apply. Lord Dilhorne held that Clause 13 when read together with Clause 28 sufficiently indicated an express agreement in favour of French law.

As well as arbitration clauses, English courts have paid regard to choice of jurisdiction clauses,[766] language used,[767] style or form of the contract,[768] currency and place of payment,[769] nationality,[770] and residence[771] of the parties in order to infer a choice of law made by the parties. However, in the leading case *Amin Rasheed Shipping Corp v Kuwait Insurance Co*,[772] the House of Lords recognised that no single factor will be sufficient in order to infer the proper law of the contract. The facts were as follows: a Liberian company resident in Dubai (plaintiffs) insured a ship with a Kuwait insurance company (defendants). When the defendants rejected a claim made by the plaintiffs, the plaintiffs sought an order to serve a writ on the defendants pursuant to RSC 0.11.[773] According to this, a writ could be granted providing the contract "is by its terms, or by implication, governed by

---

765 See comprehensive summary of the reasoning of the Lords in *Adrian Briggs* (ed.), Agreements on Jurisdiction and Choice of Law (2008) Chapter 10 432–436.

766 *The Komninos S* [1991] 1 Lloyd's Rep 370.

767 *The Leon XIII* (1883) 8 PD 121.

768 *Rossano v Manufacturer's Life Insurance Co* [1963] 2 QB 352 (insurance contract governed by law of the insurer's place of business); *Amin Rasheed Shipping Corp v Kuwait Insurance Co* [1984] AC 50 (use of an English standard form).

769 R v International Trustee for the Bondholders Aktiengesellschaft [1937] AC 500 (HL).

770 Re Missouri Steamship Co (1889) 42 Ch D 32.

771 Jacobs v Credit Lyonnais (1884) 12 QBD 589.

772 [1984] AC 50.

773 RSC, Ord 11 r 1 (1)(f)(iii) (Rules of the Supreme Court 1965). This is now substantially covered by Part 6.37(3) CPR (Civil Procedure Rules).

English law." The contract did not include an express choice of law, nor was there a clear balance of factors pointing to an implied choice of law by the parties. Factors favouring Kuwaiti law were: the insurers and head office were in Kuwait, the insurance policy was issued in Kuwait and payment of claims was to be made in Kuwait. Factors favouring English law were: English language was used in the contract, premiums were to be made in Sterling and the policy was a standard Lloyd's policy, as set out under the Marine Insurance Act 1906 (UK). The House of Lords held that the parties had intended that English law govern their contract. The inference was based on the surrounding circumstances as well as the terms of the contract itself which "point[ed] ineluctably to the conclusion that the intention of the parties was that their mutual rights and obligations under [the insurance policy] should be determined in accordance with the English law of marine insurance".[774] In other words, it was not based merely on the use of an English form, but rather on the ground that it was not possible to interpret the policy without recourse to the Marine Insurance Act 1906 and judicial interpretation of it.[775] Following this case, it can be said that the common law approach to an impliedly chosen proper law is to take account of the whole of the contract and the relevant surrounding facts. No single factor will be decisive and a weighing of the relevant factors will be necessary.

## 3. Closest and most real connection

In those cases, where there is no express choice and where the court cannot infer an implied choice of law, the problem of determining the proper law of a contract is to be solved by considering the contract as a whole in light of all the circumstances which surround it and applying the law with which it appears to have the "closest and most real connection".[776] Courts are required to ascertain how "a just and reasonable

---

774  Per Lord Diplock.

775  Note that this case concerned choice of law at the jurisdiction point and even though the House of Lords held English law was the proper law of the contract, the House of Lords also unanimously refused to serve permission to serve the defendant in Kuwait, holding that justice could equally be done there.

776  The test was adopted by the Privy Council in *Bonython v Commonwealth of Australia* [1951] AC 201, 209 (PC) (per Lord Simmonds); approved by Lord Wilberforce in *Amin Rasheed Shipping Corp v Kuwait Insurance Co* [1984] AC 50. However, origins of the test can be seen in earlier case law and authorities referred to as the "test of objective presumed intention", see *John Westlake*, A Treatise on Private International Law (1905) 22–23, 280–281. See also further references given in *Dicey & Morris*

person would have regarded the problem"[777] and what intention "ordinary, reasonable and sensible businessmen would have likely to have had if their minds had been directed to the question"[778]. This formulation of the rule is similar to the approach taken in the US Restatement of the Law (Second) and few practical differences remain between the English concept of "closest and most real connection" and the US formulation "most significant relationship". Both approaches require courts to have regard to all relevant factors surrounding the contract, which connect it to a law, presumed to be what reasonable business persons would have decided.[779]

The inquiry requires courts to ascertain only purely objective connecting factors, taking into consideration the facts of each case as they existed at the time of contracting.[780] Some uncertainty did surround the formulation and whether the search was for a connection with a country or a system of law, and whether reference should be made to the contract or the underlying transaction. The predominant view is that the appropriate search is for the system of law with which the transaction has the closest and most real connection.[781] Namely, courts should have regard to the transaction as a whole and assess which grouping of factors appears most significant in the particular case. Examples of connecting factors which may be relevant are: the domicile and residence of the parties; the national character of a corporation; the place where its principal place of business is situated; the place where the contract is concluded or where negotiations were conducted; the place

---

(15th ed.) Vol. II 1778 n 15 and 16. For a historical overview of choice of law in contract, see *Ole Lando*, The Conflict of Laws of Contracts: General Principles (1984) Recueil des Cours VI 225, 240–244 and 330–333. For cases law concerning the test, see e.g. *Re United Rlys of Havana and Regla Warehouses Ltd* [1960] Ch 52; *Tomkinson v Forst Pennsylvania Banking and Trust Co* [1961] AC 1007; *James Miller and Partners Ltd v Whitworth Street Estates (Manchester) Ltd* [1970] AC 583; *Compagnie Tunisienne de Navigation SA v Compagnie d'Armement Maritime SA* [1971] AC 572; *Coast Lines Ltd v Hudig & Veder Chartering NV* [1972] 2 QB 34 (CA); *Monterosso Shipping Ltd v International Transport Workers Federation* [1982] ICR 675 (CA); *X AG v A Bank* [1983] 2 All ER 464.

777 The Assunzione [1954] P 150 at 176 (CA); Handel Maatschappij J. Smits v English Exporters (London) Ltd [1955] 2 Lloyd's Rep 317, 322 (CA).

778 *The Assunzione* [1953] 1 WLR 929, 939. Also *Lloyd v Guibert* (1865) LR 1 QB 115.

779 Mount Albert BC v Australasian Temperance and General Assurance Society [1938] AC 224, 240.

780 Coast Lines Ltd v Hudig & Veder Chartering NV [1972] 2 QB 34, 47, 50 (CA).

781 *Dicey & Morris* (11th ed.) Vol. II 1192–1193; *Peter North/James Fawcett* (eds.), Cheshire & North's Private International Law (1992) (hereafter: *Cheshire & North* (12th ed.)) 463–464.

of performance; the style and language of a contract; the validity of contractual stipulations under one law and not the other; the nature of the subject matter or the *situs*; the head office of an international company; and any other factors which serve to localise the contract.[782]

The difficulty inherent in an objective approach to the choice of law problem is identifying the relevant factors and the weight to be given to them respectively. This is illustrated by the case *The Assunzione*,[783] in which the factors under consideration appeared to be balanced fairly evenly. The contract involved the carriage of wheat chartered by French grain merchants from Dunkirk to Venice on an Italian owned ship flying the Italian flag. The contract was formally concluded in Paris and was written in English and in an English standard form. The bills of lading were in French. Freight and demurrage were payable in Italian currency in Italy. The Court of Appeal unanimously held that Italian law was the proper law of the contract. It acknowledged that no particular factor was decisive, but that both parties had contractual obligations to carry out in Italy. Singleton LJ stated: "One must look at all the circumstances and seek to find what just and reasonable persons ought to have intended if they had thought about the matter at the time when they made the contract."

It appears that the weight to be accorded to particular factors is unpredictable; it will depend on the circumstances of each case and the nature of the contract. For example in *The Assunzione*,[784] the place of performance was held to be significant, but in cases where performance must take place in different countries,[785] or where performance is purely monetary, then this factor will not be conceded much weight. Similarly, while the place of negotiations or contracting may be a significant factor, it may not be accorded significance if those places are fortuitous.[786] The flexibility in the doctrine gained by the weighing of all relevant factors surrounding the transaction and the parties may, therefore, come at the expense of certainty and predictability. Some contracts may not have a particular connection with a particular law or the connections may be evenly balanced. Lord Denning MR in *Coast Lines Ltd v Hudig and Veder Chartering N V*,[787] noted:

---

782 Factors listed in *Cheshire & North* (12th ed.) 190.
783 [1954] P 150 (CA).
784 [1954] P 150 (CA).
785 See Jacobs v Credit Lyonnais (1884) 12 QBD 589; Bonython v Commonwealth of Australia [1951] AC 201, 209 (PC).
786 Amin Rasheed Shipping Corp v Kuwait Insurance Co [1984] AC 50; but cf. Rossano v Manufacturer's Life Insurance Co [1963] 2 QB 352.
787 [1972] 2 QB 34 at 44.

[...] there are sometimes cases where it is quite indecisive. The circumstances do not point to one country only. They point equally to two countries or even to three. What then is a legal adviser to do? What is an arbitrator or a judge to do? Is he to toss up a coin and see which way it comes down?

Traditionally, common law courts could make reference to rebuttable presumptions in order to determine the proper law, where parties had failed to choose the governing law. However, it was considered that the use of presumptions would preclude the proper consideration of each case and cause undue emphasis to be placed on one of a number of relevant connecting factors.[788] Lord Denning in *Coast Lines Ltd v Hudig and Veder Chartering N V*[789] agreed that the 'closest and most real connection' test had made the traditional presumptions redundant. However, he did decide to retain the presumption in favour of the law of the flag, but only in 'tie-break' situations when the connections were evenly balanced and the 'closest and most real connection' test failed to provide an answer. The modern English proper law approach requires a careful analysis of the particular facts of each case without the aid of predetermined presumptions and or firm guidelines to which reference may be made.

## 4. Analysis

As has been set out above, the tripartite structure of the proper law doctrine requires judges to first apply an express choice of law made by the parties. Second, in default of an express choice, the court is required to infer the applicable law the parties intended to have govern their contract. In theory this structure requires courts at the second stage to consider any subjective indications signalling the parties' intention. Only when a court cannot sufficiently identify the parties' intended choice will a court be required to continue with the third stage, namely to objectively identify the system of law with which the contract had its closest and most real connection.[790] In practice however, judges have applied the tests inconsistently.[791] In particular, the distinction between the second and third stage has often been blurred, and as illustrated by the above discussion, case law

---

788  *Cheshire & North* (11th ed.) 464–465. See also *Coast Lines Ltd v Hudig & Veder Chartering NV* [1972] 2 QB 34 at 47 (CA) (per Megaw LJ).

789  [1972] 2 QB 34 at 44.

790  *Dicey & Morris* (15th ed.) Vol. II 1777–1778.

791  *Adrian Briggs* (ed.), Agreements on Jurisdiction and Choice of Law (2008) Chapter 10 431–432. Compare also the Canadian view in *Jean Gabriel Castel*, Canadian Conflict of Laws (1997) para. 448.

demonstrates that judges have skipped straight to the third stage.[792] Lord Diplock and Lord Morris in *Compagnie D'Armement Maritime SA v Compagnie Tunisienne de Navigation SA*,[793] preferred a subjective inquiry in order to ascertain the proper law, while Lord Reid preferred the objective approach stating that: "in the absence of choice by the parties themselves, the proper law of a contract is that system of law with which the transaction has its closest and most real connection."[794] In *Amin Rasheed Shipping Corp v Kuwait Insurance Co*,[795] the House of Lords held that the parties had intended that their contract be governed by English law basing their inference on the surrounding circumstances as well as the terms of the contract.[796] However, Lord Wilberforce was of the view that an objective analysis was needed,[797] although he recognised that both the subjective and objective approaches require the court to take account of the factors surrounding the transaction and the parties and effectively merge into each other. He nevertheless reluctantly decided along with the majority that English law was the proper law despite recognising that objectively many of the factors were connected with Kuwait.

Is there then a need to distinguish between the two stages and approaches of the proper law doctrine, or can the same result always be achieved regardless of whether the court determines the proper law by inferred selection or objective selection? In the above-mentioned cases, both approaches could have achieved the same result in practice, but what if the results were different?[798] For example, a court may infer the intended law on the basis of use of certain legal terms or legal reference within the contract pointing to an otherwise *unconnected* legal system:

---

792  See e.g. *Armadora Occidental SA v Horace Mann Insurance Co* [1977] 1 WLR 520. Lord Kerr decided the proper law on the basis of the second test, which was reaffirmed on the basis of the third test. Also Lord Reid in *Compagnie D'Armement Maritime SA v Compagnie Tunisienne de Navigation SA* [1971] AC 572; and Lord Wilberforce in *Amin Rasheed Shipping Corp v Kuwait Insurance Co* [1984] AC 50, who relied on the third test whereas the other Lords applied the second test.

793  [1971] AC 572.

794  [1971] AC 572 at 608. See further, *Adrian Briggs* (ed.), Agreements on Jurisdiction and Choice of Law (2008) Chapter 10, 431–435.

795  [1984] AC 50.

796  Per Lord Diplock.

797  [1984] AC 50 at 69.

798  Cf. *Jean Gabriel Castel*, Canadian Conflict of Laws (1997) 590–591. The author argues that the end results will always be the same regardless of which formulation (subjective or objective) is applied and that attention should be focused on actual factual activity surrounding the transaction rather than terms of the contract.

"This contract is to be construed in accordance with the Australian Competition and Consumer Act 2010." Applying the second stage, a court would identify Australian law as the inferred proper law of the contract, whereas the 'closest and most real connection' test under the objective approach may not point to Australian law as the proper law of the contract based on other objective connections pointing to a different law.

A weighing of the factors is required in both stages and the factors, which are taken into consideration by the court, will be the same for both inferred and objective determination of the proper law. A sure way to avoid the court resorting to the subjective or objective determination of the governing law based on connections is to include a clearly expressed choice of law clause in the contract; if not, then it will be in the court's discretion whether an intention can be inferred or not. But the argument then becomes: if the parties had the intention that a particular law should govern the contract, then why was it not included? Attempting to give effect to what the parties had or ought to have intended is merely an arbitrary approach of the court identifying the proper law; objective connections noticeably being a more transparent and clear method of determining the most appropriate law. But on the other hand, imposing an objective proper law is harder to reconcile with the principle of party autonomy; at least in those cases where the result is dependent on the approach used. According to this view, there is still a need to have the possibility of a subjective analysis of the circumstances surrounding the transaction and the parties, and only where the parties have not made a choice and no clear inference can be drawn, should a court apply the law of the country with which the contract is most closely connected. The use of the rules when applied according to this order will provide certainty (express choice), respect the principle of party autonomy (inferred subjective choice) and give effect to the reasonable expectations of the parties (objectively ascertained choice).

## II. Reception and development of the English common law approach

The common law rules outlined above still apply in England to contracts concluded prior to 1 April 1991, but have now been replaced by the provisions of the Rome I Regulation. However, the abandonment of the common law rules was not free from controversy. In particular, the debate focused on whether it was sensible to disregard the achievements of the common law rules developed over many years and built up to reflect business realities.[799] Nevertheless, the common law rules do remain in force in many Commonwealth common law jurisdictions, including the following four.

## 1. Australia

The basic Australian conflicts rule in relation to contract choice of law is that the common law proper law doctrine will determine the governing law.[800] In 1992, the Australian Law Reform Commission produced a comprehensive report on the common law choice of law rules applicable in Australia (*ALRC* Report).[801] In the Report, the Commission confirmed that the common law doctrine of party autonomy and the parties' right to choose the law governing their contract should be upheld provided that their choice is express or can be clearly inferred from the circumstances.[802] It also confirmed that in the absence of an express or inferred choice of law, the proper law of the contract will be ascertained objectively with the 'closest and most real connection' test.[803] Although the recommendations contained in the *ALRC* Report still require legislative reform, some proposals made by the Commission seek to clarify the proper law doctrine, in particular the limitation of a choice of law and the objective ascertainment of the governing law. It has therefore been suggested that Australian courts consider the recommendations made, particularly where those solutions have found international acceptance.[804]

Australian courts have respected parties' express choice of law, permitting them to choose any legal system, regardless of any connection to the parties or the

---

799 See e.g. *Frederick Alexander Mann*, The proper law of the contract – an obituary (1991) 107 LQR 353; *Adrian Briggs*, The Formation of International Contracts (1990) LMCLQ 192.

800 See *Martin Davies/Andrew Bell/Paul Le Gay Brereton* (eds.), Nygh's Conflict of Laws in Australia (2010) 387; *Reid Mortensen/Richard Garnett/Mary Keyes* (eds.), Private International Law in Australia (2011) 437.

801 Australian Law Reform Commission *(ALRC)* Report No. 58, 1992, Choice of Law Chapter 8.

802 *ALRC* Report at para. 8.9.

803 See also e.g. Mendelson-Zeller Co v T and C Providores [1981] 1 NSWLR 366; Garstang v Cedenco JV Australia [2002] NSWSC 144.

804 Such is suggested in *Martin Davies/Andrew Bell/Paul Le Gay Brereton* (eds.), Nygh's Conflict of Laws in Australia, (2010) 389.

contract,[805] provided that it is *bona fide*, legal and not contrary to public policy.[806] In one of the few Commonwealth decisions addressing the limitation on party autonomy as established in the *Vita Food Products Inc v Unus Shipping Company Ltd* case, the court in *Golden Acres Ltd v Queensland Estates Pty Ltd*[807] was required to consider whether the parties' selection of Hong Kong law was a *bona fide* selection. The case involved an agreement between a Queensland company and a Hong Kong company concerning the sale of land in Queensland. The contract, entered into in Queensland, was in breach of the Queensland Auctioneers, Real Estate Agents, Debt Collectors and Motor Dealers Acts 1922 to 1961. The contract expressly contained a choice of law clause providing that the contract should be deemed to have been made in Hong Kong. Hoare J held that the attempted selection of Hong Kong law was for no other purpose than to avoid the operation of the Queensland law and that the express choice of law was not a *bona fide* selection.[808] He held that Queensland law should apply but made clear that the reason for applying the law was not only because it was the law of the forum but because it was the place with which the contract was most closely connected. The *ALRC* Report addressed the difficulty in applying the restriction on choice of law as established in the *Vita Food Products Inc v Unus Shipping Company Ltd* case, noting that it does not specify by reference to which law its legality is to be tested, or whose public policy must be respected.[809] The Commission recommended the adoption of a concept of 'mandatory rules', focusing on the objective effect of those rules rather than to seek an evasive motive by the parties to the contract.[810]

---

805  See e.g. *BHP Petroleum Pty Ltd v Oil Basins Ltd* [1985] VR 725, 747 (per Murray J); cf. *Queensland Estates Pty Ltd v Collas* [1971] Qd R 75 at 80–81 (per Hoare J).

806  The qualification formulated in Vita Food Products Inc v Unus Shipping Company Ltd [1939] AC 277.

807  [1969] Qd R 378 (QSC); also *Queensland Estates Pty Ltd v Collas* [1971] Qd R 75 (QSC); *Ace Insurance Ltd v Moose Enterprise Pty Ltd* [2009] NSWSC 724 at [52].

808  *Golden Acres Ltd v Queensland Estates Pty Ltd* [1969] Qd R 378 at 385. Appeal from this decision was subsequently dismissed by the High Court in *Sub nom Freehold Land Investments Ltd v Queensland Estates Pty Ltd* (1970) 123 CLR 418. Note however, that the High court held that the Queensland Act applied automatically as a mandatory law to all contracts for the sale of Queensland land, rendering the choice of law clause irrelevant. Critically, *David Kelly*, International Contracts and Party Autonomy (1970) 19 ICLQ 701, 702.

809  *ALRC* Report at para. 8.11.

810  *ALRC* Report at para. 8.12; 8.13; 8.26–8.36. See further in *Martin Davies/Andrew Bell/ Paul Le Gay Brereton* (eds.), Nygh's Conflict of Laws in Australia (2010) 402–406.

189

In 1996, the Australian High Court in *Akai Pty Ltd v People's Insurance Co Ltd*,[811] confirmed that a choice of law may be made expressly or inferred from the terms of the contract and the circumstances surrounding the case.[812] The majority of the Australian High Court cited with approval Lord Diplock's view in *Amin Rasheed Shipping Corp v Kuwait Insurance Co*,[813] but added that in the case of ambiguity of the language used in the contract, the court will be required to consider the surrounding circumstances as well as the terms and nature of the contract.[814] The *ALRC* Report recommended that in cases where the intention of the parties cannot be clearly inferred that the court should not be free to infer the choice but should instead seek to apply an objective test of the proper law.

The *ALRC* Report also noted the potential difficulty with the third stage of the proper law test, namely the problem of identifying the proper law objectively when the connecting factors are evenly balanced.[815] Drawing on international developments, in particular the approaches taken in the Rome Convention of 1980, it recommended the adoption of a presumption based on the 'characteristic performance' test.[816] This concept is novel to the common law and refers to the obligation under the contract other than the payment of money, such as the supply of goods or services.[817] This means, that where parties have not chosen a law, it should be the law of the place that has the most real and substantial connection with the contract. This will be presumed to be the place where the party to the contract that is to effect the performance that is characteristic of the contract habitually resides, unless the contract has its most real and substantial connection with another place.[818]

---

811  (1996) 188 CLR 418 at 441–442. However, the majority held that in some circumstances, courts may be required to give mandatory effect to Australian case law.

812  *Martin Davies/Andrew Bell/Paul Le Gay Brereton* (eds.), Nygh's Conflict of Laws in Australia (2010) 396 *et seq.*; *Belinda Bell*, Notes Proper Law – Ignoring the Contract? A note on Akai Pty Ltd v The People's Insurance Co Ltd (1997) 19(3) SydLawRw 400.

813  [1984] AC 50 (HL).

814  Akai Pty Ltd v People's Insurance Co Ltd (1996) 188 CLR 418 at 441.

815  *ALRC* Report at para 8.38, although the Commission admits that the problem of evenly balanced factors has not created any significant problems within Australia.

816  *ALRC* Report at para. 8.48. This test also included in the Rome Convention 1980, Art. 4(1) and the rebuttable presumption contained in Art. 4(2) and in England in the Contracts (Applicable Law) Act 1990 (UK).

817  *Cheshire & North* (14th ed.) 711–719.

818  Note that the *ALRC* Report at para. 8.71 further recommended that consumer and credit contracts be governed by the law where the consumer was when the contract was entered into, or if the goods or credit are to be supplied in another state or territory, by the law of that state or territory.

## 2. New Zealand

In New Zealand, the proper law of the contract with its three stage test will also determine which law is to apply to govern a contract.[819] The Privy Council decision in *Vita Food Products Inc v Unus Shipping Company Ltd*,[820] has been referred to or applied in several New Zealand cases, mostly within the jurisdictional stage of proceedings, but has not been discussed in any detail.[821] Thus, a New Zealand court will give effect to an express agreement, or a tacit choice of law, provided that it is *bona fide* and legal and not contrary to public policy. The factors established in English case law are to be considered when determining the proper law by inferred choice. In *NZI Insurance New Zealand Ltd v Hinton Hill & Coles Ltd*,[822] the New Zealand High Court referred to *Amin Rasheed Shipping Corp v Kuwait Insurance Co*,[823] and stated that it was not unusual for a foreign court to apply English law when interpreting contracts using an English standard form and couched in terms known to be derived from usage in the London market, and that reference must be made to established lines of English authority.[824] In *Club Mediterranee v Wendell*,[825] the New Zealand Court of Appeal also considered the terms of the contract and the place where the contract was made as conclusive indications pointing to a tacit choice of law by the parties.[826] Cooke P held that "taken

---

819 The adoption of the rule as established in *Vita Food Products Inc v Unus Shipping Company Ltd* [1939] AC 277; *Club Mediterranee NZ v Wendell* [1989] 1 NZLR 216 (CA). See also the three stage test as set out in *Lawrence Collins et al.* (eds.), Dicey and Morris on the Conflict of Laws (1980) (hereafter: *Dicey & Morris*, (10th ed.)) Vol. II 787; *Nicky Richardson*, International Contracts and the Choice of Law in New Zealand Conference Paper (2010) COBRA 2–3 September, available at: http://www.rics.org.

820 [1939] AC 277.

821 See e.g. Cornwall Properties v King [1966] NZLR 239; Campbell Motors Ltd v Storey [1966] NZLR 584 (CA); Graham v Attorney-General [1966] NZLR 937 (CA); Carey v Hastie [1968] NZLR 276 (CA); Air New Zealand Ltd v The Ship "Contship America" [1992] 1 NZLR 425 (HC); Knyett v Christchurch Casinos Ltd [1999] 2 NZLR 559 (CA).

822 [1996] 1 NZLR 203, 208 (HC).

823 [1984] AC 50 (HL).

824 *NZI Insurance New Zealand Ltd v Hinton Hill & Coles Ltd* [1996] 1 NZLR 203, 208 (HC). Note that these comments were made in the context of staying proceedings.

825 [1989] 1 NZLR 216 (CA).

826 Compare also *Longbeach Holdings Ltd v Bhanabhai & Co Ltd* [1994] 2 NZLR 28, 35 where the court was concluded that it was "probable" that New Zealand law was the proper law of the contract following its conclusion in New Zealand; or, *Governor of Pitcairn and Associated Islands v Sutton* [1995] 1 NZLR 426, where the parties

as a whole this was a contract made by parties in New Zealand, to be paid for in New Zealand currency, and that the primary obligations under it must have been intended by the parties to have been governed by New Zealand law."[827]

If parties have not chosen a law, or their choice is ineffective a court will apply the objective proper law. The New Zealand Court of Appeal adopted the formulation "closest and most real connection" in *McConnell Dowell Constructors Ltd v Lloyd's Syndicate 396*.[828] The case concerned an insurance contract, concluded in London, entered into by a group of construction companies based in New Zealand and an international consortium based in London. The contract was for the provision of first-layer cover in respect of construction projects in the Asia-Pacific region and payment for and under was to be made in New Zealand. English law had been identified as the proper law by the High Court of New Zealand and in simultaneous proceedings in England. The Court of Appeal was therefore not prepared to identify the proper law and instead assumed that the High Court judges had been correct in their findings. It tentatively held that English law was the proper law stating that the choice of law issue had not been essential for the purposes of the appeal.[829]

A more recent New Zealand High Court decision indicates a trend towards party autonomy and having the same law apply regardless of forum. In *Rimini Ltd v Manning Management and Marketing Pty Ltd*,[830] a case concerning the exercise of jurisdiction within the context of *forum non conveniens*, Randerson J said:[831]

> I do not consider in this day and age that Courts in New Zealand or Australia should shy away from applying the laws of the other country, including statute law [...] and as far as possible, Courts should seek to give effect to the laws of the other country unless it would be contrary to the law and policy of the *lex fori* to do so.

---

failed to argue against the application of New Zealand law, the Court of Appeal thus assumed that New Zealand law was the governing law.

827 *Club Mediterranee v Wendell* [1989] 1 NZLR 216 at 218–219 (CA).

828 [1988] 2 NZLR 257 at 273 the New Zealand Court of Appeal adopted the formulation in the case *Bonython v Commonwealth of Australia* [1951] AC 201 at 291. See also *Mount Albert BC v Australasian Temperance and General Mutual Life Assurance Soc Ltd* [1938] AC 224 (PC) on appeal from New Zealand, the Privy Council applied an objective test. Critically *Laurette Barnard*, Choice of Law in International Contracts – The Objective Proper Law Reconsidered (1996) 2 New Zealand Business Law Quarterly 27–49; also, *Nicky Richardson*, Choice of Law Clauses in International Contracts: Overseas Developments (1992) 5 Canterbury Law Review 126–146.

829 On this also *Laurette Barnard*, Choice of Law in International Contracts – The Objective Proper Law Reconsidered (1996) 2 New Zealand Business Law Quarterly 35.

830 [2003] 3 NZLR 22.

831 *ibid* at [47].

## 3. Canada

Canada has also followed the English common law choice of law rules upholding the proper law doctrine and the principle of party autonomy.[832] The leading English decision in *Vita Food Products Inc v Unus Shipping Company Ltd*[833] has been adopted by Canadian Courts. Hence, the primary rule is that where the parties have expressly or impliedly stipulated the law governing their contract, that chosen law will be the proper law of the contract,[834] provided it is *bona fide* and legal,[835] and is not against public policy[836]. The second rule is the English "closest and most real connection"[837] test, which will be applied to determine the proper law of the contract in the absence of the choice by the parties.[838] In the case *Canada (A.G.)*

---

832 *Melady v Jenkins SS Co.* (1909), 18 O.L.R. 251 (CA); *Wilson v Metcalfe Construction Co.* [1947] 1 W.W.R. 1089; [1947] 4 D.L.R. 472 (Alta. CA); *George C. Anspach Co. v C.N.R.* [1950] O.R. 317; [1950] 3 D.L.R. 26 (CA); *Bunge North American Grain Corp. & Fire Association of Philadelphia v S.S. "Skarp" and Owners* [1933] Ex. C.R. 75; *Montreal Trust Co. v Stanrock Uranium Mines Ltd.* [1966] 1 O.R. 258, 53 D.L.R. (2d) 594, 611 (HCJ). On the history generally, see *Jean Gabriel Castel*, Canadian Conflict of Laws (1997) 588 *et seq.*

833 [1939] 3 All ER 589; AC 277 (PC Nova Scotia).

834 See Drew Brown Ltd v The Ship "Orient Trader" and Owners [1974] SCR 1286; Long Island University v Morton (1977) 81 DLR (3d) 392 (N.S. Co. Ct.); Poly-Seal Corp v John Dale Ltd [1958] OWN 432 (HCJ); Gray v Kerslake [1958] SCR 3; Re Maritime Heating Co Ltd (1969) 2 DLR (3d) 471 (N.B.CA); AG Newfoundland v Churchill Falls (Labrador) Corp Ltd (1984) 49 Nfld. & P.E.I.R. 181 (Nfld. S.C.T.D.); Khalij Commercial Bank Ltd v Woods (1985) 17 DLR (4th) 358 (Ont. HCJ).

835 See Nike Informatic Systems Ltd v Avac Systems Ltd (1980) 105 DLR (3d) 455 (B.C.SC); Avenue Properties Ltd v First City Development Corp (1987) 32 DLR (4th) 40 (B.C.CA).

836 *Greenshields Inc. v Johnston* [1983] 3 W.W.R. 313, 119 D.L.R. (3d) 714; affd. 131 D.L.R. (3d) 234, 35 A.R. 487 (CA); and discussion of the concept of public policy in *Sangi v Sangi* [2011] B.C.SC 523 at [271] *et seq.*

837 Canadian courts have often referred to this test as the "closest and most substantial connection", see e.g. *Imperial Life Assurance Company of Canada v Segundo Casteleiro Y Colmenares* [1967] S.C.R. 443 at 448; *Cansulex Limited v Reed Stenhouse Limited* (1986), 70 B.C.L.R. (1st) 273, 18 C.C.L.I. 24 (S.C.); *Whirlpool Canada Co. v National Union Fire Insurance Co. of Pittsburgh* [2005] M.J. No. 332; *Pope & Talbot Ltd, Re* 2009, B.C.SC 1552 (No II).

838 *Bonython v Commonwealth of Australia* [1951] AC 201, 209 (PC), applied by Ritchie J in *Imperial Life Assurance Company of Canada v Segundo Casteleiro Y Colmenares*, [1967] S.C.R. 443 at 448; *Cansulex Limited v Reed Stenhouse Limited* (1986), 70 B.C.L.R. (1st) 273, 18 C.C.L.I. 24 (SC); *Canada (A.G.) v Nalleweg* (1999) 223

*v Nalleweg* (1999),[839] the Alberta Court of Appeal was required to determine the proper law of a contract. Nalleweg was a student living and attending university in British Columbia who had contracted with a Bank of British Columbia, guaranteed by the Government of Canada. When Nalleweg defaulted on his loan the federal government commenced proceedings in Alberta, where Nalleweg lived. The legal issue was whether the British Columbia or Alberta time limitation applied. According to the British Columbia law, the Government's claim had elapsed, while under Alberta law it had not. The Alberta Court of Queen's Bench held Alberta law as the applicable law. However, the Alberta Court of Appeal held that British Columbia law applied because it had the closest and most substantial connection to the contract.[840] The relevant connections considered by the court were the place of performance, the residence and place of business of the parties and the subject matter of the contract.

In the more recent case *Re Pope & Talbot Ltd*,[841] the Supreme Court of British Columbia presented a thorough and comprehensive analysis of the proper law doctrine. The case involved insurance policies issued by three different insurance

---

A.R. 89; 165 D.L.R (4th) 606 (Alta. CA); *Eastern Power Ltd v Azienda Communale Energia & Ambiente* (1999) 125 O.A.C. 54; (2000) 178 DLR (4th) 409 (Ont. CA); *Whirlpool Canada Co. v National Union Fire Insurance Co. of Pittsburgh* [2005] M.J. No. 332. Interestingly the learned author in Jean Gabriel Castel, Canadian Conflict of Laws (1997) para. 448 comments "Actually, it would be better to consider two possibilities only: where there is an express selection and where there is no express selection. The distinction between express selection and inferred selection is artificial. If the parties had wished to select the proper law they would have done so. Furthermore, except, perhaps, for the lex validitatis, the factors which are taken into consideration in determining the inferred proper law are the same as those that will enable the court to select the system of law with which the transaction has its closest and most real connection." This approach has been approved of in *Imperial Oil Ltd. v Petromar Inc.* [2002] 3 FC 190; 209 DLR (4th) 158; *JPMorgan Chase Bank v Lanner (The)* [2009] 4 FCR 109; 305 DLR (4th) 442; and *World Fuel Services Corporation v The Ship "Nordems"* 2011 FCA 73.

839　(1999) 223 A.R. 89; 165 D.L.R (4th) 606 (Alta. CA).

840　*ibid.* Alberta law rejected in particular because there was no appropriate Canadian law on time limitations. Clark, J.A. (Conrad, J.A. concurring) at 612–613 held that: "[I]t is proper that any disputes arising out of that contract be governed by the *lex loci contractus*. The proper law of the contract is the system of law which has the closest and most real connection to the contract." See also *Kenton Natural Resources v Burkinshaw* (1983), 47 A.R. 321 at 329 (QB); *243930 Alberta Ltd. v Wickham* (1990), 73 D.L.R. (4th) 474 (Ont. CA); *Jean Gabriel Castel*, Canadian Conflict of Laws (1994) 559.

841　*Pope & Talbot Ltd. (Re)*, 2009 B.C.S.C. 1552.

companies to the Pope & Talbot Group (P&T Inc., P&T Ltd.) The insurers asserted that the proper law of the insurance policies was the law of Oregon. The insured argued that the proper law of the policies was the law of British Columbia and that the language contained in the policies intended the application of *dépeçage*, or alternatively, if there was only one proper law, that it was the law of British Columbia. After consideration of the proper law doctrine and a detailed analysis of the policies, Walker J stated that the parties expressly intended the proper law of their policies to be determined in relation to the substance of the claims or matters in dispute, by the court that has taken jurisdiction. More specifically, he found that the contractual language made it clear that the parties anticipated *dépeçage*.[842] He nevertheless went on to review and weigh the following factors in order to determine proper law to be applied to the policies a) where the policy was made: all policies were deemed to have been made in BC; b) the form of the policy: concepts expressed in the policies were widely used in insurance policies issued in Canada but premium amounts and payment obligations of the insurers were expressed in US dollars; c) where the parties operations are located: the insurers head offices were located in States other than Oregon whereas the bulk of the operations of the Pope & Talbot Group were located in BC; d) the subject matter of the contract: the majority of the operations of the Pope & Talbot Group, including its employees, were located in BC at the time the policies were made; and e) where claims might be expected to arise: most of the claims were expected to arise from Canadian operations. Based on this analysis, although admitting that it was a facile approach to conclude that there was only one proper law governing each policy, Walker J reluctantly held that all three policies had the closest and most substantial connection with British Columbia.[843]

## 4. Singapore

In Singapore, the leading Privy Council case of *Vita Food Products Inc v Unus Shipping Company Ltd*[844] also provides the basis of the conflict rules on

---

842  *ibid* [55], [55], [62]. The policies were, in fact, connected to several jurisdictions: British Columbia, Ontario, Delaware, Oregon, Indiana, New Jersey, Pennsylvania, New York and Connecticut.

843  *ibid* [110] and [141], applying the factors outlined by Chief Justice McEachern in *Cansulex Limited v Reed Stenhouse Limited* (1986), 70 B.C.L.R. (1st) 273, 18 C.C.L.I. 24 (SC).

844  [1939] 3 All ER 589; AC 277 (PC Nova Scotia) affirmed by the Singapore Court of Appeal in *Peh Teck Quee v Bayerische Landesbank Girozentrale* [2000] 1 S.L.R. 148 (CA) at [12].

choice of law in contract. The English common law rules and the doctrine of party autonomy have been applied in many Singapore decisions.[845] The three stage proper law test is applied:[846] First, the court considers if the contract expressly states its governing law ("the express law"), provided it is bona fide and legal and not contrary to public policy.[847] If the contract is silent, the court proceeds to the second stage and considers whether it can infer the governing law from the intentions of the parties ("the implied law").[848] If the court is unable to infer the parties' intentions, it moves to the third stage and determines the law, which has the closest and most real connection with the contract ("the objective law").[849]

In 2003, the Law Reform Committee of the Singapore Academy of Law (Reform of the Law Concerning Choice of Law in Contract)[850] reviewed the choice of law rules in contract. The report recommended retention of the common law rules on choice of law in contract. It was of the view that an express choice of law should be upheld and that despite the deficits of the common law public policy limitation the rule does not urgently require reform.[851] The report continued that the distinction between an inferred choice of law

---

845 See e.g. Hang Lung Bank v Datuk Tan Kim Chua [1988] 2 M.L.J. 567 (HC); Foo Kee Boo v Ho Lee Investments (Pte) Ltd [1988] S.L.R. 620 (HC); Pacific Electric Wire & Cable Co Ltd & Anor v Neptune Orient Lines Ltd [1993] 3 SLR. 60 (HC); Las Vegas Hilton Corp t/a Las Vegas Hilton v Khoo Teng Hock Sunny [1997] 1 SLR 341 (CA) at [37]-[38]; Peh Teck Quee v Bayerische Landesbank Girozentrale [2000] 1 S.L.R. 148 (CA); Overseas Union Insurance Ltd v Turegum Insurance Co [2001] 3 SLR 330 at [82]; Pacific Recreation Pte Ltd v SY Technology Inc [2008] 2 SLR 491 (CA) at [35]-[37]; JIO Minerals FZC and others v Mineral Enterprises Ltd [2010] SGCA 41.

846 See recent approval in *JIO Minerals FZC and others v Mineral Enterprises Ltd* [2010] SGCA 41 at para. 79.

847 *Peh Teck Quee v Bayerische Landesbank Girozentrale* [2000] 1 S.L.R. 148 (CA); *Las Vegas Hilton Corp t/a Las Vegas Hilton v Khoo Teng Hock Sunny* [1997] 1 SLR 341 (CA), on this case see specifically Yeo Tiong Min, Are Loans for International Gambling Against Public Policy? (1997) 2 SJICL 593–608.

848 Peh Teck Quee v Bayerische Landesbank Girozentrale [2000] 1 S.L.R. 148 (CA); Overseas Union Bank v Chua Kok Kay & Anor [1993] 1 SLR 686 (HC).

849 Hang Lung Bank Ltd v Datuk Kan Tim Chua [1988] 2 M.L.J. 567 (HC); Shaik Faisal t/a Gibea v Swan Hunter Singapore Pte Ltd [1995] 1 SLR 394 (HC).

850 Report available at: http://www.sal.org.sg (Singapore Academy of Law website).

851 Law Reform Committee of the Singapore Academy of Law, Reform of the Law Concerning Choice of Law in Contract (2003) at para. 27 citing *Peh Teck Quee v Bayerische Landesbank Girozentrale* [2000] 1 S.L.R. 148 (CA) in support.

and a law identified by the "closest and most real connection" test was satisfactory and that no clarification was necessary. It stated that Singapore courts have taken a pragmatic approach to ascertaining the objective proper law where it had considered that a search for the inferred intention would be futile in the circumstances.[852] As regards the objective proper law, the Committee agreed that drawing up presumptions for various types of contract may help to clarify the "closest connection" test when the connections are evenly balanced, but refused to recommend this approach stating that the common law has worked reasonably well and that it would be impossible to fully justify the logic and rationale of any set of presumptions.[853] Recently, the Singapore Court of Appeal in *JIO Minerals FZC and others v Mineral Enterprises Ltd* [2010],[854] confirmed that the common law three stage approach is applied to determine the governing law of a contract. The court held that it was clear that the parties had not expressly chosen a law but that it was possible to determine the implied law. Citing English authority,[855] the Singapore Court of Appeal held that it is possible to infer that the parties intended that a contract be governed by the same law that governs a closely related contract. It was held that UAE law governed the parties Investment Agreement given the choice of that law in a related contract essential to the Investment Agreement, *viz*. the Exclusive Mining Agreement.[856] The court did not find it to be material that the Exclusive Mining Agreement and the Investment Agreement were between different parties but stated that "the crucial point is that the two contracts in each of those decisions were so closely related that the parties could not reasonably be considered as having intended that different laws govern the related contracts."[857]

---

852  Law Reform Committee of the Singapore Academy of Law, Reform of the Law Concerning Choice of Law in Contract (2003) para. 32.

853  See Law Reform Committee of the Singapore Academy of Law, Reform of the Law Concerning Choice of Law in Contract (2003) at para. 44.

854  SGCA 41. Note however, the sole issue on appeal was whether the Respondent's action should be stayed on the ground of *forum non conveniens*.

855  JIO Minerals FZC and others v Mineral Enterprises Ltd [2010] SGCA 41 at paras. 81 et seq.

856  The court did not find it to be material that the Exclusive Mining Agreement and the Investment Agreement were not between the same parties.

857  JIO Minerals FZC and others v Mineral Enterprises Ltd [2010] SGCA 41 at para. 85.

## III. Rome I and party autonomy – lessons for the common law?

The significant feature underpinning the English common law doctrine of the proper law is that it is premised on the principle of party autonomy: courts seek to first give effect to the express or inferred intention of the parties before objectively identifying the applicable law. After considering the approaches taken in the common law countries above, it is evident that there is substantial uniformity in the approach taken to choice of law in contract. All of the four countries addressed have adopted the English proper law doctrine. Inter-reliance on common law case law is inevitable and English decisions prior to the application of the Rome Convention have persuasive authority. But although the proper law doctrine appears to have withstood the test of time in many common law countries,[858] it has not been free from criticism. In particular, the 'closest and most real connection' test has been labelled vague, unpredictable, unworkable, and inconsistent.[859] As noted by both the *ALRC* Report and the Report of the Singapore Academy of Law, a lack of presumptions or set of principles has left the courts without any really useful aids when seeking to identify the applicable law. Recommendations made in both

---

858  Indeed its abolition in England was controversial, see e.g. *Frederick Alexander Mann*, The proper law of the contract – an obituary (1991) 107 LQR 353; *Adrian Briggs*, The Formation of International Contracts (1990) LMCLQ 192.

859  Critically see e.g. The Australian Law Reform Commission Report No. 58 1992 *Choice of Law* Chapter 8; Law Reform Committee of the Singapore Academy of Law, Reform of the Law Concerning Choice of Law in Contract (2003); *Martin Davies/Andrew Bell/Paul Le Gay Brereton* (eds.), Nygh's Conflict of Laws in Australia (2010) 399; *Jean Gabriel Castel*, Canadian Conflict of Laws (1994) 547, 553; *Otto Kahn-Freund*, General Problems of Private International Law (1974) Recueil des Cours III 139, 409–410; *Laurette Barnard*, Choice of Law in International Contracts – The Objective Proper Law Reconsidered (1996) 2 New Zealand Business Law Quarterly 27–49; also, *Nicky Richardson*, Choice of Law Clauses in International Contracts: Overseas Developments (1992) 5 Canterbury Law Review 126–146. Judges have also expressed their dissatisfaction with the test, see e.g. *Coast Lines Ltd v Hudig & Veder Chartering NV* [1972] 2 QB 34 at 44 (per Lord Denning MR) and 50–51 (per Stephenson LJ) (CA); *James Miller and Partners Ltd v Whitworth Street Estates (Manchester) Ltd* [1970] AC 583, 615 (per Lord Wilberforce; *Sayers v International Drilling Co* [1971] All ER 163, 168 (per Salmon LJ); *Amin Rasheed Shipping Corp v Kuwait Insurance Co* [1984] AC 50, 71 (per Lord Wilberforce (HL); *Stanley Kerr Holdings Pty Ltd v Gibor Textile Enterprises Ltd* [1978] NSWLR 372, 380 (per Sheppard J).

reports have drawn on and been influenced by European developments made by the Rome Convention and the Rome I Regulation.

Similar to the English proper law doctrine, the Rome I Regulation distinguishes between situations where a court may give effect to an express choice of law; subjectively ascertained choice of law; and, the situation where a court will be required to ascertain the choice of law objectively. Like the common law rules, the same order of ascertaining the governing law is required. Interestingly, the Rome I Regulation covers express choice and inferred choice under the same head. Article 3(1) Rome I, directs courts to first give effect to any express choice made by the parties.[860] The Article continues by stating that a court may also identify the law chosen by the parties if it is clearly demonstrable (inferred subjective choice). Finally, where parties are unable to establish that a choice of law has been made either expressly or "clearly demonstrated by the terms of the contract or the circumstances of the case", Article 4 Rome I designates the applicable law based on connecting factors (objectively ascertained choice).

As a result, the approach to be taken under Article 3(1) Rome I is substantially the same as that taken under the proper law doctrine and less distant to the common law when compared with the Rome Convention.[861] Both permit an inferred choice of law, which requires courts to take relevant factors into account in determining whether an intention can be implied. Under the common law, case law has established that the parties' intention to choose a particular law can be inferred from the particular terms and nature of the contract and from the general circumstances of the case. The whole of the contract and the relevant surrounding facts should be taken into consideration; no single factor will be decisive and a weighing of the relevant factors will be necessary. The *Giuliano & Lagarde* Report recognises the similarity in approach taken in the common law and lists some of the most common factors a court may take into account when interpreting the

---

860  Also made clear in Article 4(1) Rome I, under which a law will only be ascertained if it has not been chosen according to Article 3 Rome I.

861  *Adrian Briggs*, When In Rome, Choose as the Romans Choose (2009) Vol. 125 Law Quarterly Review 191–195, 194. See also Clarke J in *Egon Oldendorff v Liberia Corporation (No 2)* [1996] 1 Lloyd's Rep 380, at 388–389 when considering whether the common law rules had been affected by the Rome Convention was of the view that the proper law 'closest and most real connection' test was very similar to the test under the Convention and that the considerations made by Lord Wilberforce and Lord Diplock in the *Compagnie D'Armement Maritime SA v Compagnie Tunisienne de Navigation SA* [1971] AC 572 judgment were also relevant to the test under the Convention.

true tacit will of the parties.[862] These factors have also been considered relevant in common law case law.[863] It appears therefore, that the pre-existing English case law is still good law.

The Rome Convention, Rome I Regulation and the common law adopt an objective test where there is no express choice of law and where no choice of law can be inferred. Article 4(1) of the Rome Convention set out as a general rule that, where there is an absence of choice by the parties, the law applicable to the contract shall be governed by the law of the country with which it is 'most closely connected'. Article 4(2) Rome Convention, elaborated that the contract is most closely connected "with the country where the party who is to effect the performance which is characteristic of the contract has, at the time of conclusion of the contract, his habitual residence". It then formulated two specific presumptions identifying the most closely connected law (Article 4(3) and (4) Rome Convention) but includes an exception in Article 4(5) Rome Convention, which prevails over the other presumptions: "if it appears from the circumstances as a whole that the contract is more closely connected with another country". Similarly, the Rome I Regulation does not provide one single conflicts rule for all kinds of contract but establishes a set of different rules in order to determine the governing law. However, the Regulation presents a slightly different structure to that taken in the Convention.[864] Article 4 Rome I, starts with a list identifying eight types of contracts for which Article 4(1) Rome I determines the applicable law.[865] Article 4(2) Rome I then formulates the rule for contracts that fall outside of the list, or where elements of the contract would be covered by more than one

---

862  *Giuliano & Lagarde* Report 17. These are discussed further above under Part 1/B.I.2.b.aa) *Clearly demonstrated by the terms of the contract.*

863  See e.g. for choice of a particular forum or of a particular place of arbitration: *Tzortzis v Monark Line A/B* [1968] 1 All ER 949; 1 WLR 406 (CA) and see further references given at n 758 above, but cf *Compagnie D'Armement Maritime SA v Compagnie Tunisienne de Navigation SA* [1971] AC 572; the use of standard form governed by a particular system of law: *Whitworth Street Estates (Manchester) Ltd v James Miller and Partners Ltd* [1970] AC 583; *Amin Rasheed Shipping Corp v Kuwait Insurance Co* [1984] AC 50; previous course of dealings between parties: *JIO Minerals FZC and others v Mineral Enterprises Ltd* [2010] SGCA 41.

864  See the comprehensive analysis of both Article 4 of the Rome Convention and Rome I made by *Ulrich Magnus*, Article 4 Rome I Regulation: The Applicable Law in the Absence of Choice, in: *Franco Ferrari/Stefan Leible*, Rome I Regulation: The Law Applicable to Contractual Obligations in Europe (2009) 27–51

865  No longer referred to as presumptions but rather choice of law rules. See specific contracts set out in Article 4(1) (a)-(h) Rome I.

of contracts listed, which are to be governed by "the law of the country where the party required to effect the characteristic performance of the contract has his habitual residence."[866] Similar to the Rome Convention, Article 4(3) Rome I contains an escape clause which may operate to displace the applicable law indicated in paragraphs 1 or 2 in cases where "it is clear from all the circumstances of the case that the contract is manifestly more closely connected with a country". If it is not possible to determine the applicable law pursuant to Article 4(1) or (2) then Article 4(4) Rome I offers a 'catch-all' provision stating that the contract "shall be governed by the law of the country with which it is most closely connected." The Rome Convention, Rome I Regulation and the proper law doctrine are all based on the general principle that the law of the closest connection should govern a contract in the absence of a choice made by the parties.

Nonetheless, the approaches taken under Article 3(1) Rome I and the proper law doctrine inevitably share the same concern: problematic is identifying the distinction between an implied choice of law and a choice of law ascertained objectively and how much weight is to be accorded to the relevant connecting factors which will point to either the subjective or objective choice of law. This is a problem also encountered in the Rome II Regulation.[867] Case law has demonstrated that when there are borderline cases it will be difficult to lay down precise guidelines.[868] For example, in *American Motorists Insurance v Cellstar*,[869] the English High Court inferred the parties' intention to have Texas law as the governing law of their contract from the fact that the parties had negotiated and issued an insurance policy in Texas, despite the fact that the parties had not used a standard form clearly associated with Texas. The Court of Appeal upheld the

---

866 Recital 19 of the Rome I Regulation states that "the characteristic performance of the contract should be determined having regard to its centre of gravity." Article 19(1) Rome I defines "habitual residence" of companies and other bodies, corporate or unincorporated, as "the place of central administration", whereas the habitual residence of natural persons acting in the course of their business activity shall be their "principle place of business". The relevant point in time of determining such will be the "time of conclusion of the contract" (Article 19(3) Rome I).

867 See Article 4(1) and (3) Rome II, discussed above Part 2/B.I.1.b.bb) iii. *Accessory connection of Article 3 Rome I*. See further discussion of Article 4 Rome II in *Richard Fentiman*, The Significance of Close Connection, in: *John Ahern/William Binchy* (eds.), The Rome II Regulation on the Law Applicable to Non-Contractual Obligations (2009) 85–112

868 *Richard Plender/Michael Wilderspin*, The European Private International law of obligations (2009) 150–151.

869 [2002] EWHC 421.

judge's finding on this point. Both the decisions of the High Court and the Court of Appeal have been criticised for not inferring a choice of law, but instead choosing the law applicable on the basis of what the court thought the parties would have been likely to choose had they thought about the matter.[870] In Germany, two contrasting cases concerning building contracts demonstrate the possibility of divergent practice by the courts when dealing with this issue.[871] In the earlier judgment, reference to German building regulations and standards were interpreted as inferring a choice by the parties of German law, whereas in a case only several weeks later concerning very similar facts, it was held that the choice of law should be determined according to an objective analysis of the factors under Article 4 of the Rome Convention.

As discussed above,[872] a distinction could be drawn whereby a choice based on the subjective intention of the parties requires a court to determine that both parties were actively aware or conscious of the choice of law, whereas a choice of law that is to be ascertained objectively, should solely be based on connecting factors without the additional requirement of the 'awareness' of the parties.[873] This should apply to the objectively ascertained choice of law under Rome I, Rome II and the common law proper law doctrine. Under all regimes, courts are required to assess the nature of the contract and the individual circumstances of each case. Where the factors are evenly balanced and a conflict of connecting circumstances results it cannot be said that reliance on one of the inferences indicates a clearly demonstrated choice. In such a case, courts identifying an implied choice of law under either the proper law doctrine or Article 3(1) Rome I should instead strictly rely on the rules applicable in the absence of a choice by the parties, i.e. the 'closest and most real connection' rule or Article 4 Rome I. Still, a significant point of difference between Article 4 Rome I and the proper

---

870 *Richard Plender/Michael Wilderspin*, The European Private International law of obligations (2009) 151; *Peter Stone*, EU Private International Law: Harmonisation of Laws (2006) 278.

871 See judgments of the *Bundesgerichtshof* of 14.1.1999, VII 19/98, 1999 RIW, 537 and judgment of 25.2.1999, VII ZR 408/97, 1999 NJW, 2242.

872 See discussion above under Part 2/B.I.2.b.aa) Demonstrated with reasonable certainty by the circumstances of the case.

873 Referred to in German as *Erklärungsbewusstsein* or *Rechtswahlbewusstsein beider Parteien*, see e.g. *Junker*, in: MünchKomm (5th ed.) Art.14 marginal no. 29 and 32–33; *Thorn*, in: Palandt Art. 14 marginal no. 6; *Michael Sonnentag*, Zur Europäisierung des Internationalen außervertraglichen Schuldrechts durch die geplante Rom II-Verordnung ZVglRWiss 105 (2006) 278.

law doctrine is the provision of a set of choice of law rules in Article 4(1) Rome I. The inclusion of these rules narrows the possibility for discretion and aids judges when identifying the applicable law in the absence of a choice of law by the parties. A judge is to strictly apply the law identified in Article 4(1)(a)-(h) Rome I, and only makes reluctant use of the escape clause in very limited circumstances. In comparison, the flexibility provided for under the proper law rules has come at the price of uncertainty. In particular the objective choice of law test does not provide courts with any really useful aids or principles when seeking to identify the applicable law. The approach taken in Article 4(1) of the Rome I Regulation supports the argument made for a return to a 'presumption' based rule or a set of principles under the proper law doctrine.[874]

# B. Party autonomy in non-contractual obligations

In contrast to the long-established principle that contracting parties should be allowed to select the law to govern their contract, a similar approach in the common law was that parties had no power to agree by contract on the law to govern any tortious liability. As discussed above,[875] historically the will of the parties as a means to determine the applicable law in tort was considered to be functionally unworkable.[876] The widespread opinion was that party autonomy in the field of torts would probably not be desirable and as such, the common law tort choice of law rules reflected this attitude. In the US, the pertinent section of the Restatement (Second) addresses only the law of the state chosen by the parties to govern their *contractual* rights and duties; the question of enforceability or relevance of a pre-dispute choice of law for non-contractual claims is not uniformly answered.[877] An examination of the development of the choice of law rule for tort,

---

874  See e.g. *Laurette Barnard*, Choice of Law in International Contracts – The Objective Proper Law Reconsidered (1996) 2 New Zealand Business Law Quarterly 44 *et seq.*

875  See discussion above under Part 2/A.2. Specific justification of party autonomy in non-contractual obligations.

876  *Matthias Lehmann*, Liberating the individual from battles between states: justifying party autonomy in conflict of laws (2008) Vanderbilt Journal of Transnational Law Vol. 41 381, 387.

877  For a detailed examination of the US position, see *Symeon Symeonides*, Party Autonomy in Rome I and Rome II From a Comparative Perspective, in: *Katharina*

in particular the judicial development of the rule in the common law countries Australia, New Zealand, Canada and Singapore, will assist in explaining the current scope for party autonomy within commonwealth common law tort law.

# I. Common law choice of law in non-contractual obligations

## 1.The general double actionability rule

The traditional English double-limbed choice of law rule for tort was first formulated in the well-known case of *Phillips* v *Eyre*.[878] In the formulation by Willes J it was held that in order to found a suit in England for a wrong alleged to have been committed abroad, two conditions must be fulfilled. First, the wrong must be of such a character that it would have been actionable if committed in England (first limb); and secondly, the act must not have been justifiable by the law of the place where it was done (second limb).[879]

An uneasy relationship between these two conditions and the nature of the rule resulted. Did the application of the rule simply amount to the recognition of only those causes of action congruent with rights under the *lex fori* (a precondition to the exercise of jurisdiction), or did the two limbs contain a choice of law rule indicating which substantive law would govern the dispute? In 1971 the House of Lords in *Boys* v *Chaplin*,[880] clearly held that both limbs of the double actionability rule enunciated in *Phillips* related to choice of law and not to jurisdiction.[881] The House of Lords unanimously approved the first limb of the rule but held that, although it

---

*Boele-Woelki/Talia Einhorn/ Daniel Girsberger/Symeon Symeonides* (eds.), Convergence and Divergence in Private International Law – Liber Amicorum Kurt Siehr (2010) 540–544.

878  (1870) LR 6 QB 1 (*Phillips*).

879  *Phillips*, 28–29 where Willes J cited the case *Liverpool, Brazil and River Plate Steam Navigation Co Ltd* v *Benham*, '*The Halley*'(1868) LR 2 PC 193 as authority for the first part of the rule.

880  [1971] AC 356 (HL) (*Boys*).

881  Boys, 385–387. See also Coupland v Arabian Gulf Petroleum Co [1983] 1 WLR 1136, 1147; Metall und Rohstoff AG v Donaldson Lufkin & Jenrette Inc [1990] 1 QB 391, 446 (CA); Johnson v Coventry Churchill International Ltd [1992] 3 All ER 14. Also accepted in Australia: McKain v R W Miller & Co (South Australia) Pty Ltd (1991) 174 CLR 1; and New Zealand: Richards v McLean [1973] 1 NZLR 521, 525. However, see Tolofson v Jensen; Lucas (Litigation Guardian of) v Gagnon [1994] 3 SCR

was not necessary that the cause of action be classified as a tort action, the second limb would only be satisfied if it were "actionable" under the *lex loci delicti*.[882] This approach required the matter to be actionable as a tort under the *lex fori* and civil actionability (i.e. wrongful or not justifiable behaviour) under the *lex loci delicti*[883] – hence, also known as the double actionability rule. It appeared to provide certainty and ease of application by restricting the recognition of acts done abroad to those resulting in liability common to both legal systems but in doing so gave pre-eminence to the *lex fori*.[884]

## 2. The exception

The inflexibility of the general rule enunciated in *Phillips v Eyre* was mitigated by the creation of an exception to the rule by the House of Lords in B*oys v Chaplin*.[885] The House of Lords held that the general rule may be departed from

---

1022 (Tolofson), in which the Supreme Court of Canada regarded the first limb as jurisdictional. Discussed further below at Part 4/B.II.3. Canada.

882 *Boys*, 377, 381, and 388–389 (overruling *Machado v Fontes* [1897] 2 QB 231 (CA), where it was held that criminal liability would be sufficient). See also *Breavington v Godleman* (1988) 169 CLR 41; *Voth v Manildra Flour Mills Pty Ltd* (1990) 171 CLR 538, 570; *McKain v R W Miller & Co (South Australia) Pty Ltd* (1991) 174 CLR 1; and *Johnson v Coventry Churchill International* Ltd [1992] 3 All ER 14, 23 where it was held that availability of a claim from a statutory insurance fund in the place of a civil claim cannot satisfy the second limb.

883 *Phillips*; *Machado v Fontes* [1897] 2 QB 231 (CA). Also *Boys* at 387–389 and *Coupland v Arabian Gulf Petroleum Co* [1983] 2 All ER 434.

884 According to a *lex fori* approach, tort liability is considered akin to criminal liability and thus closely connected to the policies and interests of the forum. Restricting liability to causes of action known only to the forum is problematic. Such an approach encourages the desire of the forum to exercise control by preferring its policies and asserting its own law (in terms of recognition of causes of actions, damages and protection of the parties) to the foreign law, despite strong connections with another legal system. Moreover, the availability of overriding forum control encourages the possibility of "forum shopping" – the deliberate choice of a suitable forum by the plaintiff in order to procure the application of the most favourable law to the plaintiffs claim. Neither the *lex fori* approach, nor the problem of forum shopping will be dealt with further here. See further e.g. *Albert Ehrenzweig*, The Not So Proper Law of a Tort: Pandora's Box (1968) 17 ICLQ 1; and, *Andrew Bell*, Forum Shopping and Venue in Transnational Litigation (2003).

885 See the exception formulated in Rule 203(2) in *Dicey & Morris* (12th ed.) Vol. II at 1488. Overview of common law developments in *Yeo Tiong Min*, Tort Choice of Law Beyond the Red Sea: Wither the Lex Fori? 1 Sing J Int'l & Comp L 91, 116.

in exceptional cases on the basis of what Lord Wilberforce referred to as a "contacts or interests" analysis.[886] In *Boys*, both the defendant and the plaintiff were normally resident in England, but temporarily stationed in Malta with the British armed forces. The plaintiff (Boys) was seriously injured in a collision caused by the defendant's (Chaplin) negligent driving. The question before the House of Lords was whether the plaintiff's claim for damages should be restricted to those damages common to both systems of law,[887] or whether the damages should include general damages provided for under English law only.[888] The House of Lords unanimously agreed that on the basis of a flexible exception English law should apply, it being of no consequence that general damages were not available under the *lex loci delicti*.[889]

However, although their Lordships reached general agreement on the need for flexibility[890] and the displacement of the *lex loci delicti* in favour of the *lex fori*, the reasons for doing so were conflicting. Lord Wilberforce[891] held that English law was applicable as the proper law of the tort, stating, "nothing suggests that the Maltese state has any interest in applying the rule to persons outside of it". Similarly advocating the introduction of flexibility, Lord Hodson[892] stressed that the double actionability rule was only applicable as a "general" rule and should allow for a departure when circumstances so demand. Lord Pearson,[893] although in favour of introducing enough flexibility to avoid the potential of forum shopping, thought that the *lex fori* played a dominant role. Lord Guest and Lord Donovan,[894] taking account of the English residence of both parties, were of the view that English law should apply, as the law of the forum, governing procedural questions.

---

886  *Boys*, 389. So held with reference to the words in *Phillips*: "As a general rule" and reference also to the 1968 Draft of the American Law Institute's Restatement of the Law (Second): Conflict of Laws. See *Elsabe Schoeman*, Tort Choice of Law in New Zealand: Recommendations for Reform [2004] NZ L Rev 537–561, 544–554.

887  I.e. Special damages for incurred expenses and proved loss of earnings.

888  I.e. Damages for pain and suffering.

889  For further discussion of the case see *John O'Brien* (ed.), Conflict of Laws (1999) 388; *G. F. Karsten*, Chaplin v Boys: Another Analysis (1970) 19 Int Comp L Q 35, 37–38; *Dicey & Morris* (12th ed.) Vol. II 1494–1502, for a summary of the rule see Rule 203(1)(a) and (b).

890  Especially Lord Hodson at 378 and Lord Wilberforce at 389–393.

891  See *Boys*, at 389–393.

892  *ibid* 356, 377, 378, 380.

893  *ibid* 406.

894  *ibid* 381, 383, 405.

Following this lack of uniformity it is difficult to extract a true ratio from the decision, leaving ambiguities surrounding the degree of flexibility introduced into the general rule and little guidance as to the basis of the exception.[895] Despite this, it has been recognised as establishing two propositions. First, that the rule in *Phillips* is modified so that it now has to be asked whether the conduct of the defendant is actionable, rather than 'not justifiable' by the law of the place of the tort; and second, that the rule is one which is to be applied 'with flexibility'.[896] According to Lord Wilberforce, any tension between certainty and flexibility for a choice of law rule was to be resolved in favour of an exception flexible enough "to take account of the varying interests and considerations of policy which may arise when one or more foreign elements are present".[897] His Lordship was particularly influenced by developments in the United States, which would take account of the varying interests of states and relevant considerations of policy including the nature of the tort, the connection of the parties and occurrence to a country, the policy underlying the particular substantive rule of law in question and the system of law with the greatest interest in the application of its law to the issue.[898] The result of the introduction of an exception based on a "contacts or interest" analysis – also referred to as the "proper law approach"[899] – recognised that a particular issue between the parties may be governed by the law of the country which, with respect to that issue, has the most significant relationship with the occurrence and the parties.[900] Lord Wilberforce however, stressed that the application of an exception will not be invoked in every case or even, probably, in many cases. His Lordship went on to state that: "The general rule must apply unless clear and satisfying grounds are shown why it should be departed from and what solution, derived from what other rule, should be preferred".[901]

---

895 *Dicey & Morris* (12th ed.) Vol. II 1495; *John O'Brien* (ed.), Conflict of Laws (1999) 388.

896 *Cheshire & North* (12th ed.) 535.

897 *Boys*, 389, 391.

898 ibid 392; see also Red Sea Insurance Co Ltd v Bouygues SA [1995] 1 AC 190 (PC) (Red Sea Insurance).

899 See *John Morris*, The Proper Law of the Tort (1951) 64 Harv L Rev 881; *Dicey & Morris* (12th ed.) Vol. II 1498.

900 Compare the 1968 Draft of the American Law Institute's Restatement (Second) of the Conflict of Laws § 145(1); also formulated as Rule 203(2) in *Dicey & Morris* (12th ed.) Vol. II 1488.

901 *Boys*, 391.

In 1989, almost two decades following the reformulation of the double action-ability rule in *Boys*, the English Court of Appeal clearly confined the scope of the common law rule as being confined to torts which were in substance committed overseas.[902] As a result, those torts committed in England were governed solely by the *lex fori*. In 1995, the Privy Council in *Red Sea Insurance Co Ltd v Bouygues SA*[903] adopted and extended the "flexible exception" outlined by Lord Wilberforce in *Boys* even further. In *Red Sea Insurance*, the specific issue before the Privy Council was whether the appellants (Red Sea Insurance) could counterclaim in negligence, against a group of respondents (suppliers of building materials "PCG") for supply-ing faulty materials to one of the respondents in breach of a duty of care to another respondent, which had resulted in the appellant's economic loss. The appellants ar-gued that the loss claimed by the respondents for loss and expense incurred in the course of construction work undertaken in Saudi Arabia, was not covered by the indemnity insurance policy but if it was, that it would be entitled to recover the loss by way of subrogation from PCG. A direct cause of action against PCG in tort for the damage caused to the other respondents did not exist under the *lex fori* (Hong Kong law), while under the *lex loci delicti* (Saudi Arabian law) such a cause of ac-tion in tort was available. A cause of action allowing the appellants to directly sue PCG would only be possible through the application of the exception to the general rule requiring double actionability. The Privy Council affirmed that: (a) following *Boys v Chaplin*, an exception to the general rule as stated in *Dicey and Morris*[904] was available;[905] (b) the exception could operate to displace the *lex fori* in favour of the *lex loci delicti* and (c) the exception was not limited to specific isolated issues, but

---

902 *Metall und Rohstoff AG v Donaldson Lufkin & Jenrette Inc* [1990] 1 QB 391 (CA). The approach of the Court of Appeal in order to identify where the tort had taken place required locating the "substance" of the tort, i.e. considering the whole series of events constituting the elements of the tort and asking where in substance did the cause of action arise.

903 *Red Sea Insurance* per Lord Slynn giving the unanimous decision of the Privy Coun-cil. The case is discussed in detail by *Abla Mayss*, Statutory Reform of Choice of Law in Tort and Delict: A Bitter Pill or a Cure for the Ill? [1996] 2 Web JCLI; and *Yeo Tiong Min*, Tort Choice of Law beyond the Red Sea: Whither the *Lex Fori*? (1997) 1 Sing J Int'l & Comp L 91.

904 *Dicey & Morris* (12th ed.) Vol. II Rule 203(1) 1487–1488, which states: "But a par-ticular issue between the parties may be governed by the law of a country which, with respect to that issue, has the most significant relationship with the occurrence and the parties".

905 Red Sea Insurance, 206.

could be applied to the whole claim.[906] The most significant aspect of the subsequent elaboration of the exception in *Red Sea Insurance* is that by allowing the appellant to recover its loss despite the lack of any remedy existing under the *lex fori*, the application of the exception was extended for the first time to allow the exclusive application of the foreign *lex loci delicti*, due to an overwhelming number of connections with the law of the place where the tort occurred.[907] This additional extension of the flexible exception had not been considered in previous cases, which had only applied flexibility in order to allow the application of the *lex fori*.

Although the Privy Council in *Red Sea Insurance* served to dispel some of the uncertainty left surrounding the application of the flexible exception to the general rule following *Boys*, and strongly signified a willingness to give less prominence to the law of the forum by allowing its displacement in favour of the law of the *lex loci delicti* (even if no such claim would be available under the *lex fori*), no reference to the intention of the parties was made. The connections considered relevant in *Red Sea Insurance* were instead: the insurance policy was subject to Saudi Arabian law, the Saudi Arabian government owned the property, the project and contracts were to be carried out in Saudi Arabia, both the main and the supply contracts were subject to Saudi Arabian law, the defendant's main office was in Saudi Arabia and the breach, damage and expense of repairing the alleged damage all occurred in Saudi Arabia.[908] This identification of the connecting factors indicated a centre-of-gravity approach whereby the Privy Council focused on contractual connections rather than considering the policies underlying the substantive laws or wider factors surrounding the tort and weighing the relative significance of them. In other words, the case indicated a shift away from a policy or interest analysis,[909] instead preferring the consideration of the objective connections of the tort to the country. But just as the intention of the parties was not considered a relevant connection, a law purportedly chosen by the parties could only be accommodated in the form of an implied choice of English law evidenced by their conduct in proceedings. More specifically, where parties refrained from pleading and proving foreign law, English

---

906  *ibid*, 206–207.
907  *ibid* 207. See also *Peter North/James Fawcett*, Cheshire and North's Private International Law (1999) (hereafter: *Cheshire & North* (13th ed.)) 611–612.
908  Red Sea Insurance, 207.
909  Such an approach, which is based on the American Restatement of the Law, has been described as a 'hybrid' approach in that it is both jurisdiction-selecting and rule-selecting; see *Elsabe Schoeman*, Tort Choice of Law in New Zealand: Recommendations for Reform [2004] NZ L Rev 537, 547–554.

law would apply.[910] According to this reasoning, a choice of law in tort in the common law could be no more than a choice of law by the court.[911]

In sum, although the mechanical application of Justice Willes' formulation in *Phillips v Eyre* was mitigated by the introduction of a flexible exception, its application has left unanswered issues concerning the role (if any) for party autonomy in torts. As has been noted, no English decision challenged the proposition that a tort committed in England was subject only to English law nor did any English decision decide when a foreign tort was involved that it was possible to exclude the application of both limbs of the rule in favour of a law chosen by the parties.[912] It has been noted that following the acceptance of an exception to the rule of double actionability, it would have only been a short step for English courts to conclude that a law expressly chosen by the parties to govern their contractual relationship could also govern any non-contractual liability arising from their relationship.[913]

It remains unclear therefore, when and under what circumstances the flexible exception can be invoked. In particular, what significance should be attached to a pre-existing relationship between the parties where a choice of law for contract has been reached? Moreover, should a law purportedly chosen by the parties be taking into account as a relevant connecting factor and if so, what status should be given to it (e.g. precedence over other objective connecting factors)? In addition, if the exception can be invoked in order to give effect to a chosen law, can it be invoked in favour of a third foreign law that is neither the *lex fori* nor the *lex loci delicti*? An examination of the development of the common law rule and subsequent consideration of the possible, yet limited accommodation of party autonomy within the rule follows.

## II. Reception and application of the common law rule

The double-limbed common law choice of law rule for foreign torts has been abolished in the UK for most torts following legislative reform,[914] and more recently

---

910  *Adrian Briggs* (ed.), Agreements on Jurisdiction and Choice of Law (2008) Chapter 10, 403.

911  ibid.

912  *ibid*, Chapter 10, 404.

913  *ibid*, Chapter 2, 40–41, and at n 71 citing *Johnson v Coventry Churchill International Ltd* [1992] 3 All ER 14 suggesting that had the facts pointed to an express choice of English law in the parties' contract, this would have been the outcome.

914  Private International Law (Miscellaneous Provisions) Act 1995 (UK). The Act introduced a statutory basis for the determination of foreign torts and also applied to torts

with the adoption of the Rome II Regulation. The requirement of double action-ability has been subject to continuous academic debate and adverse comment,[915] but the lack of a clear role for the law chosen by the parties has not been a primary concern.[916] Instead, objections and calls for reform have focused on the pre-eminence given to the *lex fori* or the 'homing devices'[917] and the potential for injustice caused by the requirement for the claimant to prove that he could succeed under two legal systems. The following study of the application of the rule in the common law shows that a role for a law chosen by the parties remains minimal, or perhaps obsolete.

## 1. Australia

### a. Adoption of the common law rule

The choice of law rules applicable to cross-border tort claims in Australia, have been rules of common law inherited from the imperial British judicial

---

within the UK (s 9(6)). Compare the previous common law position distinguishing between foreign torts and torts within the UK e.g. in *Metall und Rohstoff AG v Donaldson Lufkin & Jenrette Inc* [1990] 1 QB 391 (CA). Note that section 13 of the 1995 Act specifically excluded the operation of Part III to defamation and other related claims. These are also excluded from the scope of the Rome II Regulation, see Article 1(2)(g) Rome II. As such, the common law conflict rules for tort are preserved in relation to these claims.

915 See for example *CGJ Morse*, Torts in Private International Law; A New Statutory Framework (1996) 45 ICLQ 888, 1002 n 106, who states that: "The double actionability rule has proved troublesome in every jurisdiction to which it has migrated". See also *Elsabe Schoeman*, Tort Choice of Law in New Zealand: Recommendations for Reform [2004] NZ L Rev 537–561; *Nicky Richardson*, Double Actionability and the Choice of Law (2002) 32 Hong Kong L J 497, 517; but c.f. *William Tong*, Warnings for a New Beginning Torts (Choice of Law) Bill (2005) Singapore Journal of Legal Studies 288–299.

916 *Adrian Briggs* (ed.), Agreements on Jurisdiction and Choice of Law (2008) Chapter 10 404.

917 Summarised by *Reid Mortensen*, Homing Devices in Choice of Tort Law: Australian, British and Canadian Approaches, 55 ICLQ 2006 839–878 at 841, with further references: e.g. characterisation of the issue as a non-tort claim subject to the non-tort choice of law rule of the *lex fori*; identification of the forum as the place of the tort governed by the *lex fori* as the *lex loci delicti*; characterisation of the issue as procedural to be governed by the *lex fori*; use of the flexible exception in favour of the *lex fori*; invoking public policy and applying the *lex fori* in default.

system.[918] In 1905 in the case *Potter v Broken Hill Proprietary Ltd* [1905],[919] the rule established in *Phillips v Eyre* was held to be applicable in Australia. Some Australian State courts also embraced subsequent developments in English courts in *Boys v Chaplin* and *Red Sea*.[920] However, the application of the English conflict-of-law rule in Australia as a federal dominion, caused courts not to distinguish between interstate and foreign tort claims.[921] Whereas the English common law rules of private international law were designed to apply to disputes with foreign states, Australian courts merely applied them without any consideration as to their appropriateness within the Australian federal context.[922] For almost 100 years Australian courts followed the approach taken in *Potter*.[923] Although the need to distinguish between interstate and foreign torts was recognised it was not until 1988, that the High Court in *Breavington v Godleman*[924] rejected the rule in *Phillips v Eyre* for interstate tort cases, which were instead to be governed by the *lex loci delicti*. However, the position, which had been adopted by a slim (4:3) majority by the High Court, eventually led to the court subsequently adopting a different majority and returning to the old rule in *Phillips v Eyre*.[925]

---

918  Subject to some legislation. See *Reid Mortensen*, A Common Law Cocoon: Australia and the Rome II Regulation YBPIL Vol. 9 (2007) 203–222, 204. Also *Peter Nygh*, Choice of Law in Torts in Australia (2000) YBPIL Vol. 2 55–73.

919  Potter v Broken Hill Proprietary Ltd [1905] VLR 612.

920  See e.g. *Kemp v Piper* [1971] SASR 25; *Warren v Warren* [1972] Qd R 386; *Corcoran v Corcoran* [1974] VR 164.

921  Potter v Broken Hill Proprietary Ltd [1905] VLR 612; Koop v Bepp (1951) 84 CLR 629.

922  On this see *Alex Castles*, The Reception and Status of English Law in Australia, (1963) 2 Adelaide Law Review 1–32, 9. Also dissenting judgment of Justice A'Beckett in *Potter v Broken Hill Proprietary Ltd* [1905] VLR 612, 634–635.

923  E.g. *Pedersen v Young* (1964) 110 CLR, 170 (per Windeyer J).

924  (1988) 169 CLR 41, so held by a slim 4:3 majority. Followed in *Byrnes v Groote Eylandt Mining Corporation* (1990) 19 NSWLR 13, 23, 32–33 and *Stevens v Head* (1991) 14 MVR 327, 330. The case was also referred to by the Supreme Court of Canada in *Tolofson v Jensen; Lucas (Litigation Guardian of) v Gagnon* [1994] 3 SCR 1022 at 1051–2, 1063–5 in relation to the adoption of the *lex loci delicti* rule as applicable to both interprovincial and international torts in Canada.

925  *McKain v RW Miller & Co (SA) Pty Ltd* (1991) 174 CLR 1; *Stevens v Head* (1993) 176 CLR 433. Note however, that technically the majority in both cases approved and endorsed the double actionability rule only in the obiter dicta made. Instead of deciding questions on choice of tort law, both cases concerned characterisation issues of substance and procedure.

## b. Judicial reform[926]

Reform of Australia's choice of law rules for tort came in two stages: the first stage dealt with interstate torts and was settled in the case of *John Pfeiffer Pty Ltd v Rogerson (Pfeiffer)*;[927] the second stage dealt with foreign torts and was addressed in the case *Régie Nationale des Usines Renault SA v Zhang (Renault)*.[928]

In *Pfeiffer*, the High Court of Australia firmly rejected the application of the double actionability rule for Australian interstate torts.[929] Justice Kirby, in his judgment emphasised that Australian tort law had been restricted by the "inappropriate borrowing" from English common law and "unquestioning acceptance of English jurisprudence".[930] Instead the High Court unequivocally approved the application of a strict *lex loci delicti* rule for interstate torts.[931] It held that no reference was to be had to the law of the forum or public policy constraints and that issues about damages and compensation were substantive matters to be governed by the *lex loci delicti*. Three primary reasons were given by the majority in *Pfeiffer* for adopting a universal *lex loci delicti* rule: it would give effect to the reasonable expectations of the parties;[932] recognise the importance of giving effect to local

---

926 Although this contribution focuses on common law reform, note also that the Australian Law Reform Commission had made early efforts to change the unsatisfactory position following the return to the *Phillips v Eyre* rule. In 1992 it produced a report (Choice of Law: Report No 58, Law Reform Commission, Sydney, 1992, 40–80, at 42–50), in which three options were proposed for reforming choice of tort law: the *lex causae* to be either 1) the proper law of the tort (i.e. the law of the place which has the most significant relationship with the occurrence and the parties); 2) the *lex loci delicti* with no exceptions; or 3) the *lex loci delicti* with an exception in favour of the proper law of the tort. The Commission preferred the third option, rejecting the strict *lex loci delicti* rule with no exceptions. Report discussed further in *Peter Nygh*, Choice-of-Law Rules and Forum Shopping in Australia (1995) 46 South Carolina Law Review, 899–921, especially at 918–921.

927 (2000) 172 ALR 625 (*Pfeiffer*).

928 (2002) 210 CLR 491; 187 ALR 1 (*Renault*).

929 For further commentary on intra Australian torts see e.g. *Martin Davies*, Choice of Law after the Civil Liability legislation (2008) 16 Torts Law Journal 10.

930 *Renault*, 109–110. The High Court refused to follow *Koop v Bebb* (1951) 84 CLR 629.

931 Kirby J also agreed with the general reasoning of the joint judgment: see *Pfeiffer*, 652 [106]. Further, *Ross Anderson*, International torts in the High Court of Australia (2002) 10(2) Torts Law J 132; *Gary Davis*, John Pfeiffer Pty Ltd v Rogerson; Choice of Law in Tort at the Dawning of the 21st Century (2000) 24 Melb U L Rev 982–1015.

932 *Pfeiffer* at [87], as per Gleeson CJ, Gaudron, McHugh, Gummow and Hayne JJ.

laws in force within a federation;[933] and would serve to promote certainty within the federal context.[934] The majority also explicitly rejected any application of a "flexible exception" to the *lex loci delicti*. They held that to adopt any flexible rule or exception to a universal rule would require the closest attention to identifying what criteria are to be used to make the choice of law.[935] Further, that describing the flexible rules in terms such as 'real and substantial' or 'most significant' connection with the jurisdiction would not give sufficient guidance to courts, to parties or to those such as insurers who must order their affairs on the basis of predictions about the future application of the rule.[936]

In 2002, the Australian High Court was again faced with the issue of choice of law in tort, but this time involving a foreign tort in the case *Régie Nationale des Usines Renault SA v Zhang*.[937] Two years following the decision in *Pfeiffer*, the High Court abandoned the English common law practice and theory for choice of law in all cases involving torts outside of Australia.[938] Instead, it adopted the *lex loci delicti* as the law governing the rights and liabilities and thereby brought the Australian choice of law rule for torts committed outside of Australia into line with the choice of law rule for interstate torts. Mr Zhang (the respondent) had travelled to New Caledonia, the purpose of which was to complete his application for Australian permanent residency with the Australian consulate in Noumea. Mr Zhang had hired a Renault car, and following an accident in which the car rolled, suffered serious injuries. He subsequently sought to sue several Renault companies, based in France, in New South Wales, claiming damages for negligence in respect of manufacturing faults. Renault was successful at first instance in having the proceedings stayed on the basis that the New South Wales court was an inappropriate forum.[939] However, Mr Zhang successfully appealed the stay and Renault's appeal to the Australian High Court was rejected.

Although it was recognised that the application of the double actionability rule was not a matter of contention in the case, the majority of the court nonetheless held that the double actionability rule should now be held to have no application

---

933  *ibid*, [75], [87].

934  *ibid*, [83].

935  *ibid*, [79].

936  *ibid*, [79].

937  (2002) 210 CLR 491; 187 ALR 1 (*Renault*).

938  *ibid* [60].

939  It must be shown that the forum is "clearly inappropriate"; derived from *Voth v Manildra Flour Mills Pty Ltd* (1990) 171 CLR 538.

in Australia in international torts.[940] The High Court affirmed its reasoning given in *Pfeiffer*, and extended the application of the same choice of law rule (the *lex loci delicti*) to international torts, despite absence of the significant factor of federal considerations.[941] Denying any place for the consideration of applying laws that have a real connection with the issue, the *lex loci delicti* as the universal rule was to be preferred because it would recognise the principle of comity,[942] place emphasis on activity related connections, and promote certainty in the law.[943] Consistent with its earlier judgment in *Pfeiffer*, the majority of the High Court again emphasised that for torts committed outside of Australia no regard was to be had to the law of the forum, or to any "flexible exception", instead preferring a strict application of the *lex loci delicti*.[944]

However, after considering Canadian developments the Court noted that questions, which might be caught up in the application of a flexible exception to the *lex loci delicti* may often in practice be "subsumed in the issues presented on a stay application, including one based on public policy grounds".[945] In this way public

---

940 *Renault*, [60]. See strict application of the *lex loci delicti* rule in *Blunden v Commonwealth of Australia* (2003) ALR 189, in which the High Court refused to create a special choice of law rule for torts occurring on the high seas. But compare the internet defamation case *Dow Jones & Co Inc v Gutnick* (2003) 210 CLR 575, where the High Court accepted that the 'locus' of the tort may require a flexible element, so that in the case of internet defamation the *loci delicti* is the place where the information is downloaded and read. In this respect see also the legislative developments providing for a proper choice of law rule based on the closest connection for defamatory publications within Australia: Defamation Act 2005 (NSW); Defamation Act 2005 (Vic); Defamation Act 2005 (Qld); Defamation Act 2005 (SA); Defamation Act 2005 (WA); Defamation Act 2005 (Tas); Civil Law Wrongs (Amendment) Act 2006 (ACT); Defamation Act 2005 (NT).

941 *Renault*, [75]. Previous cases had only been concerned with intranational tort proceedings. See for example: *Koop v Bebb* (1951) 84 CLR 629; *Breavington v Godleman* (1988) 169 CLR 41; 80 ALR 362; *McKain v R W Miller & Co (SA) Pty Ltd* (1991) 174 CLR 1; *Pfeiffer*.

942 *Renault*, [64] citing La Forest J in *Tolofson v Jensen; Lucas (Litigation Guardian of) v Gagnon* [1994] 3 SCR 1022.

943 *Renault*, [66].

944 *ibid* [62]-[63], [75] (per Gleeson CJ, Gaudron, McHugh, Gummow and Hayne JJ) citing the Canadian decision in *Tolofson*. Further on this, *Adrian Briggs*, The Legal Significance of the Place of a Tort (2002) 2(1) Oxford Univ Commonwealth L J 133, 134; also, *Martin Davies/Andrew Bell/Paul Le Gay Brereton* (eds.), Nygh's Conflict of Laws in Australia (2010) 423 *et seq*.

945 *Renault*, [73].

policy considerations would provide control at the jurisdiction stage of proceedings, and allow the court to invoke public policy as a basis for declining to exercise jurisdiction where necessary.[946] However, this presents a limited approach to a flexible exception having no relevance in the choice of law stage of proceedings and the consideration of the appropriate choice of law.[947]

Following the *Renault* decision, it has been argued that the recourse to forum control on questions of procedure and public policy was inevitable following the denial of the possibility of a flexible exception in the choice of law question.[948] The use of public policy to regulate the application of foreign law provides a powerful mode of forum control. But there appears little support for an approach allowing a court to invoke public policy in order to decline jurisdiction.[949] Moreover, the circumstances in which a court would exercise a stay of proceedings based on such considerations remain unclear. Use of the doctrine at the jurisdiction stage of proceedings to prevent the recognition of a foreign tort claim, cannot be linked with the idea of providing sufficient flexibility as an exception to the application of the *lex loci delicti*.[950] Even use of the doctrine at the choice of law stage cannot satisfactorily mitigate a deficient choice of law rule. The concept of public policy is vague and inherently unpredictable and resort to public policy considerations in a piecemeal fashion, in order to mitigate the unsatisfactory application of a

---

946 *Renault*, [60]: "To the extent that the first limb of [the double actionability] rule was intended to operate as a technique of *forum* control, we should frankly recognize that the question is about public policy and confront directly the issues that this may present."

947 *Anthony Gray*, Flexibility in Conflict of Laws Multistate Tort Cases: The Way Forward in Australia (2004) 23(2) U Queensland L J 435, 438; *Reid Mortensen*, Homing Devices in Choice of Tort Law: Australian, British and Canadian Approaches 55 ICLQ 2006 839, 863 *et seq*.

948 See *Adrian Briggs*, The Legal Significance of the Place of a Tort (2002) 2(1) Oxford Univ Commonwealth L J 133, 136–137. The majority in *Renault* also reserved its position on whether the issue of damages and compensation was to be regarded as substantive and therefore governed by the *lex loci delicti* in relation to foreign torts. This has left open the possibility for courts to manipulate the category of damages and compensation and resort to the *lex fori* for questions of procedure.

949 *Anthony Gray*, Flexibility in Conflict of Laws Multistate Tort Cases: The Way Forward in Australia (2004) 23(2) U Queensland L J 435, 439. The author suggests that "the High Court should elaborate on the reasons for this approach, acknowledge its departure from the United States and English jurisprudence in this area and explain precisely how 'public policy' is relevant to questions of jurisdiction, as it has suggested."

950 *Renault*, [122]. Kirby J noted that public policy would not always prevent application of inappropriate foreign laws. Compare Major J in *Tolofson*, at [84].

rigid rule, generates great uncertainty.[951] It is expected that increased use of public policy as an escape device will feature in Australian cases following the denial of a flexible exception in *Renault*.[952]

The current Australian position can be summarised as follows:

1. As a general rule the *lex loci delicti*, or the law of the place where the tort was committed governs interstate and foreign torts.
2. No exception to the *lex loci delicti* rule is available for interstate torts cases.
3. An exception to the *lex loci delicti* rule for foreign torts may only be considered at the jurisdiction stage of proceedings whereby the court can invoke public policy as a basis for declining to exercise jurisdiction where necessary.

What distinguishes the Australian approach to the tort choice of law problem from the other systems to be analysed below is the "no-exception" emphasis taken, an exception only being available as a public policy analysis in the jurisdiction stage of proceedings. Priority is given to uniformity, predictability and certainty and the application of a rigid *lex loci delicti* rule is thought to achieve this. But in a case where the parties' connection to the place of the tort is fortuitous and no other

---

951  *PB Carter*, Choice of Law in Tort and Delict (1991) 107 Law Q Rev 405, 411.
952  See also *Neilson v Overseas Projects Corporation of Victoria and Mercantile Insurance (Australia) Ltd* [2005] HCA 54. The High Court of Australia was again faced with the need to remedy the lack of a flexible exception to the *lex loci delicti* and employ other techniques in order to ensure substantive justice. It confirmed the abolition of the common law double actionability rule in *Renault* and affirmed a strict *lex loci delicti* as applicable to foreign torts. The case also raised issues associated with the *renvoi* doctrine and proof of foreign law. It overruled the decision of the Supreme Court of Western Australia in *Mercantile Mutual Insurance (Australia) v Neilson* (2004) 28 WAR 206, which had denied any application of *renvoi* and contrary to the common law rule that *renvoi* does not apply in tort (*M'Elroy v M'Allister* (1949) SC 110, at 126), the Australian court accepted a partial *renvoi*. It is noted that the application of an exception based on the parties' common residence, would have achieved the same result. For further discussion thereof see e.g. *Elsabe Schoeman*, Renvoi: Throwing (and Catching) the Boomerang – Neilson v Overseas Projects Corporation of Victoria Ltd (2006) 25 University of Queensland Law Journal 203–212; *Reid Mortensen*, Troublesome and Obscure: The Renewal of *Renvoi* in Australia (2006) 2(1) Journal of Private International Law 1; *idem*, Homing Devices in Choice of Tort Law: Australian, British and Canadian Approaches 55 ICLQ 2006 839; *Mary Keyes*, The Doctrine of *Renvoi* in International Torts: Mercantile Mutual Insurance v Neilson (2005) 13(1) Torts Law Journal 1; *idem*, Foreign Law in Australian Courts: *Neilson v Overseas Projects Corporation of Victoria* (2007) 15 Torts Law Journal 9.

connections to the place exist, the application of the *lex loci delicti*, although appealing due to its certainty and simplicity in application, is an obviously deficient choice of law rule.[953] An explicit provision for party autonomy within the tort choice of law rule has thus far not been tested in Australian courts, let alone even considered.

## 2. New Zealand

In New Zealand the rule established in *Phillips v Eyre* still provides the basis of the conflict choice of law rule in tort. The rights and liabilities of parties under a foreign tort action shall be determined by reference to the double actionability rule, requiring actionability under the *lex fori* and the *lex loci delicti commissi*. To an extent the problems associated with the forum-centric and strict requirement of double actionability, have been mitigated by the adoption of the flexible exception as formulated by the House of Lords in *Boys*[954] and the Privy Council in *Red Sea Insurance*.[955]

There are few reported cases in New Zealand concerned with international torts. This is partly due to the fact that the New Zealand accident compensation scheme seems to operate as a procedural bar under the *lex fori*, precluding any proceedings for compensatory damages.[956] However, foreign case law has indicated a trend toward regarding statutory bars as substantive.[957] As such, following the application of the exception to the double actionability rule and application of the *lex loci delicti*, a claim for compensatory damages for personal injury is a possibility.

The focus in cases where courts in New Zealand have addressed the problem of tort choice of law has primarily been on the exercise of jurisdiction within

---

953　The existing law in Australia has been described as "unsatisfactory" by *Peter Nygh*, Choice of Law in Torts in Australia (2000) YBPIL Vol. 2 55, 70. Also critical see e.g. *Friedrich Juenger*, Tort Choice of Law in a Federal System (1997) 19 Syd. LR 529; *Martin Davies*, Exactly What is the Australian Choice of Law Rule in Torts Cases? (1996) 70 ALJ 711.

954　Boys.

955　Red Sea Insurance.

956　See the New Zealand Accident Compensation Act 2001, s 317. Further, *Elsabe Schoeman/Rosemary Tobin*, The New Zealand Accident Compensation Scheme: The Statutory Bar and the Conflict of Laws (2005) 53 American Journal of Comparative Law 493–514; *Elsabe Schoeman/Rosemary Tobin*, A Holiday in New Zealand: The Implications of New Zealand's Accident Compensation Scheme (2005) IPRax 374–375.

957　Bennet v Enstrom Helicopter Corporation 679 F 2d 630 (6th Circ 1982); James Hardie & Co Pty Ltd and Another v Hall as administrator of Estate of Putt [1998] 43 NSWLR 554, 579.

the context of *forum non conveniens*,[958] rather than on true choice of law issues. Where a court is faced with an international dispute, it will first determine whether it has jurisdiction to hear the dispute and secondly, should carry out a detailed inquiry into what system of law, domestic or foreign, is to apply to govern the issue. However, in the New Zealand context this second inquiry into the search for the applicable law has been overshadowed by questions of jurisdiction. Arguably this raises questions as to the extent a New Zealand court would find itself bound by precedent when faced with a true tort choice of law issue. In addition, the examination of tort choice of law within *forum non conveniens* proceedings is problematic in the sense that a court will only carry out an extremely restricted consideration of choice of law; the focus being primarily on whether a New Zealand court has jurisdiction both over the parties and the cause of action.[959]

Despite the lack of a definitive reception of the common law double actionability rule in a true choice of law context in New Zealand, the general rule and its exception as applicable to foreign torts appears to have been accepted by New Zealand courts.[960] In 2003, the High Court in *Baxter v RMC Group Plc*[961] recognised the double actionability choice of law rule as applicable to foreign tort actions heard in a New Zealand forum. The case concerned three tort actions, one for deceit and two for conspiracy, the *leges causae* of which had to be determined to decide the issue of whether the New Zealand court was *forum non conveniens*. Justice O'Regan expressed the general tort choice of law rule and its exception as set out in *Red Sea Insurance*, in the following way:[962]

(a) A tort is actionable in New Zealand only if it is actionable both in New Zealand and England [the *locus delicti*]. If this rule (the double actionability rule) is satisfied, then the substantive law to be applied is the law of New Zealand.

---

958 Even where a New Zealand court determines that it has jurisdiction to hear a matter, a defendant might still argue that there is another country that also has jurisdiction, and that in the interests of justice the other country is the most appropriate place for the dispute to be heard. See generally *Cheshire & North* (13th ed.) 334–346.

959 *Elsabe Schoeman*, Tort Choice of Law in New Zealand: Recommendations for Reform [2004] NZ L Rev 537–561, 540, 561, who states that this strengthens the call to reformulate a certain and well-defined tort choice of law rule and argues that New Zealand should take the statutory reform route.

960 See Richards and Others v McLean and Others [1973] 1 NZLR 521; Kunzang v Gershwin Hotel, HC Auckland, CP318-SD/99, 19 September 2000, Master Faire; Starlink Navigation Ltd v The Ship "Seven Pioneer" (2001) 16 PRNZ 55; Baxter v RMC Group Plc [2003] 1 NZLR 304 (Baxter).

961 Baxter.

962 *ibid*, 318.

(b) However, if one country has the most significant relationship with the occurrence and with the parties, the substantive law of that country is to be applied.

According to the application of the double actionability rule, the governing law would have been New Zealand law. However, O'Regan J accepted the defendant's submission that English law, as the law of the country that had the most significant relationship with the occurrence and the parties, should apply. Following consideration of the relevant connecting factors, which included the parties' contractual submission to the jurisdiction of the English Courts, O'Regan J decided that apart from incidental connections with New Zealand, the substance of the torts had occurred in England. On this basis it was held that, in accordance with the exception in *Red Sea Insurance*, the *lex loci delicti* would apply. There was no analysis of the interpretation and scope of the exception, highlighting the somewhat passive acceptance of the rule by New Zealand courts and the restricted focus of choice of law for tort within the course of jurisdictional proceedings.

Following *Baxter*, the current New Zealand position can be restated as follows:

1. The common law double actionability rule, as enunciated in *Phillips v Eyre* and modified by the House of Lords in *Boys v Chaplin* and the Privy Council in *Red Sea Insurance*, is applicable to foreign tort claims heard in New Zealand.
2. On the basis of the general rule, an act done in a foreign country is actionable in New Zealand as a tort only if it is both (a) actionable as a tort according to New Zealand law (actionable under the *lex fori*); and (b) actionable according to the law of the foreign country where the act was done (actionable under the *lex loci delicti*).
3. However, on the basis of the exception, the general rule of double actionability may be departed from in an appropriate case, in which the matter is instead governed by the law of the country that has the most significant relationship with the occurrence and the parties.[963]

New Zealand is one of the few Anglo-Common Law countries, which continues to adhere to the *Phillips v Eyre* approach on the basis of double actionability, an approach that has become increasingly isolated being overturned by legislation or case law in other jurisdictions. Although subsequent application of the rule has resulted in the addition of an exception, it is based on uncertain grounds leaving the

---

963  It may govern a particular issue only: *Boys*, (head of damages); or the whole claim: *Red Sea Insurance.*

current state of tort choice of law in New Zealand in an indeterminate state.[964] As a result of the adherence to the traditional common law rule applicable to foreign torts, no provision is made for the role of a law chosen by the parties in New Zealand conflict-of-law rules.

## 3. Canada

For 50 years Canadian courts followed the Canadian decision of *McLean v Pettigrew*[965] that had applied the general rule as enunciated in *Phillips v Eyre*.[966] In 1994, a firm rejection of the English approach in favour of a Canadian reformulation of the rule was brought about by the decision of the Supreme Court of Canada in *Tolofson v Jensen; Lucas (Litigation Guardian of) v Gagnon (Tolofson)*.[967]

*Tolofson* concerned two appeals involving interprovincial car accidents, one in Saskatchewan (Tolofson) and the other in Québec (Lucas). In *Tolofson* a passenger of a car (British Columbia resident) driven by his father (British Columbia resident) was seriously injured when it collided with a car in Saskatchewan, driven by Jensen (Saskatchewan resident). The victim brought an action for damages against both his father and Jensen in British Columbia. Under Saskatchewan law, at the time of the accident, the action was time barred and a gratuitous passenger was precluded from suing the driver. In *Lucas* the passenger of a car (Ontario resident) brought an action against her husband and the driver of the other car Lavoie (Québec resident) in Ontario for personal injuries suffered following a collision. The law of Québec barred any action for damages for bodily injuries. Both cases therefore involved the determination of the applicable law in order to establish the liability of the defendants. The Supreme Court allowed both appeals. La Forest J, delivering the leading judgment of the majority, overruled *McLean v*

---

964 Critically *Elsabe Schoeman*, Tort Choice of Law in New Zealand: Recommendations for Reform [2004] NZ L Rev 537–561; *Anthony Gray*, Conflict of Laws in International Tort Cases: the need for reform on both sides of the Tasman (2006) Yearbook of New Zealand Jurisprudence 9 113–140, 137 *et seq.*

965 [1945] SCR 62.

966 *Phillips*, 28–29 as modified by *Machado v Fontes* [1897] 2 QB 231 (CA). For a discussion of the position pre *Tolofson* see *Jean Gabriel Castel*, Canadian Conflict of Laws (1997) 678–682.

967 [1994] 3 SCR 1022. For a overview see e.g. *William Tetley*, Current Developments in Canadian Private International Law (1999) 78 Can Bar Rev 152–199; *idem*, The On-Going Saga of Canada's Conflict of Law Revolution – Theory and Practice Part I (2004) IPRax 457–472 and Part II (2004) IPRax 551–561.

*Pettigrew*, dispensing with the combined effect of the English double actionability rule and holding that, in accord with the international principles of territoriality and comity, the *lex loci delicti* should henceforth govern tort choice of law.[968] The *lex loci delicti* should be applied as a general rule since it has the advantage of "certainty, ease of application and predictability" and "would seem to meet normal expectations".[969] La Forest J held that the place of the tort should be defined as the place where the wrongful act occurred, but did consider that in some cases the place where the harm ensued could be the place of the tort.[970] Following extensive discussion, the majority of the court rejected any recognition of a proper law approach that would allow application of the law of the place with which the tort is most closely connected, which would be "lacking in certainty or likely to create or prolong litigation".[971] The Court's concern with certainty was paramount and justified by reference to the underlying principles of order and fairness in private international law, and specifically that "[o]rder is a precondition to justice".[972] Thereby, for interstate tort actions any issues regarding the substantial connection to or actionability of the wrong by the law of the forum would be factors better weighed in considering the issue of *forum non conveniens*.[973]

However, with respect to foreign torts, the possible escape from the inflexible application of the *lex loci delicti* as the only applicable choice of law rule was recognised by La Forest J. It was suggested that the general conflict rule may apply less rigidly where the rule would otherwise cause injustice and acknowledged that, provided a flexible exception was very carefully defined, it might be applicable in limited circumstances.[974] Ultimately, although both appeals were

---

968 *Tolofson* at [42]: [I]t seems axiomatic to me that, at least as a general rule, the law to be applied in torts is the law of the place where the activity occurred, i.e., the *lex loci delicti* [...] That being so it seems to me, barring some recognized exception, to which possibility I will turn later, that as Willes J. pointed out in *Phillips v. Eyre*, supra, at 28, "civil liability arising out of a wrong derives its birth from the law of the place [where it occurred], and its character is determined by that law". Critically see *Peter Kincaid*, Jensen v Tolofson and the Revolution in Tort Choice of Law (1995) 74 Can Bar Rev 537.

969 *Tolofson*, [38].

970 *ibid* [37]: "[I]t may well be that the consequences would be held to constitute the wrong."

971 *ibid* [49].

972 *ibid* [51].

973 *ibid* [45], [62].

974 La Forest J noted at [40], [49] that "There might, I suppose be room for an exception where the parties are nationals or residents of the forum. Objections to an absolute rule of the *lex loci delicti* generally arise in such situations."

allowed, neither claim was successful. The majority held that time limitations were to be regarded as substantive rather than procedural in nature and thus subject to the *lex loci delicti*. Consequently, in *Tolofson* Saskatchewan law applied, the claim being barred under the Saskatchewan time bar; and in *Lucas*, the claim was barred pursuant to the applicable law of Québec. As well as the recognition of the possibility of an exception in *Tolofson*, La Forest J further acknowledged that the doctrine of public policy might also be capable of displacing the *lex loci delicti*. For interprovincial torts La Forest J stated that there was a "limited role, if any, for considerations of public policy in actions that take place wholly within Canada";[975] and, that in such cases "the application of the *forum non conveniens* rule should be sufficient."[976] However, the use of public policy as a jurisdictional forum restraint, when considering the application of the general tort choice of law rule, was recognised as applicable on the international plane.[977]

Subsequent judicial consideration of the Supreme Court's reasoning in *Tolofson* shows that courts have generally applied the *lex loci delicti* rule without any exception to interprovincial torts.[978] However, in the international context, courts have interpreted *Tolofson* as leaving some discretion to depart from the strict application of the rule if it would cause injustice. Conservative in the application of the exception, most decisions that have done so have been restricted to cases where both parties were residents of the forum and there were no other connections to the *lex loci delicti* other than that it was the place of the accident. For example, in *Hanlan v Serensky*[979] Canadian law, as the *lex fori* and the law of the parties' common residence, was applied to a tort that had occurred in the US. The majority of the court rejected the rigid adherence to the *lex loci delicti* and instead invoked a flexible exception in order to apply the *lex fori* (Canadian law).[980]

---

975   *ibid* [50].
976   ibid.
977   *ibid*. However, it has been subsequently held by the Supreme Court of Canada, that although consideration of public policy and the "real and substantial connection" test "may be sufficient to permit the court of a province to take jurisdiction over a dispute [it] may not be sufficient to for the law of that province to regulate the outcome": see *Unifund Assurance Co v Insurance Corp of British Columbia* [2003] 2 SCR 63, 68.
978   But see *Lau v Li* [2001] OJ No 1389, where the Ontario Superior Court of Justice did apply the flexible exception to an interprovincial tort.
979   [1998] 38 OR (3d) 479 (CA).
980   See critically *Janet Walker*, Are We There Yet? Towards a New Rule For Choice of Law in Tort (2000) 38 Osgoode Hall L J 331.

Similarly, in both *Wong v Wei*[981] and *Wong v Lee*,[982] Canadian courts displaced the *lex loci delicti* rule and applied the *lex fori* to govern an accident that had happened in the US. This was justified again by the great injustice that would result from the application of the law of one of the United States, where both parties were Canadian residents. Both *Wong v Wei* and *Wong v Lee* signify a willingness to displace the general rule in favour of the *lex fori*, where the application of foreign law would be significantly opposed to the social policies of the forum.[983] While displacement of the general rule was justified by reference to public policy considerations, and not specifically by the parties' common forum residence, the escape to the *lex fori* was arguably easily justified as all parties did share the same residence. Because of this, it remains unclear whether considerations of public policy would yield the same result if not all of the parties shared the common forum residence. Consequently, whether any exception to the application of the *lex loci delicti* is confined to considerations of public policy and thus restricted to the application of the *lex fori* only, or whether an exception allowing the law of a third country that is not the forum or the place of the tort to apply is possible, remains unanswered.[984]

The present position in Canadian law for tort choice of law is the following:

1. As a general rule the *lex loci delicti*, or the law of the place where the tort was committed governs interprovincial and foreign torts.[985]
2. No exception to the *lex loci delicti* rule for interprovincial torts cases.[986]
3. Where application of the *lex loci delicti* rule gives rise to injustice, the general rule may be subject to displacement on public policy grounds in favour of the

---

981  [1999] 10 WWR 296 (BC).
982  (2002), 58 OR (3d) 398 (CA). The Court cautioned on the application of the exception whenever the parties are both from the forum, which would represent a misapplication of the *Tolofson* decision.
983  Note also that in regard to the quantification of damages, the court in *Wong v Wei* at [54] held that it was a procedural matter. However, the Court noted that even if the law of California applied to the substantive law on the heads of damage, the quantification would nevertheless be determined according to the law of British Columbia because the quantification of damages is a procedural matter."
984  *Tolofson*, at [84]. Sophinka and Major JJ, agreed that the *lex loci delicti* should operate as the general rule but doubted whether a no-exceptions application of the rule would always provide the best result.
985  *Tolofson*, 1050.
986  *Tolofson*. But compare Sophinka and Major JJ at 1078.

*lex fori*.[987] This exception to the general rule may be invoked at both the jurisdiction and choice of law stage.[988]

Both the Supreme Court of Canada and the High Court of Australia have rejected any significant flexibility in the conflict-of-law rule in tort. The Canadian position illustrates that public policy often presents itself as the perfect escape device to avoid the application of foreign law, in order to achieve a result that could have been reached by a more transparent exception (for example one based on the parties' common residence). In contrast to the Australian position, Canadian courts have recognised that mere reliance on public policy at the jurisdiction stage cannot provide sufficient flexibility in order to mitigate the effect of a rigid choice of law rule, and that there is a need to provide for a flexible exception at the choice of law stage. However, like the Australian approach taken to tort choice of law, the Canadian approach also does not expressly provide for a choice of law made by the parties to be given any effect.

## 4. Singapore

### a. Adoption of the common law rule

Singapore, along with New Zealand, is one of the few common law countries that continues to apply the double actionability test. The rule, as derived from *Phillips v Eyre* and its modern formulation by the House of Lords in *Boys v Chaplin* provides the basis of the Singapore choice of law rule for civil wrongs committed abroad. Thus, an act done abroad is actionable as a tort in Singapore if it is both actionable as a tort according to the law of Singapore and the law where the act was carried out. In *Goh Chok Tong v Tang Liang Hong* [1997],[989] Lai Kew Chai J gave the first judicial endorsement of the modern tort choice of law rule applicable in Singapore.[990] The case concerned an action brought by the plaintiff against the defendant for allegedly defamatory remarks made by the defendant in Malaysia.

---

987 In some cases the 'injustice' has been a relatively minor difference between the *lex fori* and the foreign law, suggesting that courts invoke the exception as an excuse to apply local law: by *Reid Mortensen*, Homing Devices in Choice of Tort Law: Australian, British and Canadian Approaches 55 ICLQ 2006 839–878, 866. See e.g. *Gill v Gill* 2000 BCSC 870; but c.f. *Wong v Lee* (2002) 211 DLR (4th) 69 and *Somers v Fournier* (2002) 214 DLR (4th) 611.

988 Compare the Australian position given above under Part 4/B.II.1. *Australia*.

989 2 SLR 641.

990 See also the earlier case *RJ Sneddon v AG Shafe* [1947] SLR 27 which had applied *Phillips v Eyre* (1870) LR 6 QB 1.

The defendant argued, *inter alia*, that the plaintiff had failed to plead actionability as a tort under Malaysian law. The High Court accepted that the applicable law was the *lex fori*, subject to civil actionability by the *lex loci delicti*. The extension and reformulation of the double actionability rule made by the Privy Council in *Red Sea Insurance Co Ltd v Bouygues SA* was also approved by the High Court. Two years later the Court of Appeal of Singapore in *Parno v SC Marine Pte Ltd*[991] clearly confirmed that the applicable choice of law rule in Singapore with respect to torts committed overseas is that laid down in *Philips v Eyre*. It added that it was incontrovertible that the exception to the rule as formulated in *Boys v Chaplin, Johnson v Coventry Churchill*[992] and *Red Sea Insurance* is part of the law of Singapore.[993]

*b. Legislative reform efforts*

In March 2003 the Singapore Law Reform Committee presented a report entitled "Reform of the Choice of Law Rule Relating to Torts".[994] The report proposed

---

991  [1999] 4 SLR 579; [1999] SGCA 69. The plaintiff had been injured whilst working on board a dumb barge owned by the defendant. At the time of the accident, the barge was located off the coast of Myanmar where it was engaged in pile-driving operations for the purpose of constructing a jetty. The plaintiff alleged that the cause of the accident was a failure to provide a safe system of work and therefore a breach of the Factories Act of Singapore, or alternatively a breach of the duties of an employer under common law negligence. On appeal the court held that the statute did not confer extra-territorial rights to sue for a tort committed abroad. Instead, applying the double actionability rule and treating the failure to prove foreign law as giving rise to the presumption of similarity of laws, the Court of Appeal held that the act which was done in Myanmar was actionable as a tort in Singapore.

992  Johnson v Coventry Churchill International Ltd [1992] 3 All ER 14.

993  *Parno v SC Marine Pte Ltd* [1999] 4 SLR 579; [1999] SGCA 69 at [36] citing *Goh Chok Tong v Tang Liang Hong* [1997] 2 SLR 641 (HC). Note also the more recent decision of *Wing Hak Man v Bio-Treat Technology Ltd* [2009] 1 SLR (R) 446 at [26], in which the High Court referred to the "substance" test as formulated by the English Court of Appeal in *Metall und Rohstoff AG v Donaldson Lufkin & Jenrette Inc* [1990] 1 QB 391 stating that: "The test requires the court, in deciding where the alleged conspiracy took place, to "look back over the series of events" constituting the elements of the tort and ask where in substance did the cause of action arise."

994  A Report of the Law Reform Committee of the Singapore Academy of Law, 31 March 2003. The text can be accessed at: http://www.lawnet.com.sg/legal/ln2/comm/PDF/reform_of_choice_of_law.pdf. The Report also discussed reform of the law applicable to defamation, intellectual property, issues of jurisdiction, justiciability and complementary torts. Critically see, *William Tong*, Warnings for a New Beginning Torts (Choice of Law) Bill (2005) Singapore Journal of Legal Studies, 288–299.

the introduction of the Singapore Torts (Choice of Law) Act by adopting almost entirely Part III of the Private International Law (Miscellaneous Provisions) Act 1995.[995] Emphasising developments and the departure from the double actionability rule in the UK, Australia and Canada and the desire to align Singapore tort choice of law with other Commonwealth jurisdictions, the report recommended:[996]

a. That the requirement for actionability by the law of the forum be abrogated, so that the choice of law rule is the law where the act was done.[997]
b. That a flexible exception to the choice of law rule may be invoked in exceptional circumstances, allowing the court to apply the law of a country that is significantly more substantially connected with the tort.[998]

The Law Reform Committee gave five reasons justifying the abrogation of actionability by the law of the forum: that the requirement of actionability according to the law of Singapore is inappropriate to a time of global and regional dealings;[999] causes the law of Singapore to be out of alignment with the rest of the common law world; to the extent that the *lex fori* is a default law allowing parties to circumvent the problem of proof of foreign law, this role is obsolete; unknown causes under the law of the forum might be better weighed in considering the issue of *forum non conveniens* or violation of the public policy of the forum; and, the doctrine of public policy is sufficient to allow the law of the forum to be applied in order to uphold or protect the forum's vital and compelling interests.

The Report further recommended the adoption of a flexible exception to the general *lex loci delicti rule*. The formulation, adopted from section 12(1) of the UK PIL Act 1995, would require Singapore courts to determine if it is "substantially more appropriate" to apply the law advocated by the defendant or the law advocated by the plaintiff.[1000] No mention of the possibility to

---

995 The Torts (Choice of Law) Bill 2003 00/2003 (Singapore) can be viewed at: http://www.sal.org.sg.

996 Given at Executive Summary [E] and discussed at [18]-[27].

997 See section 4 Torts (Choice of Law) Bill 2003 (source: section 10 PIL Act 1995 (UK)) and section 5 Torts (Choice of Law) Bill 2003 (source: section 11 PIL Act 1995 (UK)).

998 Section 12 Torts (Choice of Law) Bill 2003 (source: section 12 PIL Act 1995 (UK)).

999 Citing Kirby J in *Regie National des Usines Renault SA v Zhang* (2002) 187 ALR 1 at [132].

1000 The Report of the Law Reform Committee of the Singapore Academy of Law, 2003 also presented alternative reform possibilities as to the scope of the exception; see [26] and [27].

allow for a choice of law made by the parties was made in the Report. Despite brief mention of concurrent developments by the European Commission and the Preliminary Draft Proposal for a Council Regulation on the Law Applicable to Non-Contractual Obligations (2002)[1001] in the Report, no consideration was given to the inclusion of provision for a choice of law made *ex ante* or *ex post* by the parties to govern the tort by the Singapore Law Reform Commission.

Despite extensive attempts advocating reform of the Singapore tort choice of law rule by the Law Reform Commission, reform of the rule does not appear to be on the agenda of the Singapore government and no further steps towards legislation have been made. Accordingly, at the present moment the double actionability rule and its exception remain law and any consideration of reform or abolishment of the rule remains with Singapore courts.

### c. Judicial development of the common law rule

Although arguments in favour of reform of the double actionability rule have yet to be tested in Singapore courts,[1002] some developments have occurred unique to Singapore tort choice of law.[1003] In 2006 the Singapore Court of Appeal in *Rickshaw Investments Ltd and Another v Nicolai Baron von Uexkull,*[1004] made several significant statements on tort choice of law. Even though the

---

1001  The purpose of this preliminary draft proposal for a Council Regulation was to launch a public debate on a future Community instrument on the law applicable to non-contractual obligations, provided for by the Vienna Action Plan (point 40(b)) and the Mutual Recognition Programme (point II.B(3)). Its purpose was to consult interested parties.

1002  But courts appear to be receptive to such arguments, see e.g. *Ang Ming Chuang v Singapore Airlines Ltd* [2005] 1 SLR 409.

1003  Compare analysis and case made for and against party autonomy in tort choice of law by *Tiong Min Yeo*, The Effective Reach of Choice of Law Agreements (2008) 20 SAcLJ 723–745, 733 *et seq.*

1004  [2006] SGCA 39. The decision and endorsement of the double actionability rule critically discussed in *William Tong*, Singapore private international law on torts: Inappropriate for modern times?, (2007) Singapore Journal of Legal Studies 405–419. The author instead advocates the adoption of the *lex loci delicti* rule. Also discussed further in *Tiong Min Yeo*, The Effect of Contract on the Law Governing Claims in Torts and Equity YBPIL Vol. 9 (2007) 459–469; *idem*, The Effective Reach of Choice of Law Agreements (2008) 20 SAcLJ 723–745, 730 *et seq.* See approval of the decision in *Vorobiev Nikolay v Lush John Frederick Peters and others* [2011] SGHC 55 at [24].

judgment of the Court of Appeal primarily focused on the application for stay of proceedings based on *forum non conveniens*,[1005] as part of that inquiry it maintained the following three points relating to tort choice of law. First, the court stated that the law in Singapore applicable to foreign torts is the double actionability rule subject to a flexible exception as accepted by the court in *Parno v SC Marine Pte Ltd*.[1006] The threshold of the exception is that it is to be strictly applied, depending on the precise facts of the case at hand.[1007] Secondly, although the court held that there was no scope to apply the flexible exception in the case, it nevertheless took a further significant step, opining that the *lex causae* of a tort could be the law of a third country, other than the *lex fori* or the *lex loci delicti*, which has the most significant relationship with the occurrence and the parties.[1008] Thirdly, even in cases where a tort was committed in Singapore only, a flexible exception may apply, in certain circumstances, leading to the application of a law other than the *lex fori*.[1009] Phang JA also stated that he did not tackle the question of whether the double actionability rule should be reformed; instead, stating that any reform is a subject for legislative reform.[1010] The double actionability rule applied to the tort claims and applied Singapore law. No consideration was given to the underlying contractual relationship of the parties.

---

1005 Further on this see detailed examination in *Adrian Briggs*, A Map or a Maze: Jurisdiction and Choice of Law in the Court of Appeal (2007) 11 SYBIL 123.

1006 [1999] 4 SLR 579; [1999] SGCA 69.

1007 *Rickshaw Investments Ltd and Another v Nicolai Baron von Uexkull* [2006] SGCA 39 at [58]. Phang JA stressed that "Singapore courts must not be quick to apply the exception unless the *lex fori* and/or the *lex loci delicti* are purely fortuitous and the application of either or both limbs of the 'double actionability rule' would result in injustice and unfairness."

1008 Rickshaw Investments Ltd and Another v Nicolai Baron von Uexkull [2006] SGCA 39 at [56]. See also Wing Hak Man and another v Bio-Treat Technology and others [2009] 1 SLR(R) 446 at [26].

1009 *ibid.* Compare the English common law position that the *lex fori* is the applicable law for torts committed in the local forum: *Szalatnay-Stacho v Fink* [1947] KB 1; *Metall und Rohstoff AG v Donaldson Lufkin & Jenrette Inc* [1990] 1 QB 391 (CA). See also Article 14(2) and (3) Rome II, which preserves the application of laws of the country with which the non-contractual obligation is solely located that cannot be derogated from by agreement.

1010 Rickshaw Investments Ltd and Another v Nicolai Baron von Uexkull [2006] SGCA 39 at [66].

More recently, in *JIO Minerals FZC and others v Mineral Enterprises Ltd* [2010],[1011] the Singapore Court of Appeal summarised the current position as follows:[1012]

1. The choice of law rule that Singapore courts apply for torts is the double action-ability rule. The double actionability rule provides that the tort must be action-able under both the *lex fori* and the *lex loci delicti*.
2. On the basis of the exception, the general rule of double actionability may be departed from in an appropriate case, in which the matter is instead governed by the law of the country that has the most significant relationship with the oc-currence and the parties.
3. Exceptionally, the double actionability rule may be displaced such that the tort may be actionable in Singapore even though it is not actionable under either the *lex loci delicti* or the *lex fori*.

In accordance with the traditional common law approach, the Singapore tort choice of law rule does not give parties the power to agree on the law, which will govern a tortious claim.[1013]

## III. The role of party autonomy in common law tort choice of law

The analysis of the current tort choice of law rules in the common law systems dis-cussed above has shown a trend to move away from a forum-based choice of law rule to a territorially-based choice of law rule. Of those countries that have departed from the double actionability rule, all have opted for the *lex loci delicti commissi* as the general rule. Indeed, prior to the Rome II Regulation, the UK PIL Act 1995 also adopted the *lex loci delicti* to replace double actionability. This trend can be briefly justified by reference to the traditional view that the nature of non-contractual

---

1011  SGCA 41; [2011] 1 SLR 391. Note however, the sole issue on appeal was whether the Respondent's action should be stayed on the ground of *forum non conveniens*.
1012  JIO Minerals FZC and others v Mineral Enterprises Ltd [2010] SGCA 41, at [88]. Recently approved by the Singapore High Court in Vorobiev Nikolay v Lush John Frederick Peters and others [2011] SGHC 55 at [24].
1013  But see *The Rainbow Joy* [2005] 3 SLR 719 at [31] where the Singapore Court of Appeal held the law of the flag as the *prima facie* applicable law to govern the claims in contract *and* tort but also noted: "where in the contract of employment the parties have specified the governing law, the contract term should prevail."

obligations connects them territorially to the rules of the place to which they are related.[1014] The lack of a consensual basis means that obligations will only arise by operation of law; it should therefore follow that such obligations be governed by the law of the place that is the location of the occurrence – the *lex loci delicti*.[1015]

In terms of a role for a choice made by the parties, it has been demonstrated above that even where reform of the tort choice of law has been undertaken, no provision for party autonomy has been advocated. This position therefore leaves only a narrow window of possibility where party autonomy may manifest. While the extent to which choice of law for non-contractual claims may be determined by the consent of the parties remains controversial, it is suggested that four general approaches may accommodate party autonomy. These four possibilities are: a) where there is no contractual relationship an *ad hoc* or *post hoc* contract including a choice of law for the resolution of disputes may apply; b) where the parties are in a contractual relationship the *lex contractus* may also apply to non-contractual liability; c) where there is no contractual relationship by use of the flexible exception; and d) a *de facto* choice of law in favour of either the *lex loci delicti* or *lex fori* may be implied.

## 1. Ad hoc or post hoc choice of law agreement

The first possibility where party autonomy may manifest in tort litigation is where, following the occurrence of the event giving rise to non-contractual liability, the parties enter into *ad hoc* or *post hoc* contract for the resolution of disputes including the choice of a governing law. This possibility proposes that where parties mutually agree on a governing law after the cause of action has arisen, that agreement should be effective.[1016] Article 14(1)(a) of the Rome II Regulation provides for the possibility to enter into an *ex post* agreement submitting their non-contractual obligations to the law of their choice. The *ex post* alternative in Rome II appears

---

1014   See further discussion on this above under Part 2/A.2. *Specific justification of party autonomy in non-contractual obligations*. Also *Mo Zhang*, Party Autonomy in Non-Contractual Obligations: Rome II and its Impacts on Choice of Law 39 Seton Hall Law Review (2009) 9–10, 11–19.

1015   *Mo Zhang*, Party Autonomy in Non-Contractual Obligations: Rome II and its Impacts on Choice of Law 39 Seton Hall Law Review (2009) 10; *Symeon Symeonides*, The American Revolution and the European Evolution in Choice of Law: Reciprocal Lessons 82 Tul L Rev (2008) 1741, 1744–1753.

1016   Similarly, *Adrian Briggs* (ed.), Agreements on Jurisdiction and Choice of Law (2008) at 43 and 406.

to rest on the rationale to encourage a greater freedom of will.[1017] Concern for protecting the weaker party to the dispute, i.e. normally the victim of the tort, is less crucial in *ex post* agreements, because after the occurrence of the tort parties are usually in a position to know of their rights and obligations. Where an *ex post* agreement is reached between the parties, it may be assumed that a weaker party would not agree to the application of a law that is unfavourable to him.[1018]

## 2. Application of the *lex contractus*

The second possibility is where parties are in a contractual relationship and have previously chosen a law to govern their contract. Any claim in tort may then be governed by the *lex contractus*, if the express choice of law clause is formulated wide enough to encompass non-contractual causes of action.[1019] Such an approach has not been precluded by cases on tort choice of law and presents an efficient solution to the choice of law problem.[1020] Although this possibility presents a 'flexible' approach to tort choice of law, it does not bring with it the usual objections to flexibility within choice of law: uncertainty and unpredictability. Parties involved in a contractual relationship would know in advance that claims, including those non-contractual claims related to the contract, will be governed by the same law. There appears no rational purpose in having a contract governed by one law and

---

1017   *Explanatory Memorandum* at 22 referring to Article 10 of the original proposal.

1018   *Cheshire & North* (14th ed.) 838; *Symeon Symeonides*, Rome II and Tort Conflicts: A Missed Opportunity (2008) 56 Am. J. Comp. L. 173, 303. See also above Part 2/A. III.2.b.bb) *Protection of weaker parties and the rights of third parties*.

1019   *Adrian Briggs* (ed.), Agreements on Jurisdiction and Choice of Law (2008) 42.

1020   See e.g. *Johnson v Coventry Churchill International Ltd* [1992] 3 All ER 14; *The Pioneer Container* [1994] 2 AC 324 (PC, HK); *Glencore International AG v Metro Trading International Inc* [2001] 1 Lloyd's Rep 284 at [37]. This approach is also advocated by *Adrian Briggs* (ed.), Agreements on Jurisdiction and Choice of Law (2008) 40, 414. In 2006 in *Trafigura Beheer BV v Kookmin Bank Co* [2006] EWHC 1450 (Comm) at [112]-[113], the English High Court clearly was of the view that at least in commercial cases, torts committed by one party against another during the course of the performance of the contract, shall be governed by the law of the underlying contractual relationship (*lex contractus*). This was decided in the context of English legislation. For further analysis of the efficiency of using the choice of law of the underlying contractual relationship to claims in tort, see e.g. *Michael J Whincop/Mary Keyes*, The Market Tort in Private International Law (1999) 19 NJILB 215.

other claims by a different, unpredicted law.[1021] For example, where one law governs a contract for the carriage of persons, it seems unreasonable that another law govern any injury caused to a passenger as a result of the negligence of the carrier. Concerns for the weaker party could be resolved in the usual way, by reference to mandatory laws and public policy. Where the parties make it clear that the choice of law clause does not extend to non-contractual claims the law governing the contractual relationship should not apply to tort claims. By way of comparison, Article 4(3) Rome II also expressly directs the court to consider the underlying contractual relationship between the parties where it exists. Permitting parties to extend their choice of law to govern non-contractual disputes arising from their underlying contractual relationship would also promote consistency between disputes resolution in an arbitration tribunal and in court.[1022] In international arbitration, parties are permitted by statute to choose the law applicable to their dispute. All four of the common law countries addressed here, have enacted legislation based on the UNCITRAL Model Law on International Commercial Arbitration, permitting parties to choose the law to govern the substance of their dispute.[1023] It appears somewhat confusing to have a choice of law clause effective to a non-contractual claim in an arbitration tribunal but not in a court. Thus, to allow a court to also apply the *lex contractus* to a claim in tort is a pragmatic and commercially sensible approach to the choice of law problem, aligning the choice of law approach with that taken in international arbitration.

## 3. Use of the flexible exception

The third possibility is similar to the preceding approach, but proposes that courts may be empowered to give effect to a choice of law made by the parties *within* the double actionability rule – by use of the flexible exception. Both Singapore and New Zealand have retained the double actionability rule and its flexible exception to depart from the general rule in an appropriate case. The matter is then instead

---

1021   *Adrian Briggs* (ed.), Agreements on Jurisdiction and Choice of Law (2008). See also The *Pioneer Container* [1994] 2 AC 324 (PC, HK); *Fiona Trust & Holding Corp v Privalov* (sub nom Premium *Nafta Products Ltd v Fili Shipping Co Ltd*) [2007] UKHL 40, [26].

1022   Similar point made by *Tiong Min Yeo*, The Effective Reach of Choice of Law Agreements (2008) 20 SAcLJ 723–745, 734–735.

1023   In Australia: International Arbitration Act 1974; New Zealand: Arbitration Act 1996; Canada: International Commercial Arbitration Act 1996; Singapore: International Arbitration Act 1994. Compare also UK Arbitration Act 1996.

governed by the law of the country that has the 'most significant relationship' with the occurrence and the parties. This possibility can be compared with the approach taken in Articles 14(1) (inferred choice of law) and 4(3) of the Rome II Regulation (the escape clause). Article 14(1) Rome II, requires courts to take circumstances of the case into account which may point to a choice of law. The factors that a court will consider are e.g. the choice of a jurisdiction or arbitration clause; the reference to a particular system of law in the contract; or, an express choice of law in a related transaction. Article 4(3) Rome II may also operate to provide for the application of a law that is connected to a pre-existing relationship between the parties, such as contract, by way of "accessory connection". In other words, although under Rome II non-commercial parties may not enter into an *ex ante* agreement, Article 4(3) Rome II may provide that the tort is manifestly more closely connected to the parties existing contractual relationship and accordingly apply the *lex contractus*. Arguably, the language used in Article 4(3) Rome II: "*the law of the country manifestly more closely connected to the tort*", is very similar to the common law flexible exception formulation: "*the law of the country that has the most significant relationship with the occurrence and the parties*". Based on this reasoning, a court could deduce a 'most significant relationship' from the parties' pre-existing contractual relationship. Accordingly, the flexible exception could work to extend the law governing the contract to also govern any questions of liability in tort arising out of, or in connection with the performance of that contract of a party to a contract to the other party.[1024] Section 12 of the UK PIL Act 1995 also contained a provision to enable a court to consider factors relating to the parties when deciding on the applicable law. The formulation in section 12(2) was intended to include a pre-existing contractual relationship between the parties.[1025] Utility of an accessory choice of law, connecting non-contractual liability to the

---

1024 See *Johnson v Coventry Churchill International Ltd* [1992] 3 All ER 14 where the court applied the law of the employment contract to a tort committed by the employer against the employee overseas using the common law exception. This issue also discussed briefly in *Adrian Briggs*, The Further Consequences of a Choice of Law (2007) 123 LQR 18 and *Peter Nygh*, Autonomy in International Contracts (1999) 240–247.

1025 Private International Law: Choice of Law in Tort and Delict, Law Commission No 193 (1990) 12–13. See Section12(2): The factors that may be taken into account as connecting a tort or delict with a country for the purposes of this section include, in particular, factors relating to the parties, to any of the events which constitute the tort or delict in question or to any of the circumstances or consequences of those events.

contractual choice of law promotes unity of applicable law, certainty and predict-ability[1026] and accords with the reasonable expectations of the parties.[1027] Never-theless, since Australia and Canada have both rejected the application of a flexible exception, this possibility would not be available.

## 4. *De facto* choice of law

The fourth, possibility is where a choice of law is brought about by the parties conduct during legal proceedings. As discussed above, a choice of law by the parties in favour of the *lex fori* can always be inferred when the parties during the course of proceedings elect not to plead or prove foreign law. The 'fact' approach to foreign law in the common law means that a failure to plead and prove or insufficiently prove foreign law will result in the application of the *lex fori*. In the absence of proof this approach, also referred to as the "presump-tion of identity", considers foreign law to the same as the law of the forum. This convenient presumption of identity has been accepted in all four common law systems analysed above. It has also been discussed above that such an ap-proach, whether in contractual or non-contractual proceedings is problematic. The conduct of the parties needs to clearly evidence an awareness and *inten-tion* to have the particular law (i.e. *lex fori*) apply to the dispute. It will not be enough if the parties were unaware of the choice or if they were under the mistaken belief that the law of the forum is applicable. A *de facto* choice of law should not be applicable unless the conduct points clearly and unequivocally to a choice of the *lex fori*. Especially where the application of such is contested, this will be indicative of a lack of consent and therefore lack of mutual choice of law by the parties. As already stated above, inferring a choice of law without an active awareness by both parties would be a mere fictitious application and recognition of party autonomy.[1028]

---

1026  Of course, where the parties have not chosen the law applicable to their contract, the determination of the applicable law will be uncertain and unpredictable.

1027  See *Jan Kropholler*, Anknüpfungssystem für das Deliktsstatut (1969) RabelsZ 601, 629–634. Also *Peter Nygh*, Autonomy in International Contracts (1999) 241 notes that this approach would avoid "jockeying for advantage", which is inherent in the Anglo-Commonwealth system. Compare Goff LJ in *Coupland v Arabian Gulf Oil* [1983] 1 WLR 1136 at 1153 stating: "The plaintiff can advance his claim, as he wishes, in contract or in tort: and no doubt he will, acting on advice, advance the claim on the basis which is most advantageous to him".

1028  See above n 567.

The examination of the four possibilities to accommodate party autonomy in the common law choice of law rule for non-contractual obligations highlights the very limited significance it is afforded. Although Singapore and New Zealand and their adherence to the double actionability rule causes them to be out of line with international developments and common practice which favours the *lex loci delicti* as the general rule, it has been seen that the rule of double actionability and its flexible exception does present more scope to accommodate a choice made by the parties. However, it is not intention of this analysis to advocate the retention of the double-limbed choice of rule. Instead it is suggested that neither the double actionability rule and its exception, nor the common law choice of law rule preferring the strict *lex loci delicti*, give sufficient weight to party autonomy within the choice of law process. The Rome II Regulation presents a historical change in the attitude towards party autonomy within non-contractual obligations. Together with the Rome I Regulation, it serves as a perfect example of the modern day development of autonomy in choice of law. It has enhanced the principle of party autonomy to be one of the leading principles in choice of law in non-contractual obligations and presents a means by which common law tort choice of law may be improved.

## IV. Rome II and party autonomy – lessons for the common law?

The Rome II Regulation offers a great opportunity to rethink traditional common law tort choice of law approaches. Its choice of law methodology and the pre-eminence given to freedom of choice provides a great platform to examine issues associated with the inclusion of the principle of party autonomy in non-contractual obligations. Most notable are the benefits that derive from an inclusion of party autonomy in non-contractual obligations within a structured choice of law regime. Legal certainty and predictability, respecting the will of the parties involved, uniformity, and flexibility are all qualities that any effective choice of law regime should make provision for. With the inclusion of party autonomy in Article 14 Rome II, the Regulation gives effect to all of these.

In order to enhance legal certainty as desired by the parties, one of the stated purposes of the Rome II Regulation is to respect the principle of party autonomy. It is believed that granting parties the power to determine the governing law will provide a fair measure of legal certainty and predictability.[1029] Parties will be able

---

1029   Rome II, Recital (31).

to predict with accuracy their rights and obligations according to the legal system they choose. It has reformed choice of law to the extent that contractual and non-contractual obligations can be dealt with in the same way.[1030] The effect of party autonomy within non-contractual obligations appears self-explanatory when considering that it is the parties' private interests and expectations that are at stake, so why shouldn't they be given the option to agree (*ex post*) or have the law already governing their relationship (*ex ante*) also apply to the non-contractual dispute. Particularly in commercial cases, parties should be given the benefit of having all obligations whether contractual or non-contractual to be governed by the same, *ex ante* agreed to law.

A further issue, particularly crucial within the conflict of laws, is the chronic struggle to find a balance between certainty and predictability on the one hand and flexibility within choice of law rules on the other. As has been discussed above, the common law approach taken in Australia and Canada to choice of law in tort is to prefer the application of a strict, pre-defined and inflexible rule. A precise and instructive rule ready to apply rather than an elastic method providing flexibility at the expense of certainty is favoured, the result being a bias towards the application of the law of the forum. But even in New Zealand and Singapore where the possibility to refer to a flexible exception within the choice of law rule for torts does exist, flexibility remains in the hands of the court, the application of which is discretionary and no direct consideration of the will of the parties is guaranteed. However, flexibility is a requirement of justice, even more so given the variable nature of torts where the interaction between the parties is unplanned and the place of the tort may be fortuitous. In the Rome II Regulation, because the parties are given the power to agree on the applicable law, the issue of flexibility becomes less significant than in a case where the choice of law is left to be determined by the courts.[1031] Only in the absence of a choice by the parties does the Regulation further stipulate the applicable law. All in all, there is less need for judicial analysis or the weighing of interests or policies of particular legal systems. It offers a clear structure in order to ascertain the applicable law without the need or indeed the possibility to resort to escape devices in order to apply the law favoured by the forum.

Any influence on the development of the common law tort choice of law through Rome II depends largely on whether the current position is seen as being

---

1030　*Mo Zhang*, Party Autonomy in Non-Contractual Obligations: Rome II and its Impacts on Choice of Law 39 Seton Hall Law Review (2009) 52.

1031　*ibid*, 53.

in need of improvement.[1032] So far, the approaches taken by the courts in Australia, New Zealand, Canada and Singapore have not been formally questioned. Despite the need to test the practicability of Rome II in respect of party autonomy in future application, the Regulation represents an attitude towards party autonomy in contemporary choice of law that the common law world should take note of.

---

1032  Although its status as EU legislation is likely to have only a minimal influence on common law development. On this also *Reid Mortensen*, A Common Law Cocoon: Australia and the Rome II Regulation YBPIL Vol. 9 (2007) 203–222, 212.

# Part 5: Conclusions

Party autonomy puts the will of the parties at the centre of the search for the applicable law. It is not the belief that a territorial connection should be the determining factor, nor that the objectively ascertained choice of law identified through objective connecting factors should be at the forefront, but rather that the will of those involved should be determinative of the applicable law. It is essential that those involved in cross-border business transactions have the confidence of knowing the possible legal consequences of their commercial activities. Both the Rome I and Rome II Regulations have elevated party autonomy to be the central rules within European private international law, reforming choice of law to the extent that contractual and non-contractual obligations can be dealt with in the same way, and thereby promoting certainty and predictability. In terms of a change brought about by the Regulations, the inclusion of party autonomy in the Rome I Regulation does not presented a significant modification of the pre-Regulation approaches taken in Germany or England. Instead, the Regulation further promotes a more uniform approach to be taken to issues in choice of law in contract, including formation, formal validity, inferring a choice of law and the restrictions to be placed on the parties' freedom to choose the applicable law. In contrast, the innovative inclusion of party autonomy in the Rome II Regulation does present a significant change to choice of law in non-contractual obligations. It signifies an increasing trend towards the recognition of the right to choose the law applicable to non-contractual obligations. It has clearly put the will of the parties at the forefront of European tort choice of law rules. More specifically, the most dramatic change to pre-Regulation tort choice of law rules has been brought about by permitting party autonomy for *ex ante* agreements, enabling parties to reach a choice of law to cover anticipatory torts. Accordingly, a choice of law reached by the parties to govern either contractual or non-contractual obligations is now managed on a methodologically similar basis in both Regulations.

The analysis of the procedural treatment and application of foreign law in Part 3, demonstrates that any significance of the *lex fori* (apart from matters of evidence and procedure) is restricted to the consideration of the validity of a choice of law and the scope and effect of mandatory laws or imperative norms on the parties' chosen law. As regards the interpretation of certain terms used within the Regulations, the role of the *lex fori* will be displaced by the required application of the *lex causae* to resolve any interpretative issues. Thereby, any inconsistent national practices should be avoided. The uniform application of Rome I and Rome II would be further supported by uniform procedural rules. A European unification of the law of procedure governing the introduction and ascertainment of foreign law seems to be the most pragmatic solution.

The exposition of the common law approach to party autonomy in light of the developments brought about by the European Regulations in Part 4, revealed that the common law approach, based on the proper law doctrine to choice of law in contract, is substantially the same as that required by Article 3(1) of Rome I. However, it has also been noted that both approaches are not free from concern. The distinction between an implied choice of law (Article 3 Rome I) and a choice of law ascertained objectively (Article 4 Rome I) is unclear; in particular, how much weight is to be accorded to the relevant connecting factors. It has been suggested that the following distinction should be drawn: an implied choice of law shall require an active awareness of the choice of law evidenced by the parties; whereas, an objectively identified choice of law shall be based solely on connecting factors without the requirement of awareness. Further, where the connecting factors are evenly balanced it has been suggested that the common law proper law doctrine should return to a 'presumption' based rule, taking note of the set of choice of law rules provided for in Article 4(1)(a)-(h) Rome I. In contrast, following exposition of the approach taken to choice of law in non-contractual obligations in the common law, it has become evident that a role for a law chosen by the parties remains minimal, if not obsolete. Although those common law systems analysed indicate a trend to move away from a forum-based choice of law rule and to instead prefer a territorially based choice of law rule, none have embraced party autonomy as a functionally workable principle within non-contractual obligations. Despite this lack of a true recognition of the freedom to choose the applicable law in tort, it has been suggested that four general approaches may still accommodate party autonomy. These are (1) by way of *ad hoc* or *post hoc* choice of law agreement; (2) by application of *the lex contractus*; (3) by use of the flexible exception to the double-actionability rule; and, (4) by recognition of a *de facto* choice of law during legal proceedings. Nevertheless, none of these approaches give sufficient weight to party autonomy. It has therefore strongly been suggested that the common law take note of the historic development brought about by inclusion of party autonomy in the Rome II Regulation. The Rome II Regulation is able to offer a clear structure in order to ascertain the applicable law. Given that choice of law clauses are extremely popular in international business transactions, certainty is promoted by permitting contractual and non-contractual obligations to be managed on a similar basis.

In conclusion, both the Rome I and Rome II Regulations have elevated party autonomy to be the central choice of law rule, indicating its practical feasibility within the choice of law process for contractual and non-contractual obligations. Not only has it become an integral part of European private international law, but many common law countries have also embraced it. Nonetheless, a true recognition of party autonomy in the common law is confined to contractual obligations and therefore within the area of non-contractual obligations the common law is lagging behind. Common law countries should seize the opportunity offered by the Rome II Regulation to reconsider and examine the issues associated with the inclusion of the principle of party autonomy within a choice of law regime. The need for common approaches and solutions at a transnational level is imperative, particularly in light of the proliferation of transborder disputes in recent years. The Rome Regulations reflect a strong trend in favour of party autonomy and demonstrate that an acceptance of the principle of party autonomy can facilitate the unification of choice of law rules within the conflict of laws, even on a global scale. It is, therefore, no exaggeration to claim that party autonomy has become the most important universal principle in the conflict of laws.

# Bibliography

## Books

Ahern, John / Binchy, William (eds.), The Rome II Regulation on the Law Applicable to Non-Contractual Obligations (Martinus Nijhoff Publishers, Leiden, 2009)

Basedow, Jürgen / Toshiyuki, Kono (eds.), An Economic Analysis of Private International Law (Mohr Siebeck, Hamburg, 2006)

Beale, Hugh (ed.), Chitty on Contracts (31st ed., Sweet & Maxwell, Vol. 1, 2012)

Beale, Joseph, A Treatise on the Conflict of Laws, Vol. 2 1080 (Baker, Voorhis & Co., New York, 1935)

Bell, Andrew, Forum Shopping and Venue in Transnational Litigation (OUP, Oxford, 2003)

Berger, Christian (et al), Stein & Jonas, Kommentar zur Zivilprozessordnung, Vol. 4 (22nd ed., Mohr Siebeck, Tübingen, 2008)

Berger, Klaus Peter, International Economic Arbitration (Kluwer Law and Taxation Publishers, Devener, 1993)

Boele-Woelki, Katharina / Einhorn, Talia / Girsberger, Daniel / Symeonides, Symeon (eds.), Convergence and Divergence in Private International Law – Liber Amicorum Kurt Siehr (Schulthess/eleven international publishing, Zürich, 2010)

Boele-Woelki, Katharina / Grosheide, W. (eds.), The Future of European Contract Law (Kluwer Law International, The Netherlands, 2007)

Briggs, Adrian (ed.), Agreements on Jurisdiction and Choice of Law (OUP, Oxford, 2008)

idem, The Conflict of Laws (OUP, Oxford, 2002)

Castel, Jean Gabriel, Canadian Conflict of Laws (2nd ed., Butterworths, Toronto 1986)

idem, Canadian Conflict of Laws (3rd ed., Butterworths, Toronto, 1994)

idem, Canadian Conflict of Laws (4th ed., Butterworths, Toronto, 1997)

Clarkson, Christopher / Hill, Jonathan, The Conflict of Laws (4th ed., OUP, Oxford, 2011)

Colinvaux, Raoul (ed.), Carver's Carriage by Sea, Vol. 1 (13th ed., Stevens, London 1982)

Collins, Lawrence et al (eds.), Dicey and Morris on the Conflict of Laws (10th ed., Sweet & Maxwell, London, 1980)

Collins, Lawrence et al (eds.), Dicey and Morris on the Conflict of Laws (11th ed., Sweet & Maxwell, London, 1987)

Collins, Lawrence et al (eds.), Dicey and Morris on the Conflict of Laws (12th ed., Sweet & Maxwell, London 1993)

Collins, Lawrence et al (eds.), Dicey & Morris on the Conflict of Laws (13th ed., Sweet & Maxwell, London, 2000)

Collins, Lawrence et al (eds.), Dicey, Morris & Collins on The Conflict of Laws (14th ed., Sweet & Maxwell, London 2006)

Collins, Lawrence et al (eds.), Dicey, Morris & Collins on The Conflict of Laws (15th ed., Sweet & Maxwell, 2012)

Cook, Walter, The Logical and Legal Bases of the Conflict of Laws (Cambridge, 1942)

Currie, Brainerd, Selected Essays on the Conflict of Laws (Duke University Press, 1963)

Davies, Martin / Bell, Andrew / Le Gay Brereton, Paul (eds.), Nygh's Conflict of Laws in Australia (8th ed., Butterworths, Chatswood NSW, 2010)

Dicey, Albert V., Conflict of Laws (2nd ed., Stevens and Sons, London, 1908)

Dickinson, Andrew, The Rome II Regulation: The Law Applicable to Non-Contractual Obligations (OUP, Oxford 2008) and updating supplement (published 2010)

Fawcett, James / Carruthers, Janeen (eds.), Cheshire, North & Fawcett Private International Law (14th ed., OUP, Oxford, 2008)

Fawcett, James / North, Peter (eds.), Cheshire, North & Fawcett Private International Law (13th ed., OUP, Oxford, 1999)

Fawcett, James / North, Peter (eds.), Cheshire, North & Fawcett Private International Law (12th ed., OUP, Oxford, 1992)

Fawcett, James / North, Peter (eds.), Cheshire, North & Fawcett Private International Law (11th ed., OUP, Oxford, 1987)

Fentiman, Richard, Foreign Law in English Courts (OUP, Oxford, 1998)

Ferrari, Franco / Leible, Stefan (eds.), Ein neues Internationales Vertragsrecht für Europa – Der Vorschlag für eine Rom I-Verordnung (Verlag Sellier, Jena, 2007)

Ferrari, Franco / Leible, Stefan, Rome I Regulation: The Law Applicable to Contractual Obligations in Europe (Verlag Sellier, Jena, 2009)

Flessner, Axel, Interessenjurisprudenz im internationalen Privatrecht (JCB Mohr, Tübingen, 1990)

244

Geeroms, Sofie, Foreign Law in Civil Litigation. A comparative and functional analysis (OUP, Oxford, 2004)

Geimer Reinhold, Internationales Zivilprozessrecht (6th ed., Kovac Verlag, Hamburg, 2009)

Graziano, Thomas Kadner, Europäisches Internationales Deliktsrecht, (Mohr Siebeck, Tübingen, 2003)

Hay, Peter / Borchers Patrick / Symeonides, Symeon, Conflict of Laws (5th ed., West, 2010)

Huber, Peter (ed.), Rome II Regulation, Pocket Commentary (Sellier, München, 2011)

Jayme, Erik (ed.), German National Reports in Civil Matters for the XIVth Congress of Comparative Law, Athens, 1994

Joseph, David, Jurisdiction and Arbitration Agreements and their Enforcement (Sweet & Maxwell, London, 2005)

Kegel, Gerhard / Schurig, Klaus, Internationales Privatrecht (9th ed., Beck Verlag, München, 2004)

Köthe, Jens, Schranken der Parteiautonomie im internationalen Deliktsrecht (Lit Verlag, Berlin, 2008)

Kroll-Ludwig, Kathrin Die Rolle der Parteiautonomie im europäischen Kollisionsrecht (Mohr Siebeck, Hamburg, 2013)

Kropholler, Jan, Internationales Privatrecht, (6th ed., Mohr Siebeck, Hamburg, 2006)

Kühne, Gerhard, Die Parteiautonomie im internationalen Erbrecht, Schriften zum deutschen und europäischen Zivil-, Handels-, und Prozessrecht, Vol. 75 (Verlag Gieseking, Bielefeld, 1973)

Leible, Stefan (ed.), Das Grünbuch zum internationalen Vertragsrecht (Sellier Verlag, München, 2004)

idem, Wege zu einem Europäischen Privatrecht – Anwendungsprobleme und Entwicklungsperspektiven des Gemeinschaftsprivatrecht, (Mohr Siebeck, Tübingen, 2005)

Lipstein, Kurt (ed.), International Encyclopaedia of Comparative Law 3, Private International Law 3 (JCB Mohr, Tübingen, 1976)

Lück, Dorothea, Neuere Entwicklungen des deutschen und europäischen internationalen Deliktsrecht (Kovac Verlag, Hamburg, 2006)

Mansel, Heinz-Peter et al. (eds.) Festschrift für E. Jayme (München, Vol. 1, 2004)

Mayss, Abla / O'Brian, John, Principles of Conflict of Laws (3rd ed., Routledge Cavendish, 1999)

McClean, David / Beevers, Kisch, The Conflict of Laws (7th ed., Sweet & Maxwell, London, 2009)

Mortensen, Reid / Garnett, Richard / Keyes, Mary, Private International Law in Australia (2nd ed., LexisNexis Butterworths, 2011)

Moser, Rudolf, Vertragsabschluß, Vertragsgültigkeit und Parteiwille im internationalen Obligationenrecht (St. Gallen, Fehr, 1948)

Neuhaus, Paul, Die Grundbegriffe des internationalen Privatrechts (2nd ed., Mohr Siebeck, Hamburg, 1976)

Nygh, Peter, Autonomy in International Contracts (OUP, Oxford, 1999)

O'Brien, John (ed.), Conflict of Laws (2nd ed., Cavendish Publishing, London, 1999)

Ost, Hartmut, EVÜ und Fact Doctrine: Konflikte zwischen europäischer IPR-Vereinheitlichung und der Stellung ausländischen Rechts im angelsächsischen Zivilprozess (Peter Lang Verlag, Frankfurt a.M, 1996)

Palandt, O. et al (eds.), Palandt, Bürgerliches Gesetzbuch (64th ed., Beck Verlag, München, 2005)

Palandt, O. et al (eds.), Palandt, Bürgerliches Gesetzbuch (69th ed., Beck Verlag, München, 2010)

Plender, Richard / Wilderspin, Michael, The European Contracts Convention (2nd ed., Sweet and Maxwell, London, 2001)

Plender, Richard / Wilderspin, Michael, The European Private International law of Obligations (3rd ed., Sweet & Maxwell, London, 2009)

Rauscher, Thomas, Internationales Privatrecht, mit internationalen und europäischen Verfahrensrecht (3rd ed., Müller Verlag, Heidelberg, 2009)

Reithmann, Christoph / Martiny, Dieter (eds.), Internationales Vertragsrecht (7th ed., Verlag Dr. Otto Schmidt, Köln, 2010)

Reithmann, Christoph, Internationales Vertragsrecht. Das internationale Privatrecht der Schuldverträge (3rd ed., Verlag Dr. Otto Schmidt, Köln, 1980)

Rogoz, Thomas, Ausländisches Recht im deutschen und englischen Zivilprozess (Diss. Univ. Erlangen-Nürnberg, Mohr Siebeck, Tübingen, 2008)

Säcker, F. J. / Rixecker, R. (eds.), Münchener Kommentar zum Bürgerlichen Gesetzbuch, Volume 10 (4th ed., Beck Verlag, München, 2006)

Säcker, F. J. / Rixecker, R. (eds.), Münchener Kommentar zum Bürgerlichen Gesetzbuch, Volume 10 (5th ed., Beck Verlag, München, 2010)

Schellack, Dirk, Selbstermittlung oder ausländische Auskunft unter dem europäischen Rechtsauskunftsübereinkommen (Duncker & Humblot, Berlin, 1998)

Steiner, Axel, Die stillschweigende Rechtswahl im Prozeß im System der subjektiven Anknüpfungen im deutschen internationalen Privatrecht (Peter Lang Verlag, Frankfurt a.M., 1998)

Stone, Peter, EU Private International Law: Harmonisation of Laws (Edward Elgar Publishing Ltd, Cheltenham, 2006)

Study Group on a European Civil Code/Research Group on EC Private Law (Acquis Group) (eds.), Principles, Definitions and Model Rules of European Private Law. Draft Common Frame of Reference (DCFR), Interim Outline Edition, 2008

Symeonides, Symeon, American Private International Law (Kluwer Law International, The Netherlands, 2008)

Thomas, R., Internationales Privatrecht, mit internationalen und europäischem Verfahrensrecht (3rd ed., C.F. Müller Verlag, Heidelberg, 2009)

Twigg-Flessner, Christian, The Europeanisation of Contract Law, (Routledge-Cavendish, London, 2008)

Vogeler, Andreas Die freie Rechtswahl im Kollisionsrecht der ausservertraglichen Schuldverhaeltnisse (Mohr Siebeck, Hambburg, 2012)

von Bar, Christian / Mankowski, Peter, Internationales Privatrecht Band 1: Allgemeine Lehren (2nd ed., Beck Verlag, München, 2003)

von Bar, Christian, Internationales Privatrecht, Band II: Besonderer Teil (Beck Verlag, München, 1991)

van den Berg, Albert Jan (ed.), International Arbitration 2006: Back to Basics? (Kluwer Law International, The Netherlands, 2007)

von Hoffmann, Bernd / Thorn, Karsten, Internationales Privatrecht (9th ed., Beck Verlag, München, 2007)

Westlake, John, A Treatise on Private International Law (London, 1858)

idem, A Treatise on Private International Law (4th ed., London, 1905)

Wolff, Martin, Private International Law (2nd ed., Clarendon Press, Oxford 1950)

Zöller, Richard / Geimer, Reinhold (eds.), Zivilprozessordnung (30th ed., Verlag Dr. Otto Schmidt, Köln, 2014)

# Articles

Alferez, Francisco, The Rome I Regulation: Much ado about nothing? (2/2008 EuL Forum), 61–79

idem, The Rome II Regulation: On the way towards a European Private International Law Code (3/2007 EuL Forum), I-82

Anderson, Ross, International torts in the High Court of Australia (2002) 10(2) Torts Law J 132

Baasch-Andersen, Camilla, Defining uniformity in Law, (2007) 12 Uniform Law Review, 5–56

Barnard, Laurette, Choice of Law in International Contracts – The Objective Proper Law Reconsidered (1996) 2 New Zealand Business Law Quarterly, 27–49

Basedow, Jürgen (et al.), Max Planck Institute for Comparative and International Private Law, Comments on the European Commission's Proposal for a Regulation of the European Parliament and the Council on the Law Applicable to Contractual Obligations (Rome I), 71 RabelsZ (2007), 225–344

idem (et al.), The Max Institute for Comparative and International Private Law, Comments on the European Commission's Green Paper on the Conversion of the Rome Convention of 1980 on the Law Applicable to Contractual Obligations into a Community Instrument and its Modernization, 68 RabelsZ (2004), 1–118

idem, Lex Mercatoria und Internationales Schuldvertragsrecht, Eine rechtsökonomische Skizze, in: Zivil- und Wirtschaftsrecht im europäischen und globalen Kontext, FS Horn (2006), 229–247

idem, Theorie der Rechtswahl oder Parteiautonomie als Grundlage des Internationalen Privatrechts, 75 RabelsZ (2011), 32–59

Bell, Belinda, Notes Proper Law – Ignoring the Contract? A note on Akai Pty Ltd v The People's Insurance Co Ltd, (1997) 19(3) SydLawRw, 400

Benecke, Martina, Auf dem Weg zu "Rom II" – Der Vorschlag für eine Verordnung zur Angleichung des IPR der außerverträglichen Schuldverhältnisse, RIW 2003, 830–837

Bertoli, Paolo, Choice of Law by the Parties in the Rome II Regulation, (2009) Rivista di Diritto Internazionale, 697–716

Boele-Woelki, Katharina Unifying and Harmonizing Substantive Law and the Role of Conflict of Laws, Collected Courses of the Hague Academy of International Law 340 (Martinus Nijhoff Publishers, 2010), 299–301

Bonomi, Andrea, Conversion of the Rome Convention into an EX Instrument: Some Remarks on the Green Paper of the EC Commission, (2003) YBPIL, 53–98

idem, Mandatory Rules in Private International Law – The quest for uniformity of decision in a global environment, (1999) YBPIL, 215

idem, Overriding Mandatory Provisions in the Rome I Regulation on the Law Applicable to Contracts, (2008) 10 YBPIL, 285–300

idem, Rome I Regulation – Some general remarks, (2008) 10 YBPIL, 171

Borchers, Patrick, Categorical Exceptions to Party Autonomy in Private International Law, (2008) 82 Tul L Rev, 1645–1661

Briggs, Adrian, A Map or a Maze: Jurisdiction and Choice of Law in the Court of Appeal (2007) 11 SYBIL, 123–132

idem, On drafting agreements on choice of law (2003), LMCLQ, 389–395

idem, The Formation of International Contracts (1990) LMCLQ, 192 idem, The Further Consequences of a Choice of Law (2007) 123 LQR, 18

idem, The Legal Significance of the Place of a Tort (2002) 2(1) Oxford Univ Commonwealth L J, 133–140

idem, When In Rome, Choose as the Romans Choose, (2009) Vol. 125 LQR, 191–195

Carter, PB, Choice of Law in Tort and Delict (1991) 107 LQR, 405

Castles, Alex, The Reception and Status of English Law in Australia (1963) 2 Adelaide Law Review, 1–32

Davies, Martin, Choice of Law after the Civil Liability legislation (2008) 17 Torts Law Journal, 104–119

idem, Exactly What is the Australian Choice of Law Rule in Torts Cases? (1996) 70 ALJ, 711–722

Davis, Gary, John Pfeiffer Pty Ltd v Rogerson; Choice of Law in Tort at the Dawning of the 21st Century (2000) 24 Melb U L Rev, 982–1015

de Boer, Th. M, Facultative Choice of Law, The Procedural Status of Choice of Law Rules and Foreign Law, Rec. des Cours (1996-I), 223–234

idem, Forum Preferences in Contemporary European Conflicts Law: The Myth of a Neutral Choice, Festschrift für Erik Jayme, Vol. I (2004), 39–55

idem, Party Autonomy and its Limitations in the Rome II Regulation, (2007) 9 YBPIL, 19

idem, The purpose of uniform choice of law rules: The Rome II Regulation, (2009) NILR, 295–332

Ehrenzweig, Albert, The Not So Proper Law of a Tort: Pandora's Box (1968) 17 Int'l & Comp L Q, 1

Einsele, Dorothee, Rechtswahlfreiheit im IPR, RabelsZ 60 (1996), 417–447

Fastrich, Lorenz, Revisibilität der Ermittlung ausländischen Rechts, ZZP 97 (1984), 423–445

Fawcett, James, Non-exclusive jurisdiction agreements in private international law (2001) LMCLQ, 234–260

Fentiman, Richard, Laws, Foreign Laws, and Facts, Current Legal Problems 2006, Vol. 59, 391–426

Flessner, Axel, Diskriminierung von grenzübergreifenden Rechtsverhältnissen im europäischen Zivilprozess, ZeuP 14 (2006), 737

idem, Fakultatives Kollisionsrecht, 34 RabelsZ (1970), 547–584

idem, Privatautonomie und Interessen im internationalen Privatrecht, am Beispiel der Forderungsabtretung, Festschrift für Canaris, 2007, 545–569

Freitag, Robert / Leible, Stefan, Das Bestimmungsrecht des Art. 40 Abs. 1 EG-BGB im Gefüge der Parteiautonomie im Internationalen Deliktsrecht, ZVglR-Wiss 99 (2000), 101–142

Frisch, David, Contractual Choice of Law and the Prudential Foundations of Appellate Review (2003) Vanderbilt Law Review, 57–112

Fuchs, Angelika, Die Ermittlung ausländischen Rechts durch Sachverständige, RIW 1995, 807–809

idem, Zum Kommissionsvorschlag einer „Rom II"-Verordnung, GPR 2003–04, 100

Gildeggen, Rainer / Langkeit, Jochen, The new Conflict of Laws Code Provisions of the Federal Republic of Germany: Introductory Comment and Translation (1986) 17 Ga J Int'l & Comp L, 229–259

Gray, Anthony, Conflict of Laws in International Tort Cases: the need for reform on both sides of the Tasman, (2006) Yearbook of New Zealand Jurisprudence, 9, 113–140

idem, Flexibility in Conflict of Laws Multistate Tort Cases: The Way Forward in Australia (2004) 23(2) U Queensland L J, 435–463

Graziano, Thomas Kadner, Das auf außervertragliche Schuldverhältnisse anzuwendende Recht nach Inkrafttreten der Rom II-Verordnung, 73 RabelsZ (2009), 1–76

Gruber, Joachim, Die Anwendung ausländischen Rechts durch deutsche Gerichte, ZRPol 1992, 6

Gruber, Urs Peter / Bach, Ivo, The Application of Foreign Law: A progress report on a new European project, 11 YBPIL (2009), 157–169

Gutteridge, Harold, Case Comment on Vita Food (1939) 55 LQR, 323

Hamburg Group for Private International Law, Comments on the European Commission's Draft Proposal for a Council Regulation on the Law Applicable to Non-Contractual Obligations, 67 RabelsZ (2003), 1–56

Harris, Jonathan, Agreements on Jurisdiction and Choice of Law: Where Next? (2009) LMCLQ, 537–561

idem, Does Choice of Law Make Any Sense? (2004) Vol. 4, 57 Current Legal Problems, 305–353

Hartley, Trevor, Pleading and Proof of Foreign Law: The Major European Systems Compared, 45 ICLQ (1996), 271–292

Hausmann, Rainer, Pleading and Proof of Foreign Law – A Comparative Analysis, (1/2008) EuL Forum, I-3

Hay, Peter, Contemporary Approaches to Non-Contractual Obligations in Private International Law (Conflict of Laws) and the European Community's 'Rome II' Regulation, (3/2007) EuL Forum, I-151

idem, From Rule-Orientation to 'Approach' in German Conflicts Law – The Effect of the 1986 and 1999 Codifications (1999) 47 Am. J. Comp. L., 633

Heiss, Helmut / Loacker, Leander Die Vergemeinschaftung des Kollisionsrechts der außervertraglichen Schuldverhältnisse durch Rom II, JBl 2007, 613–647

idem, Inhaltskontrolle von Rechtswahlklauseln in AGB nach europäischem Internationalen Privatrecht?, 65 RabelsZ (2001), 634–653

Heldrich, Andreas, Probleme bei der Ermittlung ausländischen Rechts in der gerichtlichen Praxis, FS Nakamura (1996), 243

Hill, Jonathan, Choice of Law in Contract under the Rome Convention: The Approach of the UK Courts (2004) 53 ICLQ, 325–350

Hohloch, Gerhard, Rechtswahl im internationalen Deliktsrecht, Neue ZVerkehrsR 1988, 161–168

Huber, Peter / Bach, Ivo, Die Rom II-VO. Kommissionsentwurf und aktuelle Entwicklungen, IPRax 2005, 73–83

Hüßtege, Rainer, Zur Ermittlung ausländischen Rechts: Wie man in den Wald hineinruft, so hallt es auch zurück, IPRax 2002, 292–294

Huzel, Erhard, Zur Zulässigkeit eines „Auflagenbeschlusses" im Rahmen des §293 ZPO, IPRax 1990, 77–82

Jansen, Nils / Michaels, Ralf, Die Auslegung und Fortbildung ausändischen Rechts, ZZP 116 (2003), 3–55

Jänterä-Jareborg, Maarit, Foreign Law in National Courts, Recueil des cours (2003), Vol. 304, 181–385

Jastrow, Serge-Daniel, Zur Ermittlung ausländischen Rechts: Was leistet das Londoner Auskunftsübereinkommen in der Praxis, IPRax 2004, 402–405

Jayme, Erik, Die Parteiautonomie im internationalen Vertragsrecht auf dem Prüfstand, 65. Sitzung des Institut de Droit International in Basel, IPRax 1991, 429–430

idem, Entwurf eines EU-Übereinkommens über das außervertragliche Schuldverhältnisse anwendbare Recht, IPRax 1999, 298–300

idem, Inhaltskontrolle von Rechtswahlklauseln in Allgemeinen Geschäftsbedingungen, FS Werner Lorenz (1991), 435–439

Jayme, Erik / Kohler, Christian, Europäisches Kollisionsrecht 2007: Windstille im Erntefeld der Integration, IPRax 2007, 493–499

Jörg K., Flucht vor deutschem AGB-Recht bei Inlandsverträgen: Gedanken zu Art. 3 Abs. 3 Rom I-VO und § 1051 ZPO, RIW 2010, 184–191

Jörg, G. A. Schmeding, Zur Bedeutung der Rechtswahl im Kollisionsrecht, Ein Beitrag zur funktionalen Methode nach von Mehren/Trautmann, 41 RabelsZ (1977), 299–331

Juenger, Friedrich, Conflict of Laws: A Critique of Interest Analysis, Am. J. Comp. Law 32 (1984), 1–50 idem, Tort Choice of Law in a Federal System (1997) 19 Syd. LR, 529

Junker, Abbo, Das Internationale Privatrecht der Straßenverkehrsunfälle nach der Rom II-Verordnung, JZ 2008, 169–178

idem, Das Internationale Unfallrecht nach der IPR-Reform von 1999, JZ 2000, 477–486

idem, Die freie Rechtswahl und ihre Grenzen, IPRax 1993, 1–10

idem, Empfiehlt es sich, Art. 7 EVÜ zu revidieren oder aufgrund der bisherigen Erfahrungen zu präzisieren? IPRax 2000, 65–73

idem, Reformbedarf der Rom II-Verordnung, RIW 2010 Heft 5, 257–269

Kadner Graziano, Thomas, Die Zukunft der Zivilrechtskodifikation in Europa – Harmonisierung der alten Gesetzbücher oder Schaffung eines neuen?, 2005 Zeitschrift für Europäisches Privatrecht, 523–540

Kahn-Freud, Otto, Case Comment on Vita Food (1939) 3 Modern LR, 61

idem, General Problems of Private International Law (1974) Recueil des Cours, III, 139, 409–410

Karsten, G. F., Chaplin v Boys: Another Analysis (1970) 19 Int Comp L Q 35, 37–38

Kelly, David, International Contracts and Party Autonomy (1970) 19 ICLQ, 701

Keyes, Mary, Foreign Law in Australian Courts: Neilson v Overseas Projects Corporation of Victoria (2007) 15 Torts Law Journal, 9–33

idem, The Doctrine of Renvoi in International Torts: Mercantile Mutual Insurance v Neilson (2005) 13(1) Torts Law Journal, 1

Kincaid, Peter, Jensen v Tolofson and the Revolution in Tort Choice of Law (1995) 74 Can Bar Rev, 537

Kindl, Johann, Ausländisches Recht vor deutschen Gerichten, ZZP 111 (1998), 177–203

Köndring, Jörg, Flucht vor deutschem AGB-Recht bei Inlandsverträgen: Gedanken zu Art. 3 Abs. 3 Rom I-VO und § 1051 ZPO, RIW 2010, 184–191

Kötz, Hein, Allgemeine Rechtsgrundsätze als Ersatzrecht, RabelsZ 34 (1970), 663–678

Koziol, Helmut, Comparative Law – A Must in the European Union: Demonstrated by Tort Law as an Example, (2007) Journal of Tort Law, Vol. 1, Issue 3, Article 5, 1–18, 2

Kozyris, Phaedon John, Rome II: Tort Conflicts on the Right Track! A Postscript to Symeon Symeonides' "Missed Opportunity", 56 Am. J. Comp. L. (2008), 471–498

Kralik, Winfried, Iura Novit Curia und das ausländische Recht, 3 ZfRV 75 (1962), 75

Kramer, Xandra 'The Rome II Regulation on the Law Applicable to Non-Contractual Obligations: The European private international law tradition continued' (2008) NIPR 4, 414–424

Kreuzer, Karl, Einheitsrecht als Ersatzrecht: Zur Frage der Nichtermittelbarkeit fremden Rechts, NJW 1983, 1943–1948

Kropholler, Jan, Ein Anknüpfungssystem für das Deliktstatut, 33 RabelsZ (1969), 601–653

Krüger, Hilmar, Zur Ermittlung ausländischen Rechts in Deutschland: Ein Bericht aus der Praxis, FS Nomer 2003, 357

Küster, Utz, Zur richterlichen Ermessensausübung bei der Ermittlung ausländischen Rechts, RIW 1998, 275–278

Lando, Ole / Nielsen, Peter, The Rome I Regulation, (2008) 45 CML Rev, 1687–1725

idem, The Conflict of Laws of Contracts: General Principles (1984) Recueil des Cours, VI, 225–448

idem, The EC-Draft Convention on the Law Applicable to Contractual and Non-Contractual Obligations, RabelsZ (1974), 6–55

Lehmann, Matthias, Liberating the individual from battles between states: justifying party autonomy in conflict of laws, (2008) Vanderbilt Journal of Transnational Law, Vol. 41, 381–434

idem, The State of Development of Uniform Law in the Fields of European and International Civil and Commercial Law, (7/2008 EuL Forum), 266–270

Leible, Stefan / Engel, Andreas, Der Vorschlag der EG-Kommission für eine Rom II-Verordnung – Auf dem Weg zu einheitlichen Anknüpfungsregeln für außervertragliche Schuldverhältnisse in Europa, EuZW 2004, 7–17

Leible, Stefan / Lehmann, Matthias, Die neue EG-Verordnung über das auf außervetragliche Schuldverhältnisse anzuwendende Recht ("Rom II"), 10 RIW 2007, 721–727

Leible, Stefan / Lehmann, Matthias, Die Verordnung über das auf vertragliche Schuldverhältnisse anzuwendende Recht ("Rom I"), RIW 2008, 528–543

Leible, Stefan, Außenhandel und Rechtssicherheit, ZVglRWiss 97 (1998), 286–319

idem, Parteiautonomie im IPR – Allgemeines Anknüpfungsprinzip oder Verlegenheitslösung? FS Erik Jayme (2004), 485–503

idem, Rechtswahl im IPR der außervertraglichen Schuldverhältnisse nach der Rom II-Verordnung, RIW 2008, 257–264

Lorenzen, Ernest, Validity and Effect of Contracts in the Conflict of Laws, 30 Yale LJ (1921), 655

Magnus, Ulrich / Mankowski, Peter, The Green Paper on a Future Rome I Regulation – on the Road to a Renewed European Private International Law of Contracts (2004) 103 ZvglRWiss, 131–189

Magnus, Ulrich / Mankowski, Peter, Die Rom I-Verordnung, 1 IPRax 2010, 27–44

Mankowski, Peter, Überlegungen zur sach- und interessengerechten Rechtswahl für Verträge des internationalen Wirtschaftsverkehrs, RIW 2003, 2–15

idem, Ausgewählte Einzelfragen zur Rom II-VO: Internationales Umwelthaftungsrecht, internationales Kartellrecht, renvoi, Parteiautonomie, 5 IPRax 2010, 389–492

idem, Der Vorschlag für die Rom I-Verordnung, IPRax 2006, 101–113

idem, Die Rom I-Verordnung, Änderungen im europäischen IPR für Schuldverträge, Internationales Handelsrecht 2008, 133–152

Mankowski, Peter / Kerfack, Ralf, Arrest, Einstweilige Verfügung und die Anwendung ausländsichen Rechts, IPRax 1990, 372–378

Mann, Frederick Alexander, The proper law in the Conflict of Laws, (1986) 36 ICLQ, 437

idem, The Proper Law of Contract – An Obituary (1991) 107 LQR, 353

Mann, Frederick Alexander, The Proper Law of the Contract, (1950) 3 ILQ, 60

Mansel, Heinz-Peter, Kollisions- und zuständigkeitsrechtlicher Gleichlauf der vertraglichen und deliktischen Haftung – zugleich ein Beitrag zur Rechtswahl durch Prozessverhalten, ZVglRWiss 86 (1987), 1–24

idem, Vollstreckung eines französischen Garantieurteils, IPRax 1995, 362–365

Mansel, Heinz-Peter / Thorn, Karsten / Wagner, Rolf, Europäisches Kollisionsrecht 2009: Hoffnungen durch den Vertrag von Lissabon, IPRax 1/2010, 1

Maultzsch, Felix, Rechtswahl und ius cogens im Internationalen Schuldvertragsrecht, 75 RabelsZ (2011), 60–101

Mayss, Abla, Statutory Reform of Choice of Law in Tort and Delict: A Bitter Pill or a Cure for the Ill? [1996] 2 Web JCLI

McLachlan, Campbell, Splitting the Proper Law in Private International Law, (1990) 61 BYIL, 311

Michaels, Ralf, The New European Choice-of-Law Revolution, 82 Tul. L. Rev. (2008), 1607–1644

Min, Yeo Tiong, Are Loans for International Gambling Against Public Policy? (1997) 2 SJICL, 593–608

idem, Tort Choice of Law Beyond the Red Sea: Wither the Lex Fori? 1 Sing J Int'l & Comp L, 91–116

Morris, John / Cheshire, G.G., The Proper Law of a Contract in the Conflict of Laws (1940) 56 LQR, 320

Morris, John, The Proper Law of the Tort (1951) 64 Harv L Rev, 881

Morse, Christopher, The EEC Convention on the Law Applicable to Contractual Obligations (1982) 2 YB Eur. L., 107

idem, Torts in Private International Law; A New Statutory Framework, (1996) 45 Int Comp L Q, 888

Mortensen, Reid, A Common Law Cocoon: Australia and the Rome II Regulation, 9 YBPIL (2007), 203–222

idem, Homing Devices in Choice of Tort Law: Australian, British and Canadian Approaches, 55 ICLQ 2006, 839–878

idem, Troublesome and Obscure: The Renewal of Renvoi in Australia (2006) 2(1) Journal of Private International Law, 1–26

Müller-Graf, Peter-Christian, Fakultatives Kollisionsrecht im Internationalen Wettbewerbsrecht?, 48 RabelsZ (1984), 289–318

Neuhaus, Paul Heinrich / Kropholler, Jan, Entwurf eines Gesetzes über Internationales Privat- und Verfahrensrecht, RabelsZ 44 (1980), 340–366

Nottage, Luke, Convergence, divergence and the middle way in unifying or harmonizing private law, (2004) 1 Annual German and European Law, 166–245

Nygh, Peter, Choice of Law in Torts in Australia, 2 YBPIL (2000), 55–73

idem, Choice-of-Law Rules and Forum Shopping in Australia, (1995) 46 South Carolina Law Review, 899–921

Ofner, Helmut, Die Rom II-Verordnung – Neues Internationales Privatrecht für außervertragliche Schuldverhältnisse in der Europäischen Union, ZfRV 2008, 13

Otto, Günter, Der verunglückte §293 ZPO und die Ermittlung ausländischen Rechts durch "Beweiserhebung", IPRax 1995, 299–305

Owsia, Parviz, Silence: Efficacy in Contract Formation. A Comparative View of French and English Law (1991) ICLQ, 784–806

Prebble, John, Choice of Law to Determine the Validity and Effect of Contracts: A Comparison of English and American Approaches to Conflict of Laws, (1973) Cornell Law Rev. Vo. 58 No. 3, 433

Raape, Leo, Nachträgliche Vereinbarung des Schuldstatuts, FS Boehmer (1954), 110–123

Reimann, Mathias, Codifying Tort Conflicts, The 1999 German Legislation in Comparative Perspective, (2000) 60 La. L. Rev., 1297–1319

Richardson, Nicky, Choice of Law Clauses in International Contracts: Overseas Developments, (1992) 5 Canterbury Law Review, 126–146

idem, Double Actionability and the Choice of Law (2002) 32 Hong Kong L J, 497

idem, International Contracts and the Choice of Law in New Zealand, Conference Paper (Paris, France 2010), COBRA 2–3 September, available at: http://www.rics.org

Rogerson, Pippa, Choice of Law in Tort: A Missed Opportunity?, ICLQ 44 (1995), 650–658

Roth, Wulf-Henning, Zur Wählbarkeit nichstaatlichen Rechts, Festschrift für Erik Jayme 2004, 757

Rugullis, Sven, Die antizipierte Rechtswahl in außervertraglichen Schuldverhältnissen, IPRax 2008, 319–323

Rühl, Gisela, Die Kosten der Rechtswahlfreiheit: Zur Anwendung ausländischen Rechts durch deutsche Gerichte, 71 RabelsZ (2007), 559–596

idem, Party Autonomy in the Private International Law of Contracts: Transatlantic Convergence and Economic Efficiency in: Gottschalk, E. / Michaels, R. / Rühl, G. / von Hein, J. (eds.) Conflict of Laws in a Globalised World (Cambridge CLPE Research Paper No 4/2007)

idem, Rechtswahlfreiheit im europäischen Kollisionsrecht, FS Jan Kropholler zum 70. Geburtstag, 2008, 187–210

Rushworth, Andrew / Scott, Adam, Rome II: Choice of Law for Non-Contractual Obligations, (2008) LMCLQ, 274

Samtleben, Jürgen, Der unfähige Gutachter und die ausländische Rechtspraxis, NJW 1992, 3057–3062

Schack, Haimo, Keine stillschweigende Rechtswahl im Prozeß! IPRax 1986, 272–274

idem, Rechtswahl im Prozeß?, NJW 1984, 2737

Schilken, Eberhard, Zur Rechtsnatur der Ermittlung ausländischen Rechts nach § 293 ZPO, FS Schumann, 2001, 373

Schoeman, Elsabe / Tobin, Rosemary, A Holiday in New Zealand: The Implications of New Zealand's Accident Compensation Scheme (2005) 25 IPRax, 374–375

Schoeman, Elsabe / Tobin, Rosemary, The New Zealand Accident Compensation Scheme: The Statutory Bar and the Conflict of Laws, (2005) 53 American Journal of Comparative Law, 493–514

Schoeman, Elsabe, Renvoi: Throwing (and Catching) the Boomerang – Neilson v Overseas Projects Corporation of Victoria Ltd, (2006) 25 University of Queensland Law Journal, 203–212

idem, Rome II and the substance–procedure dichotomy: crossing the Rubicon, [2010] LMCLQ, 80–93

idem, Third (Anglo-Common Law) Countries and Rome II: Dilemma or Deliverance? 2011 Journal PIL Vol. 7 No. 2, 361–392

idem, Tort Choice of Law in New Zealand: Recommendations for Reform, [2004] NZ L Rev, 537–561

Schurig, Klaus, Interessenjurisprudenz contra Interessenjurisprudenz im IPR – Anmerkungen zu Flessners Thesen, 59 RabelsZ (1995), 229–244

Siehr, Kurt, Die Parteiautonomie im Internationalen Privatrecht, FS Keller (1989), 485–510

idem, Ökonomische Analyse des internationalen Privatrechts, FS Firsching (1985), 269–273

Sommerlad, Klaus / Joachim, Schrey, Die Ermittlung ausländischen Rechts im Zivilprozeß und die Folgen der Nichtermittlung, NJW 1991, 1377–1383

Sonnentag, Michael, Zur Europäisierung des Internationalen außervertraglichen Schuldrechts durch die geplante Rom II-Verordnung, ZVglRWiss 105 (2006), 256–312

Spickhoff, Andreas, Die Produkthaftung im Europäischen Kollisions- und Zivilverfahrensrecht, FS Kropholler, 2008, 671–698

idem, Die Restkodifikation des Internationalen Privatrechts: Außervertragliche Schuldverhältnisse und Sachenrecht, (1999) NJW, 2209–2215

idem, Fremdes Recht vor inländischen Gerichten: Rechts- oder Tatfrage?, ZZP 112 (1999), 265–292

Staudinger, Ansgar / Leible, Stefan, Article 65 of the EC Treaty in the EC System of Competencies, (4/2001) EuL Forum, 225–235

Steinle, Edgar, Konkludente Rechtswahl und objektive Anknüpfung nach altem und neuem deutschen internationalen Vertragsrecht, ZvglRWiss 1994, 300

Stone, Peter, The Rome II Proposal on the Law Applicable to Non-Contractual Obligations (4/2004) EuL Forum, 213–229

Study Group on a European Civil Code/Research Group on EC Private Law (Acquis Group) (eds.), Principles, Definitions and Model Rules of European Private Law. Draft Common Frame of Reference (DCFR), Interim Outline Edition, 2008

Sturm, Fritz, Fakultatives Kollisionsrecht: Notwendigkeit und Grenzen, FS Zweigert 1981, 329–351

Symenoides, Symeon, The American Revolution and the European Evolution in Choice of Law: Reciprocal Lessons, 82 Tul L Rev (2008), 1741–1799

idem, Choice of Law in the American Courts in 2009: Twenty-Third Annual Survey, 58 Am. J. Comp. Law (2010), 221

idem, Party Autonomy in Rome I and Rome II From a Comparative Perspective, Liber Amicorum Kurt Siehr (2010), 513–550

idem, Rome II and Tort Conflicts: A Missed Opportunity (2008) 56 Am. J. Comp. L., 173, 471–488

idem, The American Choice of Law Revolution in the Courts: Today and Tomorrow, 298 Recueil des Cours 9, (2002), 34

idem, The American Revolution and the European Evolution in Choice of Law: Reciprocal Lessons, 82 Tul L Rev (2008), 1741–1799

idem, The American Revolution and the European Evolution in Choice of Law: Reciprocal Lessons (2008), available at: http://ssrn.com/abstract=1104284

idem, The First Conflicts Restatement Through the Eyes of Old: As Bad as Its Reputation?, 32 So Ill ULJ (2007), 39–82

idem, Tort Conflicts and Rome II: A View from Across (2004) FS Erik Jayme, 935–954

Tetley William, The On-Going Saga of Canada's Conflict of Law Revolution – Theory and Practice, Part I IPRax 5/2004, 457–472 and Part II IPRax 6/2004, 551–561

idem, Current Developments in Canadian Private International Law (1999), 78 Can Bar Rev, 152–199

idem, Vita Food Products Revisited, (1992) 37 RD McGill LJ, 292–316

Thorn, Karsten, Der Unternehmer im Kollisionsrecht, FS Karsten Schmidt, 2009, 1561–1580

Tillman, Christopher, The Relationship Between Party Autonomy and the Mandatory Rules in the Rome Convention, JBL 2002, 45–77

Tong, William, Singapore private international law on torts: Inappropriate for modern times?, (2007) Singapore Journal of Legal Studies, 405–419

idem, Warnings for a New Beginning Torts (Choice of Law) Bill, (2005) Singapore Journal of Legal Studies, 288–299

Trautmann, Clemens, Ausländisches Recht vor deutschen und englischen Gerichten, ZEuP 2006, 283–307

Triebel, Volker, The Choice of Law in Commercial Relations: A German Perspective, (1988) 37 ICLQ, 935–945

Verhagen, H., The Tension between Party Autonomy and European Union Law: Some observations on Ingmar GB Ltd v Eaton Leonard Technologies Inc, (2002) 51 ICLQ, 135–154

von Hein, Jan, Die Kodifikation des europäischen Internationalen Deliktsrecht – Zur geplanten EU-Verordnung über das außervertragliche Schuldverhältnisse anzuwendende Recht, ZVglRWiss. 102 (2003), 528–562

idem, Die Kodifikation des europäischen IPR vor dem Abschluss?, VersR 2007, 440–452

idem, Europäisches Internationales Deliktsrecht nach der Rom II-Verordnung, ZEuP 2009, 6–33

idem, Of Older Siblings and Distant Cousins: The Contribution of the Rome II Regulation to the Communitarisation of Private International Law, RabelsZ 73 (2009), 461–508

idem, Rechtswahl im internationalen Deliktsrecht, RabelsZ 64 (2000), 595–613

idem, Something Old and Something Borrowed, But Nothing New? Rome II and the European Choice-of-Law Evolution (2008) 82 Tul. L. Rev., 1663–1707

Wagner, Gerhard, Die neue Rom-II-Verordnung, IPRax 2008, 1–17

idem, Ein neuer Anlauf zur Vereinheitlichung des IPR für außervetragliche Schulverhältnisse auf EU-Ebene, EuZW 1999, 709

idem, Fakultatives Kollisionsrecht und prozessuale Parteiautonomie, ZEuP 1999, 6–46

idem, Internationales Deliktsrecht, die Arbeiten an der Rom II-Verordnung und der Europäische Deliktsgerichtsstand, IPRax 2006, 372–389

Wagner, Rolf, Der Grundsatz der Rechtswahl und das mangels Rechtswahl anwendbare Recht (Rom I-Verordnung), Ein Bericht über die Entstehungsgeschichte und den Inhalt der Artikel 3 und 4 Rom I-Verordnung, IPRax 2008, 377–386

idem, Zum Inkrafttreten des Gesetzes zum Internationalen Privatrecht für außervertragliche Schuldverhältnisse und für Sachen, IPRax 1999, 210–212

Walker, Janet, Are We There Yet? Towards a New Rule For Choice of Law in Tort (2000) 38 Osgoode Hall L J, 331–357

Weintraub, Russel J., Functional Developments in Choice of Law for Contracts, 187 Recueil des Cours, 1984, 239

Whincop, Michael J / Keyes, Mary, The Market Tort in Private International Law, (1999) 19 NJILB, 215–271

Wilderspin, Michael, The Rome I Regulation: Communitarisation and modernisation of the Rome Convention, ERA Forum (2008), 259–274

Woodward, William J., Contractual Choice of Law: Legislative Choice in an Era of Party Autonomy, 54 SMU Law Rev. (2001) 697–783

Yeo, Tiong Min, The Effect of Contract on the Law Governing Claims in Torts and Equity, 9 YBPIL, (2007), 459–469

idem, The Effective Reach of Choice of Law Agreements, (2008) 20 SAcLJ, 723–745

Zhang, Mo, Party Autonomy and Beyond: An International Perspective of Contractual Choice of Law, Emory International Law Review (2006), Vol. 20, 511–562

idem, Party Autonomy in Non-Contractual Obligations: Rome II and its Impacts on Choice of Law, 39 Seton Hall Review (2009), Temple University Legal Studies Research Paper No. 2009–15

# Cases

## England

Aegis Electrical and Gas International Services Co Ltd v Continental Casualty Co [2007] EWHC 1762 (Comm); [2008] Lloyd's Rep IR 17

Airways Corporation v Iraqi Airways Company and others [2002] UKHL 19

Aluminium Industrie Vaasen BV v Romalpa Aluminium Ltd [1976] 1 WLR 676 (CA)

American Motorists Insurance Co (AIMCO) v Cellstar Corp & Amor [2003] EWCA Civ 206; [2003] ILPr 370; [2002] EWHC 421

Amin Rasheed Shipping Corp v Kuwait Insurance Co [1984] AC 50 (HL)

Armadora Occidental SA v Horace Mann Insurance Co [1977] 1 WLR 520

Armar Shipping Co Ltd v Caisee Algérienne d'Assurance et de Réassurance [1981] 1 All ER 498 (CA)

Ascherberg, Hopwood & Crew Limited v Casa Musicale Sonzogno [1971] WLR 173 (CA)

Bank of Bahrain v Beximco Pharmaceuticals Ltd [2004] EWCA Civ 19; [2004] 1 WLR 1784

Boissevain v Weil [1968] 1 KB 482

Bonython v Commonwealth of Australia [1951] AC 201 (PC)

Boys v Chaplin [1971] AC 356 (HL) (Boys)

Bumper Development Corp v Commissioner of Police [1991] 1 WLR 1362

Butler Machine Tool Co Ltd v Ex-Cell-O Corporation (England) Ltd [1979] 1 All ER 965

Catalyst Recycling Ltd v Nickelhütte Aue GmbH [2008] EWCA Civ 541

Caterpillar Financial Services v SNC Passion [2004] EWHC 569

Centrax v Citibank NA [1999] EWCA Civ 892

CGU International Insurance plc v Szabo [2002] 1 All ER (Comm) 83

Coast Lines Ltd v Hudig & Veder Chartering NV [1972] 2 QB 34 (CA)

Compagnie d'Armement Maritime SA v Compagnie Tunisienne de Navigation SA [1969] 3 All ER 589; 1 WLR 1338; [1970] 3 ALL ER 71

Compania Naviera Micro SA v Shipley International Inc 'The Parouth' [1982] 2 Lloyds Rep 351

Duarte v Black and Decker Corp [2007] EWHC 2720 (QB), [2008] 1 All ER (Comm) 401

Egon Oldendorff v Libera Corporation (No 1) [1995] 2 Lloyd's Rep 64

Egon Oldendorff v Libera Corporation (No 2) [1996] 1 Lloyd's Rep 380

El du Pont de Nemours v Agnew [1987] 2 Lloyds Rep 585 (CA)

Evialis SA v SIAT [2003] EWHC 863 (Comm)

Felthouse v Bindley [1862] EWHC CP J 35

Fiona Trust & Holding Corp v Privalov (sub nom Premium Nafta Products Ltd v Fili Shipping Co Ltd) [2007] UKHL 40

Gan Insurance Co Ltd v Tai Ping Insurance Co Ltd [1999] IL Pr 729 (CA)

Gard Marine & Energy Ltd (A company incorporated under the laws of Bermuda) v (1) Lloyd Tunnicliffe (2) Glacier Reinsurance AG (A company incorporated under the laws of Switzerland) (3) Agnew [2009] EWHC 2388

Mostyn v Fabrigas (1774) 1 Cowp 161

Mount Albert Borough Council v Australasian Temperance and General Assurance Society [1938] AC 224

NV Kwik Hoo Tong Handel Maatschappij v James Findlay and Co [1927] AC 604

Owners of Cargo on Board the Morviken v Owners of the Hollandia [1983] 1 Lloyd's Rep 1 (HL)

P & O Steam Navigation Co v Shand (1865) 3 Moo PC (NS) 272

Phillips v Eyre (1870) LR 6 QB 1 (Phillips)

Phrantzes v Argenti [1960] 2 QB 19

Printing and Numerical Registering Co v Sampson (1875) LR 19 Eq 462

R v International Trustee for the Protection of Bondholders Aktiengesellschaft [1937] AC 500; [1937] 2 ALL ER 164

R v Secretary of State for Transport, ex p Factortame (No. 2) [1991] 1 AC 603 (UKHL)

Radmacher (formerly Granatino) v Granatino [2010] UKSC 42

Ralli Bros. v Compania Naviera Sota y Aznar [1920] 2 KB 287 (CA)

Re Helbert Wagg & Co Ltd [1956] Ch 323

Re Missouri Steamship Co (1889) 42 Ch D 32

Re United Rlys of Havana and Regla Warehouses Ltd [1960] Ch 52

Red Sea Insurance Co Ltd v Bouygues SA [1995] 1 AC 190 (PC) (Red Sea Insurance)

Robinson v Bland (1760) 1 Bl.W. 257

Rossano v Manufacturers' Life Insurance Co [1963] 2 QB 352 (QBD)

Rust v Abbey Life Insurance Co [1979] 2 Lloyd's Rep 355

Samcrete Egypt Engineers and Contractors SAE v Land Rover Exports Ltd [2002] EWCA Civ 2019

Sayers v International Drilling Co [1971] All ER 163

Seapremium Shipping Ltd v Seaconsortium Ltd ('The Gilian') [2001] EWHC (Admlty)

Shaker v Al-Bedrawi [2002] EWCA Civ 1452; [2003] Ch 350 (CA)

Shamil Bank of Bahrain v Beximco Pharmaceuticals Ltd [2004] EWCA Civ 19, [2004] 1 WLR 1784

Szalatnay-Stacho v Fink [1947] KB 1

Tekdata Interconnections Ltd v Amphenol Ltd [2009] EWCA Civ 1209

The Assunzione [1953] 1 WLR 929; P 150 (CA)

The Governor and Company of Bank of Scotland of the Mound v Butcher [1998] EWCA CIV 1306

The Halley (1868) LR 2 PC 193

The Komninos S [1991] 1 Lloyds Rep 370 (CA)

The Leon XIII (1883) 8 PD 121
The Pioneer Container [1994] 2 AC 324 (PC, HK)
Tiernan v The Magen Insurance Co Ltd [2000] IL Pr 517
Tomkinson v Forst Pennsylvania Banking and Trust Co [1961] AC 1007
Trafigura Beheer BV v Kookmin Bank Co [2006] EWHC 1450 (Comm)
Travelers Casualty & Surety v Sun Life of Canada [2004] EWHC 1704 (Comm)
Tryg Baltica International (UK) Ltd v Boston Compania de Seguros SA [2004] EWHC 1186 (Comm); [2005] Lloyd's Rep IR 40
Tzortzis v Monark Line A/B [1968] 1 All ER 949; 1 WLR 406 (CA)
Union Transport plc v Continental Lines SA [1992] 1 WLR 15 (HL)
Vita Food Products Inc. v Unus Shipping Co Ltd [1939] AC 277 (PC)
Welex AG v Rosa Maritime Ltd [2002] 2 Lloyd's Rep 701; [2003] 2 Lloyd's Rep 509 (CA)
Wettern Electric Ltd v Welsh Development Agency [1983] QB 796
Whitworth Street Estates (Manchester) Ltd v James Miller and Partners Ltd [1970] AC 583
X AG v A Bank [1983] 2 All ER 464

# Germany

Bundesgerichtshof judgment of 22.11.1955 – I ZR 218/53, BGHZ 19, 110
Bundesgerichtshof judgment of 14.12.1958, ZZP 71 1958, 363
Bundesgerichtshof judgment of 24.11.1960, NJW 1961, 410
Bundesgerichtshof judgment of 21.2.1962, NJW 1962, 961
Bundesgerichtshof judgment of 28.11.1963, BGHZ 40, 320
Bundesgerichtshof judgment of 23.6.1964, NJW, 2012
Bundesgerichtshof judgment of 27.3.1968, BGHZ 50
Bundesgerichtshof judgment of 14.4.1969, WM 1969, 858
Bundesgerichtshof judgment of 7.5.1969 VIII ZR 142/68, DB 1969, 1053
Bundesgerichtshof judgment of 9.7.1970 – VII ZR 70/68, BGHZ 54, 236, NJW 1970, 2021
Bundesgerichtshof judgment of 23.10.1970, NJW 1971
Bundesgerichtshof judgment of 30.3.1976, IPRspr 1976 No 2, p 8 = NJW 1976, 1581
Bundesgerichtshof judgment of 27.4.1976, NJW 1976, 1588
Bundesgerichtshof judgment of 26.10.1977, BGHZ 69, 387 = NJW 1978, 496
Bundesgerichtshof judgment of 20.3.1980, BGHZ 77, 32 = NJW 1980, 2022

Bundesgerichtshof judgment of 23.12.1981, NJW 1982, 1215

Bundesgerichtshof judgment of 15.1.1986 – VIII ZR 6/85, WM 1986, 527, 6 IP-Rax 292 (1986)

Bundesgerichtshof judgment of 15.1.1986 – VIII ZR 6/85, WM 1986, 527

Bundesgerichtshof judgment of 15.12.1986 The Lankya Abbaya [1988] IPRax 26, WM 1987 273

Bundesgerichtshof judgment of 24.3.1987, NJW 1988, 648

Bundesgerichtshof judgment of 30.9.1987 – Iva ZR 22/86, WM 1987, 1501

Bundesgerichtshof judgment of 30.9.1987, NJW-RR 1988, 159

Bundesgerichtshof judgment of 18.1.1988, NJW 1988, 1592

Bundesgerichtshof judgment of 26.10.1989 – VII ZR 153/88, NJW-RR 1990, 183

Bundesgerichtshof judgment of 12.12.1990 – VIII ZR 332/89, WM 1991, 464

Bundesgerichtshof judgment of 21.01.1991 – II ZR 50/90, NJW 1991, 1418

Bundesgerichtshof judgment of 28.1.1992, NJW 1992, 1380

Bundesgerichtshof judgment of 30.4.1992, BGHZ 118, 151, 163; NJW 1992, 2026

Bundesgerichtshof judgment of 8.5.1992, NJW 1992, 3106

Bundesgerichtshof judgment of 21.10.1992 – XII ZR 182/90, BGHZ 119, 392, NJW, 1993, 385

Bundesgerichtshof judgment of 7.4.1993, NJW 1993, 2305

Bundesgerichtshof judgment of 12.5.1993, NJW 1993, 2753

Bundesgerichtshof judgment of 8.11.1994, NJW 1995, 1032

Bundesgerichtshof judgment of 20.9.1995 – VIII 52/94, WM 1995, 2073, BGHZ 130, 371

Bundesgerichtshof judgment of 14.11.1996 NJW 1997, 1150

Bundesgerichtshof judgment of 28.1.1997, RIW 1997, 426

Bundesgerichtshof judgment of 14.1.1999, RIW 1999, 537

Bundesgerichtshof judgment of 14.1.1999, VII 19/98, 1999 RIW, 537

Bundesgerichtshof judgment of 25.2.1999, in NJW 1999, 2242

Bundesgerichtshof judgment of 25.2.1999, VII ZR 408/97, 1999 NJW, 2242

Bundesgerichtshof judgment of 19.1.2000 – VIII ZR 275/98, NJW-RR 2000, 1002

Bundesgerichtshof judgment of 7.12.2000 VII ZR 404/99, NJW 2001, 1936

Bundesgerichtshof judgment of 30.1.2001, WM 2001, 502 = IPRax 2002, 302

Bundesgerichtshof judgment of 19.9.2001, NJW 2002, 1209

Bundesgerichtshof judgment of 23.4.2002, BGH NJW-RR 2002, 1359

Bundesgerichtshof judgment of 23.6.2003, NJW 2003, 2685

Bundesgerichtshof judgment of 23.6.2003, NJW 2003, 2685

Bundesgerichtshof judgment of 25.1.2005, NJW-RR 2005, 1071

Bundesgerichtshof judgment of 13.12.2005, NJW 2006, 762

Landesgericht Berlin judgment of 9.11.1994, NJW-RR 1995, 754 = IPRspr. 1994 Nr. 42
Oberlandesgericht Karlsruhe judgment of 30.3.1979, RIW 1979, 642
Oberlandesgericht Hamburg judgment of 30.12.1985, RIW 1986, 462
Oberlandesgericht Hamm judgment of 9.6.1995, NJW-RR 1996, 179
Oberlandesgericht München judgment of 9.8.1995, RIW 1996, 955 (956) = IPRax 1997, 3 (40) = IPRspr. 1995 Nr. 38 (68)
Oberlandesgericht Düsseldorf judgment of 19.12.1997, NJW-RR 1998, 1716
Oberlandesgericht Düsseldorf judgment of 16.7.2002 NJW-RR 2003, 1610

## European Court of Justice

Case C-133/08 Intercontainer Interfrigo SC (ICF) v Balkenende Oosthuizen BV, MIC Operations BV ECR I-000 (6.10.2009)
Case C-159/02 Turner v Grovit [2004] ECR I-3565
Case C-21/76 Handelskwekerij G. J. Bier BV v Mines de potasse d'Alsace SA NJ [1976] ECR I-1735
Case C-38/98 Régie Nationale des Usines Renault SA v Maxicar SpA [2000] ECR I-2973
Case C-381/98 Ingmar GB Ltd v Eaton Leonard Technologies Inc [2000] ECR I-9305
Case C-7/98 Krombach v Bamberski [2000] ECR I-1935; [2001] QB 709

## Australia

Akai Pty Ltd v People's Insurance Co Ltd (1996) 188 CLR 418
BHP Petroleum Pty Ltd v Oil Basins Ltd [1985] VR 725
Blunden v Commonwealth of Australia (2003) ALR 189
Breavington v Godleman (1988) 169 CLR 41
Byrnes v Groote Eylandt Mining Corporation (1990) 19 NSWLR 13
Corcoran v Corcoran [1974] VR 164
Dow Jones & Co Inc v Gutnick (2003) 210 CLR 575
Garstang v Cedenco JV Australia [2002] NSWSC 144
Golden Acres Ltd v Queensland Estates Pty Ltd [1969] Qd R 378
Ace Insurance Ltd v Moose Enterprise Pty Ltd [2009] NSWSC 724
James Hardie & Co Pty Ltd and Another v Hall as administrator of Estate of Putt [1998] 43 NSWLR 554
John Pfeiffer Pty Ltd v Rogerson (2000) 172 ALR 625 (Pfeiffer)

Kay's Leasing Corp v Fletcher (1964) 64 SR (NSW) 195
Kemp v Piper [1971] SASR 25
Koop v Bepp (1951) 84 CLR 629
McKain v R W Miller & Co (South Australia) Pty Ltd (1991) 174 CLR 1
Mendelson-Zeller Co v T and C Providores [1981] 1 NSWLR 366
Mercantile Mutual Insurance (Australia) v Neilson (2004) 28 WAR 206
Neilson v Overseas Projects Corporation of Victoria and Mercantile Insurance (Australia) Ltd [2005] HCA 54
Pedersen v Young (1964) 110 CLR
Potter v Broken Hill Proprietary Ltd [1905] VLR 612
Queensland Estates Pty Ltd v Collas [1971] Qd R 75
Régie Nationale des Usines Renault SA v Zhang (2002) 210 CLR 491; 187 ALR 1 (Renault)
Stanley Kerr Holdings Pty Ltd v Gibor Textile Enterprises Ltd [1978] NSWLR 372
Stevens v Head (1991) 14 MVR 327
Stevens v Head (1993) 176 CLR 433
Sub nom Freehold Land Investments Ltd v Queensland Estates Pty Ltd (1970) 123 CLR 418
Voth v Manildra Flour Mills Pty Ltd (1990) 171 CLR 538
Warren v Warren [1972] Qd R 386

# New Zealand

Air New Zealand Ltd v The Ship "Contship America" [1992] 1 NZLR 425 (HC)
Baxter v RMC Group Plc [2003] 1 NZLR 304 (Baxter)
Campbell Motors Ltd v Storey [1966] NZLR 584 (CA)
Carey v Hastie [1968] NZLR 276 (CA)
Club Mediterranee NZ v Wendell [1989] 1 NZLR 216 (CA)
Cornwall Properties v King [1966] NZLR 239
Governor of Pitcairn and Associated Islands v Sutton [1995] 1 NZLR 426
Graham v Attorney-General [1966] NZLR 937 (CA)
Knyett v Christchurch Casinos Ltd [1999] 2 NZLR 559 (CA)
Kunzang v Gershwin Hotel, HC Auckland, CP318-SD/99, 19 September 2000
Longbeach Holdings Ltd v Bhanabhai & Co Ltd [1994] 2 NZLR 28
McConnell Dowell Constructors Ltd v Lloyd's Syndicate 396 [1988] 2 NZLR 257
NZI Insurance New Zealand Ltd v Hinton Hill & Coles Ltd [1996] 1 NZLR 203, 208 (HC)

Richards and Others v McLean and Others [1973] 1 NZLR 521

Rimini Ltd v Manning Management and Marketing Pty Ltd [2003] 3 NZLR 22

Starlink Navigation Ltd v The Ship "Seven Pioneer" (2001) 16 PRNZ 55

# Canada

243930 Alberta Ltd. v Wickham (1990), 73 D.L.R. (4th) 474 (Ont. CA)

AG Newfoundland v Churchill Falls (Labrador) Corp Ltd (1984) 49 Nfld. & P.E.I.R. 181 (Nfld. S.C.T.D.)

Avenue Properties Ltd v First City Development Corp (1987) 32 DLR (4th) 40 (B.C.CA)

Bunge North American Grain Corp. & Fire Association of Philadelphia v S.S. "Skarp" and Owners [1933] Ex. C.R. 75

Canada (A.G.) v Nalleweg (1999) 223 A.R. 89; 165 D.L.R (4th) 606 (Alta. CA)

Cansulex Limited v Reed Stenhouse Limited (1986), 70 B.C.L.R. (1st) 273, 18 C.C.L.I. 24 (SC)

Dominion Glass Co v The Ship Anglo Indian [1944] SCR 409; [1944] 4 DLR 721

Drew Brown Ltd v The Ship "Orient Trader" and Owners [1974] SCR 1286

Eastern Power Ltd v Azienda Communale Energia & Ambiente (1999) 125 O.A.C. 54; (2000) 178 DLR (4th) 409 (Ont. CA)

George C. Anspach Co. v C.N.R. [1950] O.R. 317; [1950] 3 D.L.R. 26 (CA)

Gill v Gill 2000 BCSC 870

Gray v Kerslake [1958] SCR 3

Greenshields Inc. v Johnston [1983] 3 W.W.R. 313, 119 D.L.R. (3d) 714; affd. 131 D.L.R. (3d) 234, 35 A.R. 487 (CA)

Hanlan v Serensky [1998] 38 OR (3d) 479 (CA)

Imperial Life Assurance Company of Canada v Segundo Casteleiro Y Colmenares, [1967] S.C.R. 443

Imperial Oil Ltd. v Petromar Inc. [2002] 3 FC 190; 209 DLR (4th) 158

JPMorgan Chase Bank v Lanner (The) [2009] 4 FCR 109; 305 DLR (4th) 442

Kenton Natural Resources v Burkinshaw (1983), 47 A.R. 321 at 329 (QB)

Khalij Commercial Bank Ltd v Woods (1985) 17 DLR (4th) 358 (Ont. HCJ)

Lau v Li [2001] OJ No 1389

Long Island University v Morton (1977) 81 DLR (3d) 392 (N.S. Co. Ct.)

McLean v Pettigrew [1945] SCR 62

Melady v Jenkins SS Co. (1909), 18 O.L.R. 251 (CA)

Montreal Trust Co. v Stanrock Uranium Mines Ltd. [1966] 1 O.R. 258, 53 D.L.R. (2d) 594, 611 (HCJ)

Nike Informatic Systems Ltd v Avac Systems Ltd (1980) 105 DLR (3d) 455 (B.C.SC)

P & O Steam Navigation Co v Shand (1865) 3 Moo PC (NS) 272

Poly-Seal Corp v John Dale Ltd [1958] OWN 432 (HCJ)

Pope & Talbot Ltd, (Re) 2009, B.C.S.C. 1552 (No II)

Re Maritime Heating Co Ltd (1969) 2 DLR (3d) 471 (N.B.CA)

Sangi v Sangi [2011] B.C.S.C. 523

Somers v Fournier (2002) 214 DLR (4th) 611

Tolofson v Jensen; Lucas (Litigation Guardian of) v Gagnon [1994] 3 SCR 1022 (Tolofson)

Unifund Assurance Co v Insurance Corp of British Columbia [2003] 2 SCR 63

Whirlpool Canada Co. v National Union Fire Insurance Co. of Pittsburgh [2005] M.J. No. 332

Wilson v Metcalfe Construction Co. [1947] 1 W.W.R. 1089; [1947] 4 D.L.R. 472 (Alta. CA)

Wong v Lee (2002), 58 OR (3d) 398 (CA)

Wong v Wei [1999] 10 WWR 296 (BC)

World Fuel Services Corporation v The Ship "Nordems" 2011 FCA 73


# Singapore

Ang Ming Chuang v Singapore Airlines Ltd [2005] 1 SLR 409

Foo Kee Boo v Ho Lee Investments (Pte) Ltd [1988] SLR 620 (HC)

Goh Chok Tong v Tang Liang Hong [1997] 2 SLR 641

Hang Lung Bank Ltd v Datuk Kan Tim Chua [1988] 2 MLJ 567 (HC)

JIO Minerals FZC and others v Mineral Enterprises Ltd [2010] SGCA 41; [2011] 1 SLR 391

Las Vegas Hilton Corp t/a Las Vegas Hilton v Khoo Teng Hock Sunny [1997] 1 SLR 341 (CA)

Overseas Union Bank v Chua Kok Kay & Anor [1993] 1 SLR 686 (HC)

Overseas Union Insurance Ltd v Turegum Insurance Co [2001] 3 SLR 330

Pacific Electric Wire & Cable Co Ltd & Anor v Neptune Orient Lines Ltd [1993] 3 SLR 60 (HC)

Pacific Recreation Pte Ltd v SY Technology Inc [2008] 2 SLR 491 (CA)

Parno v SC Marine Pte Ltd [1999] 4 SLR 579; [1999] SGCA 69

Peh Teck Quee v Bayerische Landesbank Girozentrale [2000] 1 SLR 148 (CA)

Rickshaw Investments Ltd and Another v Nicolai Baron von Uexkull [2006] SGCA 39

RJ Sneddon v AG Shafe [1947] SLR 27

Shaik Faisal t/a Gibea v Swan Hunter Singapore Pte Ltd [1995] 1 SLR 394 (HC)

The Rainbow Joy [2005] 3 SLR 719

Vorobiev Nikolay v Lush John Frederick Peters and others [2011] SGHC 55

Wing Hak Man v Bio-Treat Technology Ltd [2009] 1 SLR(R) 446

# United States

Babcock v Jackson [1963] 2 Lloyd's Rep 286, 12 NY 2d 473, 240 NYS 2d 743, New York Court of Appeals

Bennet v Enstrom Helicopter Corporation 679 F 2d 630 (6th Circ 1982)

Wayman v Southard 23 US (10 Wheat.) 1 (1825)

# Legislation/Conventions/Treaties/Directives referred to

Arbitration Act 1996 (New Zealand)

Arbitration Act 1996 (UK)

Auslands-Rechtsauskunftsgesetz (AuRAG) from 5 July 1974, BGBl. 1974 I, 1433

Australian: Defamation Act 2005 (NSW; Defamation Act 2005 (NT); Defamation Act 2005 (Qld); Defamation Act 2005 (SA); Defamation Act 2005 (Tas); Defamation Act 2005 (Vic); Defamation Act 2005 (WA)

Belgium Wetboek van International Privaatrecht (Belgium PIL Act)

Bundesgesetz über das internationale Privatrecht – IPR-Gesetz (Austrian PIL Act)

Bundesgesetz über das internationale Privatrecht – IPR-Gesetz (Swiss PIL Act)

Bundesgesetz über das Internationale Privatrecht – IPR-Gesetz (Lichtenstein PIL Act)

Civil Law Wrongs (Amendment) Act 2006 (ACT)

Civil Procedure Rules 1998 UK (CPR) and its accompanying Practice Direction (CPR PD 16)

Consumer Protection Act 1987 (UK)

Contracts (Applicable Law) Act 1990 (UK)

Convention on the law applicable to contractual obligations (Rome Convention) (OJ L 266, 1 [9.10.1980])

Convention on the Settlement of Investment Disputes between States and Nationals of other States, Washington DC, March 18 1965 575 U.N.T.S. 159

Council Directive 85/374/EEC of 25 July 1985 on the approximation of the laws, regulations and administrative provisions of the Member States concerning liability for defective products (OJ L/210 [7.08.1995])

Council Directive 93/13/EEC of 5 April 1993 on Unfair Terms in Consumer Contracts (OJ L/095 [24.4.1993])

Council Regulation (EC) No 44/2001 of 22 December 2000 on jurisdiction and the recognition and enforcement of judgments in civil and commercial matters (OJ L12 [16.1.2001])

Council Regulation (EC) No 864/2007 on the law applicable to non-contractual obligations (Rome II) (OJ L199/40 [31.7.2007])

Council Regulation (EC) No 593/2008 on the law applicable to contractual obligations (Rome I) (OJ L177/6 [4.7.2008])

Council Regulation (EC) No 4/2009 of 18 December 2008 on jurisdiction, applicable law, recognition and enforcement of decisions and cooperation in matters relating to maintenance obligations (OJ L 7/1 [10.1.2009])

Council Regulation (EC) No 1259/2010 of 20 December 2010 implementing enhanced cooperation in the area of the law applicable to divorce and legal separation (OJ L343 [29.12.10])

Council Regulation (EC) No 650/2012 of 4 July 2012 on jurisdiction, applicable law, recognition and enforcement of decisions and acceptance and enforcement of authentic instruments in matters of succession and on the creation of a European Certificate of Succession (OJ L201 [27.7.2012])

European Convention on International Commercial Arbitration, Geneva, April 21 1961, 48 U.N.T.S. 159

First Council Directive 73/239/EEC of 24 July 1973 on the coordination of laws, regulations and administrative provisions relating to the taking-up and pursuit of the business of direct insurance other than life assurance, OJ L 228, 16.8.1973, p 3. Directive as last amended by Directive 2005/68/EC of the European Parliament and of the Council (OJ L 323 [9.12.2005])

Gesetz über das internationale Privatrecht – IPR-Gesetz (Lichtenstein PIL Act)

Gesetz zum Internationalen Privatrecht für außervertragliche Schuldverhältnisse und das Sachenrecht vom 21.5.1999, BGBl. I 1026

Gesetz zur Neuregelung des IPR vom 25.7.1986, BGBl. I/1986, 1142

Grundgesetz – GG (German Basic Law)

Hague Convention of 1 August 1989 on the Law Applicable to Succession to the Estates of Deceased Persons

Hague Convention of 14 March 1978 on the Law Applicable to Matrimonial Property Regimes

Hague Convention of 15 June 1955 on the Law Applicable to International Sale of Goods

Hague Convention of 22 December 1986 on the Law Applicable to Contracts for the International Sale of Goods

Handelsgesetzbuch – HGB (German Commercial Code)

International Arbitration Act 1974 (Australia)

International Arbitration Act 1994 (Singapore)

International Commercial Arbitration Act 1996 (Canada)

Newfoundland Carriage of Goods by Sea Act 1932

Private International Law (Miscellaneous Provisions) Act 1995 (UK)

Produkthaftungsgesetz of 15 December 1989 (German Product Liability Act)

Restatement of the Law, Conflict of Laws (1933) as adopted and promulgated by the American Law Institute at Washington, D.C., May 1934

Restatement of the Law (Second): Conflict of Laws (1971) as adopted and promulgated by the American Law Institute at Washington, D.C., May 1969

Rules of the Supreme Court 1965 (UK)

Treaty establishing the European Economic Community (EEC) of 25 March 1957 (entry into force 1958)

Treaty of Amsterdam Amending the Treaty on European Union, the Treaties Establishing the European Communities and Certain Related Acts of 10 November 1997 (OJ C 340/01 42)

Treaty on European Union (TEU) of 7 February 1992 (OJ C 191 [29/07/1992])

Treaty on the Functioning of the European Union (TFEU) (OJ C 115/47 [9/5/2008])

Unfair Contract Terms Act 1977 (UK)

United Nations Convention on Contracts for the International Sale of Goods Vienna, 11 April 1980, Document Number 98–9 (1984), UN Document Number A/CONF 97/19, 1489 UNTS 3.

Wet conflictenrecht onrechtmatige daad of 11 April 2001 (Dutch PIL Act)

Wetboek van International Privaatrecht (Belgian PIL Act)

Zivilprozessordnung (ZPO) (German Code of Civil Procedure)


# Proposals and Reports referred to

1st Reading Report of the EP JURI Committee on the proposal for a Regulation on the law applicable to non-contractual obligations (Rapporteur: Diana Wallis) (EP document A6–0211/2005 FINAL 27.6.2005)

Amended Proposal for a European Parliament and Council Regulation on the Law Applicable to Non-Contractual Obligations ("Rome II") COM (2006) 83 final, 21 February 2006 (Commission Amended Proposal)

Australian Law Reform Commission Choice of Law (ALRC): Report No 58, Law Reform Commission, Sydney, 1992, 40–80

Commission Opinion on the European Parliament's amendments to the Council Common Position (COM (2007) 126 final 14.3.2007)

Communication from the Commission concerning the Council's Common Position (COM (2006) 566 final [27.9.2006]

Council Common Position for adopting a regulation of the European Parliament and of the Council on the law applicable to non-contractual obligations (Rome II) (OJ C 289/68 [28.11.2006])

Draft regulation (unpublished) proposed by the Groupe Européen de Droit International Privé (GEDIP) Proposition pour une convention européenne sur la loi applicable aux obligations non contractuelles (Texte adopté lors de la réunion de Luxembourg du 25–27 septembre 1998)

Draft Report on the proposal for a regulation of the European Parliament and of the Council on the law applicable to non-contractual obligations ("Rome II") (COM(2003)0427 – C5–0338/2003 – 2003/0168(COD)) of 11.11.2004 (Rapporteur: Diana Wallis)

European Commission, Amended proposal for a Regulation on the law applicable to non-contractual obligations (Rome II) (COM (2006) 83 final) 21.2.2006)

European Commission, Proposal for a Regulation on the law applicable to non contractual obligations (Rome II) (COM (2003) 427 final of 22 July 2003 22.7.2003)

European Parliament legislative resolution on the proposal for a regulation of the European Parliament and of the Council on the law applicable to non-contractual obligations ("Rome II") COM (2003) 0427 06.07.2005, OJ C157E Vol. 49

Explanatory Memorandum of the Commission of the European Communities accompanying the European Commission, Proposal for a Regulation on the law applicable to non contractual obligations (Rome II) (COM (2003) 427 final of 22 July 2003 22.7.2003)

Giuliano, M. & Lagarde, P., Report on the Convention on the Law Applicable to Contractual Obligations, Official Journal of the European Union, OJ C 282 (1.10.1980) (hereafter Giuliano & Lagarde Report)

Green Paper on Conflict of Laws in Matters Concerning Matrimonial Property Regimes, including the question of jurisdiction and mutual recognition COM (2006) 400 final 17.7.2006

Green Paper on the Conversion of the Rome Convention 1980 on the law applicable to contractual obligations into a Community Instrument and its modernisation COM (2002) 654 14.1.2003

House of Lords European Union Committee, 8th Report of Session 2003–4, HL Paper 66

Law Commission (Working Paper No. 87) Private International Law: Choice of Law in Tort and Delict (Joint Working Paper – Scottish Law Commission Consultative Memorandum No. 62)

Magnus, Ulrich / Mankowski, Peter, Joint Response on the Green Paper on the Conversion of the Rome Convention on the Law Applicable to Contractual Obligations into a Community Instrument and its Modernisation, COM (2002) 654 final

Ministry of Justice (UK), Guidance on the law applicable to contractual obligations (Rome I), February 2010

Ministry of Justice, Rome I – Should the UK Opt in? Consultation Paper CP05/08, April 2, 2008

Parliament Council Conciliation Committee: Agreement on regulation on the law applicable to non-contractual obligations (Rome II) 16.5.2007, 9713/07 (Presse 111)

Preliminary Draft Proposal for a Council Regulation on the Law Applicable to Non-Contractual Obligations (2002)

Principles of European Contract Law, Commission on European Contract Law ("Lando-Commission") 1999 (PECL)

Project JLS/CJ/2007-I/03, Principles for a Future EU Regulation on the Application of Foreign Law (Madrid Principles)

Proposal for a Regulation of the European Council on the Law Applicable to Non-Contractual Obligations ("Rome II") COM (2003) 427 final, 22.7.2003

Proposal for a Regulation of the European Parliament and of the Council on the law applicable to non-contractual obligations (ROME II) – Outcome of the European Parliament's first reading (Strasbourg, 4 to 7 July 2005)

Proposal for a Regulation of the European Parliament and the Council on the law applicable to contractual obligations (Rome I) COM (2005) 650 final of 15.12.2005

Recommendation for Second Reading on the Council common position for adopting a regulation of the European Parliament and of the Council on the law applicable to non-contractual obligations (Rome II) <DocRef>(9751/7/2006 – C60317/2006 – 2003/0168(COD)) 22.12.2006 (Rapporteur: Diana Wallis)

Report on the proposal for a regulation of the European Parliament and of the Council on the law applicable to non-contractual obligations ("Rome II"), COM (2003)0427 – C5–0338/2003 – 2003/0168(COD) of 27 June 2005

Singapore Law Reform Committee Reform of the Choice of Law Rule Relating to Torts A Report of the Law Reform Committee of the Singapore Academy of Law, 31 March 2003

Statement of the Councils Reasons (accompanying the Council's Common Position) OJ C 289E, 28.11.2006

The Torts (Choice of Law) Bill 2003 00/2003 (Singapore)

UNIDROIT Principles of International Commercial Contracts 2010 (PICC), International Institute for the Unification of Private Law

# Appendix 1

REGULATION (EC) No 593/2008 OF THE EUROPEAN
PARLIAMENT AND OF THE COUNCIL

of 17 June 2008

on the law applicable to contractual obligations (Rome I)

THE EUROPEAN PARLIAMENT AND THE COUNCIL OF THE EUROPEAN UNION,

Having regard to the Treaty establishing the European Community, and in particular Article 61(c) and the second indent of Article 67(5) thereof,

Having regard to the proposal from the Commission,

Having regard to the opinion of the European Economic and Social Committee ([1]),

Acting in accordance with the procedure laid down in Article 251 of the Treaty ([2]),

Whereas:

(1) The Community has set itself the objective of maintaining and developing an area of freedom, security and justice. For the progressive establishment of such an area, the Community is to adopt measures relating to judicial cooperation in civil matters with a cross-border impact to the extent necessary for the proper functioning of the internal market.

(2) According to Article 65, point (b) of the Treaty, these measures are to include those promoting the compatibility of the rules applicable in the Member States concerning the conflict of laws and of jurisdiction.

(3) The European Council meeting in Tampere on 15 and 16 October 1999 endorsed the principle of mutual recognition of judgments and other decisions of judicial authorities as the cornerstone of judicial cooperation in civil matters and invited the Council and the Commission to adopt a programme of measures to implement that principle.

(4) On 30 November 2000 the Council adopted a joint Commission and Council programme of measures for implementation of the principle of mutual recognition of decisions in civil and commercial matters ([3]). The programme identifies measures relating to the harmonisation of conflict-of-law

---

1 OJ C 318, 23.12.2006, p. 56.
2 Opinion of the European Parliament of 29 November 2007 (not yet published in the Official Journal) and Council Decision of 5 June 2008.

3 OJ C 12, 15.1.2001, p. 1.

rules as those facilitating the mutual recognition of judgments.

(5) The Hague Programme (⁴), adopted by the European Council on 5 November 2004, called for work to be pursued actively on the conf lict-of-law rules regarding contractual obligations (Rome I).

(6) The proper functioning of the internal market creates a need, in order to improve the predictability of the outcome of litigation, certainty as to the law applicable and the free movement of judgments, for the conflict-of-law rules in the Member States to designate the same national law irrespective of the country of the court in which an action is brought.

(7) The substantive scope and the provisions of this Regulation should be consistent with Council Regulation (EC) No 44/2001 of 22 December 2000 on jurisdiction and the recognition and enforcement of judgments in civil and commercial matters (⁵) (Brussels I) and Regulation (EC) No 864/2007 of the European Parliament and of the Council of 11 July 2007 on the law applicable to non-contractual obligations (Rome II) (⁶).

(8) Family relationships should cover parentage, marriage, affinity and collateral relatives. The reference in Article 1(2) to relationships having comparable effects to marriage and other family relationships should be interpreted in accordance with the law of the Member State in which the court is seised.

(9) Obligations under bills of exchange, cheques and promissory notes and other negotiable instruments should also cover bills of lading to the extent that the obligations under the bill of lading arise out of its negotiable character.

(10) Obligations arising out of dealings prior to the conclusion of the contract are covered by Article 12 of Regulation (EC) No 864/2007. Such obligations should therefore be excluded from the scope of this Regulation.

(11) The parties' freedom to choose the applicable law should be one of the cornerstones of the system of conflict-of-law rules in matters of contractual obligations.

(12) An agreement between the parties to confer on one or more courts or tribunals of a Member State exclusive jurisdiction to determine disputes under the contract should be one of the factors to be taken into account in determining whether a choice of law has been clearly demonstrated.

(13) This Regulation does not preclude parties from incorporating by reference into their contract a non-State body of law or an international convention.

(14) Should the Community adopt, in an appropriate legal instrument, rules of

---

4  OJ C 53, 3.3.2005, p. 1.
5  OJ L 12, 16.1.2001, p. 1. Regulation as last amended by Regulation (EC) No 1791/2006 (OJ L 363, 20.12.2006, p. 1).
6  OJ L 199, 31.7.2007, p. 40.

substantive contract law, including standard terms and conditions, such instrument may provide that the parties may choose to apply those rules.

(15) Where a choice of law is made and all other elements relevant to the situation are located in a country other than the country whose law has been chosen, the choice of law should not prejudice the application of provisions of the law of that country which cannot be derogated from by agreement. This rule should apply whether or not the choice of law was accompanied by a choice of court or tribunal. Whereas no substantial change is intended as compared with Article 3(3) of the 1980 Convention on the Law Applicable to Contractual Obligations (7) (the Rome Convention), the wording of this Regulation is aligned as far as possible with Article 14 of Regulation (EC) No 864/2007.

(16) To contribute to the general objective of this Regulation, legal certainty in the European judicial area, the conf lict-of-law rules should be highly foreseeable. The courts should, however, retain a degree of discretion to determine the law that is most closely connected to the situation.

(17) As far as the applicable law in the absence of choice is concerned, the concept of 'provision of services' and 'sale of goods' should be interpreted in the same way as when applying Article 5

of Regulation (EC) No 44/2001 in so far as sale of goods and provision of services are covered by that Regulation. Although franchise and distribution contracts are contracts for services, they are the subject of specific rules.

(18) As far as the applicable law in the absence of choice is concerned, multilateral systems should be those in which trading is conducted, such as regulated markets and multilateral trading facilities as referred to in Article 4 of Directive 2004/39/EC of the European Parliament and of the Council of 21 April 2004 on markets in financial instruments (28), regardless of whether or not they rely on a central counterparty.

(19) Where there has been no choice of law, the applicable law should be determined in accordance with the rule specified for the particular type of contract. Where the contract cannot be categorised as being one of the specified types or where its elements fall within more than one of the specified types, it should be governed by the law of the country where the party required to effect the characteristic performance of the contract has his habitual residence. In the case of a contract consisting of a bundle of rights and obligations capable of being categorised as falling within more than one of the specified types of contract, the characteristic performance

---

7   OJ C 334, 30.12.2005, p. 1.

8   OJ L 145, 30.4.2004, p. 1. Directive as last amended by Directive 2008/10/EC (OJ L 76, 19.3.2008, p. 33).

of the contract should be determined having regard to its centre of gravity.

(20) Where the contract is manifestly more closely connected with a country other than that indicated in Article 4(1) or (2), an escape clause should provide that the law of that other country is to apply. In order to determine that country, account should be taken, inter alia, of whether the contract in question has a very close relationship with another contract or contracts.

(21) In the absence of choice, where the applicable law cannot be determined either on the basis of the fact that the contract can be categorised as one of the specified types or as being the law of the country of habitual residence of the party required to effect the characteristic performance of the contract, the contract should be governed by the law of the country with which it is most closely connected. In order to determine that country, account should be taken, inter alia, of whether the contract in question has a very close relationship with another contract or contracts.

(22) As regards the interpretation of contracts for the carriage of goods, no change in substance is intended with respect to Article 4(4), third sentence, of the Rome Convention. Consequently, single-voyage charter parties and other contracts the main purpose of which is the carriage of goods should be treated as contracts for the carriage of goods. For the purposes of this Regulation, the term 'consignor' should

refer to any person who enters into a contract of carriage with the carrier and the term 'the carrier' should refer to the party to the contract who undertakes to carry the goods, whether or not he performs the carriage himself.

(23) As regards contracts concluded with parties regarded as being weaker, those parties should be protected by conflict-of-law rules that are more favourable to their interests than the general rules.

(24) With more specific reference to consumer contracts, the conflict-of-law rule should make it possible to cut the cost of settling disputes concerning what are commonly relatively small claims and to take account of the development of distance-selling techniques. Consistency with Regulation (EC) No 44/2001 requires both that there be a reference to the concept of directed activity as a condition for applying the consumer protection rule and that the concept be interpreted harmoniously in Regulation (EC) No 44/2001 and this Regulation, bearing in mind that a joint declaration by the Council and the Commission on Article 15 of Regulation (EC) No 44/2001 states that 'for Article 15(1)(c) to be applicable it is not sufficient for an undertaking to target its activities at the Member State of the consumer's residence, or at a number of Member States including that Member State; a contract must also be concluded within the framework of its activities'. The declaration also states that 'the mere fact that an Internet site is

accessible is not sufficient for Article 15 to be applicable, although a factor will be that this Internet site solicits the conclusion of distance contracts and that a contract has actually been concluded at a distance, by whatever means. In this respect, the language or currency which a website uses does not constitute a relevant factor.'.

(25) Consumers should be protected by such rules of the country of their habitual residence that cannot be derogated from by agreement, provided that the consumer contract has been concluded as a result of the professional pursuing his commercial or professional activities in that particular country. The same protection should be guaranteed if the professional, while not pursuing his commercial or professional activities in the country where the consumer has his habitual residence, directs his activities by any means to that country or to several countries, including that country, and the contract is concluded as a result of such activities.

(26) For the purposes of this Regulation, financial services such as investment services and activities and ancillary services provided by a professional to a consumer, as referred to in sections A and B of Annex I to Directive 2004/39/EC, and contracts for the sale of units in collective investment undertakings, whether or not covered by Council Directive 85/611/EEC of 20 December 1985 on the coordination of laws, regulations and administrative provisions relating to undertakings for collective investment in transferable securities

(UCITS) (⁹), should be subject to Article 6 of this Regulation. Consequently, when a reference is made to terms and conditions governing the issuance or offer to the public of transferable securities or to the subscription and redemption of units in collective investment undertakings, that reference should include all aspects binding the issuer or the offeror to the consumer, but should not include those aspects involving the provision of financial services.

(27) Various exceptions should be made to the general conflict-of-law rule for consumer contracts. Under one such exception the general rule should not apply to contracts relating to rights in rem in immovable property or tenancies of such property unless the contract relates to the right to use immovable property on a timeshare basis within the meaning of Directive 94/47/EC of the European Parliament and of the Council of 26 October 1994 on the protection of purchasers in respect of certain aspects of contracts relating to the purchase of the right to use immovable properties on a timeshare basis (¹⁰).

(28) It is important to ensure that rights and obligations which constitute a financial instrument are not covered by the general rule applicable to consumer contracts, as that could lead to

---

9   OJ L 375, 31.12.1985, p. 3. Directive as last amended by Directive 2008/18/EC of the European Parliament and of the Council (OJL 76, 19.3.2008, p. 42).

10   OJ L 280, 29.10.1994, p. 83.

different laws being applicable to each of the instruments issued, therefore changing their nature and preventing their fungible trading and offering. Likewise, whenever such instruments are issued or offered, the contractual relationship established between the issuer or the offeror and the consumer should not necessarily be subject to the mandatory application of the law of the country of habitual residence of the consumer, as there is a need to ensure uniformity in the terms and conditions of an issuance or an offer. The same rationale should apply with regard to the multilateral systems covered by Article 4(1)(h), in respect of which it should be ensured that the law of the country of habitual residence of the consumer will not interfere with the rules applicable to contracts concluded within those systems or with the operator of such systems.

(29) For the purposes of this Regulation, references to rights and obligations constituting the terms and conditions governing the issuance, offers to the public or public take-over bids of transferable securities and references to the subscription and redemption of units in collective investment undertakings should include the terms governing, inter alia, the allocation of securities or units, rights in the event of over subscription, withdrawal rights and similar matters in the context of the offer as well as those matters referred to in Articles 10, 11, 12 and 13, thus ensuring that all relevant contractual aspects of an offer binding the issuer or the offeror to the consumer are governed by a single law.

(30) For the purposes of this Regulation, financial instruments and transferable securities are those instruments referred to in Article 4 of Directive 2004/39/EC.

(31) Nothing in this Regulation should prejudice the operation of a formal arrangement designated as a system under Article 2(a) of Directive 98/26/EC of the European Parliament and of the Council of 19 May 1998 on settlement finality in payment and securities settlement systems ([11]).

(32) Owing to the particular nature of contracts of carriage and insurance contracts, specific provisions should ensure an adequate level of protection of passengers and policy holders. Therefore, Article 6 should not apply in the context of those particular contracts.

(33) Where an insurance contract not covering a large risk covers more than one risk, at least one of which is situated in a Member State and at least one of which is situated in a third country, the special rules on insurance contracts in this Regulation should apply only to the risk or risks situated in the relevant Member State or Member States.

(34) The rule on individual employment contracts should not prejudice the application of the overriding mandatory provisions

---

11    OJ L 166, 11.6.1998, p. 45.

of the country to which a worker is posted in accordance with Directive 96/71/EC of the European Parliament and of the Council of 16 December 1996 concerning the posting of workers in the framework of the provision of services ([12]).

(35) Employees should not be deprived of the protection afforded to them by provisions which cannot be derogated from by agreement or which can only be derogated from to their benefit.

(36) As regards individual employment contracts, work carried out in another country should be regarded as temporary if the employee is expected to resume working in the country of origin after carrying out his tasks abroad. The conclusion of a new contract of employment with the original employer or an employer belonging to the same group of companies as the original employer should not preclude the employee from being regarded as carrying out his work in another country temporarily.

(37) Considerations of public interest justify giving the courts of the Member States the possibility, in exceptional circumstances, of applying exceptions based on public policy and overriding mandatory provisions. The concept of 'overriding mandatory provisions' should be distinguished from the expression 'provisions which cannot be derogated from by agreement' and should be construed more restrictively.

(38) In the context of voluntary assignment, the term 'relationship' should make it clear that Article 14(1) also applies to the property aspects of an assignment, as between assignor and assignee, in legal orders where such aspects are treated separately from the aspects under the law of obligations. However, the term 'relationship' should not be understood as relating to any relationship that may exist between assignor and assignee. In particular, it should not cover preliminary questions as regards a voluntary assignment or a contractual subrogation. The term should be strictly limited to the aspects which are directly relevant to the voluntary assignment or contractual subrogation in question.

(39) For the sake of legal certainty there should be a clear definition of habitual residence, in particular for companies and other bodies, corporate or unincorporated. Unlike Article 60(1) of Regulation (EC) No 44/2001, which establishes three criteria, the conflict-of-law rule should proceed on the basis of a single criterion; otherwise, the parties would be unable to foresee the law applicable to their situation.

(40) A situation where conflict-of-law rules are dispersed among several instruments and where there are differences between those rules should be avoided. This Regulation, however, should not exclude the possibility of inclusion of conflict-of-law rules relating to contractual obligations in provisions of Community law with regard to particular matters.

---

12  OJ L 18, 21.1.1997, p. 1.

This Regulation should not prejudice the application of other instruments laying down provisions designed to contribute to the proper functioning of the internal market in so far as they cannot be applied in conjunction with the law designated by the rules of this Regulation. The application of provisions of the applicable law designated by the rules of this Regulation should not restrict the free movement of goods and services as regulated by Community instruments, such as Directive 2000/31/EC of the European Parliament and of the Council of 8 June 2000 on certain legal aspects of information society services, in particular electronic commerce, in the Internal Market (Directive on electronic commerce) ([13]).

(41) Respect for international commitments entered into by the Member States means that this Regulation should not affect international conventions to which one or more Member States are parties at the time when this Regulation is adopted. To make the rules more accessible, the Comission should publish the list of the relevant conventions in the Official Journal of the European Union on the basis of information supplied by the Member States.

(42) The Commission will make a proposal to the European Parliament and to the Council concerning the procedures and conditions according to which Member States would be entitled to negotiate and conclude, on their own behalf, agreements with third countries in individual and exceptional cases, concerning sectoral matters and containing provisions on the law applicable to contractual obligations.

(43) Since the objective of this Regulation cannot be sufficiently achieved by the Member States and can therefore, by reason of the scale and effects of this Regulation, be better achieved at Community level, the Community may adopt measures, in accordance with the principle of subsidiarity as set out in Article 5 of the Treaty. In accordance with the principle of proportionality, as set out in that Article, this Regulation does not go beyond what is necessary to attain its objective.

(44) In accordance with Article 3 of the Protocol on the position of the United Kingdom and Ireland, annexed to the Treaty on European Union and to the Treaty establishing the European Community, Ireland has notified its wish to take part in the adoption and application of the present Regulation.

(45) In accordance with Articles 1 and 2 of the Protocol on the position of the United Kingdom and Ireland, annexed to the Treaty on European Union and to the Treaty establishing the European Community, and without prejudice to Article 4 of the said Protocol, the United Kingdom is

---

13   OJ L 178, 17.7.2000, p. 1.

not taking part in the adoption of this Regulation and is not bound by it or subject to its application.

(46) In accordance with Articles 1 and 2 of the Protocol on the position of Denmark, annexed to the Treaty on European Union and to the Treaty establishing the European Community, Denmark is not taking part in the adoption of this Regulation and is not bound by it or subject to its application.

HAVE ADOPTED THIS REGULATION:

## CHAPTER I

## SCOPE

### Article 1

### Material scope

1. This Regulation shall apply, in situations involving a conflict of laws, to contractual obligations in civil and commercial matters.

It shall not apply, in particular, to revenue, customs or administrative matters.

2. The following shall be excluded from the scope of this Regulation:

(a) questions involving the status or legal capacity of natural persons, without prejudice to Article 13;

(b) obligations arising out of family relationships and relationships deemed by the law applicable to such relationships to have comparable effects, including maintenance obligations;

(c) obligations arising out of matrimonial property regimes, property regimes of relationships deemed by the law applicable to such relationships to have comparable effects to marriage, and wills and succession;

(d) obligations arising under bills of exchange, cheques and promissory notes and other negotiable instruments to the extent that the obligations under such other negotiable instruments arise out of their negotiable character;

(e) arbitration agreements and agreements on the choice of court;

(f) questions governed by the law of companies and other bodies, corporate or unincorporated, such as the creation, by registration or otherwise, legal capacity, internal organisation or winding-up of companies and other bodies, corporate or unincorporated, and the personal liability of officers and members as such for the obligations of the company or body;

(g) the question whether an agent is able to bind a principal, or an organ to bind a company or other body corporate or unincorporated, in relation to a third party;

(h) the constitution of trusts and the relationship between settlors, trustees and beneficiaries;

(i) obligations arising out of dealings prior to the conclusion of a contract;

(j) insurance contracts arising out of operations carried out by organisations other than undertakings referred to in Article 2 of Directive 2002/83/EC of the European Parliament and of the Council of 5 November 2002 concerning life assurance ([14]) the object of which is to provide benefits for employed or self employed persons belonging to an undertaking or group of undertakings, or to a trade or group of trades, in the event of death or survival or of discontinuance or curtailment of activity, or of sickness related to work or accidents at work.

3. This Regulation shall not apply to evidence and procedure, without prejudice to Article 18.

4. In this Regulation, the term 'Member State' shall mean Member States to which this Regulation applies. However, in Article 3(4) and Article 7 the term shall mean all the Member States.

### Article 2

### Universal application

Any law specified by this Regulation shall be applied whether or not it is the law of a Member State.

---

14  OJ L 345, 19.12.2002, p. 1. Directive as last amended by Directive 2008/19/EC (OJ L 76, 19.3.2008, p. 44).

## CHAPTER II

### UNIFORM RULES

### Article 3

### Freedom of choice

1. A contract shall be governed by the law chosen by the parties. The choice shall be made expressly or clearly demonstrated by the terms of the contract or the circumstances of the case. By their choice the parties can select the law applicable to the whole or to part only of the contract.

2. The parties may at any time agree to subject the contract to a law other than that which previously governed it, whether as a result of an earlier choice made under this Article or of other provisions of this Regulation. Any change in the law to be applied that is made after the conclusion of the contract shall not prejudice its formal validity under Article 11 or adversely affect the rights of third parties.

3. Where all other elements relevant to the situation at the time of the choice are located in a country other than the country whose law has been chosen, the choice of the parties shall not prejudice the application of provisions of the law of that other country which cannot be derogated from by agreement.

4. Where all other elements relevant to the situation at the time of the choice are located in one or more Member States, the parties' choice of applicable law other than that of a Member State shall not prejudice the application of provisions of Community law, where appropriate as implemented in

the Member State of the forum, which cannot be derogated from by agreement.

5. The existence and validity of the consent of the parties as to the choice of the applicable law shall be determined in accordance with the provisions of Articles 10, 11 and 13.

## Article 4

### Applicable law in the absence of choice

1. To the extent that the law applicable to the contract has not been chosen in accordance with Article 3 and without prejudice to Articles 5 to 8, the law governing the contract shall be determined as follows:

(a) a contract for the sale of goods shall be governed by the law of the country where the seller has his habitual residence;

(b) a contract for the provision of services shall be governed by the law of the country where the service provider has his habitual residence;

(c) a contract relating to a right in rem in immovable property or to a tenancy of immovable property shall be governed by the law of the country where the property is situated;

(d) notwithstanding point (c), a tenancy of immovable property concluded for temporary private use for a period of no more than six consecutive months shall be governed by the law of the country where the landlord has his habitual residence, provided that the tenant is a natural person and has his habitual residence in the same country;

(e) a franchise contract shall be governed by the law of the country where the franchisee has his habitual residence;

(f) a distribution contract shall be governed by the law of the country where the distributor has his habitual residence;

(g) a contract for the sale of goods by auction shall be governed by the law of the country where the auction takes place, if such a place can be determined;

(h) a contract concluded within a multilateral system which brings together or facilitates the bringing together of multiple third-party buying and selling interests in financial instruments, as defined by Article 4(1), point (17) of Directive 2004/39/EC, in accordance with non-discretionary rules and governed by a single law, shall be governed by that law.

2. Where the contract is not covered by paragraph 1 or where the elements of the contract would be covered by more than one of points (a) to (h) of paragraph 1, the contract shall be governed by the law of the country where the party required to effect the characteristic performance of the contract has his habitual residence.

3. Where it is clear from all the circumstances of the case that the contract is manifestly more closely connected with a country other than that indicated in paragraphs 1 or 2, the law of that other country shall apply.

4. Where the law applicable cannot be determined pursuant to paragraphs 1 or 2, the contract shall be governed by the law of the country with which it is most closely connected.

## Article 5

### Contracts of carriage

1. To the extent that the law applicable to a contract for the carriage of goods has not been chosen in accordance with Article 3, the law applicable shall be the law of the country of habitual residence of the carrier, provided that the place of receipt or the place of delivery or the habitual residence of the consignor is also situated in that country. If those requirements are not met, the law of the country where the place of delivery as agreed by the parties is situated shall apply.

2. To the extent that the law applicable to a contract for the carriage of passengers has not been chosen by the parties in accordance with the second subparagraph, the law applicable shall be the law of the country where the passenger has his habitual residence, provided that either the place of departure or the place of destination is situated in that country. If these requirements are not met, the law of the country where the carrier has his habitual residence shall apply.

The parties may choose as the law applicable to a contract for the carriage of passengers in accordance with Article 3 only the law of the country where:

(a) the passenger has his habitual residence; or

(b) the carrier has his habitual residence; or

(c) the carrier has his place of central administration; or

(d) the place of departure is situated; or

(e) the place of destination is situated.

3. Where it is clear from all the circumstances of the case that the contract, in the absence of a choice of law, is manifestly more closely connected with a country other than that indicated in paragraphs 1 or 2, the law of that other country shall apply.

## Article 6

### Consumer contracts

1. Without prejudice to Articles 5 and 7, a contract concluded by a natural person for a purpose which can be regarded as being outside his trade or profession (the consumer) with another person acting in the exercise of his trade or profession (the professional) shall be governed by the law of the country where the consumer has his habitual residence, provided that the professional:

(a) pursues his commercial or professional activities in the country where the consumer has his habitual residence, or

(b) by any means, directs such activities to that country or to several countries including that country,

and the contract falls within the scope of such activities.

2. Notwithstanding paragraph 1, the parties may choose the law applicable to a contract which fulfils the requirements of paragraph 1, in accordance with Article 3. Such a choice may not, however, have the result of depriving the consumer of the protection afforded to him by provisions that cannot be derogated from by agreement by virtue of the law which, in the absence of choice, would have been applicable on the basis of paragraph 1.

3. If the requirements in points (a) or (b) of paragraph 1 are not fulfilled, the law applicable to a contract between a consumer and a professional shall be determined pursuant to Articles 3 and 4.

4. Paragraphs 1 and 2 shall not apply to:

(a) a contract for the supply of services where the services are to be supplied to the consumer exclusively in a country other than that in which he has his habitual residence;

(b) a contract of carriage other than a contract relating to package travel within the meaning of Council Directive 90/314/EEC of 13 June 1990 on package travel, packageholidays and package tours ([15]);

(c) a contract relating to a right in rem in immovable property or a tenancy of immovable property other than a contract relating to the right to use immovable properties on a timeshare basis within the meaning of Directive 94/47/EC;

(d) rights and obligations which constitute a financial instrument and rights and obligations constituting the terms and conditions governing the issuance or offer to the public and public take-over bids of transferable securities, and the subscription and redemption of units in collective investment undertakings in so far as these activities do not constitute provision of a financial service;

(e) a contract concluded within the type of system falling within the scope of Article 4(1)(h).

## Article 7

### Insurance contracts

1. This Article shall apply to contracts referred to in paragraph 2, whether or not the risk covered is situated in a Member State, and to all other insurance contracts covering risks situated inside the territory of the Member States. It shall not apply to reinsurance contracts.

2. An insurance contract covering a large risk as defined in Article 5(d) of the First Council Directive 73/239/EEC of 24 July 1973 on the coordination of laws, regulations and administrative provisions relating to the taking-up and pursuit of the business of direct insurance other than life assurance ([16]) shall be governed by the law chosen by the parties in accordance with Article 3 of this Regulation.

To the extent that the applicable law has not been chosen by the parties, the insurance contract shall be governed by the law of the country where the insurer has his habitual residence. Where it is clear from all the circumstances of the case that the contract is manifestly more closely connected with another country, the law of that other country shall apply.

3. In the case of an insurance contract other than a contract falling within paragraph 2,

---

15  OJ L 158, 23.6.1990, p. 59.

16  OJ L 228, 16.8.1973, p. 3. Directive as last amended by Directive 2005/68/EC of the European Parliament and of the Council (OJ L 323, 9.12.2005, p. 1).

only the following laws may be chosen by the parties in accordance with Article 3:

(a) the law of any Member State where the risk is situated at the time of conclusion of the contract;

(b) the law of the country where the policy holder has his habitual residence;

(c) in the case of life assurance, the law of the Member State of which the policy holder is a national;

(d) for insurance contracts covering risks limited to events occurring in one Member State other than the Member State where the risk is situated, the law of that Member State;

(e) where the policy holder of a contract falling under this paragraph pursues a commercial or industrial activity or a liberal profession and the insurance contract covers two or more risks which relate to those activities and are situated in different Member States, the law of any of the Member States concerned or the law of the country of habitual residence of the policy holder.

Where, in the cases set out in points (a), (b) or (e), the Member States referred to grant greater freedom of choice of the law applicable to the insurance contract, the parties may take advantage of that freedom.

To the extent that the law applicable has not been chosen by the parties in accordance with this paragraph, such a contract shall be governed by the law of the Member State in which the risk is situated at the time of conclusion of the contract.

4. The following additional rules shall apply to insurance contracts covering risks for which a Member State imposes an obligation to take out insurance:

(a) the insurance contract shall not satisfy the obligation to take out insurance unless it complies with the specific provisions relating to that insurance laid down by the Member State that imposes the obligation. Where the law of the Member State in which the risk is situated and the law of the Member State imposing the obligation to take out insurance contradict each other, the latter shall prevail;

(b) by way of derogation from paragraphs 2 and 3, a Member State may lay down that the insurance contract shall be governed by the law of the Member State that imposes the obligation to take out insurance.

5. For the purposes of paragraph 3, third subparagraph, and paragraph 4, where the contract covers risks situated in more than one Member State, the contract shall be considered as constituting several contracts each relating to only one Member State.

6. For the purposes of this Article, the country in which the risk is situated shall be determined in accordance with Article 2(d) of the Second Council Directive 88/357/ EEC of 22 June 1988 on the coordination of laws, regulations and administrative provisions relating to direct insurance other than

life assurance and laying down provisions to facilitate the effective exercise of freedom to provide services ([17]) and, in the case of life assurance, the country in which the risk is situated shall be the country of the commitment within the meaning of Article 1(1) (g) of Directive 2002/83/EC.

## Article 8

### Individual employment contracts

1. An individual employment contract shall be governed by the law chosen by the parties in accordance with Article 3. Such a choice of law may not, however, have the result of depriving the employee of the protection afforded to him by provisions that cannot be derogated from by agreement under the law that, in the absence of choice, would have been applicable pursuant to paragraphs 2, 3 and 4 of this Article.

2. To the extent that the law applicable to the individual employment contract has not been chosen by the parties, the contract shall be governed by the law of the country in which or, failing that, from which the employee habitually carries out his work in performance of the contract. The country where the work is habitually carried out shall not be deemed to have changed if he is temporarily employed in another country.

3. Where the law applicable cannot be determined pursuant to paragraph 2, the contract shall be governed by the law of the country where the place of business through which the employee was engaged is situated.

4. Where it appears from the circumstances as a whole that the contract is more closely connected with a country other than that indicated in paragraphs 2 or 3, the law of that other country shall apply.

## Article 9

### Overriding mandatory provisions

1. Overriding mandatory provisions are provisions the respect for which is regarded as crucial by a country for safeguarding its public interests, such as its political, social or economic organisation, to such an extent that they are applicable to any situation falling within their scope, irrespective of the law otherwise applicable to the contract under this Regulation.

2. Nothing in this Regulation shall restrict the application of the overriding mandatory provisions of the law of the forum.

3. Effect may be given to the overriding mandatory provisions of the law of the country where the obligations arising out of the contract have to be or have been performed, in so far as those overriding mandatory provisions render the performance of the contract unlawful. In considering whether to give effect to those provisions, regard shall be had to their nature and purpose and to the consequences of their application or nonapplication.

---

17    OJ L 172, 4.7.1988, p. 1. Directive as last amended by Directive 2005/14/EC of the European Parliament and of the Council (OJ L 149, 11.6.2005, p. 14).

## Article 10

### Consent and material validity

1. The existence and validity of a contract, or of any term of a contract, shall be determined by the law which would govern it under this Regulation if the contract or term were valid.

2. Nevertheless, a party, in order to establish that he did not consent, may rely upon the law of the country in which he has his habitual residence if it appears from the circumstances that it would not be reasonable to determine the effect of his conduct in accordance with the law specified in paragraph 1.

## Article 11

### Formal validity

1. A contract concluded between persons who, or whose agents, are in the same country at the time of its conclusion is formally valid if it satisfies the formal requirements of the law which governs it in substance under this Regulation or of the law of the country where it is concluded.

2. A contract concluded between persons who, or whose agents, are in different countries at the time of its conclusion is formally valid if it satisfies the formal requirements of the law which governs it in substance under this Regulation, or of the law of either of the countries where either of the parties or their agent is present at the time of conclusion, or of the law of the country where either of the parties had his habitual residence at that time.

3. A unilateral act intended to have legal effect relating to an existing or contemplated contract is formally valid if it satisfies the formal requirements of the law which governs or would govern the contract in substance under this Regulation, or of the law of the country where the act was done, or of the law of the country where the person by whom it was done had his habitual residence at that time.

4. Paragraphs 1, 2 and 3 of this Article shall not apply to contracts that fall within the scope of Article 6. The form of such contracts shall be governed by the law of the country where the consumer has his habitual residence.

5. Notwithstanding paragraphs 1 to 4, a contract the subject matter of which is a right in rem in immovable property or a tenancy of immovable property shall be subject to the requirements of form of the law of the country where the property is situated if by that law:

(a) those requirements are imposed irrespective of the country where the contract is concluded and irrespective of the law governing the contract; and

(b) those requirements cannot be derogated from by agreement.

## Article 12

### Scope of the law applicable

1. The law applicable to a contract by virtue of this Regulation shall govern in particular:

(a) interpretation;

(b) performance;

(c) within the limits of the powers conferred on the court by its procedural law, the consequences of a total or partial breach of obligations, including the assessment of damages in so far as it is governed by rules of law;

(d) the various ways of extinguishing obligations, and prescription and limitation of actions;

(e) the consequences of nullity of the contract.

2. In relation to the manner of performance and the steps to be taken in the event of defective performance, regard shall be had to the law of the country in which performance takes place.

## Article 13

### Incapacity

In a contract concluded between persons who are in the same country, a natural person who would have capacity under the law of that country may invoke his incapacity resulting from the law of another country, only if the other party to the contract was aware of that incapacity at the time of the conclusion of the contract or was not aware thereof as a result of negligence.

## Article 14

### Voluntary assignment and contractual subrogation

1. The relationship between assignor and assignee under a voluntary assignment or contractual subrogation of a claim against another person (the debtor) shall be governed by the law that applies to the contract between the assignor and assignee under this Regulation.

2. The law governing the assigned or subrogated claim shall determine its assignability, the relationship between the assignee and the debtor, the conditions under which the assignment or subrogation can be invoked against the debtor and whether the debtor's obligations have been discharged.

3. The concept of assignment in this Article includes outright transfers of claims, transfers of claims by way of security and pledges or other security rights over claims.

## Article 15

### Legal subrogation

Where a person (the creditor) has a contractual claim against another (the debtor) and a third person has a duty to satisfy the creditor, or has in fact satisfied the creditor in discharge of that duty, the law which governs the third person's duty to satisfy the creditor shall determine whether and to what extent the third person is entitled to exercise against the debtor the rights which the creditor had against the debtor under the law governing their relationship.

## Article 16

### Multiple liability

If a creditor has a claim against several debtors who are liable for the same claim, and one of the debtors has already satisfied the claim in whole or in part, the law governing the debtor's obligation towards the creditor also governs the debtor's right to claim recourse from the other debtors. The other debtors may rely on the defences they had against the creditor to the extent allowed by the law governing their obligations towards the creditor.

## Article 17

### Set-off

Where the right to set-off is not agreed by the parties, set-off shall be governed by the law applicable to the claim against which the right to set-off is asserted.

## Article 18

### Burden of proof

1. The law governing a contractual obligation under this Regulation shall apply to the extent that, in matters of contractual obligations, it contains rules which raise presumptions of law or determine the burden of proof.

2. A contract or an act intended to have legal effect may be proved by any mode of proof recognised by the law of the forum or by any of the laws referred to in Article 11 under which that contract or act is formally valid, provided that such mode of proof can be administered by the forum.

## CHAPTER III

## OTHER PROVISIONS

### Article 19

### Habitual residence

1. For the purposes of this Regulation, the habitual residence of companies and other bodies, corporate or unincorporated, shall be the place of central administration.

The habitual residence of a natural person acting in the course of his business activity shall be his principal place of business.

2. Where the contract is concluded in the course of the operations of a branch, agency or any other establishment, or if, under the contract, performance is the responsibility of such a branch, agency or establishment, the place where the branch, agency or any other establishment is located shall be treated as the place of habitual residence.

3. For the purposes of determining the habitual residence, the relevant point in time shall be the time of the conclusion of the contract.

## Article 20

### Exclusion of renvoi

The application of the law of any country specified by this Regulation means the application of the rules of law in force in that country other than its rules of private international law, unless provided otherwise in this Regulation.

## Article 21

### Public policy of the forum

The application of a provision of the law of any country specified by this Regulation may be refused only if such application is manifestly incompatible with the public policy (ordre public) of the forum.

## Article 22

### States with more than one legal system

1. Where a State comprises several territorial units, each of which has its own rules of law in respect of contractual obligations, each territorial unit shall be considered as a country for the purposes of identifying the law applicable under this Regulation.

2. A Member State where different territorial units have their own rules of law in respect of contractual obligations shall not be required to apply this Regulation to conflicts solely between the laws of such units.

## Article 23

### Relationship with other provisions of Community law

With the exception of Article 7, this Regulation shall not prejudice the application of provisions of Community law which, in relation to particular matters, lay down conflict-of-law rules relating to contractual obligations.

## Article 24

### Relationship with the Rome Convention

1. This Regulation shall replace the Rome Convention in the Member States, except as regards the territories of the Member States which fall within the territorial scope of that Convention and to which this Regulation does not apply pursuant to Article 299 of the Treaty.

2. In so far as this Regulation replaces the provisions of the Rome Convention, any reference to that Convention shall be understood as a reference to this Regulation.

## Article 25

### Relationship with existing international conventions

1. This Regulation shall not prejudice the application of international conventions to which one or more Member States are parties at the time when this Regulation is adopted and which lay down conflict-of-law rules relating to contractual obligations.

2. However, this Regulation shall, as between Member States, take precedence over conventions concluded exclusively between two or more of them in so far as such conventions concern matters governed by this Regulation.

## Article 26

### List of Conventions

1. By 17 June 2009, Member States shall notify the Commission of the conventions referred to in Article 25(1). After that date, Member States shall notify the Commission of all denunciations of such conventions.

2. Within six months of receipt of the notifications referred to in paragraph 1, the Commission shall publish in the Official Journal of the European Union:

(a) a list of the conventions referred to in paragraph 1;

(b) the denunciations referred to in paragraph 1.

## Article 27

### Review clause

1. By 17 June 2013, the Commission shall submit to the European Parliament, the Council and the European Economic and Social Committee a report on the application of this Regulation. If appropriate, the report shall be accompanied by proposals to amend this Regulation. The report shall include:

(a) a study on the law applicable to insurance contracts and an assessment of the impact of the provisions to be introduced, if any; and

(b) an evaluation on the application of Article 6, in particular as regards the coherence of Community law in the field of consumer protection.

2. By 17 June 2010, the Commission shall submit to the European Parliament, the Council and the European Economic and Social Committee a report on the question of the effectiveness of an assignment or subrogation of a claim against third parties and the priority of the assigned or subrogated claim over a right of another person. The report shall be accompanied, if appropriate, by a proposal to amend this Regulation and an assessment of the impact of the provisions to be introduced.

### Article 28

#### Application in time

This Regulation shall apply to contracts concluded after 17 December 2009.

## CHAPTER IV

## FINAL PROVISIONS

### Article 29

#### Entry into force and application

This Regulation shall enter into force on the 20th day following its publication in the Official Journal of the European Union.

It shall apply from 17 December 2009 except for Article 26 which shall apply from 17 June 2009.

This Regulation shall be binding in its entirety and directly applicable in the Member States in accordance with the Treaty establishing the European Community.

Done at Strasbourg, 17 June 2008.

For the European Parliament
The President
H.-G. PÖTTERING

For the Council
The President
J. LENARČIČ

# Appendix 2

REGULATION (EC) No 864/2007 OF THE EUROPEAN PARLIAMENT
AND OF THE COUNCIL

of 11 July 2007

on the law applicable to non-contractual obligations (Rome II)

THE EUROPEAN PARLIAMENT AND THE COUNCIL OF THE EUROPEAN UNION,

Having regard to the Treaty establishing the European Community, and in particular Articles 61(c) and 67 thereof,

Having regard to the proposal from the Commission,

Having regard to the opinion of the European Economic and Social Committee ([1]),

Acting in accordance with the procedure laid down in Article 251 of the Treaty in the light of the joint text approved by the Conciliation Committee on 25 June 2007 ([2]),

---

1    OJ C 241, 28.9.2004, p. 1.
2    Opinion of the European Parliament of 6 July 2005 (OJ C 157 E, 6.7.2006, p. 371), Council Common Position of 25 September 2006 (OJ C 289 E, 28.11.2006, p. 68) and Position of the European Parliament of 18 January 2007 (not yet published in the Official Journal) European Parliament Legislative Resolution of 10 July 2007 and Council Decision of 28 June 2007.

Whereas:

(1) The Community has set itself the objective of maintaining and developing an area of freedom, security and justice. For the progressive establishment of such an area, the Community is to adopt measures relating to judicial cooperation in civil matters with a cross-border impact to the extent necessary for the proper functioning of the internal market.

(2) According to Article 65(b) of the Treaty, these measures are to include those promoting the compatibility of the rules applicable in the Member States concerning the conflict of laws and of jurisdiction.

(3) The European Council meeting in Tampere on 15 and 16 October 1999 endorsed the principle of mutual recognition of judgments and other decisions of judicial authorities as the cornerstone of judicial cooperation in civil matters and invited the Council and the Commission to adopt a programme of measures to implement the principle of mutual recognition.

(4) On 30 November 2000, the Council adopted a joint Commission and

Council programme of measures for implementation of the principle of mutual recognition of decisions in civil and commercial matters (³). The programme identifies measures relating to the harmonisation of conflict-of-law rules as those facilitating the mutual recognition of judgments.

(5) The Hague Programme (⁴), adopted by the European Council on 5 November 2004, called for work to be pursued actively on the rules of conflict of laws regarding non-contractual obligations (Rome II).

(6) The proper functioning of the internal market creates a need, in order to improve the predictability of the outcome of litigation, certainty as to the law applicable and the free movement of judgments, for the conflict-of-law rules in the Member States to designate the same national law irrespective of the country of the court in which an action is brought.

(7) The substantive scope and the provisions of this Regulation should be consistent with Council Regulation (EC) No 44/2001 of 22 December 2000 on jurisdiction and the recognition and enforcement of judgments in civil and commercial matters (⁵) (Brussels I) and the instruments dealing with the law applicable to contractual obligations.

(8) This Regulation should apply irrespective of the nature of the court or tribunal seised.

(9) Claims arising out of acta iure imperii should include claims against officials who act on behalf of the State and liability for acts of public authorities, including liability of publicly appointed office-holders. Therefore, these matters should be excluded from the scope of this Regulation.

(10) Family relationships should cover parentage, marriage, affinity and collateral relatives. The reference in Article 1(2) to relationships having comparable effects to marriage and other family relationships should be interpreted in accordance with the law of the Member State in which the court is seised.

(11) The concept of a non-contractual obligation varies from one Member State to another. Therefore for the purposes of this Regulation non-contractual obligation should be understood as an autonomous concept. The conflict-of-law rules set out in this Regulation should also cover non-contractual obligations arising out of strict liability.

(12) The law applicable should also govern the question of the capacity to incur liability in tort/delict.

(13) Uniform rules applied irrespective of the law they designate may avert the risk of distortions of competition between Community litigants.

---

3    OJ C 12, 15.1.2001, p. 1.
4    OJ C 53, 3.3.2005, p. 1.
5    OJ L 12, 16.1.2001, p. 1. Regulation as last amended by Regulation (EC) No 1791/2006 (OJ L 363, 20.12.2006, p. 1).

(14) The requirement of legal certainty and the need to do justice in individual cases are essential elements of an area of justice. This Regulation provides for the connecting factors which are the most appropriate to achieve these objectives. Therefore, this Regulation provides for a general rule but also for specific rules and, in certain provisions, for an 'escape clause' which allows a departure from these rules where it is clear from all the circumstances of the case that the tort/delict is manifestly more closely connected with another country. This set of rules thus creates a flexible framework of conflict-of-law rules. Equally, it enables the court seised to treat individual cases in an appropriate manner.

(15) The principle of the lex loci delicti commissi is the basic solution for non-contractual obligations in virtually all the Member States, but the practical application of the principle where the component factors of the case are spread over several countries varies. This situation engenders uncertainty as to the law applicable.

(16) Uniform rules should enhance the foreseeability of court decisions and ensure a reasonable balance between the interests of the person claimed to be liable and the person who has sustained damage. A connection with the country where the direct damage occurred (lex loci damni) strikes a fair balance between the interests of the person claimed to be liable and the person sustaining the damage, and also reflects the modern approach to civil liability and the development of systems of strict liability.

(17) The law applicable should be determined on the basis of where the damage occurs, regardless of the country or countries in which the indirect consequences could occur. Accordingly, in cases of personal injury or damage to property, the country in which the damage occurs should be the country where the injury was sustained or the property was damaged respectively.

(18) The general rule in this Regulation should be the lex loci damni provided for in Article 4(1). Article 4(2) should be seen as an exception to this general principle, creating a special connection where the parties have their habitual residence in the same country. Article 4(3) should be understood as an 'escape clause' from Article 4(1) and (2), where it is clear from all the circumstances of the case that the tort/delict is manifestly more closely connected with another country.

(19) Specific rules should be laid down for special torts/delicts where the general rule does not allow a reasonable balance to be struck between the interests at stake.

(20) The conflict-of-law rule in matters of product liability should meet the objectives of fairly spreading the risks inherent in a modern high-technology society, protecting consumers' health, stimulating innovation, securing undistorted competition and facilitating

trade. Creation of a cascade system of connecting factors, together with a foreseeability clause, is a balanced solution in regard to these objectives. The first element to be taken into account is the law of the country in which the person sustaining the damage had his or her habitual residence when the damage occurred, if the product was marketed in that country. The other elements of the cascade are triggered if the product was not marketed in that country, without prejudice to Article 4(2) and to the possibility of a manifestly closer connection to another country.

(21) The special rule in Article 6 is not an exception to the general rule in Article 4(1) but rather a clarification of it. In matters of unfair competition, the conflict-of-law rule should protect competitors, consumers and the general public and ensure that the market economy functions properly. The connection to the law of the country where competitive relations or the collective interests of consumers are, or are likely to be, affected generally satisfies these objectives.

(22) The non-contractual obligations arising out of restrictions of competition in Article 6(3) should cover infringements of both national and Community competition law. The law applicable to such non-contractual obligations should be the law of the country where the market is, or is likely to be, affected. In cases where the market is, or is likely to be, affected in more than one country, the claimant should be able in certain circumstances to

choose to base his or her claim on the law of the court seised.

(23) For the purposes of this Regulation, the concept of restriction of competition should cover prohibitions on agreements between undertakings, decisions by associations of undertakings and concerted practices which have as their object or effect the prevention, restriction or distortion of competition within a Member State or within the internal market, as well as prohibitions on the abuse of a dominant position within a Member State or within the internal market, where such agreements, decisions, concerted practices or abuses are prohibited by Articles 81 and 82 of the Treaty or by the law of a Member State.

(24) 'Environmental damage' should be understood as meaning adverse change in a natural resource, such as water, land or air, impairment of a function performed by that resource for the benefit of another natural resource or the public, or impairment of the variability among living organisms.

(25) Regarding environmental damage, Article 174 of the Treaty, which provides that there should be a high level of protection based on the precautionary principle and the principle that preventive action should be taken, the principle of priority for corrective action at source and the principle that the polluter pays, fully justifies the use of the principle of discriminating in favour of the person sustaining the damage. The question of when the person seeking compensation

can make the choice of the law applicable should be determined in accordance with the law of the Member State in which the court is seised.

(26) Regarding infringements of intellectual property rights, the universally acknowledged principle of the lex loci protectionis should be preserved. For the purposes of this Regulation, the term 'intellectual property rights' should be interpreted as meaning, for instance, copyright, related rights, the sui generis right for the protection of databases and industrial property rights.

(27) The exact concept of industrial action, such as strike action or lock-out, varies from one Member State to another and is governed by each Member State's internal rules. Therefore, this Regulation assumes as a general principle that the law of the country where the industrial action was taken should apply, with the aim of protecting the rights and obligations of workers and employers.

(28) The special rule on industrial action in Article 9 is without prejudice to the conditions relating to the exercise of such action in accordance with national law and without prejudice to the legal status of trade unions or of the representative organisations of workers as provided for in the law of the Member States.

(29) Provision should be made for special rules where damage is caused by an act other than a tort/delict, such as unjust enrichment, negotiorum gestio and culpa in contrahendo.

(30) Culpa in contrahendo for the purposes of this Regulation is an autonomous concept and should not necessarily be interpreted within the meaning of national law. It should include the violation of the duty of disclosure and the breakdown of contractual negotiations. Article 12 covers only non-contractual obligations presenting a direct link with the dealings prior to the conclusion of a contract. This means that if, while a contract is being negotiated, a person suffers personal injury, Article 4 or other relevant provisions of this Regulation should apply.

(31) To respect the principle of party autonomy and to enhance legal certainty, the parties should be allowed to make a choice as to the law applicable to a non-contractual obligation. This choice should be expressed or demonstrated with reasonable certainty by the circumstances of the case.

Where establishing the existence of the agreement, the court has to respect the intentions of the parties. Protection should be given to weaker parties by imposing certain conditions on the choice.

(32) Considerations of public interest justify giving the courts of the Member States the possibility, in exceptional circumstances, of applying exceptions based on public policy and overriding mandatory provisions. In particular, the application of a provision of the law designated by this Regulation which would have the effect of causing non-compensatory exemplary or punitive

damages of an excessive nature to be awarded may, depending on the circumstances of the case and the legal order of the Member State of the court seised, be regarded as being contrary to the public policy (ordre public) of the forum.

(33) According to the current national rules on compensation awarded to victims of road traffic accidents, when quantifying damages for personal injury in cases in which the accident takes place in a State other than that of the habitual residence of the victim, the court seised should take into account all the relevant actual circumstances of the specific victim, including in particular the actual losses and costs of after-care and medical attention.

(34) In order to strike a reasonable balance between the parties, account must be taken, in so far as appropriate, of the rules of safety and conduct in operation in the country in which the harmful act was committed, even where the non-contractual obligation is governed by the law of another country. The term 'rules of safety and conduct' should be interpreted as referring to all regulations having any relation to safety and conduct, including, for example, road safety rules in the case of an accident.

(35) A situation where conflict-of-law rules are dispersed among several instruments and where there are differences between those rules should be avoided. This Regulation, however, does not exclude the possibility of inclusion of conflict-of-law rules relating to non-contractual obligations in provisions of Community law with regard to particular matters.

This Regulation should not prejudice the application of other instruments laying down provisions designed to contribute to the proper functioning of the internal market in so far as they cannot be applied in conjunction with the law designated by the rules of this Regulation. The application of provisions of the applicable law designated by the rules of this Regulation should not restrict the free movement of goods and services as regulated by Community instruments, such as Directive 2000/31/EC of the European Parliament and of the Council of 8 June 2000 on certain legal aspects of information society services, in particular electronic commerce, in the Internal Market (Directive on electronic commerce) (6).

(36) Respect for international commitments entered into by the Member States means that this Regulation should not affect international conventions to which one or more Member States are parties at the time this Regulation is adopted. To make the rules more accessible, the Commission should publish the list of the relevant conventions in the Official Journal of the European Union on the basis of information supplied by the Member States.

(37) The Commission will make a proposal to the European Parliament and the

---

6    OJ L 178, 17.7.2000, p. 1.

Council concerning the procedures and conditions according to which Member States would be entitled to negotiate and conclude on their own behalf agreements with third countries in individual and exceptional cases, concerning sectoral matters, containing provisions on the law applicable to non-contractual obligations.

(38) Since the objective of this Regulation cannot be sufficiently achieved by the Member States, and can therefore, by reason of the scale and effects of this Regulation, be better achieved at Community level, the Community may adopt measures, in accordance with the principle of subsidiarity set out in Article 5 of the Treaty. In accordance with the principle of proportionality set out in that Article, this Regulation does not go beyond what is necessary to attain that objective.

(39) In accordance with Article 3 of the Protocol on the position of the United Kingdom and Ireland annexed to the Treaty on European Union and to the Treaty establishing the European Community, the United Kingdom and Ireland are taking part in the adoption and application of this Regulation.

(40) In accordance with Articles 1 and 2 of the Protocol on the position of Denmark, annexed to the Treaty on European Union and to the Treaty establishing the European Community, Denmark does not take part in the adoption of this Regulation, and is not bound by it or subject to its application,

HAVE ADOPTED THIS REGULATION:

CHAPTER I

SCOPE

Article 1

Scope

1. This Regulation shall apply, in situations involving a conflict of laws, to non-contractual obligations in civil and commercial matters. It shall not apply, in particular, to revenue, customs or administrative matters or to the liability of the State for acts and omissions in the exercise of State authority (acta iure imperii).

2. The following shall be excluded from the scope of this Regulation:

(a) non-contractual obligations arising out of family relationships and relationships deemed by the law applicable to such relationships to have comparable effects including maintenance obligations;

(b) non-contractual obligations arising out of matrimonial property regimes, property regimes of relationships deemed by the law applicable to such relationships to have comparable effects to marriage, and wills and succession;

(c) non-contractual obligations arising under bills of exchange, cheques and promissory notes and other negotiable instruments to the extent that the obligations under such other negotiable instruments arise out of their negotiable character;

(d) non-contractual obligations arising out of the law of companies and other bodies corporate or unincorporated regarding matters such as the creation, by registration or otherwise, legal capacity, internal organisation or winding-up of companies and other bodies corporate or unincorporated, the personal liability of officers and members as such for the obligations of the company or body and the personal liability of auditors to a company or to its members in the statutory audits of accounting documents;

(e) non-contractual obligations arising out of the relations between the settlors, trustees and beneficiaries of a trust created voluntarily;

(f) non-contractual obligations arising out of nuclear damage;

(g) non-contractual obligations arising out of violations of privacy and rights relating to personality, including defamation.

3. This Regulation shall not apply to evidence and procedure, without prejudice to Articles 21 and 22.

4. For the purposes of this Regulation, 'Member State' shall mean any Member State other than Denmark.

## Article 2

### Non-contractual obligations

1. For the purposes of this Regulation, damage shall cover any consequence arising out of tort/delict, unjust enrichment, negotiorum gestio or culpa in contrahendo.

2. This Regulation shall apply also to non-contractual obligations that are likely to arise.

(a) an event giving rise to damage shall include events giving rise to damage that are likely to occur; and

(b) damage shall include damage that is likely to occur.

## Article 3

### Universal application

Any law specified by this Regulation shall be applied whether or not it is the law of a Member State.

## CHAPTER II

### TORTS/DELICTS

## Article 4

### General rule

1. Unless otherwise provided for in this Regulation, the law applicable to a non-contractual obligation arising out of a tort/delict shall be the law of the country in which the damage occurs irrespective of the country in which the event giving rise to the damage occurred and irrespective of the country or countries in which the indirect consequences of that event occur.

2. However, where the person claimed to be liable and the person sustaining damage both have their habitual residence in the same country at the time when the damage occurs, the law of that country shall apply.

3. Where it is clear from all the circumstances of the case that the tort/delict is manifestly more closely connected with a country other than that indicated in paragraphs 1 or

2, the law of that other country shall apply. A manifestly closer connection with another country might be based in particular on a pre-existing relationship between the parties, such as a contract, that is closely connected with the tort/delict in question.

## Article 5

### Product liability

1. Without prejudice to Article 4(2), the law applicable to a non-contractual obligation arising out of damage caused by a product shall be:

(a) the law of the country in which the person sustaining the damage had his or her habitual residence when the damage occurred, if the product was marketed in that country; or, failing that,

(b) the law of the country in which the product was acquired, if the product was marketed in that country; or, failing that,product was marketed in that country.

However, the law applicable shall be the law of the country in which the person claimed to be liable is habitually resident if he or she could not reasonably foresee the marketing of the product, or a product of the same type, in the country the law of which is applicable under (a), (b) or (c).

2. Where it is clear from all the circumstances of the case that the tort/delict is manifestly more closely connected with a country other than that indicated in paragraph 1, the law of that other country shall apply. A manifestly closer connection with

another country might be based in particular on a pre-existing relationship between the parties, such as a contract, that is closely connected with the tort/delict in question.

## Article 6

### Unfair competition and acts restricting free competition

1. The law applicable to a non-contractual obligation arising out of an act of unfair competition shall be the law of the country where competitive relations or the collective interests of consumers are, or are likely to be, affected.

2. Where an act of unfair competition affects exclusively the interests of a specific competitor, Article 4 shall apply.

3. (a) The law applicable to a non-contractual obligation arising out of a restriction of competition shall be the law of the country where the market is, or is likely to be, affected.

(b) When the market is, or is likely to be, affected in more than one country, the person seeking compensation for damage who sues in the court of the domicile of the defendant, may instead choose to base his or her claim on the law of the court seised, provided that the market in that Member State is amongst those directly and substantially affected by the restriction of competition out of which the non-contractual obligation on which the claim is based arises; where the claimant sues, in accordance with the applicable rules on jurisdiction, more than one defendant in that court, he or she can only choose to base his or her claim on the law of that court if the restriction of competition on which the claim against each of these defendants relies directly and substantially affects also the market in the Member State of that court.

4. The law applicable under this Article may not be derogated from by an agreement pursuant to Article 14.

## Article 7

### Environmental damage

The law applicable to a non-contractual obligation arising out of environmental damage or damage sustained by persons or property as a result of such damage shall be the law determined pursuant to Article 4(1), unless the person seeking compensation for damage chooses to base his or her claim on the law of the country in which the event giving rise to the damage occurred.

## Article 8

### Infringement of intellectual property rights

1. The law applicable to a non-contractual obligation arising from an infringement of an intellectual property right shall be the law of the country for which protection is claimed.

2. In the case of a non-contractual obligation arising from an infringement of a unitary Community intellectual property right, the law applicable shall, for any question that is not governed by the relevant Community

instrument, be the law of the country in which the act of infringement was committed.

3. The law applicable under this Article may not be derogated from by an agreement pursuant to Article 14.

## Article 9

### Industrial action

Without prejudice to Article 4(2), the law applicable to a non-contractual obligation in respect of the liability of a person in the capacity of a worker or an employer or the organisations representing their professional interests for damages caused by an industrial action, pending or carried out, shall be the law of the country where the action is to be, or has been, taken.

## CHAPTER III

## UNJUST ENRICHMENT, NEGOTIORUM GESTIO AND CULPA IN CONTRAHENDO

## Article 10

### Unjust enrichment

1. If a non-contractual obligation arising out of unjust enrichment, including payment of amounts wrongly received, concerns a relationship existing between the parties, such as one arising out of a contract or a tort/delict, that is closely connected with that unjust enrichment, it shall be governed by the law that governs that relationship.

2. Where the law applicable cannot be determined on the basis of paragraph 1 and

the parties have their habitual residence in the same country when the event giving rise to unjust enrichment occurs, the law of that country shall apply.

3. Where the law applicable cannot be determined on the basis of paragraphs 1 or 2, it shall be the law of the country in which the unjust enrichment took place.

4. Where it is clear from all the circumstances of the case that the non-contractual obligation arising out of unjust enrichment is manifestly more closely connected with a country other than that indicated in paragraphs 1, 2 and 3, the law of that other country shall apply.

## Article 11

### Negotiorum gestio

1. If a non-contractual obligation arising out of an act performed without due authority in connection with the affairs of another person concerns a relationship existing between the parties, such as one arising out of a contract or a tort/delict, that is closely connected with that non-contractual obligation, it shall be governed by the law that governs that relationship.

2. Where the law applicable cannot be determined on the basis of paragraph 1, and the parties have their habitual residence in the same country when the event giving rise to the damage occurs, the law of that country shall apply.

3. Where the law applicable cannot be determined on the basis of paragraphs 1 or 2, it shall be the law of the country in which the act was performed.

4. Where it is clear from all the circumstances of the case that the non-contractual obligation arising out of an act performed without due authority in connection with the affairs of another person is manifestly more closely connected with a country other than that indicated in paragraphs 1, 2 and 3, the law of that other country shall apply.

## Article 12

### Culpa in contrahendo

1. The law applicable to a non-contractual obligation arising out of dealings prior to the conclusion of a contract, regardless of whether the contract was actually concluded or not, shall be the law that applies to the contract or that would have been applicable to it had it been entered into.

2. Where the law applicable cannot be determined on the basis of paragraph 1, it shall be:

(a) the law of the country in which the damage occurs, irrespective of the country in which the event giving rise to the damage occurred and irrespective of the country or countries in which the indirect consequences of that event occurred; or

(b) where the parties have their habitual residence in the same country at the time when the event giving rise to the damage occurs, the law of that country; or

(c) where it is clear from all the circumstances of the case that the non-contractual obligation arising out of dealings prior to the conclusion of a contract is manifestly more closely connected with a country other than that indicated in points (a) and (b), the law of that other country.

3. Any reference in this Regulation to:

Applicability of Article 8

For the purposes of this Chapter, Article 8 shall apply to non-contractual obligations arising from an infringement of an intellectual property right.

## CHAPTER IV

## FREEDOM OF CHOICE

### Article 14

### Freedom of choice

1. The parties may agree to submit non-contractual obligations to the law of their choice:

(a) by an agreement entered into after the event giving rise to the damage occurred;

or

(b) where all the parties are pursuing a commercial activity, also by an agreement freely negotiated before the event giving rise to the damage occurred.

The choice shall be expressed or demonstrated with reasonable certainty by the circumstances of the case and shall not prejudice the rights of third parties.

2. Where all the elements relevant to the situation at the time when the event giving rise to the damage occurs are located in a country other than the country whose law has been chosen, the choice of the parties shall not prejudice the application of provisions of the law of that other country which cannot be derogated from by agreement.

3. Where all the elements relevant to the situation at the time when the event giving rise to the damage occurs are located in one or more of the Member States, the parties' choice of the law applicable other than that of a Member State shall not prejudice the application of provisions of Community law, where appropriate as implemented in the Member State of the forum, which cannot be derogated from by agreement.

## CHAPTER V

## COMMON RULES

### Article 15

### Scope of the law applicable

The law applicable to non-contractual obligations under this Regulation shall govern in particular:

(a) the basis and extent of liability, including the determination of persons who may be held liable for acts performed by them;

(b) the grounds for exemption from liability, any limitation of liability and any division of liability;

(C) the law of the country in which the damage occurred, if the the remedy claimed;

(d) within the limits of powers conferred on the court by its procedural law, the measures which a court may take to prevent or terminate injury or damage or to ensure the provision of compensation;

(e) the question whether a right to claim damages or a remedy may be transferred, including by inheritance;

(f) persons entitled to compensation for damage sustained personally;

(g) liability for the acts of another person;

(h) the manner in which an obligation may be extinguished and rules of prescription and limitation, including rules relating to the commencement, interruption and suspension of a period of prescription or limitation.

## Article 16

### Overriding mandatory provisions

Nothing in this Regulation shall restrict the application of the provisions of the law of the forum in a situation where they are mandatory irrespective of the law otherwise applicable to the non-contractual obligation.

## Article 17

### Rules of safety and conduct

In assessing the conduct of the person claimed to be liable, account shall be taken, as a matter of fact and in so far as is appropriate, of the rules of safety and conduct which were in force at the place and time of the event giving rise to the liability.

## Article 18

### Direct action against the insurer of the person liable

The person having suffered damage may bring his or her claim directly against the insurer of the person liable to provide compensation if the law applicable to the non-contractual obligation or the law applicable to the insurance contract so provides.

## Article 19

### Subrogation

Where a person (the creditor) has a non-contractual claim upon another (the debtor), and a third person has a duty to satisfy the creditor, or has in fact satisfied the creditor in discharge of that duty, the law which governs the third person's duty to satisfy the creditor shall determine whether, and the extent to which, the third person is entitled to exercise against the debtor the rights which the creditor had against the debtor under the law governing their relationship.

## Article 20

### Multiple liability

If a creditor has a claim against several debtors who are liable for the same claim, and one of the debtors has already satisfied the claim in whole or in part, the question of that debtor's right to demand compensation from the other debtors shall be governed by the law applicable to that debtor's non-contractual obligation towards the creditor.

## Article 21

### Formal validity

A unilateral act intended to have legal effect and relating to a non-contractual obligation shall be formally valid if it satisfies the formal requirements of the law governing the non-contractual obligation in question or the law of the country in which the act is performed.

## Article 22

### Burden of proof

1. The law governing a non-contractual obligation under this Regulation shall apply to the

extent that, in matters of non-contractual obligations, it contains rules which raise presumptions of law or determine the burden of proof.

2. Acts intended to have legal effect may be proved by any mode of proof recognised by the law of the forum or by any of the laws referred to in Article 21 under which that act is formally valid, provided that such mode of proof can be administered by the forum.

## CHAPTER VI

## OTHER PROVISIONS

### Article 23

### Habitual residence

1. For the purposes of this Regulation, the habitual residence of companies and other bodies, corporate or unincorporated, shall be the place of central administration.

Where the event giving rise to the damage occurs, or the damage arises, in the course of operation of a branch, agency or any other establishment, the place where the branch, agency or any other establishment is located shall be treated as the place of habitual residence.

2. For the purposes of this Regulation, the habitual residence of a natural person acting in the course of his or her business activity shall be his or her principal place of business.

### Article 24

### Exclusion of renvoi

The application of the law of any country specified by this Regulation means the application of the rules of law in force in that country other than its rules of private international law.

### Article 25

### States with more than one legal system

1. Where a State comprises several territorial units, each of which has its own rules of law in respect of non-contractual obligations, each territorial unit shall be considered as a country for the purposes of identifying the law applicable under this Regulation.

2. A Member State within which different territorial units have their own rules of law in respect of non-contractual obligations shall not be required to apply this Regulation to conflicts solely between the laws of such units.

### Article 26

### Public policy of the forum

The application of a provision of the law of any country specified by this Regulation may be refused only if such application is manifestly incompatible with the public policy (ordre public) of the forum.

### Article 27

### Relationship with other provisions of Community law

This Regulation shall not prejudice the application of provisions of Community law which, in relation to particular matters, lay down conflict-of-law rules relating to non-contractual obligations.

### Article 28

### Relationship with existing international conventions

1. This Regulation shall not prejudice the application of international conventions

to which one or more Member States are parties at the time when this Regulation is adopted and which lay down conflict-of-law rules relating to non-contractual obligations.

2. However, this Regulation shall, as between Member States, take precedence over conventions concluded exclusively between two or more of them in so far as such conventions concern matters governed by this Regulation.

## CHAPTER VII

## FINAL PROVISIONS

### Article 29

### List of conventions

1. By 11 July 2008, Member States shall notify the Commission of the conventions referred to in Article 28(1). After that date, Member States shall notify the Commission of all denunciations of such conventions.

2. The Commission shall publish in the Official Journal of the European Union within six months of receipt:

(i) a list of the conventions referred to in paragraph 1;

(ii) the denunciations referred to in paragraph 1.

### Article 30

### Review clause

1. Not later than 20 August 2011, the Commission shall submit to the European Parliament, the Council and the European Economic and Social Committee a report on the application of this Regulation. If necessary, the report shall be accompanied by proposals to adapt this Regulation. The report shall include:

(i) a study on the effects of the way in which foreign law is treated in the different jurisdictions and on the extent to which courts in the Member States apply foreign law in practice pursuant to this Regulation;

(ii) a study on the effects of Article 28 of this Regulation with respect to the Hague Convention of 4 May 1971 on the law applicable to traffic accidents.

2. Not later than 31 December 2008, the Commission shall submit to the European Parliament, the Council and the European Economic and Social Committee a study on the situation in the field of the law applicable to non-contractual obligations arising out of violations of privacy and rights relating to personality, taking into account rules relating to freedom of the press and freedom of expression in the media, and conflict-of-law issues related to Directive 95/46/EC of the European Parliament and of the Council of 24 October 1995 on the protection of individuals with regard to the processing of personal data and on the free movement of such data ([7]).

### Article 31

### Application in time

This Regulation shall apply to events giving rise to damage which occur after its entry into force.

---

7  OJ L 281, 23.11.1995, p. 31.

Article 32

Date of application

This Regulation shall apply from 11 January 2009, except for Article 29, which shall apply from 11 July 2008.

This Regulation shall be binding in its entirety and directly applicable in the Member States in accordance with the Treaty establishing the European Community.

Done at Strasbourg, 11 July 2007.

For the European Parliament

The President

H.-G. PÖTTERING

For the Council

The President

M. LOBO ANTUNES

Commission Statement on the review clause (Article 30)

The Commission, following the invitation by the European Parliament and the Council in the frame of Article 30 of the 'Rome II' Regulation, will submit, not later than December 2008, a study on the situation in the field of the law applicable to non-contractual obligations arising out of violations of privacy and rights relating to personality. The Commission will take into consideration all aspects of the situation and take appropriate measures if necessary.

Commission Statement on road accidents

The Commission, being aware of the different practices followed in the Member States as regards the level of compensation awarded to victims of road traffic accidents, is prepared to examine the specific problems resulting for EU residents involved in road traffic accidents in a Member State other than the Member State of their habitual residence. To that end the Commission will make available to the European Parliament and to the Council, before the end of 2008, a study on all options, including insurance aspects, for improving the position of cross-border victims, which would pave the way for a Green Paper.

Commission Statement on the treatment of foreign law

The Commission, being aware of the different practices followed in the Member States as regards the treatment of foreign law, will publish at the latest four years after the entry into force of the 'Rome II' Regulation and in any event as soon as it is available a horizontal study on the application of foreign law in civil and commercial matters by the courts of the Member States, having regard to the aims of the Hague Programme. It is also prepared to take appropriate measures if necessary.

**STUDIEN ZUM VERGLEICHENDEN UND INTERNATIONALEN RECHT**

Herausgeber: Bernd von Hoffmann (†), Erik Jayme und Heinz-Peter Mansel

Band 59 Aleksandar Jaksic: Arbitration and Human Rights. 2002.

Band 60 Islamisches und arabisches Recht als Problem der Rechtsanwendung. Symposium zu Ehren von Professor Emeritus Dr. iur. Omaia Elwan. Veranstaltet vom Institut für ausländisches und internationales Privat- und Wirtschaftsrecht der Universität Heidelberg und der Gesellschaft für Arabisches und Islamisches Recht e.v. Herausgegeben von Herbert Kronke, Gert Reinhart und Nika Witteborg. 2001.

Band 61 Patrick Fiedler: Stabilisierungsklauseln und materielle Verweisung im internationalen Vertragsrecht. 2001.

Band 62 Werner Mangold: Die Abtretung im Europäischen Kollisionsrecht. Unter besonderer Berücksichtigung des spanischen Rechts. 2001.

Band 63 Eike Dirk Eschenfelder: Beweiserhebung im Ausland und ihre Verwertung im inländischen Zivilprozess. Zur Bedeutung des US-amerikanischen discovery-Verfahrens für das deutsche Erkenntnisverfahren. 2002.

Band 64 Bernd Ehle: Wege zu einer Kohärenz der Rechtsquellen im Europäischen Kollisionsrecht der Verbraucherverträge. 2002.

Band 65 Heiko Lehmkuhl: Das Nacherfüllungsrecht des Verkäufers im UN-Kaufrecht. 2002.

Band 66 Jochen Nikolaus Schlotter: Erbrechtliche Probleme in der Société Privée Européenne. IPR-Harmonisierung im einheitlichen Europäischen Rechtsraum. 2002.

Band 67 Konrad Ost: Doppelrelevante Tatsachen im Internationalen Zivilverfahrensrecht. Zur Prüfung der internationalen Zuständigkeit bei den Gerichtsständen des Erfüllungsortes und der unerlaubten Handlung. 2002.

Band 68 Tobias Bosch: Die Durchbrechungen des Gesamtstatuts im internationalen Ehegüterrecht. Unter besonderer Berücksichtigung deutsch-französischer Rechtsfälle. 2002.

Band 69 Ursula Philipp: Form im amerikanischen Erbrecht. Zwischen Formalismus und harmless error. 2002.

Band 70 Christian Stefan Wolf: Der Begriff der wesentlich engeren Verbindung im Internationalen Sachenrecht. 2002.

Band 71 André Fomferek: Der Schutz des Vermögens Minderjähriger. Ein Vergleich des deutschen und des englischen Rechts unter Berücksichtigung des schottischen und irischen Rechts. 2002.

Band 72 nicht erschienen

Band 73 Markus Dreißigacker: Sprachenfreiheit im Verbrauchervertragsrecht. Der Verbraucher im Spannungsfeld zwischen kultureller Identität und Privatautonomie. 2002.

Band 74 Vassiliki Myller-Igknay: Auskunftsansprüche im griechischen Zivilrecht. Auswirkungen im deutsch-griechischen Rechtsverkehr sowie im deutschen internationalen Privat- und Verfahrensrecht. 2003.

Band 75 Stefan Bruinier: Der Einfluss der Grundfreiheiten auf das Internationale Privatrecht. 2003.

Band 76 Nika Witteborg: Das gemeinsame Sorgerecht nichtverheirateter Eltern. Eine Untersuchung im soziologischen, rechtsgeschichtlichen, verfassungsrechtlichen, rechtsvergleichenden und internationalen Kontext. 2003.

Band 77 Peter Stankewitsch: Entscheidungsnormen im IPR als Wirksamkeitsvoraussetzungen der Rechtswahl. 2003.

Band 78 Jan Wilhelm Ritter: Euro-Einführung und IPR unter besonderer Berücksichtigung nachehelicher Unterhaltsverträge. Eine Untersuchung mit Blick auf das deutsche, französische und schweizerische Recht. 2003.

Band 79 Wolf Richard Herkner: Die Grenzen der Rechtswahl im internationalen Deliktsrecht. 2003.

Band 174    Manuela Krach: Scheidung auf Mexikanisch. Das materielle Recht der Scheidung im Mehr-rechtsstaat Mexiko unter Berücksichtigung von Eheschließung und Ehewirkungen. 2011.

Band 175    Vanessa Sofia Wagner: Verkehrsschutz beim redlichen Erwerb von GmbH-Geschäfts-anteilen. Ein Vergleich des Rechts für Gesellschaften mit beschränkter Haftung in Deutschland, England und Italien. 2011.

Band 176    Alexander Swienty: Der Statutenwechsel im deutschen und englischen internationalen Sachenrecht unter besonderer Betrachtung der Kreditsicherungsrechte. 2011.

Band 177    Kathrin Süß: Streitbeilegungsmechanismen im Verbraucherrecht. Unter besonderer Be-rücksichtigung der australischen Rechtsordnung. 2011.

Band 178    Efe Direnisa: Die materielle Rechtskraft im deutschen und türkischen Zivilverfahrensrecht. 2012.

Band 179    Julia Faenger: Leistungsunabhängige Nebenpflichten zum Schutz des Integritätsinteresses im deutschen und französischen Recht. Eine rechtsvergleichende Betrachtung ausgehend von den Rücksichtspflichten des § 241 Abs. 2 BGB. 2012.

Band 180    Dorothea Heine: Das Kollisionsrecht der Forderungsabtretung. UNCITRAL-Abtretungs-konvention und Rom I-Verordnung. 2012.

Band 181    Lisa B. Möll: Kollidierende Rechtswahlklauseln in Allgemeinen Geschäftsbedingungen im internationalen Vertragsrecht. 2012.

Band 182    Jutta Jasmin Uusitalo: Einbeziehung von AGB im unternehmerischen Geschäftsverkehr zwischen Deutschland und Finnland. 2012.

Band 183    Darya Alikhani Chamgardani: Der Allgemeine Teil des iranischen Schuldvertragsrechts. Im Spannungsverhältnis zwischen rezipiertem französischen und traditionellem islamischen Recht. 2013.

Band 184    Volker Anton: Aktuelle Entwicklungen des Bankgeheimnisses im Rechtsvergleich unter besonderer Berücksichtigung seiner exterritorialen Wirkungen. Deutschland, Luxemburg, Österreich, Schweiz und Liechtenstein. 2013.

Band 185    Charlotte Wilhelm: Die Regelung der Geld- und Warenkreditsicherheiten nach dem deut-schen Recht im Vergleich zum Draft Common Frame of Reference (DCFR). 2013.

Band 186    Michael Nehmer: Erbunwürdigkeit und Elternunterhalt im Internationalen Privatrecht. Eine historisch-rechtspolitische Betrachtung. 2013.

Band 187    Pınar Şamiloğlu-Riegermann: Türkisches und deutsches Vertragshändlerrecht im Rechts-vergleich. 2014.

Band 188    Elvan Er: Realsicherheiten des türkischen Mobiliarsachenrechts. Eine Darstellung des geltenden türkischen Rechts unter vergleichender Berücksichtigung des deutschen und schweizerischen Kreditsicherungsrechts. 2014.

Band 189    Maya Mandery: Party Autonomy in Contractual and Non-Contractual Obligations. A Euro-pean and Anglo-Common Law perspective on the freedom of choice of law in the Rome I Regulation on the law applicable to contractual obligations and the Rome II Regulation on the law applicable to non-contractual obligations. 2014.

www.peterlang.com